Mar 19, 2006

Joe,

May you draw closer to the Lord with each passing day!

Your Brother In Christ

Ed.

W9-AXX-163

"Preach the Word; be prepared in season and out of season." – 2 Tim 4:2

# GREAT DAYS WITH THE GREAT LIVES

PROFILES IN CHARACTER FROM
CHARLES R. SWINDOLL

**W PUBLISHING GROUP**
A Division of Thomas Nelson Publishers
*Since 1798*

www.wpublishinggroup.com

GREAT DAYS WITH THE GREAT LIVES

Copyright © 2005, Charles R. Swindoll.

All rights reserved. No portion of this book may be reproduced, stored in a retrieval system, or transmitted in any form or by any means—electronic, mechanical, photocopy, recording, or any other—except for brief quotations in printed reviews, without the prior written permission of the publisher.

Published by W Publishing Group, a Division of Thomas Nelson, Inc., P.O. Box 141000, Nashville, Tennessee, 37214.

Published in association with Yates & Yates, LLP, Attorney and Counselors, Orange, California.

W Publishing Group books may be purchased in bulk for educational, business, fundraising, or sales promotional use. For information, please email SpecialMarkets@ThomasNelson.com.

All Scripture quotations, unless otherwise indicated, are taken from New American Standard Bible (NASB). Copyright © 1960, 1962, 1963, 1968, 1971, 1973, 1975, 1977 by The Lockman Foundation, La Habra, California. Used by permission.

Other Scripture references are from the following sources:

Quotations designated MSG are from the Message copyright © by Eugene H. Peterson, 1993, 1994, 1995, 1996. Used by permission of NavPress Publishing Group.

Quotations designated NIV are from The Holy Bible, New International Version. Copyright © 1973, 1978, 1984, International Bible Society. Used by permission of Zondervan Bible Publishers.

The New King James Version (NKJV), copyright © 1979, 1980, 1982, Thomas Nelson, Inc., Publishers.

Produced with the assistance of The Livingstone Corporation (www.LivingstoneCorp.com). Project staff includes Linda Taylor and Dana Veerman.

Editorial Staff: Shady Oaks Studio, 1507 Shirley Way, Bedford, TX 76022.

Library of Congress Cataloging-in-Publication Data
Swindoll, Charles R.
  Great days with the great lives / Charles Swindoll.
    p.  cm.
ISBN 0-8499-0043-3
    1. Devotional calendars.  2. Bible—Biography—Meditations.  I. Title.
    BV4811.S977   2006
221.9'22—dc22                                          2005031113

*Printed in the United States of America*
05  06  07  08  09  10  QW  9  8  7  6  5  4  3  2  1

# Publications by Charles R. Swindoll

BOOKS FOR ADULTS

Active Spirituality

Bedside Blessings

Behold . . . The Man!

The Bride

Come Before Winter

Compassion: Showing We Care in a
  Careless World

The Darkness and the Dawn

Cultivating Purity in an Impure World

David: A Man of Passion and Destiny

Day by Day

Dear Graduate

Dropping Your Guard

Elijah: A Man of Heroism and Humility

Encourage Me

Esther: A Woman of Strength and Dignity

Fascinating Stories

The Finishing Touch

Five Meaningful Minutes a Day

Flying Closer to the Flame

For Those Who Hurt

Getting Through the Tough Stuff

Getting Through the Tough Stuff
  Workbook

God's Provision

The Grace Awakening

The Grace Awakening Devotional

The Grace Awakening Workbook

Growing Deep in the Christian Life

Growing Strong in the Seasons of Life

Growing Wise in Family Life

Hand Me Another Brick

Home: Where Life Makes Up Its Mind

Hope Again

Improving Your Serve

Intimacy with the Almighty

Job: A Man of Heroic Endurance

Job: Interactive Study Guide

Joseph: A Man of Integrity and
Forgiveness

Killing Giants, Pulling Thorns

Laugh Again

Leadership: Influence That Inspires

Living Above the Level of Mediocrity

Living Beyond the Daily Grind,
  Books I and II

The Living Insights Study Bible,
  general editor

Living on the Ragged Edge

Living on the Ragged Edge Workbook

Make Up Your Mind

Man to Man

Moses: A Man of Selfless Dedication

The Mystery of God's Will

Paul: A Man of Grace and Grit

The Quest for Character

Recovery: When Healing Takes Time

The Road to Armageddon

Sanctity of Life

Simple Faith

Simple Trust

So, You Want to Be Like Christ?

So, You Want to Be Like Christ?
  Workbook

Starting Over

Start Where You Are

Strengthening Your Grip

Stress Fractures

Strike the Original Match

The Strong Family

Suddenly One Morning

Swindoll's Ultimate Book of
  Illustrations and Quotes

Three Steps Forward, Two Steps Back

Victory: A Winning Game Plan for  Life

When God is Silent

Why, God?

Wisdom for the Way

You and Your Child

# INTRODUCTION

*O*ur world is desperately in need of models worth following. Authentic heroes. People of integrity, whose lives inspire us to do better, to climb higher, to stand taller. This has always been true.

Maybe that explains why biographies of great men and women have fascinated me throughout my life. I can still remember the first Bible I owned because of the colorful pictures of various characters interspersed through its pages. Each one loomed larger than life as I relived each drama, imagining the sounds, entering into the action-packed scenes portrayed on the pages. I still find delight in reentering those scenes from antiquity. My soul is stirred and my heart inspired as those saints of old, people of "whom the world was not worthy" (Heb. 11:38) play out their lives, make their mistakes, accomplish incredible feats, and finally pass on into glory. What encouragement! What enrichment!

The words of the Russian poet, Boris Pasternik, come to mind, "It is not revolutions and upheavals that clear the road to new and better days, but someone's soul inspired and ablaze."[1] It is my hope that you will be enlightened and encouraged from beginning each new and better day spending time with the Great Lives you'll discover in this daily devotional. Since our world is desperately in need of models worth following, here are ten deserving of our time and attention to help us endure the uncertain challenges of the future.

—Chuck Swindoll
*Frisco, Texas*

*Joseph: A Man of Integrity & Forgiveness*

# GOD'S TRAINING MANUAL

### ✦ *Read Genesis 37:1–4* ❦

*B*efore we get better acquainted with Joseph, let's take a quick glance at some background information. It will help if you remember that his biography falls neatly into three distinct segments.

*Birth to Seventeen Years (Genesis 30:24–37:2).* During this time Joseph's family was in transition—everyone was unsettled, on the move. A low-level antagonism was brewing as his family clashed and argued in jealousy and hatred.

*Seventeen to Thirty Years (Genesis 37:2–41:46).* This second segment occurs as Joseph reaches young manhood. It seems as though his life becomes out of control. Enslavement, unfair accusation, and imprisonment assault him.

*Thirty Years to Death (Genesis 41:46–50:26).* Joseph's last eighty years are years of prosperity and reward under God's blessing. He had the classic opportunity to get even with his brothers, to ruin them forever, but he refused. Instead he blessed, protected, and forgave.

God constantly uses the lives of Bible characters to teach us, to encourage us, to warn us. Who can forget the impact of the truths lived out in the lives of David and Esther, of Moses and Elijah, of Peter and Paul? It's impossible to leave truth in the theoretical realm when you see it revealed in the lives of real-life men and women. That is what these divinely inspired biographies do; they distill truth and weave it into the fabric of everyday living. God's training manual is full of lives that inspire and instruct.

Romans 15:4 states, "For whatever was written *in earlier times* was written for our instruction, that through perseverance and the encouragement of the Scriptures we might have hope" (emphasis added). This reference to "earlier times" encompasses all the truths written in the Old Testament. And if I read this verse correctly, there are two basic reasons God has allowed us to have the Old Testament available for study and application: first, for present instruction, and second, for future hope. God has given us this information so that our minds can learn the truth about Him and about life, and so that we will be encouraged to persevere in the future.

# LESSONS IN ADVERSITY

### ❧ *Read Genesis 37:5–35* ❧

This is a good time to call to mind several lessons we can learn from Jacob's family and Joseph's adversity.

The first is obvious. *No enemy is more subtle than passivity.* When parents are passive, they may eventually discipline, but by then the delayed reaction is often carried out in anger. Passivity waits and waits until finally, when it can wait no longer, it comes down with both feet! When that happens, children are not disciplined, they are brutalized. Passivity not only blinds us to the here and now, it makes us inconsistent.

There's a second lesson we learn from Joseph's teenage struggles. *No response is more cruel than jealousy.* Solomon was right when he said, "Jealousy is cruel as the grave" (Song of Solomon 8:6, RSV). Jealousy, if allowed to grow and fester, leads to devastating consequences. If you allow jealousy to rage within your family or between your children, you are asking for trouble. At some point, it will manifest itself in detrimental ways.

Enough of the negatives. Let's find in all this at least one magnificent lesson of hope: *No action is more powerful than prayer.* I realize that the biblical story does not state that Jacob turned to God in prayer, but surely, he did so! How else could he have gone on with his life? Where else could he have turned for hope?

The same can be said for you and me. Prayer brings power to endure. Those who are older are a source of wisdom for young parents and for children and grandchildren. Single men and women also have much to offer, whether within their own extended families or within the family of the church. Broken, hollow lives can find new strength to recover. It's at this point I would say that Joseph, without question, turned his situation over to God, even as the caravan made its way toward Egypt. Surely he knew, even at seventeen, that his only hope would come through God's faithful intervention! Surely, he cried out to the One who, alone, was in sovereign control of his future! And so must we!

# TEMPTATIONS OF PROSPERITY

*Read Genesis 37:36; 39:1–6*

T he sovereign God of Israel was intimately involved in Joseph's life. He guided him. He gave him facility in the Egyptian language. On top of all that, he gave him favor in the eyes of Potiphar. Clearly, God was the secret of Joseph's success. Luck had nothing to do with it.

Joseph didn't have to tell Potiphar that the Lord was with him; Potiphar could see it for himself. "Now his master saw that the LORD was with him" (v. 3). Furthermore, Joseph didn't use his spirituality as a manipulative tool to get benefits from his boss. Simply because the Lord caused all that Joseph did to prosper, Joseph found favor in his sight. Notice, it doesn't say that Joseph asked favors from Potiphar; he *found* favor with Potiphar.

With greater success comes greater measures of trust, which, by the way, lead to greater times of unguarded vulnerability. Regarding the latter, F. B. Meyer writes insightfully,

> We may expect temptation in the days of prosperity and ease rather than in those of privation and toil. Not on the glacier slopes of the Alps, but in the sunny plains of the Campagna; not when the youth is climbing arduously the steep ladder of fame, but when he has entered the golden portals; not where men frown, but where they smile sweet exquisite smiles of flattery—it is there, it is there, that the temptress lies in wait! Beware!

What a wise exhortation! This warning is not of concern to the person who is down and out. Its message is addressed to the successful, to the up-and-coming executive, to the man or woman on the way to the top of the heap, to the individual who is experiencing the bene-fits and favor of God, who is reaping the benefits of increased privacy and trust. Thomas Carlyle, the Scottish essayist, was right when he said, "Adversity is sometimes hard upon a man, but for one man who can stand prosperity, there are a hundred that will stand adversity." The temptations that accompany prosperity are far greater (and far more subtle) than those that accompany adversity.

# RUN FOR YOUR LIFE!

### ❧ *Read Genesis 39:6—18* ❧

T he appeal of sensual lust works like a magnet, drawing two "sudden and fierce" forces toward each other—inner desire and an outer bait. Let's face it, you can't escape the bait if you live in the real world. In fact, even if you somehow manage to shut yourself away from the real world, your mind will not let you escape the outer bait. But keep in mind that there is no sin in the bait. The sin is in the bite. When the lust of another tempts you to give in to your own lust, so much so that your resistance weakens, you have been enticed. You have given in to the lure of temptation. The secret of victory is modeled beautifully by Joseph. He refused to weaken. He continued to resist.

Potiphar's wife dropped the bait day after day after day. And each time Joseph refused to take it. "No, no, no!" he replied. Not only did he not listen to her, it got to where he did not even want to be near her. She was not safe to be around.

Joseph had rebuffed her time and time again, refusing to yield to her advances. Finally, she set a trap for him.

Joseph had come into the house to do his work one day. He noticed the house was quiet. There were no servants nearby. She was alone with Joseph in the house, and she again made her move. Only this time she would not take no for an answer. She went beyond verbal advances and physically grabbed hold of Joseph. She held on so tightly that when he jerked away from her and dashed out into the street, he left his outer robe in her hands.

What a clear image! What a practical spotlight on truth from Joseph's life. What strong biblical counsel. Whenever the New Testament lingers on the subject of sensual temptation, it gives us one command: RUN! It does not tell us to reason with it. It does not tell us to think about it and claim verses. It tells us to FLEE! I have discovered you cannot yield to sensuality if you're running away from it. So? Run for your life! Get out of there! If you try to reason with lust or play around with sensual thoughts, you will finally yield. You can't fight it. That's why the Spirit of God forcefully commands, "Run!"

# THE PERSONAL RAMIFICATIONS

*Read Genesis 39:19–23*

*I*magine what must have been going through Joseph's mind at this point, shortly after he was incarcerated. He was not only innocent, he had resisted blatant temptation over and over again. (He'd never read Genesis 41. He didn't know what the final outcome would be. He didn't know that in a matter of years he would be prime minister of Egypt.) All the man knew at this painful moment was that he had done what was right and had suffered wrong for it. Time dragged by. Days turned into months. He was, again, unfairly rejected—forgotten—totally helpless.

But somehow, in the midst of this unfair situation, Joseph sensed that Jehovah's hand was in all this. "Joseph, you're Mine. Just wait. I'm with you. I'm not ignoring you or rejecting you. You will be a better man, Joseph, because of this accusation against you. I'm not through preparing you for My service."

It may be that you are facing temptation right now. Perhaps you have already yielded. A few of my readers may be thinking, *Preach it, brother, I need to hear it. So far I've resisted the lure of sensual temptation, and I need help to keep standing strong.* But not one person reading this can say, "I don't know what you're talking about, Chuck. I've never encountered anything like this in my entire life."

You and I need to discern the times in which we live. We are living in an era that attempts to stretch grace to heretical extremes. I see it and hear it virtually every week of my life. So allow me to say this very straight: The greatest gift you can give to your marriage partner is your purity, your fidelity. The greatest character trait you can provide your spouse and your family is moral and ethical self-control. Stand firm, my friend. Refuse to yield. Joseph did and so can you. So *must* you!

Whatever your situation, no matter how alluring or pleasurable or momentarily delightful the bait looks, don't linger. Claim the supernatural strength that comes from knowing Jesus Christ and, operating under the control of His power, stand strong in His might. Right now, this very moment, determine to be a Joseph. Make up your mind to join God's ranks—and from this day forward, *resist*.

Otherwise, *you will yield.* It's only a matter of time.

# HIS UNKNOWN WAYS

### ✢ *Read Genesis 39:19–23* ✢

*J*f anybody knew about unfair treatment, about a false accusation, about being an innocent victim on the receiving end, it was Joseph.

First, *he received unfair treatment from his family.* His brothers hated him, wanted to kill him, but sold him into slavery instead. Next, *his circumstances were unexpectedly restricted.* He became a slave in a land where he didn't even know the language. One minute he was a seventeen-year-old boy with his whole life before him, and the next he was totally at the mercy of—actually the property of—some stranger. Following all that, he was falsely accused. After earning the favor of his master, Potiphar, the master's wife tried to seduce Joseph. When he didn't submit to her wishes, she lied and said, "This slave tried to rape me." As a result of her lies, *he was unjustly put in prison and abandoned.*

Remember those words from Isaiah's pen as he repeats God's message?

"For My thoughts are not your thoughts,
Neither are your ways My ways," declares the LORD.
"For as the heavens are higher than the earth,
So are My ways higher than your ways,
And My thoughts than your thoughts." (Isaiah 55:8–9)

Look carefully at the contrasts. There is a vast difference between "My thoughts" and "your thoughts" says the Lord. "My ways" are not like "your ways." They are higher; they are far more profound, deep, mysterious—and I would add, *surprising.*

Our human ways are based on what seems fair. We firmly believe that when someone does what is right, rewards and blessings result. When someone does what is wrong, there are serious consequences, even punishment. But that's our way, not necessarily God's way. At least not immediately. He's been known to allow unfair treatment to occur in the lives of absolutely innocent folks—for reasons far more profound and deep than they or we could have imagined. How slowly He steps in!

# GOD'S STRATEGY

*Read Genesis 39:21–23*

*T*wice we read in that short account, "The Lord was with Joseph." Joseph began to see the hand of God in his prison experience. In what could have been the direst of positions, the dreariest of places, Joseph prospered. Because of this, he was freed up to be used by God strategically in the lives of at least two men. Amazingly, he prospered in prison—of all places.

False accusations put Joseph in prison, but it was the Lord who stayed near him and nurtured his soul while he was there. As a result, Joseph found favor even in the eyes of the chief jailer—what we might call the prison warden—to the point where the man trusted Joseph to supervise all the other prisoners. The warden trusted and respected Joseph so much that he "did not supervise anything under Joseph's charge because the Lord was with him; and whatever he did, the Lord made to prosper."

You see, the Lord God remained first in Joseph's life; He was the focus of his life. The lens of God's will stood between Joseph and his circumstances, enabling Joseph to see God in them, to read God in them—and enabling God to use him in them.

When a dungeon experience comes, the quickest and easiest response is to feel that you've been forgotten by God. I don't know if you read the cartoon "Ziggy," but I enjoy him—maybe because he often says the very things I've been thinking! One of my favorites shows Ziggy, with his big nose and bald head, standing on a mountain and staring far above him. The sky is dark, and there is one lonely cloud up there. Ziggy yells, "Have I been put on hold for the rest of my life?"

You've felt like that, haven't you? "Lord, will You ever answer?" How often the heavens seem more like cold brass than God's loving abode. We cry out, but nothing comes in return.

Make no mistake about it, Joseph didn't deserve jail, but he responded to it beautifully. That's the marvel of the story. First and foremost in his life was his vital and consistent relationship with his Lord. And because of that, God used him in strategic and significant ways.

# MINISTRY IN PAIN

### ✦ *Read Genesis 40:1—3* ✦

*A* cupbearer was the person who tasted the wine and food of the king before he ate or drank. That way, if it was poisoned, "So long, cupbearer," but "Long live Pharaoh"! He also would not allow poorly prepared food to be served to the pharaoh since he was responsible for watching the monarch's diet. This led to a very close relationship, a relationship of trust between the two men. Often the king of the land would confide in the cupbearer. If you recall, Nehemiah was the cupbearer to the king of his day and had a close, personal relationship with him. In many ways, the cupbearer was the most trusted man of the court. If that trust was ever broken, serious consequences followed.

Something like that must have happened, because the cupbearer to Pharaoh landed in jail—as had also the king's baker. (He was another person on whom the pharaoh relied, because whatever he prepared passed into the mouth of the Egyptian ruler.) The specifics of what had happened to bring about this falling out and punishment, we're never told. All we know is that they "offended their lord" and he was "furious with his two officials." Maybe the biscuits fell that morning, and later there were too many jalapeños in the chili, and the cupbearer didn't warn Pharaoh! It must have been related to the food because their jobs were interrelated. But whatever it was, it made Pharaoh so angry that he said, "Get out of my sight!" and had them both thrown in jail. And since God's ways are deep and profound, it happened to be the same jail where Joseph was imprisoned.

Isn't it remarkable how often God brings alongside us people who are going through, or have gone through, similar experiences? Isn't it amazing, when we are hurting, God brings alongside us others who understand our pain? That is certainly true here. Joseph and these two men may have ended up in prison for different reasons, but they found themselves in the same place, sharing similar miseries. And out of his own painful experience, Joseph was able to minister to them.

# A Positive Attitude

### ❧ *Read Genesis 40:4–19* ❧

*I* smile as I read this, because if anybody ought to have had a sad face, it should have been Joseph. His plight was much worse than theirs. They were there on a whim of the Pharaoh and surely would not be there forever. But Joseph had been accused by the chief executioner's wife and didn't know if he'd ever see the light of day. But in spite of his own circumstance, he noticed the plight of these two men.

When your heart is right, even though the bottom may have dropped out of your life, it is remarkable how sensitive you can be to somebody else in need. They don't even have to spell it out. Rather than saying, "You think you've got a lot to complain about, listen to my tale of woe!" Joseph said, "How come you're so sad today, guys? What's wrong?" I admit it may be stating the obvious to ask this in a dungeon, but it shows Joseph's ability to think beyond his own immediate cares and needs in order to minister mercy to others.

One of the beautiful things about the right attitude is that, with it, every day has sunshine. You don't have to have cloudless days for there to be sunshine days.

Actually, it's rather amazing that Joseph would want to have anything to do with dreams. The last time he did that, remember what happened? He told his brothers about his dreams and it was "Operation Pit City." He wound up in an Egyptian slave market. You'd think he would say, "Not me, man! I'm off of dreams forever." But not Joseph. He said, "Oh, really? A dream, huh? Tell me about it."

That's what a positive attitude will do. It gets you beyond common hurdles. It will clear the deck. It will free you from hang-ups. It will show you an opportunity for ministry you never would have touched with a ten-foot pole.

# GOD AT WORK

### ✤ *Read Genesis 40:20–23* ✤

*P*ain, when properly handled, can shape a life for greatness. History is replete with stories of those whose struggles and scars formed the foundation for remarkable achievements. In fact, it was because of their hardship they gained what they needed to achieve greatness.

For a long time in my life, I wrestled with that concept. It seemed to be a cruel philosophy. Why should anyone need to suffer? What do you mean, "There are benefits that come only through struggles?" I have now come full circle. I agree with A. W. Tozer, who said, "It is doubtful whether God can bless a man greatly until He has hurt him deeply."[2] I could mention numerous examples, but certainly no life evidences this truth more clearly than the life of Joseph.

For the most part, Joseph's experiences thus far have been somber. He may have been born a favored son, but his life was filled with disappointment, mistreatment, and rejection, with fear and false accusations, with slavery and abandonment. We left Joseph alone in prison as we ended the previous chapter. Now, after a gap of two full years, we pick up his story again.

Remember, when we left him, he had told the cupbearer two years earlier, "Now that I've told you the meaning of your dream, don't forget me. Keep me in mind when things go well with you, and when you get promoted. Please do me the kindness of mentioning me to Pharaoh, and get me out of this place. Remember me." But the cupbearer failed to remember or mention Joseph. Only three days after Joseph said this, the man was released and restored to his former position as chief cupbearer to Pharaoh. He promptly forgot all about his days in the dungeon, as well as his cell mate, Joseph.

Two full years passed after that event—a long time to be forgotten. We may find ourselves asking, "After all Joseph had been through, why would something like this happen?" He had been obedient to God and was earlier promoted because "God was with him." The answer is that God was still at work in his life. The same is true for you.

# GRACE TO ENDURE

### *Read Genesis 40:20—41:1*

*W*hen Joseph saw the cupbearer taken from the prison, he must have thought, *Now's my chance! This guy has Pharaoh's ear. He'll get me out of here.* We don't know whether Joseph knew what happened to these men, but when their release came within the predicted time, he must have figured that, with God's help, he had given the correct interpretation of the dreams. So he waited hopefully for his opportunity to be released and set free.

Instead of being remembered and rewarded, he was forgotten for two more years. It's easy to overlook that little fact buried in the midst of all these dream sequences and their interpretations. But for two years after the cupbearer left, Joseph remained buried in that dungeon. Notice the emphasis: two *full* years. Two long, monotonous, miserable years!

What did Joseph think about during that time? The human tendency would be: *Will I be on hold forever, Lord? In fact, it seems like You have forgotten me!* No, there was none of that. This remarkable man, victimized again and again, continued to wait—to trust—to hope—to lean on God.

Listen to me, victims of mistreatment; more importantly, please listen to God's truth. He has a hundred different messages to give you during a hundred different dungeon experiences. He knows just the right message at just the right time, and all it takes to receive it is a sensitive, obedient, trusting heart. A heart that says, "Lord, God, help me now. Right at this moment. Deliver me from my own prison. Help me to see beyond the darkness, to see Your hand. As I am being crushed, remold me. Help me to see You in this abandonment, this rejection." Pray that prayer. Turn your trial into trust as you look to God to tenderly use that affliction, that dungeon, that abandonment for His purpose.

God has not abandoned you. He may be silent, but He has not forgotten you. He never left. He understands the heartache brought on by the evil which He mysteriously permits so that He might bring you to a tender, sensitive walk with Him. God is good, Jesus Christ is real—your present circumstances notwithstanding. My prayer is that He will do for you what He did for Joseph.

May He give you the grace to endure.

# DARKNESS BEFORE THE DAWN

*Read Genesis 40:20—41:1*

The process of discovering, processing, purifying, and shaping gold is a lengthy, painstaking process. Affliction is gold in the making for the child of God, and God is the one who determines how long the process takes. He alone is the Refiner.

This is where Joseph was when we left him. He is still in process. His gold is still being refined. His heart is still being broken by affliction and abandonment.

Those *two full years* for Joseph were neither exciting nor eventful. They represented a long, dull, monotonous, unspectacular, slow-moving grind. Month after month after month of . . . well, *nothing*. Not even the Genesis account attempts to make those years seem meaningful. Because they weren't.

That's what it's like when you're in a period of waiting. Nothing's happening! Wait. Wait. Wait. Wait.

On the other hand, it only *seems* like nothing is happening. In reality, a whole lot is happening. Events are occurring apart from our involvement. Furthermore, *we* are being strengthened. We are being established. We are being perfected. We are being refined. into pure gold.

We're back to my earlier comment—Joseph is being shaped for greatness. All whom God uses greatly are first hidden in the secret of His presence, away from the pride of man. It is there our vision clears. It is there the silt drops from the current of our life and our faith begins to grasp His arm. Abraham waited for the birth of Isaac. Moses didn't lead the Exodus until he was eighty. Elijah waited beside the brook. Noah waited 120 years for rain. Paul was hidden away for three years in Arabia. The list doesn't end. God is working while His people are waiting, waiting, waiting. Joseph is being shaped for a significant future.

That's what's happening. For the present time, nothing. For the future, everything!

# THE TURNING POINT

### *Read Genesis 41:1–16*

*A*fter those two full years, Joseph experienced a turning point in his life—on a day that seemed like any other day. That morning dawned like every other morning over the previous two years. Just like the morning that dawned before Moses saw the burning bush. Just like the morning that dawned before David was anointed by Samuel as the king-elect. For Joseph, just another dungeon day—except for one little matter Joseph knew nothing about: the night before Pharaoh had a bad dream.

The king of the land had a dream, and in it he saw seven fat, sleek cattle coming up out of the marshy Nile delta. Then seven ugly, gaunt, starving cows came up from the same river and devoured the fat, sleek cows.

Pharaoh awoke, perhaps thinking that huge meal he'd eaten before he went to bed wasn't setting too well on his stomach. Before long he fell back to sleep, and his dream continued. This time he saw a stalk of grain with seven plump and healthy ears. But then seven lean ears, scorched from the east wind, sprang up and devoured the seven healthy ears of grain.

When Pharaoh heard that there was someone around who could tell him what this troubling dream meant, he naturally said, "Go get the man."

"And Pharaoh said to Joseph, 'I have had a dream, but no one can interpret it; and I have heard it said about you, that when you hear a dream you can interpret it.' Joseph then answered Pharaoh, saying, 'It is not in me; God will give Pharaoh a favorable answer'" (Genesis 41:15–16).

Talk about humility. Talk about absolute integrity. This was Joseph's moment in court, his golden opportunity to say, "Do you realize that I could have been out of that place two years ago if that dummy standing right over there hadn't forgotten me?" But there was none of that.

You know why Joseph could be so humble and speak so openly? Because his heart had been broken. Because he had been tried by the fire of affliction. Because while his external circumstances seemed almost unbearable during those years, his internal condition had been turned into pure gold. We are now witnessing the benefits of enduring affliction with one's eyes on God.

# Humility When Promoted

### ✣ *Read Genesis 41:17–40* ✣

T here stood Joseph right before him, meeting all the requirements. But even then, when it seemed appropriate for Joseph to volunteer, he restrained. The king, however, knew Joseph was the man for the job.

Who isn't impressed with Joseph's self-control? Refusing to manipulate the moment or drop hints, he simply stood there and waited. Somehow in the loneliness of his recent years, abandoned and forgotten in prison, he had learned to let the Lord have His way, in His time, for His purposes. Absent of selfish ambition, Joseph refused to promote himself. How refreshing—how rare!

How many of us have maneuvered or plotted to get our own way, only to live to regret it? One of the most embarrassing memories many people have is the day they got what they schemed and manipulated to acquire—only to see it dissolve right in their hands. That was not the kind of promotion Joseph wanted.

If God was in it, God would do it. That's precisely what happened here. God was in it, and God did it. Pharaoh said to Joseph, "Since God told you all this, there is obviously no one as discerning or as wise as you. Therefore, I'm putting you in command of everything. The only person you answer to—the only person with more authority—is me. You're second in command. You're now my prime minister." Do you know what Pharaoh saw in Joseph? Gold.

The word *discernment* suggests the ability to have shrewd insight into a situation and act constructively in times of need. Joseph was a man who could do this and much, much more. He understood how to assess a situation and make the right decisions, even under pressure. He understood this, because it was through pressure that he had been refined into gold.

# TENDER MERCIES

### ❧ *Read Genesis 41:41–46* ❧

*P*haraoh swept his hand out wide, so as to include all that vast land of Egypt, and said, "It's all yours, Joseph." Then he took off his signet ring and put it on Joseph's hand.

You know what that ring signified, don't you? It was the platinum charge card of that day. It was the way the king stamped the invoices, the laws, or anything else he wanted to verify or validate with his seal. Now Joseph had that ring on his finger, placed there by the Pharaoh himself. Joseph wore the authority of the king's imprint.

Joseph's Cinderella-like promotion was incredible. But when God determines the time is right, that's the way He operates.

*When the reward comes, thank God without pride.* Only God can bring you through and out of the dungeon. Only God can reward you for your faithfulness. If He has, be grateful, not proud. Remember, with humility, that it is God who has put you there.

Some of you are on the verge of promotion and you don't even know it, because God doesn't announce His appointments in advance. What you have to do, while you wait, is to believe His promises. While in the darkness of your dungeon, by faith, trust him to bring the light of a new dawn. In the winter of your discontent, believe there'll be a spring.

The God of Joseph will stay beside us during the dungeon days; He will not forsake or forget us. He will be there during the blast of the winter storm, holding out the promise of springtime. He will be there through the darkest night, quietly reminding us of the promise of morning light.

Joseph learned that a broken and contrite heart is not the end, but the beginning. Bruised and crushed by the blows of disappointment and unrealized dreams, he discovered that God had never left his side. When the affliction ended, he had been refined, and he came forth as gold. He had become a person of greater stability, of deeper quality, of stronger character. God's promises are just as much for us as they were for Joseph. His grace is still at work. His tender mercies accompany us from the pit to the pinnacle.

# Don't Panic . . . Trust

### ⚓ *Read Genesis 41:41–46* ⚓

*T*his is an excellent opportunity to shift the scene for a moment and look at all this from the perspective of the guy who's out working in the fields, moving stones for one of those interminable, ever-ongoing pyramid projects. He knows nothing at all about what's just happened in the dungeon and throne room. All he knows is that some young upstart, some foreigner, has maneuvered his way into Pharaoh's good graces. And he is being told, "Bow your knee to this man!"

"Oh, man, look at that!" whispers the workman. "Who does he think he is? Who did he bribe to get all this? He must know somebody. That's the way it is up there in the court."

Given that same situation, we'd probably think the same thing. Back in the Vietnam era, we often heard the phrase, "Never trust anyone over thirty." Today, given the large segment of aging populace, we are more likely to hear, "Never trust anyone *under* thirty."

But what we can't see from our limited perspective is what God has been doing on the inside. That worker in the field doesn't know—doesn't have the slightest idea—what has gone on before in Joseph's life, nor is he even aware of his years in the dungeon. He doesn't know about Joseph's faithfulness when nobody else was around.

Joseph has been appointed, chosen, selected, prepared, and refined into gold by Almighty God. That's how he has come to wear the ring. That's how he has come to get the robe, the necklace, and the chariot. That's why others are saying, "Bow the knee." Joseph himself isn't saying that; others are.

I wonder what Joseph was thinking at that moment?

I believe he was saying to himself over and over, "Praise be to God." I think he was tallying up all the things God had taught him in the past thirty years, things God also wants to teach us.

*During the waiting period, trust God without panic.* Count on Him to handle the cupbearers of your life, the people who forget you, the people who break their promises. It's God's job to deal with the cupbearers of your past. It's your job to be the kind of servant He has designed you to be. Be faithful during the waiting periods of life. God will not forget you or forsake you.

# FORGIVE AND FORGET

### ❧ *Read Genesis 41:47—52* ❧

God guided the writer of Genesis to reveal the truth about most every area of Joseph's colorful life. He allows us to see what the man was really like inside, even what he was thinking. We can sum it up in one sentence: his heart was humble before God.

Why does the writer add these details? First, I think he wants us to know that Joseph was monogamous. He didn't fall into the trap of polygamy, like so many surrounding him—even his own family. He had one wife, and she bore him two sons. Second, and more important, the writer wants us to realize the significance found in the names of Joseph's sons. Both names are a play on words. The New International Version footnotes state, "*Manasseh* sounds like and may be derived from the Hebrew word for *forget*," and "*Ephraim* sounds like the Hebrew for *twice fruitful*."

In naming his sons as he did, Joseph proclaimed openly that God had made him forget all his troubles, even those in his father's household. Above and beyond that, God had made him fruitful in a land and in circumstances that had brought him nothing but trouble. How humble of Joseph to acknowledge that!

The memories were still there, lodged deep in the creases beneath his cranium, but when relief finally came, God made him forget the pain, the anguish of what had happened.

It is very tempting to try to get revenge on the Reubens and the Judahs and the Dans and the Mrs. Potiphars from our past. To get back at those who have stung us and stripped us and hurt us with evil deeds and ugly words. Instead, we must give birth to a Manasseh. Could it be that it's time to ask the Lord God to erase the stings in your memory? *Only He can do that.* Then it will be time to go on to give birth to an Ephraim. To remember how God has abundantly blessed us. Talk about a positive, affirming name: "God has made me fruitful." But it doesn't stop there. With the plural ending, this word conveys the idea of double benefit—multiple blessings. It's what we would call "superabundance." And it was God who did it all.

# GIVING FOR HIS GLORY

### ✦ *Read Genesis 41:53–57* ✦

*I*f I read these verses correctly, this was a widespread famine such as the world had never known, for it says, "The famine was spread over all the face of the earth."

In these circumstances, what did Joseph do? He didn't hoard the storehouses of plenty for himself and his family, or for the royal household, or even for the land of Egypt. He opened those great vaults and released the contents to anyone who needed food. "The people of all the earth came to Egypt to buy grain from Joseph." This was a man who never took advantage of his privileges, his authority, or his financial resources.

He is continuing to walk humbly before his Lord. He has earthly power, but his integrity is still in place, and he freely shares his abundance with others in need. That helps in our evaluation, doesn't it? We cannot help but admire those who reap the rewards of righteousness because God prospers them, when they, in turn, provide for others in need.

I want to go on record here and state that I personally believe that some of the choicest saints in the family of God are those who have walked in integrity as God has blessed them with wealth by His grace, and they use it for God's glory. Ministries I have been a part of have benefited immensely not only from those who have little of this world's goods, but also from the Josephs of this and previous generations.

To the wealthy Josephs that God is raising up in this generation and the next, may you continue to walk with Him. May you generously use your affluence and authority for His glory, and your influence and success to make His Word and truth known.

God *can* use our authority and our abundance and our promotion as He did with Joseph. But before He can, we need to humble ourselves before God's mighty hand and say, "Jesus Christ, I need You. I have all of this to account for, and I can't take any of it with me. Please use me as you see fit." With authority comes the need for *accountability*. With popularity comes the need for *humility*. With prosperity comes the need for *integrity*. Joseph passed all three tests with flying colors.

Those who model the same depth of character mixed with wisdom deserve our respect and affirmation.

# TAKING RESPONSIBILITY

*Read Genesis 42:1–24*

*P*ut yourself in Joseph's sandals. How must he have felt as he heard their words? So far as his brothers were concerned, he no longer existed! He was buried in the graveyard of their memories. He was "no more." Out of sight, out of mind, gone forever.

Three times Joseph accused them of being spies. Then, in one of their responses, they unwittingly gave him information he wanted. They told him that his father and Benjamin were still alive!

We can imagine what was surging through Joseph's mind: "I wonder if Benjamin is healthy and strong? And what about my father? Is he too old to remember? Oh, how I long to see my entire family. How tempted I am to tell them who I am—they'll be shocked! What I really wonder about is the condition of their hearts."

Joseph chose Simeon as hostage and had him put in shackles there in his brothers' presence. Why did Joseph pick Simeon? We might think he would have chosen the firstborn, but that was Reuben, who had tried to save Joseph's life back at the pit when they all teamed up against him. Perhaps Joseph remembered Reuben's attempt to intervene on his behalf, and instead chose the second eldest brother, Simeon, to remain behind.

"Then they said to one another, 'Truly we are guilty concerning our brother, because we saw the distress of his soul when he pleaded with us, yet we would not listen; therefore this distress has come upon us'" (Genesis 42:21).

In the original language, the "we" in their conversation is emphatic! "We are guilty . . . we saw the distress of his soul . . . we would not listen."

The first step toward softening a seared conscience is taking responsibility for one's own personal guilt. The brothers did not blame their father for being passive. They did not blame their brother Joseph for being proud or arrogant or favored. They did not diminish the wrong by saying they were too young to know any better. They used the right pronoun when they agreed together, "We are responsible! There is no one else we can blame!"

# GUILTY

### ✦ *Read Genesis 42:21—24* ✦

When you have done wrong to someone and haven't gone through the necessary process to make things right with them and with God—when you haven't fully dealt with your transgression—you become the victim of the very distress that you put that person through. "We feel the same distress that we caused him and saw in his face."

Do you remember Edgar Allan Poe's short story *The Telltale Heart?* In it the murderer couldn't sleep because he kept hearing the beating heart of his victim down in his basement. He wasn't hearing the victim's heart, of course; he was hearing his own heart, pounding in his chest, reverberating through his skull. His own guilt awoke him, tortured him, and finally led to the revelation that he was the murderer.

The brothers' crime was now more than two decades old, but they still felt the distress of it. Time doesn't erase distress. We have evidence of that in our own lives. We know from experience the inescapable reminders of our guilt. The emotional entanglements brought about by the consequences of our own sin can be so devastating that we become physically sick.

We're not left to wonder what Joseph felt when he heard his brothers' words, when he heard them admit their guilt over what they had done. We are told he had to leave the room so he could weep. What tears of relief and joy! He understood well one of the reasons they were breaking. They had been in the dungeon for three days, and he knew what that was like. He had spent years in a dungeon. He knew what that could do to a person. He also knew that when God comes to tap on stooped shoulders and to break a guilty heart, He does not stop with a slight nudge or mild reproof.

The long-outstanding bills were coming due for Joseph's brothers. And as their debt rose ever higher before their eyes, they openly admitted, "We are guilty!"

# New Perspective

### ❧ *Read Genesis 42:25—28* ❧

oseph's brothers wanted to get out of Egypt, like, fast. When the sacks of grain were loaded on their donkeys, they immediately began their journey back to Canaan. But something happened on the first night they stopped to rest and feed and water the animals. When one of the brothers opened a sack to get food for his donkey, he saw that the money he had paid to the prime minister of Egypt was tucked into the top of the bag.

"I can't believe this!" he exclaimed. "Look! My money has been returned. It's here in the sack."

The other brothers quickly opened their sacks and discovered that their money had been returned to them also.

Instead of being happy about this surprise, however, they were frightened. "Their hearts sank, and they turned trembling to one another." The Hebrew word that is translated "trembling" is the same word used in 1 Samuel 14:15 to describe a giant earthquake. It's also used in Genesis 27:33 to describe the trembling of Isaac when he learned that his son Jacob had stolen Esau's birthright. In fact, we read there that Isaac "trembled violently." He shook, literally! That's what Joseph's brothers began to do. They began to shake. They began to tremble as they looked at one another. It was then they said, "What is this that God has done to us?"

I love that statement. Not only are they now feeling the full brunt of their own guilt, they are also sensing God's hand in this. "What is God doing?"

When God softens a seared conscience *we begin to gain a different perspective.* Sometimes we become victims of the kind of treatment we have meted out to someone else. When the harm, the hurt, or the pain that we brought on someone else is visited upon us, something begins to change within us. God begins to break through our hard shell and soften our hearts that had become calloused.

# A HORIZONTAL VIEWPOINT

### ✤ *Read Genesis 42:29–38* ✤

*W*hen Jacob learned what had happened, the old gentleman shriveled in fear. Rather than saying, "Thank God, He is at work. Men, He loves us and watches over us. In His care we are all safe," he responded negatively and horizontally. His sons had not only returned with the food they needed, but also with all of their money. They had been given grain from Egypt free of charge. All the prime minister had asked was that they prove they were not spies by returning with their youngest brother and claiming Simeon who had been left as a hostage. Yet Jacob saw none of this as God's provision. He froze in fear and focused on a worst-case scenario.

As soon as he heard they had left their brother in Egypt, he jumped to the conclusion that Simeon was dead. "Joseph is dead. Simeon is dead. Everything is against me," he moaned. He began to sound paranoid and self-pitying. "All these things are against me!"

Last time I checked, Jacob was supposed to be the patriarch of the clan, the spiritual leader. Yet, with a quick glance behind the scenes, as we sneak a peek through the back door of the tent, we see Jacob as he really is.

It's one thing for us to sit with this book in hand and read the story, knowing what the outcome will be, and say with a shrug, "I'll tell you this, I sure wouldn't have done that. I would have trusted God if I had been in that situation." But would you really? Well, then why didn't you trust Him last week? What was it that kept you from seeing God's hand in that matter you couldn't handle last month? Call to mind your most recent major test. Did you rest calmly in Him? Or did you push the panic button out of fear?

Negative thinking. A horizontal viewpoint. A closed mind to something that is unexpected and new. That's why we tend to panic. Because, humanly speaking, you and I have been programmed toward defeat. We have formed habits of response that leave God out of the picture. We don't actually announce it in those words, we just model it and rationalize around it by calling it something else. And aren't we relieved God didn't put our biography into print?

# GOD'S DIRECTIONS

### ✤ *Read Genesis 43:1–12* ✤

*J*udah put it on the line. "You can't continue to delay and deny the situation. I'll take responsibility for Benjamin's life. If anything happens to him, I will bear the consequences for the rest of my days. Come on, Dad, let's cooperate. If we hadn't delayed this long, we could already have been down there and back twice with food."

Judah offered to take the blame, even though blaming is a futile exercise. Yelling at darkness doesn't make it light. But we like to blame. "Dad," said Judah, "if you want to blame somebody, blame me. But let Benjamin go. Man, we're dying here."

Aging Jacob reluctantly gave in. He responded with what I would call tolerance and uncertainty. First he denied and delayed. Then came blame and deceit. And now, finally, tolerance and uncertainty. The old man was one tough nut to crack!

Perhaps his response went something like this: "Oh, all right. If you have to do it, then here's the procedure I want you to follow." See his attitude? And then he reverted to another old pattern. He ordered them to take gifts, things that were native to Canaan. If he had lived in the days of Solomon, he would have claimed Proverbs 21:14: "A gift in secret subdues anger, and a bribe in the bosom, strong wrath."

Years before, he had done that with his brother, Esau, and it had worked. It might work with the Egyptian prime minister too.

Jacob could see all kinds of schemes, but he still refused to see God's hand at work. He could not say, "Look, boys, we don't know what all this means, but we do know that we're confused and we need God's help. Let's trust God for protection and insight on this. Let's ask Him to give us direction on what to do."

Parents, this is an appropriate time for me to urge you to call your families to prayer. "Hey, kids, let's pray about this before we leave the breakfast table." Or, "Let's spend some time Saturday morning asking God for direction in this situation. We don't know what to do." Maybe one of your sons or daughters is edging into rebellion. Listen to them. Listen longer than normal. Try hard not to butt in. Admit it when you're not sure how to respond. Then sit down and pray together, asking for God's direction.

# A VERTICAL FOCUS

### 🌿 *Read Genesis 43:13—15* 🌿

*I* wonder what those ten men, those ten grown sons of Jacob, talked about during that journey from Canaan to Egypt? I have an idea that it might have been the same things we would have talked about had we been in their sandals. I also believe these men were beginning to be broken. Perhaps they spoke of how much they missed their brother, Joseph. With Benjamin now among them, maybe they felt this was a good time to express their sorrow over their past actions and, together, sincerely request El Shaddai's power and protection. I so want to believe that God was starting to melt their hearts before Him! In fact, that's the beauty of this story as it progresses. We're led to wonder what exactly they were thinking. We so desperately want to cut to the chase to see the happy ending, but we must wait. Because there's always something to learn along the way.

When we're on our journey from Canaan to Egypt, we tend to be negative rather than positive. We tend to view life horizontally rather than vertically. We tend to be resistant rather than open to that which is new and unexpected. We need some course-correction techniques to break those habits!

I can think of at least three that have worked for me:

*Recognize and admit your negative mentality.* So much of the cure is in the confession. Immediate correction begins with honest admission.

*Force a vertical focus until it begins to flow freely.* I have never seen a habit just lie down, surrender, and die; we have to make a conscious effort if we hope to break longstanding habits. If you are negative today, chances are very good that when you wake up tomorrow morning you're still going to be negative. Force a vertical focus.

*Stay open to a new idea for at least five minutes.* Don't try it for an entire day; you might panic. Just take on your day five minutes at a time. When something new, something unexpected, confronts you, don't respond with an immediate "Nope! Never!" Wait five minutes. Hold off. Tolerate the possibility for five minutes. You will be surprised at the benefit of remaining open.

# CALMING RESPONSE

*Read Genesis 43:16—23*

uilt always does a number on us. It certainly did on Joseph's brothers. Though, standing before an unnamed, soft-spoken servant from Egypt, whom they had never really known throughout their lives, they poured out their confession.

"We don't know how the money got back in our sacks the first time, but here it is. We've brought it all back. We also brought additional money to buy more food. That's why we're here . . . to buy food."

I love the steward's reassuring response: "Be at ease," he told them. The Hebrew Bible says, simply, "Shalom." The steward, who knew their well-known language, used their word for peace. He said, in effect, "Hey, shalom, men—be at peace. Settle down. Don't be afraid." And then this Egyptian even witnessed to them about their God. "Your own God is the one who put the treasure in your sacks. Nobody thinks you stole it. I know what happened; I was the one who put it there. I was the one who had your money. It was a treasure from Elohim, the God of your father."

They were in agony, wondering when the other shoe was going to drop. Instead, the steward said, "Shalom! Elohim has done it again." What a reproof! And, by the way, what an interesting surprise that this Egyptian steward understood such sound theology. No doubt, it was the result of Joseph's influence through the years. He personifies what we considered earlier—vertical perspective.

Joseph's brothers had never thought to relate the return of their money to the abundant grace of God. Why? Because guilt had kept them from seeing God's hand of grace in their lives. (It always does!) Yet the unmerited favor of God had been demonstrated in abundance to them: grain in abundance, money in abundance. And now their brother Simeon is restored to them, healthy and whole. Mercy in abundance.

# STRENGTH TO WEEP

### *Read Genesis 43:24–30*

S uddenly, this great man, this strong-hearted and efficient prime minister of a mighty nation, collapsed inside. Like the rest of us, great men and women encounter those times in life when they can no longer restrain their emotions. Composure flies away, and feelings take control. That was what happened to Joseph at this long-awaited moment in time. It is at such sacred crossroads words fail us. Often we need to get alone to gain our composure. Joseph did.

"And Joseph hurried out for he was deeply stirred over his brother, and he sought a place to weep; and he entered his chamber and wept there" (Genesis 43:30).

Can't you imagine the scene? All of a sudden, the handsome, confident leader of millions has rushed to his bedroom and collapsed in sobs. All those years passed in review. All the loneliness. All the loss. All the seasons and birthdays and significant occasions without his family. It was too much to contain, like a rushing river pouring into a lake, swelling above the dam. His tears ran, and he heaved with great sobs. All of a sudden, he was a little boy again, missing his daddy.

There have been times in my own life when I've had doubts, when I've stumbled over great cracks that appeared in my world. I've had those times when I climbed into my own bed and wept, crying out to God, just as you have. Such is life, especially when you decide to be real rather than protect some kind of super-confident image. It's comforting to realize we're in good company in times like that, isn't it?

Joseph was a great and powerful man, admittedly, but he was also a real human being with real human emotions, who could step out of the corridors of power and have the strength to weep his heart out.

# A BANQUET OF GRACE

*Read Genesis 43:31–34*

*J*oseph's brothers were astonished at the way they were being treated. They had expected any number of things to happen to them, including possible death, but certainly not this. Now here they were, seated according to age, dining with the prime minister. And what a feast! They were served fresh garden salads, thick T-bone steaks, fried okra, overstuffed baked potatoes, cornbread, black-eyed peas, and big glasses of iced tea (if Egypt was anything like Texas)! Besides that, the prime minister unloaded more food from his own table.

Benjamin, interestingly, was served portions five times the size of the other men. Those hungry Hebrews must have thought they'd died and gone to glory. Benjamin himself may have thought, *I know I'm thin, but this is ridiculous. What's going on here?*

By now Joseph was totally oblivious. *This is Benjamin! My brother!* He was so ecstatic, so overjoyed that he just kept piling on the food. Sounds like something an older brother would do for one he hasn't seen in ages, doesn't it? Especially, when the elder is full of forgiveness and grace!

Amazing, isn't it, how Joseph's acts of grace freed up everyone around the tables. At the outset, there were feelings of anxiety and dread as guilt held them in its grip. Their fear had known no bounds as they returned to Egypt, wondering what they would face.

Within a brief span of time, they found themselves treated kindly, sitting around a banquet table loaded with food, and, of all things, relaxing in the joyful presence of royalty. What relief! Better than that, what grace! They were the recipients of favor they hadn't earned and kindness they didn't deserve. And they were overloaded with an abundance of provisions they could never repay. Is anyone surprised they were astonished and no longer afraid? Their fear was now displaced by grace. Why? One reason—Joseph. This great man, though not as yet known to them to be their brother, determined to forgive their mistreatment and, instead, demonstrate great grace. Rather than remind them of their wrongs and force them to pay for their cruelty and injustices from years gone by, he showed them favor to the maximum extreme. This reunion was really a banquet of grace—on full display—thanks to Joseph, a man of integrity and forgiveness.

# A REFLECTION OF CHRIST

### ❧ *Read Genesis 43:33–34* ❧

*J*oseph's life offers us a magnificent portrayal of the grace of God as He came to our rescue in the Person of His Son, Jesus. So many come to Him, like Joseph's guilty brothers, feeling the distance and fearing the worst from God, only to have Him demonstrate incredible generosity and mercy. Instead of being blamed, we are forgiven. Instead of feeling guilty, we are freed. And instead of experiencing punishment, which we certainly deserve, we are seated at His table and served more than we can ever take in.

For some, it's too unreal. So we desperately plead our case, only to have Him speak kindly to us—promising us peace in our own language. We then try to fend off His anger by bargaining with Him, thinking our hard work and sincere efforts will pay Him back for all those evil past deeds we're guilty of. But to our astonishment, He never even considered our attempts important enough to mention. What we had in mind was earning just enough to silence our guilt, but what He had in mind was overwhelming us with such an abundance we'd realize we can never, ever repay.

What a beautiful picture of Christ at the cross, bearing the sins we committed, forgiving us in the process. Isn't such grace amazing? The One who was rejected is the same One who goes the limit to get us reunited with Him.

Therefore the LORD longs to be gracious to you,
And therefore He waits on high to have compassion on you.
For the LORD is a God of justice;
How blessed are all those who long for Him. (Isaiah 30:18)

Do you long for Him? I've got great news! In an even greater way—greater than you could ever imagine—He longs to be gracious to you. He is offering you all the things you hunger for. The table is loaded, and He is smiling, waiting for you to sit down and enjoy the feast He prepared with you in mind. Have a seat—grace is being served.

# FINAL EXAM, PART ONE

### ❦ *Read Genesis 44:1—16* ❦

The sons of Jacob were not far from the city when they looked back and saw the prime minister's steward overtaking them. Once he caught up, he accused them of stealing from the Egyptian leader. "How could you do such a deceitful deed, after having been treated so well?"

They did not hesitate to let the steward examine their sacks of food, beginning with Reuben, the oldest. But lo and behold, when the steward got all the way down to the youngest, he found the silver cup in Benjamin's sack!

They had to return to the city with the steward, of course, where they were immediately ushered into the prime minister's presence. There, Judah did the talking.

This confession from Judah's mouth was amazing. But this was precisely what Joseph had been waiting for; this was why he had given the final exam. They passed. In fact all the brothers made straight A's on the first part of the test.

In speaking for his brothers, Judah did not attempt to justify himself or the others, nor does he try to pass the blame off onto Benjamin. Unlike before, they didn't turn on Benjamin and reject him as they had Joseph so many years ago. Judah says, in no uncertain terms, they were all guilty.

Given their history, this is an amazing admission. A real change had begun in their attitude. Think about the fact that these words were coming from the mouth and heart of *Judah!*

Joseph wanted to know whether his brothers were able to read the hand of God into daily life, even in things that seemed unfair. Even in misfortune and death. He wanted to see if their vertical scope was clear. And now he heard this confession coming out of Judah's mouth, who laid the guilt on all their shoulders. "Before God we have been found out. We are guilty! Our iniquity has been discovered."

I believe that in his confession Judah was actually going back over twenty years earlier and was referring to those days when they not only hated their brother Joseph but turned against him and sold him into slavery. Had it not been for Reuben, they would have murdered him. This now haunted these men. Judah had begun to realize that God did not overlook an unrepented offense.

# FINAL EXAM, PART TWO

### ✒ *Read Genesis 44:17–34* ✒

This was Joseph's second part of the final exam. First came the vertical test. Had his brothers gotten to the place where they read the hand of God into their daily life? Yes. They had demonstrated this in their attitude. Next came the horizontal test. Which would they choose, themselves or Benjamin? Had there been any change in their hearts over the years?

So Joseph said, "I would never punish all of you for one man's crime. The cup has been found in your youngest brother's possession, so he is the one I will punish. He will forfeit his freedom and become my slave. The rest of you, go in peace. You can return to your father."

Following this pronouncement comes a shocking speech: "Now, therefore, please let your servant remain instead of the lad a slave to my lord, and let the lad go up with his brothers. For how shall I go up to my father if the lad is not with me, lest I see the evil that would overtake my father?" (Genesis 44:33–34).

Do you realize who is saying this? Again, it is *Judah*. These "unexcelled" words were coming from the same man who, twenty years earlier, proposed without remorse, "Here comes that dreamer, Joseph. Let's kill him and say that a ferocious animal devoured him." Shortly after that cold-blooded proposal, he rationalized, "What will we gain if we kill our brother and cover up his blood? Let's sell him to the slave traders instead."

Yet here he is now, pleading for his youngest brother. Added to that, he is pleading on behalf of his aging father.

A few years earlier, Judah could not have cared less what his father thought, since his father had always shown favoritism to Rachel's sons. In fact, the violence and cruelty Judah and his brothers perpetrated against Joseph was an indirect act of cruelty committed against their father.

Now, of all things, this same man is exhibiting a sacrificial attitude. "Take me instead. But send Benjamin back home. I cannot bear to imagine such grief that would overtake my father." No, it's not the same man; Judah has changed.

No doubt about it. All his brothers were becoming transformed men, and Joseph recognized this. Repentance had done its work.

# GRACE TO THE GUILTY

### *Read Genesis 45:1–8*

Humanly speaking, the average individual, when faced with people who have done them such grievous wrong, would likely frown and demand, "Drop to your knees and stay there! You think you know what humiliation is all about. You wait until I'm through with you. I've been waiting all these torturous years for this moment!"

But not Joseph. He, too, was a changed man. He was God's man, which means he was a great man. And so, with the arm of the Lord supporting him, he could look into his brothers' anxious eyes and say, in all sincerity, "Do not be grieved or angry with yourselves because you sold me into slavery. It was not you who sent me here, but God. He sent me before you to preserve life." Allow me a moment to interrupt the flow of events and ask you: Did he operate from the vertical perspective, or what?

"But God!" Those two words change *everything*.

Joseph could never have spoken such words of reassurance if he had not fully forgiven his brothers. You cannot genuinely embrace a person you've not fully forgiven. Joseph did not see his brothers as enemies, because his perspective had been changed. "You didn't send me here," he said. "God sent me here. And He sent me here for a reason—to preserve life."

I love that. In today's terms: "Men, it wasn't you who pulled this off; it was God. It was my sovereign Lord who saw far into the future and saw the needs of this world and chose me to be His personal messenger to solve the famine problem of the future. You thought you were doing evil to me. But I'll tell you, it was God who worked outside your evil intentions to preserve life."

And he says it again, "Now, therefore, it was not you who sent me here, but God." *But God!* Underline that. "God sent me." Joseph was a man who operated his life—continually—with divine perspective.

# ATTITUDE ADJUSTMENT

### ✤ *Read Genesis 45:8—9* ❦

*O*n top of his forgiveness and reassurance, he "made them an offer they couldn't refuse." He urged them to return and bring their father to this land, where they could enjoy relief from their barren existence.

Joseph said, "Brothers, I have seen a change in your lives. You care about our father and one another, and you never did before. You care about Benjamin, more than even your own lives. What a change!"

Attitude is so crucial in the life of the Christian. We can go through the Sunday motions, we can carry out the religious exercises, we can pack a Bible under our arms, and sing familiar songs from memory, yet we can still hold grudges against the people who have wronged us. In our own way—and it may even be with a little religious manipulation—we'll get back at them. But that is not God's way. Here, He shows us the right way. He gives us the example of Joseph, great man that he was, being supportive, merciful, gracious, generous, and unselfish. He's not through showing how deeply he cares for them. Look at this next scene!

"Then he fell on his brother Benjamin's neck and wept; and Benjamin wept on his neck. And he kissed all his brothers and wept on them, and afterward his brothers talked with him" (Genesis 45:14–15).

*I would imagine* they "talked with him!" They had about twenty-five years' worth of talking to do. And I am confident that every time they went back and started to rehearse their wrongs, Joseph stopped them. "We're not going there. That was then, this is now. God had a plan, and it's all worked out for our good and His glory. Let's talk about that."

The late great preacher, John Henry Jowett, used to say that a minister doesn't deserve an hour to preach a sermon if he can't give it in one sentence. So let me give you this sermon in a sentence: Greatness is revealed mainly in our attitude.

# WALK BY FAITH

### ⚜ *Read Genesis 45:10—15* ⚜

*I*f you're under the impression that you are going to be great because of some accomplishment you've achieved but harbor wrong attitudes, you're in for a terrible jolt. Greatness comes in the sweet-spirit attitudes of humility and forgiveness toward others. Joseph sets before us a magnanimous example. How beautifully forgiving he was, how generous in his mercy.

It takes God to make the heart right. When I have a wrong attitude, I look at life humanly. When I have a right attitude, I look at life divinely. That's the real beauty of Joseph's life. That's the kernel of truth his life represents. He was great, mainly because of his attitude.

And there are specific lessons that grow out of that single truth. Let me offer at least three for your consideration.

First: *When I'm able, by faith, to see God's plan in my location, my attitude will be right.* God sent me . . . God sent me . . . God sent me. Not until you can relax and see God in your present location will you be useful to Him. A positive theological attitude will do wonders for your geographical latitude.

Second: *When I'm able, by faith, to sense God's hand in my situation, my attitude will be right.* I don't begin the day gritting my teeth, asking, "Why do I have to stay in this situation?" Instead, I believe that He made me the way I am and put me where I am to do what He has planned for me to do.

Third: *When I'm able, by faith, to accept both location and situation as good, even when there's been evil in the process, my attitude will be right.* When I can say with Joseph, "but God meant it for good," then I become a trophy of grace.

Joseph shows us that the only way to find happiness in the grind of life is to do so *by faith.* A faith-filled life means all the difference in how we view everything around us. It affects our attitudes toward people, toward location, toward situation, toward circumstances, toward ourselves. Only then do our feet become swift to do what is right.

You say you want to be considered great some day? Here's the secret: walk by faith, trusting God to renew your attitude.

# THE NATURE WITHIN

### ✣ *Read Genesis 45:16—28* ✣

*J*oseph's brothers not only had plenty to eat on the way, but had also been given new clothing. They had all that they needed—and they once again had it in abundance! These men must have really looked like something when they returned to Canaan, a land drying up under those lingering years of famine.

Notice, however, the one directive Joseph gave them: "Don't get into an argument on the journey!" He knew those men, didn't he? I can't help but smile at times in these biblical stories when little tidbits like that are inserted. Centuries may come and go, but human nature stays pretty much the same. It's impossible to erase depravity.

Not very many men can carry a full cup without its disturbing their equilibrium. Sudden wealth or promotion can be a tottering experience, both for the recipient and those surrounding him or her. Superiority, inferiority, arrogance, and jealousy can easily begin to hold sway. If you question that, check on those who win the lottery. Very few can handle the financial windfall.

Joseph had given his brother Benjamin more than he had given to the other brothers. He gave them all provisions and gave each of them new garments, but he gave Benjamin three hundred shekels of silver and five new garments. No doubt Joseph remembered well what had happened years before when he had been given more than the others, but he had his own reasons for giving Benjamin these items. He didn't want that to result in a fight. "So don't argue about it!" he told his brothers.

I think it is safe to say that we are to trust one another, but we are never to trust one another's nature. That's one of the reasons parents give their children the warnings that they do. Parents understand their children's natures better than their offspring do. It's not a question of trust; it's a matter of knowing the nature within.

# GOD IN THE MOVE

*Read Genesis 46:1–7*

*Y*es, old Jacob had learned some hard lessons about what happened when he did not talk with God and walk with God. Therefore, he wanted to be sure that God was in this. This was a big move for all the family. Thankfully, by now, Jacob had matured into a seasoned and wise old man. He stopped and waited, willing to learn whether the move to Egypt would be accompanied by the presence and blessing of God.

It must have been a great moment when, in the night, he was awakened by the voice of God, calling, "Jacob, Jacob."

"Here I am," he replied quietly.

"I am God, the God of your father, Isaac. Don't be afraid to go down to Egypt, for it is there that I will make you a great nation. I will go down to Egypt with you, and I will also bring you back to this land again. And your son Joseph will be with you when you die."

This is a major moment not only for Jacob and his family, but for all of Israel. This is an early prophetic reference to Israel's great Exodus from Egypt. Go back and read the Lord's words to Jacob once again. Notice the promise, "I will also surely bring you up [to this land] again."

Making a major move can be one of the most insecure times we face in life. Pulling up roots in one place and trying to put them down in another can be not only fearful but depressing. That's why I think it's wise to pause here and understand the value of Jacob's hearing God's voice of approval. I've known people who have taken years to adjust—and some who simply never adjust. For the Christian this is heightened by a sense of wonder over whether God is in the move. And even when we feel assured that God is in it, we can still experience times of uncertainty and displacement. I'm referring not only to a geographical move but also to a career change or a domestic move from single to married. Big, big changes! The assurance that God is with us during such alterations in lifestyle and adjustment periods is terribly important.

As children of God, we're to listen to the voice of God and ask, *Is God in this? Does this please Him?*

# FINAL FAMILY REUNION

### ✧ *Read Genesis 46:28–30* ✧

T hink of what it must have been like. After more than two decades, Jacob once more held the son that he had given up for dead. After all he had been through, Joseph embraced his aging father—the man he had missed so much, the one he feared he would never see again. He could feel the bones across his back as he held the old man in his arms. How long it had been! How much he had missed him! There the two men stood, staring into each other's eyes. Weeping one moment, laughing the next. *What a grand family reunion.*

Jacob said the only fitting thing as soon as he could control himself: "Now let me die, since I have seen your face, that you are still alive" (Genesis 46:30).

There is another type of reunion noted in Scripture—*the final, ultimate family reunion* that is the hope of every child of God.

On that day, we'll all hear the blast of a trumpet. I know some who expect to hear the melodious strings of a harp. Not me. I expect to hear the lonely whine of a harmonica—because my dad is there in glory, awaiting my arrival. And on that "great gettin'-up morning," our entire family will be reunited forever in the presence of the Lord.

The reality is, though, that no matter how precious your memories, it does not matter the way you were. What matters is the way you are. No amount of solid family ties will fit you for heaven. Only through Christ will you be included in His family roll call.

We can be thankful for the recording chamber of our memories that keeps us young. But what we really need at this important moment is the deep assurance that we are His. Only then can we look forward in hope to that ultimate and final family reunion.

# LOYALTY TEST

### ✦ *Read Genesis 46:31–34* ✦

*J*oseph efficiently thought through a plan of operation that would get his family settled. He rehearsed the plan with those who were involved and then, as we will see in a moment, presented the plans to his boss for final approval. Joseph never assumed that he could just go ahead with his plans, despite his high level of authority and responsibility. He always deferred to his employer.

One complaint that I often hear leveled against Christian employees who work for Christian employers is presumption—the expectation of special treatment because they're members of the same spiritual family. They expect certain privileges, higher salaries, or vacation perks or other benefits, not because they have earned or deserve them, but simply because they serve the same Lord. We see no such spirit of entitlement happening with Joseph.

Joseph knew how the Egyptians thought and reacted. He had not only worked with Pharaoh but had thoroughly studied and observed the man and his people. That explains why he warned his brothers, "Look, shepherds are loathsome to these people. You're not in Canaan anymore, you're in Egypt. And when you're in Egypt, you have to think like an Egyptian. So I want you to tell Pharaoh that you are keepers of livestock." This was the truth. He wasn't asking them to lie, but to avoid using a word or concept—shepherd—that was repugnant to Pharaoh and his people.

Joseph settled his family in the choicest part of the land of Egypt, in an area located in the fertile Nile Delta, as Pharaoh had ordered him to do.

Do you serve under someone else's authority? Obviously, most of us do. How's your spirit, your attitude, toward that person to whom you answer? Having the right attitude or spirit of cooperation can be especially tough if the person to whom you answer is a difficult individual or an incompetent leader, one whose weaknesses you know all too well. This is not only a test of your personal loyalty, but a test of your emotional maturity.

# INNOVATIVE PLANNING

*Read Genesis 47:1—26*

*J*oseph had an innovative plan, something that had never been done before. "In order for the land to produce, we must spread out over this land," he said. Prior to this they had been settled in only a few well-populated regions. Those places represented their homes, their work, their farms, their neighborhoods. They were asked to relinquish all that. That took some selling—an awful lot of convincing. But Joseph managed it, and he spread the people out across the land of Egypt.

Leadership calls for the stretching of creativity. If you are a leader, you will occasionally find yourself up against a blank wall. It's big and intimidating and usually tall and slick. You can't push through it, climb over it, or see your way around it. That's when it gets exciting! That's when innovative juices start to flow and you begin to think about possible ways to get beyond that wall. Innovation and creativity (not to mention courage) team up, determined to find an answer and a way.

Jesus Christ carried out the most innovative, creative plan this world will ever know. From the virgin birth to the death and the resurrection to the soon-coming of Christ, the plan of Almighty God is packed with innovation and creativity. It had never been done before. It will never be done again. It was a once and for all Master Plan only the Creator could envision.

As He did with Joseph, the Father does with us. In His great arrangement of life, He does not discount man's sin; He deals with it. He deals with the hard questions of life. Not questions like how do I make a living, but how do I make a life? Not how do I spend my time, but how will I spend eternity? And not so much how do I get along with the person who sits next to me, but ultimately, how do I get along with God? When we answer the hard questions correctly, all the others fall into place.

May we be models of diligence, honesty, compassion, creativity. May our work be an extension of our integrity. And may each one of us who names the name of Christ as our Lord be a positive influence on those around us and a faithful representative and ambassador for Him who loved us and gave Himself for us.

# The Test of Integrity

*Read Genesis 47:18—25*

*T*he people came to Joseph with their hands empty and open, and he responded by upholding their dignity and treating them with respect. And keep in mind, he had everything, but they had nothing. "Our money is gone! Our food is gone!" They were completely at Joseph's mercy.

He didn't shrug his shoulders and give them a handout. He didn't put them on welfare. Instead, he told them to bring him what they had—their livestock—and in exchange he would give them food.

A year later, with the famine still going strong, all of their livestock were gone, and they were back on their knees with their hands empty and open, saying, "Help us, Joseph. What do we do now? Buy our land for food. Buy us—we will serve Pharaoh. Only help us get through these awful years." In their desperation, they put themselves entirely at Joseph's mercy.

What is striking is that Joseph did not abuse that power—not once! God had raised him up from slavery, and he never forgot how marvelous a deliverance that was. To whom much has been given, much is required.

Arthur Gordon, writing for a national periodical, says this about the importance of personal integrity:

> Year after year businessmen study college records, screen applicants, and offer special inducement to proven people. What are they after, really? Brains? Energy? Know-how? These things are desirable, sure. But they will carry a person only so far. If he is to move to the top and be entrusted with command decisions, there must be a plus factor, something that takes mere ability and doubles or trebles its effectiveness. To describe this magic characteristic there is only one word: integrity.[3]

Integrity keeps your eyes on your own paper during the test. Integrity makes you record and submit only true figures on your expense account. Integrity keeps your personal life pure and straight. Integrity restrains us from taking unfair advantage of others.

# FINAL PROMISE

### ✦ *Read Genesis 47:27–31* ✦

Swear to me, Joseph—promise me this," Jacob said. "Place your hand under my thigh and swear." Making promises to the dying is nothing unusual. That is still done today. Frequently I have heard spouses or children tell of promises they made to a dying mate or a parent. But what about this strange gesture of placing one's hand under the thigh of another? What's that all about?

Brown, Driver, and Briggs, old but still reputable authorities on the Hebrew text, suggest that this sealing of the promise was done by placing the hand beneath the lower back or beneath the buttocks. Joseph promised to do as his father asked, and he also indicated this symbolically by placing his hand under Jacob. It was an oath-taking posture common at that time.

"Promise me before our God, Joseph, that you will bury me back in my father's land. Promise to bury me over there in Canaan, the land of our people, not here in Egypt. God brought us to Egypt so we could survive the famine, but I want to be buried in the land of our forefathers, along with Abraham and Isaac and Leah. Take me back there. Don't bury me in Egypt. Swear before God that will not happen." And Joseph swore to keep this promise to his father.

On Jacob's tombstone, Joseph could have placed the words: "He worshiped." Years earlier, of course, "He deceived" might have seemed more appropriate, but now that Jacob was almost a century-and-a-half old, he had come a long way with God. At the end of his life, one of his final acts was to worship the God he had both wrestled with and served. In his old age he urged Joseph to remember that Canaan—not Egypt—was the Promised Land, so he made his son promise to make his final grave there.

# LASTING IMPACT

### ❧ *Read Genesis 48:5, 10—11, 14—16* ❧

*B*ecause Joseph had been a special son to Jacob, Joseph's sons were special to their grandfather as well. The NIV study notes on this portion of the text state that Jacob, at his death, adopted Joseph's first two children as his own and in doing that divided Joseph's inheritance in the land of Canaan between them. "Joseph's first two sons would enjoy equal status with Jacob's first two sons [Reuben and Simeon] and in fact would eventually supersede them. Because of an earlier sinful act, Reuben would lose his birthright to Jacob's favorite son, Joseph, and thus to Joseph's sons."

All of this becomes greatly significant later in the history of the nation of Israel, and it makes this last scene with Jacob and his grandsons extremely important.

Perhaps it is my own practical nature, but I see something of great value for us here also. It has to do with how and where Jacob died in contrast to how and where we die. Jacob died on his own bed, at home. Rarely does that occur today. We have fallen upon strange times. Birth has become more and more of a family affair, often with the entire family being present in the "birth suite" when the baby is born. Wonderful change from the way things used to be! On the other hand, death has become relegated more and more to the cold and sometimes uncaring comfort of professionals and the sterile environment of a busy hospital, and, later, the funeral home or graveside chapel. Only in recent years have we begun to see the hospice movement growing, where people are allowed to spend their last days at home with those they love alongside to support them and encourage them in their final earthly journey.

Joseph's sons were with their grandfather as he approached those final moments. They felt his hand on their foreheads and heard his tender, wise words of blessing. "May God bless the nation as He blesses you." What a moment! Perhaps Manasseh and Ephraim were kneeling beside their granddad. What a lasting impact for good on the lives of those two young men!

# THOSE FINAL MOMENTS

*❦ Read Genesis 49:1–33 ❧*

*D*espite his age and infirmity, Jacob's memory was nothing short of remarkable. He could name each one of his boys, and he could describe their individual natures and recall with pertinent detail the lives they had lived. Although he had not always disciplined them appropriately or wisely, he knew his sons well. No doubt the Lord assisted at this touching moment of his life by providing the prophetic insight passed on by this aging father. From the firstborn, Reuben, through the youngest, Benjamin, Jacob blessed not only his sons, but the twelve tribes that would descend from them.

After this, Jacob gave them specific instructions about where he was to be buried, in keeping with the promise Joseph had made to him earlier. And then, this beautiful statement: "When Jacob finished charging his sons, he drew his feet into the bed and breathed his last, and was gathered to his people" (Genesis 49:33).

Those who have eternal hope, though grieving over the instant loss death brings and the painful absence that follows, must remember and will be comforted by the realization that when the believer is taken from this life, he or she is gathered into the place of the saints. As it says, Jacob was "gathered to his people." Absent from the body, face to face with the Lord. How simple yet how sacred the moment. With one quiet and final sigh, the old patriarch joined those eternal ranks.

John Donne, seventeenth-century English poet, was not only one of that country's great poets but also one of her most celebrated preachers. He wrote eloquently about death:

> All mankinde is of one Author, and is one volume; when one Man dies, one Chapter is not torne out of the booke, but translated into a better language; and every Chapter must be so translated. God emploies several translators: some peeces are translated by age, some by sicknesse, some by warre, some by justice; but God's hand is in every translation; and his hand shall binde up all our scattered leaves againe, for that Librarie where every booke shall lie open to one another.

God translates the life of an individual after death, and only then can we measure the significance of that life.

# LED BY GRACE

### ❧ *Read Genesis 50:1–21* ❧

*A*m I in God's place?" Joseph asked them. Had he been a lesser man, he could have played "king of the mountain" and filled the role of God. "Grace killers" do that sort of thing. They exploit the power they have over others. They play a cruel and unfair game when they have someone cornered, someone who is vulnerable and at their mercy.

Joseph refused to do that. He didn't do it earlier at their reunion, and he doesn't do it now. In his obedience to God, he was restrained by feelings of tender mercy as he communicated God's grace. "Am I in God's place?" he asked his brothers, saying, in effect, "Brothers, listen to me. Let's get this cleared up for the last time. I know what you did, and I know what you meant by it. I know you meant to do me evil. Okay? I understand all that. That was your plan. But God had other plans, and He turned the results of your evil intentions into something good. At one time I did not understand all this, but that time is long past. Get this straight—God meant it all for good." Joseph never stood taller than at this moment in his life. As Churchill would say, it was his "finest hour."

Guard your heart when you have the power to place guilt on someone else. Refuse to rub their nose in the mess they've made. Remember the father of the Prodigal Son. Best of all, remember Joseph. "Don't be afraid," he comforted them kindly. "I will provide for you and your children."

I love the words of George Robinson's timeless hymn: "Led by grace that love to know." It is especially pertinent here, because it so beautifully describes Joseph, who, like Christ, had a love that would not cease.

Joseph was led by grace. He spoke by grace. He forgave by grace. He forgot by grace. He loved by grace. He remembered by grace. He provided by grace. Because of grace, when his brothers bowed before him in fear, he could say, "Get on your feet! God meant it all for good."

*Moses: A Man of Selfless Dedication*

# THE HINGE OF HISTORY

### ✤ *Read Exodus 1:1–22* ✤

*B*aby Moses opened his eyes on a world very different from our own. Although neither his mother nor father knew it, the birth of this man-child launched a series of events that would change the course of nations and shape the destiny of millions. History would turn like a hinge on that birth. The world would never be quite the same again.

The day came, after the deaths of Joseph and the Pharaoh who had promoted him, that a new Pharaoh stepped onto the throne. He, too, ruled, then passed the crown to the next Pharaoh. Finally, after several centuries, the name Joseph became virtually unknown. Few remembered the famine. Less recalled the golden oceans of stored grain. No one recollected how a wise, young Jewish prime minister had stepped out of obscurity to save the day. That was ancient history. Irrelevant. And the bilateral policy established between Joseph and some long-gone Pharaoh? Completely forgotten.

This new Pharaoh despised the growing Hebrew population. How had they even come to be there? No one knew for sure; the reports had been filed away in some obscure, dusty archive.

But one thing about these multiplying Hebrews could not be ignored: They seemed to pose a threat. And a threatened Pharaoh was not a pleasant Pharaoh to have around.

The Egyptians looked upon the growing number of Israelites (a "mighty people," Pharaoh called them) with dread. The Hebrew word translated "dread" is *kootz*. It means "to have an abhorrence for and horror, a sickening feeling." When the officers of Egypt noted the swelling population of Hebrews from month to month and year to year, they felt sick in the pit of their stomachs. Had there been coffee shops in those days, John and Jane Egyptian might have sat at those little round tables and said over their lattes, "Man, this problem is getting out of hand. Our demographic plan isn't working. We've got to stop their growth! If we don't limit these foreigners now, they'll be running the country in a few years."

And so the hammer blows fell as the brutality increased.

When Pharaoh saw that the harsh conditions of slavery didn't achieve his ends, he turned up the persecution dial yet one more terrible notch.

Infanticide.

# GOD KNOWS

### ✦ *Read Exodus 1:1–22* ✦

The Egyptians' insecurity and abhorrence for their Jewish neighbors eventually led to savagery. I find that interesting. It strikes me that if you are prone to violent anger and brutality, it might be wise for you to back off and ask yourself what you're afraid of. Throughout my years of ministry, I have sadly noted how brutal people are often driven by fear. Fear of loss. Fear of humiliation. Fear of exposure. Fear of weakness. Fear of losing control.

The Egyptians wallowed in that kind of fear. Fear of losing their land drove them to ever more vicious acts of injustice. Once you've decided to starve or beat or mistreat one person, it becomes easy to persecute a whole population. Note what happened next: "The Egyptians compelled the sons of Israel to labor rigorously; and they made their lives bitter with hard labor in mortar and bricks and at all kinds of labor in the field, all their labors which they rigorously imposed on them" (vv. 12–13).

These people [the Hebrews] found themselves in terrible straits, but God had promised, "I'll send a deliverer." When times grow hard it is easy to leap to the conclusion that God has forgotten His promises. The Book of Exodus shows us that when God says, "I promise you something," He never forgets it. You may forget. I may forget. A whole nation may forget. But God cannot forget.

Do you ever imagine that your hard, harsh moments and tests escape God's notice? You may become so discouraged, so filled with acute pain, that you begin to think God couldn't be aware of your circumstances, or, if He is aware, then obviously He doesn't care.

God is always aware. And He cares very deeply. As we will see, He will do whatever it takes to rescue His people. It may be by calling someone home to Himself, or it may be by splitting an ocean right down the middle so you can walk through on dry ground. His deliverance may not arrive on your timetable or in the manner you expect it, but it will arrive at the best time, the right time. God will not abandon His own.

# COURAGE IN THE FACE OF KINGS

*Read Exodus 1:1–22*

According to Pharaoh's instructions, the Hebrew midwife was to watch closely as the baby emerged. She was immediately to discover the sex of the child as it came forth from the womb and to snuff out its life if she noticed it was a male—possibly suffocating the little boy before he ever uttered his first cry.

Then the midwife could say, "Oh, I'm so sorry. This one was stillborn."

What a heinous, murderous plan! Frankly, it comes very close—within a few seconds, as a matter of fact—to the present heinous practice known as "partial birth abortion." These midwives, however, remained staunchly pro-life! What heroines! These ladies feared God more than they feared the laws of the king. Actually, their alibi contained some humor. The word "vigorous" literally means "lively." They told a frowning, unhappy Pharaoh, "My, oh my, King, these women are fast. When we hear they're about to give birth, we rush over to the house and zip, pop, it's over! The baby's already there, and then what can we do?"

Pharaoh, who may not have appreciated the graphic details of childbirth any more than I do, bought the whole thing. Who was he to argue with these strong-hearted midwives? Thankfully, these two courageous women, as Scripture would later say of Moses' own parents, "were not afraid of the king's edict" (Hebrews 11:23).

Praise God for such courageous people of faith. To this day, from Africa to China to the Middle East, that same courage shines out like a beacon. All over the world as you read these words, God's people are being hounded and persecuted for their allegiance to Jesus Christ. And they are standing fast in the face of edicts from kings, presidents, generals, and party commissars. They are saying, "No, we won't do the things you are asking us to do. We refuse to deny our Lord." And they are paying the ultimate price.

# WE MUST OBEY GOD

### Read Exodus 1:1—22

*W*hen we come to passages like the first chapter of Exodus, we are reminded that God's law always comes before man's law. Scripture does not teach blind-and-blanket submission. The fact is, there is a time to submit, and there's also a time to resist.

Before we run with that principle too far, however, a word of caution may be in order. The Exodus passage does not teach children to disobey their parents, wives to usurp their husband's leadership in the home, or anyone to reject ethical authority. But the passage does make one thing clear: submission to civil authority has limits. As Peter once told the Jewish ruling council, "We must obey God rather than men" (Acts 5:29).

In other words, when the king's edict directly violates God's clearly stated will, we ought to fear God, even as a couple of brave ladies named Shiphrah and Puah feared God. And they, being dead, still speak. Scripture tells us that God honored the faith of these midwives. It says, "The people multiplied, and became very mighty. And it came about because the midwives feared God, that He established households for them" (1:20–21).

The midwives valued God's favor more than that of Pharaoh. Motivated by a deep and abiding reverence for the living God, they refused to obey the king's wicked edict. When that king told them to violate God's basic principle, the preservation of life, they refused to do so.

Pharaoh's directive, barbarous as it was, has its contemporary equivalent . . . in reverse. In Communist China today, couples are allowed only one child. When many women learn the sexes of their babies, they either carry them to term or immediately abort. If it's a boy, he lives. If it's a baby girl, she is frequently terminated.

The date on the calendar may have changed since the days of the Exodus, but human nature has not. Apart from the redeeming work of Christ, our hearts are desperately wicked. Cruelty existed in Moses' day, and cruelty exists today. Tyrants ruled in the ancient world, and tyrants rule in our day. Injustice hurt the innocent in Pharaoh's time, in Herod's time, and still in our sophisticated twenty-first-century world.

But in the days of Exodus there also lived men and women ready to stand alone for righteousness, even in the face of death, just as there are today. God always has His remnant.

# HAVE FAITH, HAVE A PLAN

*Read Exodus 2:1–10*

*J*ochebed had faith. She also thought through a very creative plan. I'd like to pause to reflect on this tension between careful planning and full-hearted faith. Are they mutually exclusive? Not on your life! Yet to talk to some believers, you might be led to think otherwise.

I've counseled with unemployed men and women who tell me, "I'm just waiting on the Lord to provide a job."

"Fine," I reply. "And where have you placed your resumé?"

"Well, I'm not going that route. I'm just waiting on God."

"Oh really?" I say. "Then I hope you don't mind remaining jobless for awhile."

The old motto of soldiers during the Revolutionary War applies to many areas of life: "Trust in God, but keep your powder dry!" In other words, place your life in the Savior's hands, but stay at the ready. Do all that you can to prepare yourself for battle, understanding that the ultimate outcome rests with the Lord God.

To walk by faith does not mean you stop *thinking*. To trust God does not imply becoming slovenly or lazy or apathetic. What a distortion of biblical faith! You and I need to trust God for our finances, but that is no license to spend foolishly. You and I ought to trust God for safety in the car, but we're not wise to pass on a blind curve. We trust God for our health, but that doesn't mean we can chain smoke, stay up half the night, and subsist on potato chips and Twinkies without consequences.

Acting foolishly or thoughtlessly, expecting God to bail you out if things go amiss, isn't faith at all. It is *presumption*. Wisdom says to do all you can within your strength, then trust Him to do what you cannot do, to accomplish what you cannot accomplish. Faith and careful planning go hand-in-hand. They always have.

# GOD'S TIMING

### ❦ *Read Exodus 2:11–14* ❧

'm convinced Moses was doing more than grandstanding. I believe he was absolutely sincere. He didn't see himself murdering a cruel slave-driver as much as courageously striking a blow for God's people. The desire to do something right overcame him. His problem? *He dedicated himself to the will of God, but not to the God whose will it was.*

Let that thought sink in. You and I can become so dedicated to the will of God, we can be so driven by a blind sense of purpose, that we might inadvertently take matters into our own hands and leave God completely out of the loop. Been there, done that?

Did that cruel taskmaster need to be punished? Yes. Was it wrong to beat that Hebrew as he did? Certainly. But when Moses stepped in and began his own Operation Deliverance, he was energized by the flesh, not the Spirit.

How easily this can happen to good people, to men and women with the highest motives and the best of intentions. Picture this: You're a gifted and highly qualified teacher. In your heart, you ache to be in front of a classroom again. With all your soul, you want to feel that lectern beneath your hands and the minds of those eager students absorbing your knowledge. And suddenly, seemingly out of the blue, an opportunity presents itself. If you don't watch it, my friend, you'll find yourself elbowing your way through that "open door."

But all the while, God waits for you to seek His counsel. If you act without discerning His timing, you may lose the smile of divine favor. He will not bless what He has not ordained. You may truly sense that God has something for you to accomplish in a certain area. But if you aren't vigilant, if you aren't daily humbling yourself before Him, seeking His face, discerning His timing, operating under the Spirit's control, you may push and force your way prematurely into that place where God wanted you, but you will not have arrived in His own time.

# GOD GETS IT DONE

### ❧ *Read Exodus 2:11–14* ❧

*M*oses looked this way, and he looked that way. Isn't it interesting? He didn't look up, did he? He looked in both directions horizontally, but he ignored the vertical. And what did he do with the results of his murderous anger? Scripture says "he hid the Egyptian in the sand."

Invariably, when you act in the flesh, you have something to cover up. You have to bury your motive. You have to hide a contact you made to manipulate the plan. You have to conceal a lie or half-truth. You have to backtrack on a boast. You have to cover up the evidence your fleshly procedure created. It's just a matter of time before truth catches up with you. The sand always yields its secrets.

This is a good time to emphasize that the capable and gifted are also cursed with vulnerability. The highly qualified live on the cutting edge of the enemy's subtle attack—the very adversary who prods you to act in the flesh, to do the right thing at the wrong time. And how does he operate? Most of us know the drill.

You find yourself moved by a sense of need. You utter a foolish vow, like Jepthah, and live to regret it for the rest of your days. You hurry the process along, as Abram and Sarai did, and later find yourself with an Ishmael on your hands, mocking the child of promise.

Neglecting to ask God's counsel, neglecting to seek God's timing, you step in to handle things prematurely. And by and by, you've got a mess on your hands. You're stuck with a corpse, with a shovel in your hands and a shallow grave at your feet.

You know the odd thing about it all? Most of us aren't very clever at cover-ups anyway. It amazes me that Moses couldn't even bury an Egyptian right. Makes me wonder if he left the guy's toes sticking out of the sand. He failed simply to cover up the corpse.

But what about years and years later, when God took charge and Moses acted according to His timing? Was God able to cover up the Egyptians? God buried their entire army under the Red Sea—horses, weapons, chariots, and all! When God's in it, the job gets done. With the Lord in charge, failure flees.

# LET'S MOVE ON

### Read Exodus 2:11–14

According to Exodus 2:12, Moses hid the body of the slain Egyptian. But by the next day, it was all over the papers. They found the Egyptian. Five inches of loose sand hid nothing.

Hiding wrong, Moses now had to admit, does nothing to erase wrong. And I am convinced that from that moment on Moses determined never to hide anything again. He would be transparent. He would speak his heart, regardless of the risks of vulnerability. He would no longer hide.

Sometime in my ministry, I am going to gather up enough courage to have a testimony time where the only thing we'll share is our failures. Wouldn't that be different? Ever been to a testimony meeting where everybody else seemed to be on Cloud 39, and you were in Tunnel Number 7? One after another is talking about soaring in the heavenlies, while you're counting gum wrappers in the gutter. Why don't we visit the other side? Why not hand the microphone around and say, "When was the last time you took a nosedive? Can you share with others what it was like to experience a major disappointment?"

Far from being a downer, I've got a hunch that might prove to be a major encouragement to a group of people who feel all alone in their struggles. So many of us feel as though we have to hide our failures, believing no one else could have possibly failed as we have. Some are even afraid to tell God about it, fearing He might be as put off as we imagine others will be.

But He isn't like that at all, is He? When we take a tumble, and cry out to Him in our shame and our distress, the psalmist says He "inclines His ear" to us. He bends over to listen. We say, "Oh, Father, I've failed! I've failed terribly. Look at what I've done!" It is then He puts His arms around us, just as a loving earthly father would do. He then says, "I accept you just as you are. I agree that what you have done was wrong, as you've confessed it to Me. Now, My son, My daughter, let's move on."

# HEAT BUT NO LIGHT

### ✦ *Read Exodus 2:11–14; Acts 7:20–29* ❧

*M*oses believed he was to be the deliverer, many years before he received his recommission at the burning bush. He assumed everyone else would realize it too.

The passage goes on to tell us, "On the following day he appeared to them as they were fighting . . ." (Acts 7:26).

Now why did he go back to the scene of the crime? I think he returned to carry out his plan. He'd proved his loyalty to the Hebrews by striking down an Egyptian official. That was Plan A. Now for Plan B. He would return to the scene of his action and rally the troops. But they didn't listen to his counsel. In fact, they didn't respect him at all. "But the one who was injuring his neighbor pushed him away, saying, 'Who made you a ruler and judge over us?'" (Acts 7:27).

How those words must have stung a man who had just risked everything.

It's a pretty simple plan, isn't it? A meat-and-potatoes sort of proposition. If you're a spiritual leader, spiritual people will follow you. That's true of any leader. If you've got the goods, people follow. But they didn't follow Moses. At that point, the prince of Egypt led a lonely one-man parade. The bills of the flesh are now coming due.

Let's level with each other. Have you ever experienced something like that? Most of us have been there. You get all ready to pull off something big for God. You set goals. You spend time and money. You tell a bunch of people. But as painful as it may be for us to admit it, goals not bathed in prayer or brought before the Lord in humility turn out to be downright useless. They don't go anywhere. They don't accomplish anything. They generate heat but no light. And you're left with confusion and defeat.

Bottom line: If you are moving in the energy of the flesh, your efforts are doomed to fail. But when you trust the Lord God to give you the next step, when you wait in humility upon Him, He will open the doors or close them, and you'll get to rest and relax until He says, "Go."

# BUMPS IN THE ROAD

### ❧ *Read Exodus 2:11–15* ❧

irst surprise. Next confusion, followed by fear, like icy fingers around the heart. When Moses' well-kept secret hit the primetime networks, he got the shakes. And acting on fear, the biblical account states that "he fled from the presence of Pharaoh." Why did he run? Verse 15 tells us, "Pharaoh tried to kill Moses." Now that Moses had tipped his hand and shown his true loyalties, Pharaoh couldn't stomach having such a threat around. In the king's eyes, a disloyal and out-of-control prince was better off dead. What awful repercussions grew out of Moses' ill-considered action.

It is very possible that you, too, have been forced to deal with such consequences. Your track record may reflect a pattern of great ambition but little knowledge. Great desire but little discernment. Great aspirations but little humility. Great zeal but little wisdom. And so you have to run the rabbit trails right to the bitter dead-ends, one after another. You've run faster each time, but never succeeded. None has taken you where you wanted to go. And if the truth were known, your impulsive actions have resulted in an unbearable situation.

In my book, there's only one thing worse than being at the end of a self-directed life, and that's being in the middle of one.

You say, "Well, I'm in my thirties, I ought to know better than that." Moses was forty.

You say, "Hey, I'm no novice! I've got education and training like you wouldn't believe!" Better than Moses? Remember, by this time in his career, he was "educated in all the learning of the Egyptians."

Our impressive resumé is part of the problem. Sometimes we're educated beyond our own intelligence. We know more than we're safe to handle! The truth is, when you rely on the flesh to get a job done, you don't need more schooling. You don't need another degree. You don't need more training seminars. Plain and simple, you need *wisdom*. So do I. So do all of God's people.

But discerning wisdom takes time. It takes some major bumps in the road. It takes enduring some failures and swallowing big and bitter doses of humility. Welcome to reality.

# SIT DOWN!

### ✢ *Read Exodus 2:11–15* ✢

*M*oses was a frightened and disillusioned fugitive running, escaping for his very life. His vaunted education now meant nothing to him. His knowledge of hieroglyphics and Egyptian culture gave him no comfort. His military victories seemed hollow. Thanks to his rash act of violence, that same military wanted to kill him. And with every step, he probably groaned within himself over his untimely deed, saying things like, "Life is over. God can never, *never* use me. I'm absolutely finished."

Maybe that's where you are today as you read these words. This man Moses lived thousands of years ago, but the situation I've just described may seem as contemporary to you as today's stale bread in your kitchen. You say, "I've worked so hard. Tried so many things. Pushed myself so relentlessly. But it's gotten me nowhere. Nothing has worked for me. It's curtains."

Believe it or not, you may be closer than ever in your life to a spiritual breakthrough. You won't quit running in the flesh until you get to the endless, waterless sand dunes. When you finally get there, when you finally stumble to a stop in the pitiful shade of some sun-scorched rock, you will be saying to yourself, "Will God ever, ever use me?" And there you'll sit.

*When the self-life finally sits down, the well of a new life lies near.* When will we ever learn that? Highly qualified, capable people prefer to be on the move; sitting down goes against the grain. Yet when that broken forty-year-old named Moses finally slumped to the ground at the end of a self-driven life, fresh, cool drinking water was available right next to him.

Sit down. That's right, my friend, *sit down!*

You have run far enough. You have pushed long enough. You have fought, demanded, and manipulated your way for too many years. God has finally grabbed your attention. He is saying, "Quit! Stop! Let Me handle it! Sit there on the hot sands of the desert where you have brought yourself. Look at what lies next to you. It is a well, full of fresh water." Soon it will be God's delight to bring up the bucket and refresh your soul. Sit still. Stay there. Be quiet. Listen.

# SHRINK-WRAPPED SALVATION

### ✣ *Read Exodus 2:15–25* ✣

*M*oses took a forty-story fall. As we pick up the biblical account, he's a heavy-hearted, bruised-and-battered soul who has come to a sudden stop at the bottom. In a matter of mere days, he has stepped off the top of the pyramid as Pharaoh-designate and down to a bedraggled, penniless fugitive on the backside of Zipville.

Living as we do in a product-oriented culture, we like to package our faith too. We prefer to sell a slick, shrink-wrapped version of salvation that includes prosperity and peace, endless happiness here and now, and heaven by and by. While there is nothing wrong with teaching principles that can result in genuine, God-given success, there is something wrong if we neglect to mention the *process*, which must inevitably include times of defeat and failure.

I wouldn't have to go back very far on my calendar to revisit a week where I missed the mark—missed the whole target—more than I hit close to the bull's eye. And I don't have to be a prophet to proclaim that you have experienced the same. Of course you have. You may be having such a week even as you read these words.

What I'd like to know is who erected such a happily-ever-after standard of perfection in the first place? God knows very well we aren't able to produce perfection; that's why Jesus, the perfect Son of God, graciously died in our place. That's why He gave us a position of perfect righteousness in Him, reminding us by contrast that our own daily experience will constantly fall short.

If you're waiting for a seamless, blemish-free week, friend, you're going to wait in vain. There is no such thing. And until we learn how to derive lessons from seasons of failure and loss, we will keep repeating those failures—digging ourselves into an ever deeper hole—rather than moving on as we grow up.

What you and I need is the reminder of the *process* that leads to times of victory and success. Then, with memories of those golden moments shining in our minds, we'll learn how to avoid some of those valleys, or how to climb out of them more quickly. That process, I believe, is every bit as important as the product.

# SPIRITUAL ENDS

### *Read Exodus 2:15—25*

Spiritual ends are never achieved by carnal means. Back in Egypt, as you may recall, Moses had "looked this way and that," then murdered an Egyptian and buried him with sand. As we have already noted, Moses may have thought he was following God's plan in that moment, but he never bothered to check signals. He certainly never prayed before he struck the blow. We have no record that he sought God's face before taking that significant step. As a result, the bottom fell out of Moses' dreams like a soggy cardboard box. It was the biggest setback of his life.

The fact is, you cannot sow a fleshly seed and reap a spiritual plant. You cannot plant a carnal act and grow spiritual fruit. If you manipulate and connive and scheme and lie to get yourself to the top, don't thank God for the promotion! God knows, as you know, that you maneuvered and pulled strings and buried those carnal carcasses in the soil to get yourself promoted. So when you get that bigger office and the key to the executive washroom, don't give Him the credit. He doesn't want it. Your fingerprints are all over that scheme, not His.

At times we say to the Lord, "Thanks for that, Father." And the Lord must answer back, "Who? Me? I didn't pull that off. That was your doing." You cheat on an exam, make a good grade, and thank God for the "A." You fudge on your income tax, get a nice refund, and thank Him for the extra cash you can give to the building fund.

It doesn't work that way, friend. He says to you, "This isn't My doing. This is your plan."

As Moses was sitting by that well, I can imagine a still, small voice cutting through his musings. "Don't thank Me, Moses, that an Egyptian lies buried in the sand. You did that. And fleshly acts like that can never advance My plans. It was carnal, Moses, from start to finish. And you know it."

He did know it. He realized it most keenly when he had come back to the Hebrews the next day and tried to take leadership—only to be mocked and rejected. And then the whole scheme came unhinged, and he had to take to his heels. Thankfully, Moses learned that first lesson well.

# SELFLESS DEDICATION

### ❧ *Read Exodus 2:15–25* ❧

*M*oses, the Prince of Egypt, alias Prince Charming, watering animals? Why? Because Moses had just choked down the biggest wedge of humble pie you can imagine. By now, the man was ready to do anything. Isn't it interesting, though, that in this incident Moses was allowed to be a deliverer on an immensely smaller scale? Earlier, he had thought he was going to deliver a nation. He had grand dreams and mighty schemes. But this time God said, "You want a job as deliverer? Then stand up and do it, son. Start here. There are seven women here in Midian who need a champion at this moment."

Moses could have shrugged it off. He could have said, "Aw forget it. I'm out of the delivery business. Let someone else do the job." But he didn't. It was here Moses took his first steps in becoming a man of selfless dedication. The young women would later tell their father, "An Egyptian delivered us from the hand of the shepherds, and what is more, he even drew the water for us and watered the flock" (v. 19).

That thought moves me. If you can't do the good you would, do the good you can. You may have had big-time plans in your life—major league dreams that haven't panned out. You were going to write a best-selling book, but the opportunities just haven't come along. Are you willing to write for your church newsletter?

Maybe you wanted to teach in seminary or Bible school, but the pressures of life forced you in a different direction. Are you willing to teach a fourth-grade Sunday school class? Are you up for leading a small group Bible study? Is it really the teaching that draws your heart, or is it the prestige that goes along with the position?

Failure, you see, teaches us a servant's attitude. And what does a servant do? He does "the next task." She does what is available and ready for her to do. Those without such an attitude resist getting their hands dirty. They never want to get involved in the messy part of working with people. They always want the polished part, the popular part. But the tough stuff behind the scenes? Well, give that to someone else.

God, however, will use our failures and setbacks to cultivate within us a servant's heart. That's step one. It's all part of the process.

# LIVING IN OBSCURITY

### ❧ *Read Exodus 2:16–25* ❧

*P*ay close attention to that last sentence. "Moses was willing to dwell with the man." How good that is. Here is a man he had never met; an obscure desert priest and shepherd, who had spent a lifetime raising sheep (and daughters!) in the desolate patch of land known as Midian. "And he gave his daughter Zipporah to Moses. Then she gave birth to a son, and he named him Gershom, for he said, "I have been a sojourner in a foreign land" (vv. 21–22).

Moses, who would have been in line to marry an exotic Cleopatra-type beauty back in Egypt, settled down with a shepherdess. And when she gave birth to their firstborn, Moses gave him an unusual name: Gershom. It means "a sojourner." That's what Moses had become—a sojourner in a distant land, forgotten and obscure. He came into Midian not knowing anyone, not knowing the ropes, not even knowing where he was going to live. But when Jethro said, "Young man, would you like to live with us?" Moses replied, "Yes, I would. I'll live anywhere."

Let me ask you directly: Are you willing to be obscure? A servant's mindset will teach you what that attitude is all about. To put it in simple terms, in the Body of Christ some people are called to be the toes. Not everyone can be a right hand, an eye, or an ear. Some people have to be the toe, or the heel, or the kidney, or the liver. These members are (hopefully) seldom seen. But just let one of them stop functioning for awhile and watch out! The whole body is in trouble.

Moses was willing to be obscure, to dwell apart from the limelight, to accept his new status. I ask again: Are you? God will use failure in your life to break down that strong desire in your heart to see your name in lights. And when he finally breaks you of that lust for recognition, He may place you before the lights like you could never have imagined. But then it won't matter. You won't care if you're prime time or small time, center stage or backstage, leading the charge or cooking the food. You're just part of the King's army. People of selfless dedication are mainly available. That's plenty!

# THROUGH IT ALL

### ❧ *Read Exodus 2:15–25* ❧

*Y*ou'd better believe that Moses, though tucked away in a corner of that waste-land, heard the latest news from the travelers in caravans making their way up from Egypt through the Midian desert. When Moses learned the Hebrews were crying out, his heart must have turned over within him. But unlike before, he rested and relied upon God. He didn't try to organize a rescue party. He didn't slip back into Egypt as an assassin or saboteur. Not him! He'd learned that lesson.

Do you know who it is who keeps erecting all those unrealistic standards in your life? Do you know who keeps raising the bar beyond all hope of clearing it?

It's you. You do. And so do I. Our Heavenly Father doesn't. The psalmist tells us, "He knows our frame. He remembers that we are dust." We think we're finished because of our failures, but God says, "No, you're just getting started. Press on!"

Our problem isn't that we've failed. Our problem is that we haven't failed enough. We haven't been brought low enough to learn what God wants us to learn. We're still trying to redeem Egypt single-handedly.

So what are you trying to prove? Who are you trying to impress? Why don't you step off that treadmill and just be yourself? Plead with the Spirit of God to prepare you, then use you, however He pleases, dark side and all. You'll be amazed how that takes the pressure off.

This very moment, you and I are the recipients of a gift from One who loves us just the way we are: warts, cracks, failures, and all. Since it is a gift, you might as well open your hands and receive it. Look, there—that's your name on the tag, just underneath the ribbon.

The gift is called grace.

# A MAJOR IN OBSCURITY

### ✺ *Read Exodus 3:1* ✺

The desert is a place of obscurity. Moses had to cope with being a nobody. All his adolescent and adult life, he had been a big-time somebody. The spotlight followed his every move, much as the contemporary spotlight follows Britain's Prince William and Prince Harry. Every time Moses stood, people looked up expectantly. Every time he addressed them, people stopped talking and listened. Every time he strolled through the streets, heads turned.

Sheep don't do that. You can say whatever you want, you can turn backflips while reciting poetry, and the flock won't be impressed at all. They'll go right on feeding their faces. As much as you and I may appreciate wool sweaters and wool socks, sheep are basically unintelligent and unresponsive animals. And Moses had the pleasure of their company for four long decades of his life.

Perhaps you identify with this situation. As you read, you're nodding your head. You are taking some course work in obscurity yourself; you find yourself struggling every day with the limitations you've had to endure. You have been forced by the very nature of the desert to give up many of the privileges, perks, and activities you once enjoyed and held most dear. Now you're "just getting by," subsisting on the absolute basics of life. That is God's plan, my friend. And if you would graduate from His school of the desert, you must take classes in obscurity; it is the first required course of the school.

Amy Carmichael, one of my favorite poets, wrote these words:

Before the winds that blow do cease,
Teach me to dwell within Thy calm:
Before the pain has passed in peace,
Give me, my God, to sing a psalm.
Let me not lose the chance to prove
The fullness of enabling love.
Oh, love of God, do this for me:
Maintain a constant victory.[4]

Here is the unvarnished truth: If you don't learn to live peacefully with obscurity, you will repeat that course until you do. You cannot skip this one and still graduate.

# A MAJOR IN DISCOMFORT

### *Read Exodus 3:1; Acts 7:29–30*

otice carefully how the process took place through those years of desert learning, because it is the same with you and me. God must break through several hard, exterior barriers in our lives before He can renovate our souls. His persistent goal is to break through to the inner person. As David acknowledged, "Behold, You desire truth in the innermost being, and in the hidden part You will make me know wisdom" (Psalm 51:6).

What are those resistant layers in our hearts, and how does He break through to that hidden part? First, He finds pride. And He uses the sandpaper of obscurity to remove it ever so gradually.

Then He finds us gripped by fear—dread of our past, anxiety over our present, and terror over what may lie ahead—and He uses the passing of time to remove that fear. We learn that things aren't out of hand at all; they're in His hand.

He next encounters the barrier of resentment—the tyranny of bitterness. He breaks down that layer with solitude. In the silence of His presence, we gain a fresh perspective, gradually release our cherished rights, and let go of the expectations that held us hostage.

Finally, He gets down to the basic habits of living, he penetrates our inner person, and there He brings discomfort and hardship to buff away that last layer of resistance. Why? So that He might renovate us at the very core of our being.

Reach for the hand of your Guide! He is Lord of the desert. Make that *your* desert. The most precious object of God's love is His child in the desert. If it were possible, you mean more to Him during this time than at any other time. You are as the pupil of His eye. You are His beloved student taking his toughest courses. While testing you, He loves you with an infinite amount of love.

Jesus walked through the desert first. He felt its heat. He endured its loneliness. He accepted its obscurity. He faced down Satan himself while the desert winds howled. And you can be sure He will never, ever forget or forsake the one who follows Him across the sand.

# AN ORDINARY DAY

### *Read Exodus 3:1–3*

This was the day when God decided to break a forty-year silence. Pause and let that sink in! Through four decades in Midian, we have no record of God's speaking to Moses. Not even once. The day that was going to shatter that silence, however, dawned like every other day in the wilderness. The night before, as he was sleeping out under those bright desert stars with his flock, perhaps under the looming shoulder of Sinai, he saw no meteor flash across the sky. He heard no voice. No angel tapped him on the shoulder at breakfast that morning and said, "Pay attention, Moses. God speaks today."

There were no hints, no premonitions, no special signs to alert him to the fact that God Himself would break the silence that day and change his life forever. It was just your common, ordinary, garden-variety day-shift with the sheep. Nothing more. Nothing less. Nothing else.

That is the way God works. Without a hint of warning, He speaks to ordinary people on ordinary days. In other words, it will happen on an ordinary day. People will be getting married and buried. There will be problems, and there will be needs. Some people will be driving buses, others will be riding in them. Some will be on the way home from work, tuned in to talk radio. Others will be in the checkout line at the grocery store, impatiently wondering why the person ahead of them is taking so long to write that check. Some will be boarding an airplane, others stepping out of a subway.

And suddenly, the Son will come! There will be a flash in the sky, a shout, the staccato blast of a trumpet, and in the twinkling of an eye, it will be over. There will be no previous warning.

Don't look for some brilliant aura to come over you early in the morning, and a booming angelic voice announcing, "This is the day!" If that happened, you might pull the covers over your head and never get out of bed.

God works by simply stepping into an ordinary day of life and saying what He wants to say. It's a meat-and-potatoes kind of proposition. Here's what needs doing, and you're the person who's going to do it, *so get after it!*

# I'M HERE

### ✤ *Read Exodus 3:4* ✤

*I* think one of the most important words in this verse is the very first one. *When.* The Hebrew word means "at the same time." That goes back to verse 3, where Moses said, "I must turn aside."

When did God speak to Moses? At the same moment when Moses turned aside. Now that's simple, isn't it? Moses stopped his forward motion, stepped aside from his responsibilities for only a few brief seconds, and headed in another direction. He moved toward the event that had captured his attention.

And God says, "What's it going to take? What will finally persuade you to stop in your tracks for a minute, turn aside, and consider this event in your life?" What's it going to take before you say, "I'm going to check this out. I'm going to find out what all of this might be saying to me."

Moses did just that, and when he did, he came face to face with his destiny. It was not until Moses turned aside that God spoke. Yet even at that moment, I do not believe it had dawned on the man that God was speaking. As far as Moses was concerned, a *bush* was speaking. God hadn't introduced Himself yet. Moses had simply heard his name coming out of a flaming shrub and answered back.

"Moses! Moses!" the voice said.

And do you know what Moses answered? The original Hebrew reveals that he spoke only one word: *hinaynee*, which could be rendered, "I'm here," or, in our terms, "It's me."

Believe it or not, that's all God wanted to hear. It's still true today. That's all He wants to hear from you when He speaks. Don't kid yourself; He's not impressed with *you*; He's checking out your humility, your sensitivity, your availability. He's looking for someone who will slow down long enough to check out a burning bush. And when He calls, all He asks is a simple acknowledgement. *I'm here, Lord. All present and accounted for.*

# FLAMMABLE BUSHES

### ❧ *Read Exodus 3:4–10* ❧

W hat was God's larger message to Moses in that moment? Release your imagination for a few moments. It might have included some thoughts such as these: "Moses, forty years ago you were a fine looking bush, impressed with all your own foliage. You had long, strong branches and lush, green leaves. But when your bush started burning, it was gone in less than forty-eight hours. Your grand scheme went up in flames, charring your dreams and consuming your ambitions along with it. There was nothing left, was there? That was your life, Moses. And then you ran like a scared rabbit across the border to get away from the Egyptian lynch mob.

"You thought you were a choice, top-quality bush before that happened, and now you don't think you're worth much at all. Listen, man, *any bush will do as long as I, the great God of all grace, am in the bush!* I want to use you, Moses. Stand still, and let Me set you on fire!"

What does it take to qualify as a bush that God will use? You have to be dried up and thorny. *Okay, I qualify.* You have to be dusty and dirty. *All right, I'm there.* You've got to be ordinary. *Right. That's me all over. What else, Lord?*

You have to be burnable. God is looking for flammable bushes. There are some good looking bushes and shrubs out there in Christendom that won't burn at all. They're made out of asbestos. You couldn't set 'em on fire with a welding torch. Napalm wouldn't even do the job. These are beautiful replicas of beautiful plants, but they won't burn. Which means they are of no use to God.

The truth is, any old bush will do as long as God is in the bush. That's what He was saying to Moses. "I want you to burn for Me as no man has burned before. You've been dried out and well-seasoned in this howling wasteland through these years. I wanted you dried out! And I have pruned away from you all those things you used to hang on to, and that meant so much to you. I have reduced you to a simple love for Me. That's all you have to offer now, Moses, and that is all I want."

# HARD OF HEARING

### ✤ *Read Exodus 3:4–22* ✤

*M*oses had been resistant for forty years, telling himself all that time that his was a lost cause. Now, when God came with a direct, simple call, the old shepherd couldn't handle it. In fact, he wouldn't let himself believe he might still be useful to God. "Therefore, come now, and I will send you to Pharaoh, so that you may bring My people, the sons of Israel, out of Egypt" (Exodus 3:10).

Now that wasn't complicated, was it? The Lord spoke in a tongue Moses could understand. He gave him a simple, two-fold command. First, He said to Moses, "I will send you." And second, "You will bring My people out." That was the plan.

Notice, please, that this was not a multiple choice arrangement. It wasn't even an invitation. *It was a call.* God does not speak and ask our advice regarding His plan. God makes declarations. He doesn't open up the scene for a rap session or a dialogue. He doesn't call in a blue-ribbon panel of consultants to suggest viable options.

He speaks, and that is that.

At very unique junctures of our lives, God says to us, "Now, My child, I have *this* in mind for you. I know that you have knotted things up in the past. And I know that you may knot things up in the future. But as far as today, right now, this is My plan for you. Now go. I'm sending you, and I will be with you."

God told him that he would be an instrument in the deliverance, but *God Himself* would be the deliverer. Huge difference. In God's calling, He has a plan; but He never expects *you* to carry out that plan. He's going to pull it off. He simply wants you to be the instrument of action. After all, it is His reputation that's at stake, not yours. All He asks is that you give yourself to Him as a tool He can pick up and use. That's all.

# AND THE ANSWER IS . . .

*❦ Read Exodus 4:1–10 ❧*

*B*ut Lord," Moses was saying, "I can't be Your spokesman in this situation. Why, I wouldn't have any answers when those guys started firing questions at me."

Before we consider the Lord's response, stop and think about that lame excuse for a moment. It has a familiar ring to it, doesn't it? It's a pretext mouthed by many believers today. "Lord, I can't do that, because I'll get in a verbal corner and won't know how to handle it. Somebody will ask me, 'What about the heathen in Africa?' or 'How did they fit dinosaurs into Noah's ark?' I'll get tongue-tied. I won't know what to say, and I'll appear ridiculous and foolish in the eyes of other people. No, I can't do that, Lord. You can see that, can't You? I just don't have all the answers."

Maybe you remember what it was like in high school or college to have a teacher or professor who stranded himself out on a logical limb. He found himself in the wrong, everyone knew it, and yet he stubbornly refused to admit it. What did you do? Chances are, you began to bear down on him, sawing off that flimsy limb with a set of sharp-toothed facts. Why did you do that? Because there is something inside of us that wants the other person simply to admit, "Yeah, I was wrong."

I have never lost respect for any individual who replied to a question with the answer, "I just don't know." On the other hand, I have lost a great deal of respect for those who knew they were wrong, and knew that I knew they were wrong, but could not bring themselves to admit it.

Direct question: Why do we feel we have to have all the answers at our fingertips? Straight answer: Pride. Pride says, "If I don't have a ready comeback, if I say 'I don't know,' they'll laugh at me." But that's not true at all. Intelligent, thoughtful people won't laugh; they will realize that *no one* has all the answers.

# GOING IT ALONE

### ✦ *Read Exodus 4:11—17* ✦

*D*o you know what God did? He accommodated Moses' desire. But the compromise was less than the best; brother Aaron proved to be an albatross around his neck. It was Aaron who got impatient while Moses was on the mountain and created a golden calf for the people to worship. It was he who told the people, "This is your god, O Israel, who brought you up from the land of Egypt" (Exodus 32:4).

As you read these words, you may sense God's nudge to step out on faith in a plan that seems risky at best. You don't have all the answers. You don't know the hows and whys and wherefores of what God has in mind. From a human point of view, the prospects look rather bleak. Do you know what our tendency is? It's to take someone with us. Somehow, that keeps us from having to put our full trust in the Lord's plan; we can lean on that gifted friend or companion we've brought along with us.

How many men have gone into a business partnership and lived to regret the day they chose that partner? How many women have engaged in pursuits with a companion they wish they had never asked to join them? God's call is a serious, individual matter. While I believe with all my heart in accountability, God's call does not lend itself to the buddy system or to group excursions. And before you bring any other individual along with you to fulfill that call, or before you join a team, you must make absolutely certain in your heart that each one has the same vision beating in his or her heart that you do.

If not, then take this advice, my friend: Go it alone. Follow God's voice without distraction.

God was finally willing to say to Moses, "All right, all right, have it your way. I'll send Aaron, too, but it isn't My best, Moses. The day will come when you will wish you'd followed My call on your own. You don't really need Aaron; all you need is Me."

# LEAVE OF ABSENCE

*Read Exodus 4:18*

*V*erse 18 features a glimpse into Moses' humanity and God's patience. Then Moses departed and returned to Jethro his father-in-law and said to him, "Please, let me go, that I may return to my brethren who are in Egypt, and see if they are still alive." And Jethro said to Moses, "Go in peace."

Moses left just a few things out of that account, don't you think? Moses says, "Dad, I want to go see if any of my buddies down in Egypt are still alive. I've been at this forty years now. Do you mind if I take a little time off? You know, check out the pyramids, take a ride on the Nile, that kind of stuff."

And Jethro says, "Fine. Have a good time. Take off, son."

Somehow, Moses couldn't bring himself to say, "Uh, Jethro, there was this bush out in the desert, and there was this voice in the bush, and well, the upshot is I'm going to lead the whole nation of Israel in an Exodus out of slavery and deliver them to Canaan." He just couldn't say that. But God, in His grace, doesn't slap Moses' hand. He doesn't say, "Knock it off, Moses! Tell him the whole story." He lets Moses cover his departure with kind of a broad-brush, nebulous explanation.

Somehow, that touches my heart. God is full of grace. Moses was packing his bags for Egypt, and God let it go at that. All He asks of us is a willing heart. He doesn't expect perfection. He doesn't expect you to have all the answers, all the ability, or all the courage. He doesn't even require you to spell out each detail of His call. He just asks you to be available, and take that first step of faith in the direction He's pointing.

# COVERING HOME BASE

### 🐦 *Read Exodus 4:18* 🐦

*M*oses, you'll remember, approached his father-in-law Jethro and asked permission to return to Egypt. He certainly didn't tell Jethro everything at that point, but he let the man know there was something stirring in his heart. After years and years of virtual silence about his life and background back in Egypt, Moses said to Jethro, "It's time for me to go back. There's some unfinished business that needs attention."

When you have heard the voice of God calling you in a new direction—confirming that direction through His Word, through events, and through the wisdom of godly counselors—the result of that thought process needs to be communicated with your family. This is especially true if you are young. Why? *Because your family has not had the benefit of the burning bush.* You've heard God's voice; that's not true for them. They may not know or understand what God has said to you. They still feel like you should be going in a previously agreed-upon direction, and now you seem to be talking about a whole new set of plans. Those kinds of major course changes can seem upsetting, or even frightening, to those who care about you, especially parents. You need to be gracious enough to give them some helpful information on how God has changed your direction.

This exchange between these two men leads me to two principles worth considering. First of all, when God crystallizes a plan for your life, perhaps nudging you in a new direction, be extremely sensitive how you communicate that to others. Don't assume they know all you know about the process. Don't expect them to greet the idea with immediate acceptance and open arms. Give them the courtesy of time and space to think things through. Communicate your thoughts with tenderness, care, and understanding.

The second thing to notice is that this plan flowed. When you are in the center of God's will, my friend, it *flows.* It doesn't have to be forced. Moses said, "Jethro, may I go?" And Jethro replied, "Go in peace." Moses could move into what would prove to be a difficult ministry knowing things back home were just fine.

It is a very humbling experience to be moving in the direct current of God's will. But it can also bring fresh assurance.

# YOU ARE HIS CONCERN

*Read Exodus 4:19–20*

*I*sn't God gracious? We have a Lord who knows our hearts, knows our thoughts, and knows our fears. When Moses had left Egypt forty years before there were those who sought his life. He was probably featured at the top of the Egyptian version of The Ten Most Wanted list.

Naturally, Moses had not forgotten. He was a family man now, headin' west with the wife and kids, and that potential danger must have been weighing on his mind. It was part of the reason he had been reluctant to go in the first place. But when he finally made the decision to embrace God's will, he determined to make the journey in spite of those concerns. He told the Lord, in effect, "Lord, I'm going to trust You with all my heart. I'm not going to lean on my own understanding. In all my ways I'm going to recognize You and let You take care of the obstacles."

So he set his face toward Egypt and began putting one foot in front of another, in obedience to God. Before he stepped outside the borders of Midian, however, the Lord did something for His servant. He said to him, "Oh, by the way, Moses, you remember all those who sought your life in Egypt? Don't be anxious about them. They're all dead. They can't hurt you now."

What a sight that little family must have been as they headed down the desert road. His wife, Zipporah, was on the donkey, the two kids were cavorting on ahead, and a few of the family's belongings were probably tied on the donkey's back. They were on their way, leaving a steady job, family, security, and the familiarity of their surroundings. Midian wasn't much, but it had been their home for forty years. And now they were on their way to Egypt—on their way to the Exodus. What faith!

Have you stepped out on faith like that recently? Have you made a move, followed the nudging of God, into realms you wouldn't have even dreamed of five years ago? He will honor your faith as you trust Him in that kind of walk. Those who remain in the false security of Midian never get to experience what Moses experienced on that winding highway to Egypt— the sense of moving in the strong current of God's will and plan. Press on!

# THE STAFF OF GOD

*Read Exodus 4:21–23*

God was saying to his servant, "Moses, you simply go before Pharaoh and deliver the goods. He won't like it. He won't want it. Just bear in mind that even his stubborn, hardened heart is not outside My will." In the following verse, the Lord gave Moses specific instructions of what to say when he rammed into that brick wall. "Then you shall say to Pharaoh, 'Thus says the LORD, "Israel is My son, My first-born. So I said to you, 'Let My son go, that he may serve Me'; but you have refused to let him go. Behold, I will kill your son, your firstborn"'" (Exodus 4:22–23).

To put it into the vernacular, that was a gutsy message. You walk out of the desert into a new land, get an audience with the king, stand before him eyeball to eyeball, and say, "Pharaoh, God says to let His people go. But because you will refuse to do that, your own son will die."

Wow! What a tough thing to say. Yet, it was the Lord's own words. It was a good thing Moses had already settled the issue of obedience to his Lord back in Midian. Moses didn't argue; Scripture doesn't report so much as a flinch. Forty years in the wilderness had changed the man. He was ready to be God's mouthpiece, whatever the consequences. In fact, from that moment on, he seemed to have a quiet confidence in his dealings with the feisty Pharaoh. Knowing he was in the nucleus of God's will, he must have felt invincible.

We could call any work done in the will of God "the work of righteousness." And in doing that work, you will be surrounded by peace. Deep within you, in the very outworking of that service and that obedient walk, you will enjoy quietness and confidence. The original Hebrew term rendered "confidence" here might be better termed "security." The King James Version translates it "assurance."

In other words, there will be a quiet, secure confidence when you are walking in His will. There will be an invincible sense of inner assurance, gently and humbly accepted. Every believer in Jesus Christ longs to experience such assurance. It comes from being in the flowing current of His will. It envelopes us when we do God's will, God's way.

# SOUL BROTHERS

*Read Exodus 4:27–28*

God knew Moses felt lonely in that moment. God knew His man needed some human companionship. Perhaps before Moses felt his first pang of loneliness, God was already moving to meet his need. Aaron was Moses' big brother, his senior by three years. And the Lord sought this brother out and said to him, "Aaron, go to Moses' side now. He's on a long, wilderness road, heading for Egypt. Your younger brother has been through some tough things. He needs a soul brother, right now."

Moses said, "Aaron, listen to this. You'll never believe it. There I was, out with the sheep one day, just like a thousand other days before. And all of sudden—whoosh!—this bush caught fire, and it wouldn't stop burning. So I stopped and stared. And as I got closer—Aaron, listen to this, man—God was speaking from that bush! And here's what He told me."

If Aaron doubted a single word of the account, Scripture never mentions it. In fact, he was already prepared to believe every word Moses told him. Hadn't God called him out of Egypt to meet his younger brother in the desert? So Aaron listened, nodded his head, and said, "That's great, Moses. I'm with you, bro."

Do you have a closeness with your brother or a kindred spirit in your sister? Do you have a friend with whom you can face the realities of your life?

You may have lots of friendships in your life, but you'll probably never have more than a couple of friends on that deeper, spiritual, soul-to-soul level. You can tell such a friend anything that God is doing in your life, and you'll find a warm reception and deep affirmation. If you don't have such a friendship, tell God about your longing. He's the same God who moved Aaron's heart down in Egypt while Moses was walking alone on the desert road. And remember, the best way to find such a friend is to be such a friend.

# MISUNDERSTOOD

### ❧ *Read Exodus 4:29—5:21* ❧

*A* bad day just got worse! Moses couldn't believe it. Disappointment turned to disillusionment. Where had he gone wrong? He had taken God at His word, stood before Pharaoh, and repeated—almost word perfectly—what God had told him to say. He said the right words, at the right time, to the right person, spoken in the right way. And now the wheels seemed to be falling off the wagon. The very people he had longed to help (for over forty years) were now cursing him for increasing their hardships and anguish. "Why did you come, Moses? It was bad enough before you showed up. Now, our lives are in danger."

Being misunderstood hurts all the way to the bone. Maybe you've felt that sting recently. You did the right things in the right way, but someone misjudged you, reading motives into your acts or words that you never intended. And now you live under that cloud, unable to change the minds of those who have turned against you.

Moses came before the Lord asking those two questions most of us ask when we find ourselves under intolerable pressure: *Why?* and *How?*

We begin by saying, "Why? Why me? Why now? Why this?" And then we ask, "How? How in the world am I going to get through this or out of that?"

As one who has also spoken those words numerous times in my life's journey, I find myself very encouraged by how the Lord responded to Moses. He didn't say, "Back off, Moses. You should be ashamed of yourself." I love it that the Lord never slaps you or shames you when you come to Him. He never pushes you away when you bring an aching, honest question that cries out for an answer.

Isn't that great of God? Instead of criticizing Moses for asking "Why?" the Lord says, "Just you wait, son. Pharaoh's been reading too many of his own press clippings. He thinks he's a god, but there is only one God, and he'll find that out soon enough. For a brief period it will seem to you that he's in charge. But don't kid yourself, Moses. I alone am the Lord."

# "Watch Me Work"

### 🐾 *Read Exodus 5:22—6:12* 🐾

*M*oses felt as low as a slug's belly. Way down there. He still hadn't rid himself of the idea that he was supposed to be the deliverer, and that he was somehow failing. How many times had God explained it to him? Yet, like many of us, he had trouble keeping a grip on the Lord's assurances.

What was Moses to do now? The message was a rerun of the last one: "Go, tell Pharaoh king of Egypt to let the sons of Israel go out of his land" (v. 11).

"Go to *Pharaoh*, Lord? My own people just bought me a one-way ticket caravan back to Midian, and You want me to go back to Pharaoh? R-r-r-e—m-m-m-em—ber m-m-me? I'm the guy who can't t-t-t-talk. Shoot, I'd mess up a rock fight, Lord. I can't get it together. I'm at the end of my rope. How in the world are You going to pull this off?"

Moses didn't know it at the moment, but he'd put before the Lord the best proposition yet. *I'm at the end of my rope. How are you going to do it?*

Before we go any further, I'd like to underline a major truth in this world of ours that I don't pretend to understand. Here it is: the best framework for the Lord God to do His most ideal work is when things are absolutely impossible and we feel totally unqualified to handle it. That's His favorite circumstance. Those are His ideal working conditions.

In spite of the Lord's assurances, things kept going from bad to worse for Moses. He'd already gotten the worst of it in a meeting with Pharaoh, and now, in a subsequent parley with the Israelites, he found himself fresh out of credibility. They would no longer listen to him.

Time after time, He brings us to our absolute end and then proves Himself faithful. That, my friend, is not only the story of my life, it's the story of the Bible in a nutshell.

# SHORTCUTS TO FUTILITY

### ✒ *Read Exodus 6:2–29* ✒

So many times you and I miss the opportunity to watch the Lord work in mighty and miraculous ways. Why? Because instead of "standing still" and watching Him pull off our deliverance, we seek out the carnal alternative. We look for the back-door escape, a fleshly shortcut.

Notice how God handled His man, Moses. Without rebuke, the Lord gave Moses two pieces of counsel. One related to His person; the other related to His work. He told Moses who He was, and then He told him what He was going to do. And the *order* in the Lord's response is as important as the facts themselves.

Right off the top, He repeated the message from the burning bush, saying, "I am" five different times in Exodus chapter 6.

"I am the LORD . . . " (v. 2)

"I am the LORD . . . " (v. 6)

"I am the LORD . . . " (v. 7)

"I am the LORD . . . " (v. 8)

"I am the LORD . . . " (v. 29)

Time after time He punctuated His message to Moses by saying, "Look, Moses, your eyes are in the wrong place (again). Get your eyes back on Me (again). Remember who I am (again)."

Who is the Lord? Ask the prophet Isaiah. Troubled and sick at heart over the moral condition of his nation, Isaiah glanced toward the sky one day and "saw the Lord sitting on a throne, high and lifted up" (Isaiah 6:1 NKJV). That's all he needed to see. He fixed his eyes on the Lord, and, suddenly, his whole perspective changed.

If you have been a believer for any length of time, you will have heard these words over and over. But that's all right; here they are again. *Until your eyes are fixed on the Lord, you will not be able to endure those days that go from bad to worse.*

# I WILL NOT RETREAT

*Read Exodus 6:13*

*R*ight after God told Moses what He would do, He said to him, "You must believe it. I command you to do this thing." "Now the LORD spoke to Moses and Aaron about the Israelites and Pharaoh king of Egypt, and he commanded them to bring the Israelites out of Egypt" (v. 13 NIV).

God was saying, "This is going to happen. The Israelites will come out of Egypt. This isn't wishful thinking or a nice sentiment. I intend to bring it to pass. Get ready to execute the plan."

So often the arrow that penetrates our soul at the weakest point is our unbelief. We know in our heads what God has said, but it takes faith to put it into gear, to get out there and start practicing what He has told us to do. Then and there, at that split-second of hesitation, the battle is won or lost.

This is how we need to pray, even when we feel as if we never want to pray again: "Lord, I don't feel like praying right now, but hear my prayer anyway. Lord, I will believe You, even though the tide is rising, and I'm already on tip-toe. I will believe You, even though it seems like it's taking You forever to keep Your promise. I will believe You, even though I've come to the ragged end of my strength, the dregs of my hope, the broken shards of my plans. I will not look for a shortcut. I will not rely on a carnal option. I will not retreat from the battle. I will believe You!"

God's promise to Moses is the same to us: "Because I am who I am, I will do what is best for you." There isn't a day on this side of eternity, no matter how grim, that can't be improved by clinging to that reassuring thought.

# PLAGUES THAT PREACH

### *Read Exodus 6:28—10:29*

*I*'m convinced this dreadful display of judgment in Egypt, this battle between a righteous, holy God and the stubborn heart of Pharaoh, has at least two major truths to teach us.

First, when God judges, He does a thorough job of it.

Second, it is a fearful thing to fall into the hands of the living God.

Let's make this painfully personal. You may be in the danger zone as you read these words. You have played fast and loose with your life, ignoring warning after warning. You have shoved aside essential truths for so long that your heart has become hardened. And the longer you harden it, the more difficult it is to allow God's light to finally break through.

But there's a bright side to this dark story. When God blesses, He holds nothing back. It's called *grace*. God's grace rescued the children of Israel in the land of Goshen. As dark as it became in Egypt, the Hebrews were flooded with light. They were a city on a hill, shining through the night, if only Pharaoh had eyes to see it.

You may be one who has enjoyed God's great grace and favor in your life—His protection, provision, daily blessings, and unmerited favor fill your days. You can thank God for a place in the land of Goshen. You enjoy God's protection—a careful plan which distinguishes you from those who live under His wrath. Believe me, nothing in this life or the next is more serious and sobering than the wrath of God. Some are broken—blessedly broken—by that wrath. Others only harden.

Life's plagues are tough to endure—painful to the core. But God has no desire to leave us alone in our pain and distress. Habakkuk once cried out to God, "In wrath, remember mercy."

And the Lord has done just that. Jesus, who endured God's wrath to the uttermost on the cross, now invites us to walk arm in arm with Him through the rest of our days. He is our faithful, ever-present Friend. No earthly catastrophe can ever separate us from the grip of His grace or the legacy of His love. Gratefully thank Him for both today.

# THE ESSENTIAL INGREDIENT

### ✤ *Read Exodus 11:1–10* ✤

T he main point, the central ingredient of Exodus 11 and 12, is *obedience*. God spoke, some people heard and did what God said. As a result, God used them in His plan at that time in history.

God knew in advance what use that silver and gold would be put to when the new nation arrived at Mount Sinai out in the desert. God already had something in mind that no one had ever dreamed of yet—the Tabernacle, the Tent of Meeting where the Israelites would meet in close proximity with the awesome holy God who had delivered them.

At this point, God didn't tell them why they would need those precious metals. He just said, "Ask for them," and they did. It's called *obedience*.

Isn't that encouraging? Earlier, we read about Moses' bad day. The ex-shepherd was under the gun, snarled at by the king and thoroughly hated by the Hebrew leadership. But now we read that he was "greatly esteemed" in Egypt *by the Egyptians*. From the court of Pharaoh on down to the man on the street, people were saying, "Now there's a great man."

Do you know why that was true? Because Moses stood all alone and trusted God (he obeyed), and the Lord gave him favor in their eyes. The Lord delights to do that. Remember Proverbs 16:7? "When a man's ways are pleasing to the LORD, He makes even his enemies to be at peace with him." We see that borne out yet again in this amazing development.

That may be the very word you need from the Lord today. Perhaps in your work you have come to an impasse; there's an issue of integrity at stake, and you've determined not to compromise. Because of your stand for Christ, you find that you are resented. I want to assure you that if you handle your situation wisely and tactfully, God will see to it that in the eyes of those who are now your enemies, you will one day be esteemed. They will respect your stand because you are standing alone, doing what is right.

# HISTORICAL OBEDIENCE

### ❧ *Read Exodus 12:1–28* ❧

*T*he instruction Moses gave was to be passed along from generation to generation. After he finished with these specific instructions, Scripture says, "And the people bowed low and worshiped. Then the sons of Israel went and did so; just as the LORD had commanded Moses and Aaron, so they did" (vv. 27–28).

We're back again to the key word: *obedience.*

Pharaoh did not—would not—obey. As a result, he exposed both himself and his nation to the judgment of the Lord. The Hebrews, however, heard the Lord's Word through Moses and did obey, right down to the smallest detail. As a result, they experienced a great deliverance. They *made* history, while Pharaoh *became* history.

I would like to apply some of these thoughts before we press on. My personal conviction is that our greatest struggle is not in the realm of understanding the will of God; it's in the realm of *obeying* the God whose will it is. To be painfully honest, when you and I look back over our lives, we do not find ourselves puzzled and mystified about God's will nearly as much as we find ourselves stubborn and resistant to the One who was directing our steps. Our problem wasn't that we didn't know; our problem was that we knew but weren't willing to follow through.

That's the basic struggle of the Christian life. The clear truth of God is set before us time and time again. It's available to us, we read it, we hear it explained from a pulpit, in a Christian book, or on a Christian radio program, and we sense the Holy Spirit whispering, *Yes, this means you.* We understand Him clearly . . . but we resist. When the chips are down, our tendency is to say, "I've got it planned another way." Looking back, we wonder, "Why didn't I obey?" Or, "Why didn't I follow God's call?"

At some juncture in our lives—maybe at several junctures—we need to ask ourselves those questions. You may say, "Well, Chuck, he's not calling everyone to that task." I know that. But that's not the issue here. We're not talking about everyone. The question is, how do *you* know He isn't calling *you?*

# HISTORICAL JOY

*Read Exodus 12:29–30; Psalm 105:26–38*

*I*sn't that great? Rather than sadness and fear, there was exhilaration that night. The sweet fragrance of freedom was in the wind. We love to sing the hymn, "O for a thousand tongues to sing, my great Redeemer's praise." If you think that sounds good, how about, "O for two million tongues to sing!" You could hear those voices echo far away into the distant reaches of the empty desert as Moses led the way, and the joyous throng followed. Great clouds of dust billowed as Jacob's children walked out of Egypt, walked out of their chains and away from their bondage.

Just think of that day or night when you came to know the Lord Jesus as your Savior. Can you recapture the emotions of that moment? Remember when that friend gave you the Good News about God's provision for sin and His offer of eternal life? Remember when you realized it was really for *you?* Remember when that pastor or teacher explained the gospel, and for the first time it really made sense? Remember when your dad or mom sat down with you in your bedroom and explained the truth about sin and Christ and eternity, and you said, "Tonight's the night"?

Was that a harsh, hard experience? Admittedly, you left all the familiar things of Egypt behind you, but don't forget you also left your chains! You left your years of slavery of sin's domination, and then you began to taste of God's provision. You began to drink from the deep wells of His grace. Nothing ever tasted so sweet and so refreshing.

It's not over, friend. There's more out there. His plan goes a lot deeper than getting you out of Egypt. Getting you into His family was Plan A. Getting you into His will, for your whole life—that's Plan B. And maybe that's where you are as you read these words. You find yourself about to step into unknown territory and follow God where you have never been before. Looking at it through the eyes of the ancient Hebrews, you're about to make history. Good for you!

# "Do Not Fear!"

### 🌿 *Read Exodus 12:31—14:14* 🌿

Humanly speaking, predicaments are terrible experiences. If you stay in one long enough, you will begin to question the very roots of your faith. By and by you'll begin to look for someone to blame; usually it'll be somebody in leadership.

That's why I am extremely impressed with Moses' response. He didn't say, as most are prone to say, "God helps those who help themselves." People think that familiar saying comes from the Bible. It doesn't. It's from the pit. No, God helps *the helpless!*

Note Moses' more biblical response in verse 13: "Do not fear!" What strange counsel. Can't you hear his fellow Israelites? "Hey, Moses, the Egyptians are around the corner. They've got chariots and bows and arrows and pointy spears. And you're saying, 'Don't fear'? What's the matter with you, man? Do you need a change in your eyeglass prescription? Can't you see they're coming? God, save us from this near-sighted shepherd!"

"Oh, I see them fine," Moses replied. "But I'm still saying to you, 'Don't fear!'"

But Moses isn't done. After telling them not to be afraid, he has a second piece of counsel for his followers: "Stand still." And a third: "Watch." And a fourth: "The Lord will fight for you while you keep silent."

Now, there's a prescription for people in an inescapable predicament! Don't be afraid, stand still, watch God come through, quit talking. The hardest is the fourth, because we just *have* to complain or tell somebody what a predicament we're in. But God doesn't need to be informed. He knows the predicament. He is simply waiting for us to calm down and keep silent.

When you are in a cul-de-sac, led by God to that tight place, it is there you will discover some phenomenal surprises designed just for you. That's why Moses said, "Look, let's stand still. There's a great blessing here for us that we'll miss if we turn tail and run."

You know the common response to panic? First, we become afraid. Second, we run. Third, we fight. Fourth, we tell everybody.

God's counsel is just the opposite. Don't be afraid. Stand still. Watch Him work. Keep quiet. It's then that He does His best work on our behalf. He takes over! He then handles our predicament opposite the way we'd do it. The Lord is tapping His foot, waiting for us to wait.

# THE HIGHWAY TO THE PROMISED LAND

### ❧ *Read Exodus 4:15—22* ❧

*H*ad we been in charge of the Red Sea project, we would have handled it differently. Our group of engineers would have pushed back that water a week in advance. We would have installed great, massive fans to dry out the land. We would have erected huge neon signs. Somebody would have brought in concession stands to handle the hot dogs and drinks. You see, when people do it, the project takes on all the trademarks of market-driven hot-shots. The supernatural is easily eclipsed by human ingenuity.

That's not God's plan. When He wants you cornered, outnumbered. And there are no signs. There is no slick ad campaign. There are no great human resources to trust in. There's just an uncrossable Red Sea and an encroaching army of impossibilities. So you wait. And time passes. He will fight His way at His time. Bite your nails all you want to—He's in no hurry.

Do you feel cornered right now? Up against it? Overwhelmed? Listen, child of God, your predicament is by His design. It takes those dark and dreary streets of heartache and those dead-end feelings of intimidation to prepare you for the glorious days of deliverance.

Perhaps you're a single adult. Those can be frustrating, hard years and lonely times. More than anything you'd like to find a spouse.

Or maybe you're married. You can be so involved in making a living that you fail to make a life, and then the time is gone.

Or perhaps you feel backed into some physical cul-de-sac, where you've languished for weeks, months, maybe years. . . . still in that wheelchair.

Listen carefully. Read this slowly. Coming to the Red Sea is just as much a part of His plan as crossing it. It may well be that the Lord is breaking a habit born in Egypt, a habit that has no business living in Canaan. Those habits are tough to break. The tears flow as God works in His time. But in the burning of those tears, God becomes very significant and real. And we realize, at last, that a predicament in God's hands finally leads to a highway to the Promised Land.

# SING IT OUT!

### ✦ *Read Exodus 4:23—15:22* ✦

*A*fter God drowned Pharaoh's entire army in the sea, for the first time in history Israel found herself living in the Egyptian desert, out in the open, completely on her own. The Hebrews had begun their journey to the land of Canaan. God had proven Himself faithful; the nation had walked through the sea on dry land. How awestruck they must have been! As a result, they sang a song of great praise to God. All the way from verse 1 to verse 21 of Exodus 15 they continue to sing.

Have you ever done that? Have you ever, on the spur of the moment, scratched out a song of praise to the Lord? I recommend it to you; it's actually an exciting experience. You say, "Well, Chuck, that's fine for you, but I'm not some kind of eloquent, creative poet. I don't have that gift. Words don't flow through me like that."

Really? How do you know if you never try? The next time you go through an experience, and God proves Himself faithful, stop and think, *Maybe I could write a song.* (Even if it's for an audience of One.) That's how praise songs are born. Why not compose one today?

On the heels of this Hebrew song of triumph and gratitude comes a word denoting a particular time: *"then."* When? After the Red Sea. After the first flush of freedom. After their wonderful song of praise. Scripture records, "*Then* Moses led Israel from the Red Sea, and they went out into the wilderness of Shur."

What a description of the Christian life! All of us have been through the Red Sea. Spiritually speaking, believers have all been placed in God's family through the cross. We have come to know the Lord Jesus. And in coming to know Him, we have been delivered for the first time from bondage to the old life. How glorious! Freed from the domination of our old master, we have been given a new song, a new life, a new beginning. But in this beginning we quickly discover we must endure some wilderness experiences. Looking back, we later realize they were deserts designed by God for a very real purpose. But what a come-down after our Red Sea conversion.

# BABY STEPS

*Read Exodus 15:22–27*

*A*s we consider Israel's first days in the wilderness, perhaps we should remind ourselves of where the Hebrew nation is in Exodus 15. They began their journey in the land of Goshen. If you have a map of that area handy, you might want to glance over it as you pinpoint their location. The Red Sea (or Sea of Reeds) is north of the Gulf of Suez. They crossed that sea, then began a south-southeasterly journey toward Mount Sinai. But before they arrived at the mount of God, they reached the wilderness of Shur in the northernmost section of the Sinai Peninsula. That's where the cloud and fire led Israel into the wilderness, with the shepherd Moses out in front of the flock. It was a vast expanse of desolation stretching south to the wilderness of Etham.

So that's where the Hebrews were. But *why* were they there? If God took the people through the Red Sea, couldn't He take them immediately to the lush land of Canaan? Of course! If He was able to part the waters, and enable them to walk on dry land, and deliver them from the Egyptians, wasn't He also able to move them swiftly to the borders of milk-and-honey-land? Absolutely! God can do anything. If He can take you and me through our conversion, He can hasten our journey across this earthly desert and swiftly deposit us into heaven. No problem . . . but He doesn't.

Why does God put us through wilderness experiences before Canaan? For one thing, He wants to test us. That's why God led Israel into the wilderness, according to Deuteronomy 8:2: "You shall remember all the way which the LORD your God has led you in the wilderness these forty years, that He might humble you, testing you, to know what was in your heart, whether you would keep His commandments or not." (Read that again . . . only this time, slowly.)

God puts us in the wilderness to humble us, to test us, to stretch our spiritual muscles. Our earthly wilderness experiences are designed to develop us into men and women of faith. Let's face it, our spiritual roots grow deep only when the winds around us are strong. Take away the tests, and we become shallow-rooted, spiritual wimps. But bring on the wilderness winds, and it's remarkable how we grow as our roots dig deeply into faith.

# THE TEST OF TIME

### ❧ *Read Exodus 16:1—36* ❧

*T*ime has passed. If you read the previous passage in chapter 15 with a careful eye, you observe that it took them only three days to find the water they now enjoyed. But now it's been a month and a half—more than forty days! I call that the test of time. There they are in the midst of the wilderness with their unrealistic expectations. "We thought we were through with those parched days in the wilderness. We were already there *three days*. Why do we have to go back?"

And guess what? Out rushed the complaints: "The whole congregation of the sons of Israel grumbled against Moses and Aaron in the wilderness" (16:2). Why were they grumbling? Again, they were looking back. Listen to their words in verse 3: "Would that we had died by the LORD's hand in the land of Egypt, when we sat by the pots of meat, when we ate bread to the full; for you have brought us out into this wilderness to kill this whole assembly with hunger" (v. 3).

Sound like your response? If so, it's time to learn a timeless lesson. If you focus on the past, it won't be long before complaints start oozing from your lips. You will remember a long-ago time, bathed in the hazy, rosy glow of memory, when something was easier and more comfortable than it is today. And as you compare then to now, I guarantee it, you will grumble.

It hurts to endure life's trials, and it hurts worse to repeat such episodes. Yet, without those deep hurts, we have very little capacity to receive godly counsel or make forward progress toward maturity. The test of time is perhaps the most rugged of all.

Over the long haul, God is honing us through such tests. Stretching us. Breaking us. Crushing us. Reducing us to an absolute, open-armed trust, where we say, "Lord, I have come to the end of my own flesh. If You wish me to die in this wilderness, here is my life. Take it. I refuse to look back and complain about where I find myself at this moment." Moses had learned to wait. His congregation needed to learn as well. How about you?

# THE WILDERNESS CYCLE

### ✤ *Read Exodus 17:1–16* ✤

*E*ach of us has his or her own wilderness cycle. Some struggle with a quiver full of small children at home. Others have no children. Your test may not be related to the home at all; it may be connected to your employment. Perhaps you're wrestling with relationships; you're abrasive and have difficulty with people. That's why God keeps you with people and grinds away so that your long-standing Egyptian habit might be altered. With others it's finances; you live continually under the gun of insufficient funds. Maybe it's a problem related to academics and school issues. That's your wilderness.

Your wilderness does not separate from you merely because you fly several thousand miles to some other spot. Wherever you go, your Egyptian appetite accompanies you. God is in the business of not only putting you through the Red Sea at salvation, but in getting you to Canaan by way of the wilderness. Conversion is often a brief trip to the altar, but maturity is always married to time.

Remember that this week. You have never lived the seven days in front of you, and you will never live them again. Life is like a coin. Spend it any way you want to, but you can spend it only once. God would like you to learn from your experience in the wilderness. He wants to change your appetite, change your habits, change your style, and, in the process, change your entire life.

As I've been writing, such deep, inward changes do not suddenly occur; they begin at the cross, where you lay down your arms and accept God's gift, Jesus Christ. Now may be your time to say, "Lord Jesus, this is Your moment. I give You my heart, my life, as Your child."

May we never forget the lessons of history, whether they be our personal history or the history of ancient Israel. And may we heed the words of my high-school history teacher, Mrs. Allen, "There are two things that you can do with history: you can ignore it, or you can learn from it."

Learning from the past may be hard, but continuing in ignorance is expensive. Better to learn those priceless lessons today than to search for pennies in the scorching wilderness tomorrow.

# DELEGATE THE WORKLOAD

### *Read Exodus 18:1–27*

The Christian worker is a strange breed. He or she wants it to look as if the work is terribly hard. In fact, the more difficult and strained the look, the better. Christian workers are notorious for what I call the "tired blood" look, better known as the overburdened and outdated "missionary image," or, better stated, the exhausted "over-burdened religious image." They usually carry an old, worn-out Bible, and walk with a slump, listing to port. They seldom smile—sort of a "please pity me" image. Makes me want to gag.

I don't mean to be super critical. The tragic reality is, some of these folks *are* overworked and hardly have enough to live on. But I believe you can be in full-time ministry without having to resemble the poor-me stereotype.

The happiest people on earth ought to be those of us in God's service. And we ought to *look* like it. We have every reason to smile more than anyone else. Even though our work is terribly serious, we ought to have more fun and have a better time doing it than anybody in any other career or calling. I think an individual in cross-cultural ministry or a local pastor ought to be able to enjoy his or her taste in music and live it up, just like anybody else.

Frankly, those who look as if they've just finished their last piece of bread do not minister very effectively, certainly not to me. Those who minister to me, and those to whom I think I minister, are men and women who truly enjoy life. We really don't need to spend all our time on the negative of life; there are enough heart-breaking experiences to go around for all of us.

Please don't misunderstand me. Ministry is not an easy calling. There *are* times when you must work longer than you should. And those times can occur back to back. But we don't need to remind most pastors of the need to work harder. We need a reminder of another sort. "You're making your job harder than it should be. Share the load. Lighten up! Your work can be easier. Let us help you get these things done."

# A GOD TOO SMALL?

*❧ Read Exodus 19:1–15 ❧*

S o deep, so profound must be this respect for God's holy presence that no one was even to *touch* the mountain. The people were to wait upon God to speak to Moses and hear the Lord's words through the Lord's servant.

What a needed reminder! This story makes it clear that we live in a day of pitifully shallow concepts of God. Some of today's contemporary Christian music leaves the impression that God is our buddy—a great pal to have in a pinch. A film star once said of God, "He's my great Big Daddy upstairs." One pop song asks, "What if God were just a slob like us?" That is not the biblical view of God. That is a human being's feeble attempt to make God relevant.

The Puritans, that rigorous people of old, possessed a solidly biblical concept of God. Do you know why it is so crucial for us to recover such a respectful understanding? Because a shallow view of God leads to a shallow life. Cheapen God and you cheapen life itself. Treat God superficially, and you become superficial. But hold God in profoundest respect, and it is remarkable how deep the roots of your spiritual life grow.

God is holy. Exalted. He is the only wise God, the Creator, the Maker, the sovereign Lord. He is the Master. He tells me what to do, and I have no safe option but to do it. He offers no alternative, no multiple choice. We have but one directive, and that it is to do His will. We reaffirm that truth in our times with Him.

But not today. Today He's our pal, our understanding buddy, our ever-available bellboy. No, He is not! The Lord is our God. He does not bow to our hurried pace, but in silence He waits for us to meet *His* demands. And once we slow down enough to meet Him, He is pleased to add incredible spiritual depth to our otherwise shallow lives.

What has been *your* concept of the Lord? Who is *your* God? Be honest, now. Does He look anything like the God of Mount Sinai?

# A HEALTHY FEAR

### *Read Exodus 19:16—25*

*W*hat a magnificent experience! If you live in an area shaken by earthquakes, you feel a little ripple now and then, get a funny feeling, and then life returns to normal. But how often do you see a granite mountain shaking, or hear constant thunder rumbling from lightning strikes between clouds and earth, or shrink before the long blasts of heavenly trumpets announcing that God is ready to meet you?

Just your regular, ho-hum quiet time, right? In no way. Can you imagine how Moses felt when the Lord said to Moses, "Come up, Moses"? Wow! If you were Moses, what would you do now? How would you do it? How could you carry on? I'll tell you how: with fear and trembling Moses made that historic journey up into the clouds. He'd stood before a burning bush, but that was nothing compared to this epochal experience. The writer of Hebrews says, "So terrible was the sight, that Moses said, 'I am full of fear and trembling'" (Hebrews 12:21).

A healthy fear of God will hold us in awe and do much to deter us from sin. When we have a proper fear of the living Lord, we live a cleaner life. Any born-again person who sins willfully has momentarily blocked out any fear of God. You and I can do that. When we actively engage in sin, we consciously put aside what we know to be the truth about God. We deliberately suppress the knowledge of Him in our hearts and minds. We lie to ourselves by saying, "We'll get by. God won't mind so much." Yet God used Moses to reveal to His people a reverential and healthy fear of the Almighty.

When you come to that understanding, and God's light breaks into your life like the pure whitewater of a rushing river, you learn to thoroughly hate and dread those actions that will plunge you again into darkness. The psalmist expressed that thought with these words: "How sweet are your words to my taste, sweeter than honey to my mouth! I gain understanding from your precepts; therefore I hate every wrong path. Your word is a lamp to my feet and a light for my path" (Ps. 119:103–105 NIV).

# WRITTEN INSTRUCTIONS

### ❧ *Read Exodus 19:16—20:26* ❧

*W*hy did God want to meet with Moses? The text gives us two good and healthy reasons:

*To establish a healthy fear of the Almighty.* "Moses said to the people, 'Do not be afraid; for God has come in order to test you, and in order that the fear of Him may remain with you, so that you may not sin'" (Exodus 20:20).

*To communicate written instructions for the people.* "Now the LORD said to Moses, 'Come up to Me on the mountain and remain there, and I will give you the stone tablets with the law and the commandment which I have written for their instruction.' So Moses arose with Joshua his servant, and Moses went up to the mountain of God" (Exodus 24:12–13).

Isn't it great that God gave His people written instructions to obey? This is the first time in all of history that God *wrote down* His Word. Until the time of Moses, the written Word of God did not exist. But now, here it was. And to think, you and I possess those written words! What an awesome and majestic thought. How we take that privilege for granted.

Back before the collapse of the atheistic Soviet Union, my friend John Van Diest represented the Evangelical Christian Publishers Association at the Moscow Book Fair. The authorities had granted them reluctant permission to hand out a limited number of Russian language New Testaments, and long lines of people waited in line to receive a copy. When the supplies were exhausted, one desperately disappointed man asked if he might have one of the empty boxes that had once held those Testaments.

"But there's nothing in there!" John protested. "The Bibles are all gone!" With tears glistening in his eyes, the man replied, "Then I at least want the box." The Bible was so precious to this man that he treasured the cardboard box that had held the Scriptures. May our eyes be opened to the astonishing privilege that is ours to hold the complete written Word of God in our very hands.

# DOING TIME

*Read Exodus 24:12; 25:1–9*

N ow we know why God met with Moses. But what did He reveal? Verse 12 tells us: He revealed *His written word*. The first thing God gave to this man who met with Him was His truth in written form.

No one has ever had in his possession a more valuable document than this. Moses possessed the very autograph of Deity—the *autographa* etched in stone by God's own finger.

God gave His people the Word of God that they might know His mind and obey. He gave them the design for the tabernacle that He might come and dwell among them. He didn't want to remain aloof high up on a mountain. He wanted to make Himself accessible and available, but, in keeping with His own design, He would dwell in a sacred place within the tabernacle.

Moses is a man who met with God. He learned that it takes discipline and preparation to do so. It's one thing to know what to do; it's quite another to actually do it. How many of us take a course on prayer but rarely pray, or learn the techniques of evangelism but seldom share our faith? In this account of Moses' life, we may have learned little new, but we have been confronted with some profound reminders from God's Word. We do not need a creative new technique nearly as much as a swift kick in the pants. We need a rebuke from the Holy Spirit, because we are so slothful and slow and sleepy when it comes to climbing that mountain and meeting for half an hour with the Lord.

May He do a work in spite of us! Despite our bad track record, may He stop us this moment with the reminder that we could become far stronger men and women of God if we would only maintain a time of meeting with Him.

It may be on a craggy mountain peak, in a closet, or as with my own mother, in a locked bathroom with a "Do not disturb" sign on the door. God isn't particular in the least about the place you choose or the amount of time you spend. All He wants is you.

# NOT INDISPENSABLE

### ✎ *Read Numbers 11:24–30* ✎

These young men were jealous for Moses' role. They said, "Moses, you can't let 'em get away with that. You're the prophet. What are Eldad and Medad doing in there? Who do they think they are, prophesying like that? That's your job." So Joshua says, "General Moses, sir, put a stop to it."

I love it that Moses is more broad-shouldered than that. He replies securely, without a hint of jealousy, "Are you jealous for my sake? Would that all the LORD'S people were prophets, that the LORD would put His Spirit upon them" (v. 29)! Talk about unselfish. There wasn't an ounce of jealousy or insecurity in that man of God.

Are you pursuing godliness? Do you want to count for Christ? Has God gifted you for service? If so, somewhere along the line, you will face the peril of jealousy, the feeling of being "indispensable" to some particular ministry. And some around you will plant seeds of jealousy in your heart that will tempt you to feel indispensable. You'll think, *What's she doing up there? I could teach better than she.* Or, *you know, that man bears watching. He's trying to take over. Everybody knows I'm the leader.* Or, *I can't afford to step down. I started this organization.* Ever heard those words or something similar? Ever said them yourself? Those are words of petty jealousy and proud indispensability.

Listen to me! *Everybody* can afford to step down if God's enthroned. Some of the most jealous, suspicious people in the world are so-called Christian public figures enamored with their own press clippings. It's vital to them that they drop the right names and be seen by the right people and have others think well of them. They crave fame. And God help the one whose fame crowds theirs!

You're not indispensable. I'm not indispensable. Nobody is indispensable, except the Lord Jesus Christ. He's the head. He's the Preeminent One. He's the founder. He's in first place. And when He moves one out and brings in another or demotes one and sets up another, He calls the shots. That is His sovereign right. The problem arises when we get to thinking *we're* sovereign. My friend, He put you where He wanted you. He gave you that job. He can take it away just as fast as He gave it. Faithfully do your work, lie low, and exalt Christ.

# ANGER'S BITTER FRUIT

### ✣ *Read Numbers 20:1–13* ✣

N ow, wait a minute! Did we miss something? Where did Moses get the okay to deliver that scathing address? The truth is, He didn't. Then where did it come from? From anger. *Brimming* with hostility and reacting in unbelief, he takes that rod and preaches an angry sermon to the people. His short fuse prompts him to take advantage of an opportunity to level these rebels with enraged verbiage.

I think there's even a hint of blasphemy here. "Shall *we* bring water out of the rock?" he asks. But Moses, when did *you* ever bring water out of a rock? Isn't *God* the one who summons water? True enough. But when you give in to rage, you sort of black out; you set aside your right mind and are driven by the unchecked emotions of anger. So the text states, Moses "lifted up his hand and *struck* the rock *twice* with his rod" (20:11, italics mine).

God had told him to *speak* to the rock; Moses *struck* it, not just once, but *twice*. And I frankly doubt whether he even cared if water came. He probably hoped it wouldn't. He was so angry, he wanted their throats to stay dry. He wanted them to choke and writhe in their thirst. "Do you think we'll give *you* water, you low-life scumbags? Hah!" So he belts the rock—Wham! Wham!—and much to his surprise, out flows fresh water. Scripture tells us that "water came forth abundantly, and the congregation and their beasts drank" (v. 11). Absolutely amazing! Amazing *grace!*

But that's the way God's grace works, isn't it? Have you ever acted in rash unbelief, and yet God went ahead and opened up the door in spite of you? Talk about ultra humiliation. It happens when you're out to lunch spiritually, when you're walking in the flesh and you know it. You know when it began, and you know the depth and intensity of your carnality, but God graciously gives you what is best anyway. It's remarkable, isn't it, this thing called grace? It was grace that brought forth that clear stream of fresh water for the rebellious Israelites, as well as for ill-tempered Moses.

# GOD OF ALL MY MOMENTS

### ✦ *Read Numbers 20:1–13* ✦

ouldn't you love the ability to go back in time and change something you did or said? I know there have been moments in my life—awful moments when I acted on the impulse of the flesh—that I would dearly love to call back. But alas, I cannot.

Don't you imagine, during those days prior to his homegoing, Moses would have cheerfully given his right arm to relive that incident at the rock? *"Oh Lord, if I could only back up and do that all over! I would have cried out for Your help to control my anger. I would have been more concerned for Your glory. I would have done exactly as You instructed."*

But he couldn't go back. In a single moment of rage, he forfeited his right to lead Israel. He threw away his opportunity to enter the Promised Land.

The sad fact is, we cannot go back. None of us can. We cannot undo sinful deeds or unsay sinful words. We cannot reclaim those moments when we were possessed by rage, lust, cruelty, indifference, or hard-headed pride. Like Moses, we may be forgiven for those sins and have them blotted out of our record by the blood of Christ. Even so, we must live with the consequences of our words and our actions. What we sow, the Scriptures warn, we will also reap.

No, we can't go back. Our gracious Lord has covered our past with His own blood, given on the cross for us. David reminds us that, "As far as the east is from the west, so far has He removed our transgressions from us" (Psalm 103:13).

But we *can* learn to walk much closer with Him, day by day, hour by hour, moment by moment. We *can* keep short accounts with Him and lean on the Holy Spirit to guard our hearts and shield us from destructive, life-shattering sins. He will do it. He has promised to provide us with a way of escape so that we can bear up under any temptation (Hebrews 10:13)—*any* temptation at *any* moment.

If this becomes our way of life, my friend, when God says speak to the rock, we *will* speak, not strike. And the water that flows from those moments of obedience will refresh a multitude, including ourselves, with no aftertaste of regret.

# A Shepherd's Heart

### ✦ *Read Numbers 27:12–23* ✦

*M*oses asks for a man "who will go out and come in before them, who will lead them out and bring them in, that the congregation of the LORD may not be like sheep which have no shepherd" (v. 17). In other words, "Lord, we need a man who realizes he must be in touch with the people before he can minister to them. He needs to be a people person."

Moses was saying, "These people don't need a mystic. They don't need a man pre-occupied by his love for research, as important as that may be. These folks don't really need a super-efficient CEO or a brilliant organizational genius. They need a *shepherd*. They need a man who knows people, who will minister to people, understand people, and know how to guide people."

In whatever capacity you might minister—as a Bible teacher, as a student preparing for the ministry, as a woman of God ministering in your area of giftedness—your ministry is primarily *people,* not shuffling papers, not crunching numbers, not making phone calls, not writing letters, not planning programs, or noodling over strategies for the next decade. Of course, all of those things must be done. I must sign and/or write an average of forty to fifty letters a week and get involved in planning sessions too. Administrative details need to be handled. (As few as I can get by with!)

Do you know the most common thing I hear from individuals just beginning to come to our church? They want very much to get to know some of us on staff, and they'll say, "You don't know me, but I come on Sunday to hear you preach." And they almost apologize, as if to say, "Hey, I'm sorry to take your time, but I just want to shake your hand." I go out of my way to say to each one, "You are as important as anybody else in this entire church. There is no insignificant member of the family of God." I don't say this to make a good public relations statement or to make a good impression. I say it because I believe it—because it's true. Whoever you are, whatever you do, you are special before the God who has chosen you.

# GOD OF EVERY DETAIL

*Read Numbers 27:12–23; Deuteronomy 34:9*

*I* am always amazed to hear how the Lord uses His Word in the lives of His people. I don't know your circumstances. I don't know how God intends to use this episode from the life of Moses in your own life.

It may be that these words fall on a very hungry heart. Or perhaps you have been strengthened and encouraged with the thought that you're very special to God, that none of His children are insignificant. Or maybe you're engaged in the awesome task of finding a man or a woman for a position that carries a great weight of responsibility, and you've been reminded that you are dependent, more than ever, on God to locate His Joshua. Or perhaps *you* are that Joshua, and you've been asked to accept a responsibility broader than you ever dreamed.

Whatever your circumstances, I want to remind you that our heavenly Father cares about areas of your life that would seem insignificant to a distant deity. He's never too busy to hear your hurts, to wipe away your tears, to whisper words of encouragement, and to put His big shoulder under your load. He's the God who cares about the details.

As I write these words, I'm praying that our sovereign God might be a very personal comfort to you this week. I pray especially for you who are wrestling with loneliness and discouragement. Even though you're surrounded by people, deep within there's an ache. Friend, God can meet your need as only He can, even as He did in the heart of Moses just a few hours before the great man's death.

If you're God's Joshua, you don't need to worry that you'll be forgotten. You don't need to worry that the shadow of your predecessor will eclipse you and your ministry in the years to come. In fact, you don't need to worry about *anything*. If you're God's Joshua, you're right where you ought to be. Remind yourself that He is sovereign. He has everything under His control. He will have His way in His time, for His glory, which includes your life, your position, and your future. Worrying over any of that is a waste. He's got *every detail* covered—every one.

Think of it this way: there's no such thing as God's being *almost* sovereign.

# THREE SECRETS REVEALED

### ✦ *Read Deuteronomy 34:1–12* ✦

hen we read this part of [Moses'] epitaph and think of all the mighty power and all the miracles that Moses did, many of us tend to think, *Moses is in another league. I can't touch him. This life I've observed amounts to just another theoretical study. It almost mocks me, because I'm light years from Moses.*

What a colossal error we make if we come to such a faulty deduction. Moses was unique, certainly, but he was just a man in the service of God. Still, we can learn much of personal benefit from his life and death.

*The secret of fulfillment in life is involvement.*

When you're planning on retirement, don't plan on checking out with people or with God's Word. If you do, you'll be moving away from that which is eternal, and that's the wrong direction, my friend. So stay in touch. Give until you don't have anything else to give, and then tap into God's reservoirs and give some more. This is what lengthens the meaning and purpose—and sometimes the years—of life.

*The secret of reality in life is humility.*

If involvement gives life length, then humility gives it breadth. Moses presents us with a beautiful picture of real humanity mixed with deep humility and genuine godliness. Moses never believed his own press reports. He never got lost in his own track record. He never got up in the morning to see what the headlines had to say about his performance the day before. He stayed real, believable, and humble.

*The secret of happiness in life is perspective.*

If involvement gives life length and humility gives it breadth, then perspective gives life depth.

Death comes to all of us. And unless our Lord comes in the clouds for us first, that day of departure will arrive . . . maybe sooner, maybe later. We have no control over that, but we do have control over the way we live, right up to the moment we leave this planet.

Moses teaches us that, regardless of whether we live or die, God remains worthy of our praise. It must be our goal, then, as it was the goal of Moses, to bring honor to Him, whether by life or by death.

*David: A Man of Passion & Destiny*

# HOW'S YOUR HEART?

### *Read 1 Samuel 13:1—14*

When God scans the earth for potential leaders, He is not on a search for angels in the flesh. He is certainly not looking for perfect people, since there are none. He is searching for men and women like you and me, mere people made up of flesh, bone, and blood. But He is also looking for certain qualities in those people, like the qualities He found in David.

The first quality God saw in David was *a heart for God*. "The Lord has sought out . . . a man after His own heart." What does it mean to be a person after God's own heart? Seems to me, it means that you are a person whose life is in harmony with the Lord. What is important to Him is important to you. What burdens Him burdens you. When He says, "Go to the right," you go to the right. When He says, "Stop that in your life," you stop it. When He says, "This is something I want you to change," you come to terms with it because you have a heart for God. That's bottom-line biblical Christianity.

When you are deeply spiritual, you have a heart that is sensitive to the things of God. A parallel verse in 2 Chronicles confirms this: "For the eyes of the LORD move to and fro throughout the earth that He may strongly support those whose heart is *completely* His" (2 Chronicles 16:9, emphasis added).

What is God looking for? He is looking for men and women whose hearts are completely His—*completely*. That means there are no locked closets. Nothing's been swept under the rugs. That means that when you do wrong, you admit it and immediately come to terms with it. You're grieved over wrong. You're concerned about those things that displease your heavenly Father. You long to please Him in your actions. You care about the motives behind your actions. That's having a heart for God, and that's the first quality David had. Do you have a heart for God?

# PEOPLE PANIC . . . GOD PROVIDES

### ✛ *Read 1 Samuel 15:1–19* ✛

The tragic story of King Saul is that he never, ever fully repented of his sin. Saul's greatest concern was his image, how he looked before the people. Even after Samuel gave him a break, Saul took advantage of it and continued in that same vein until the day he took his own life. How sad is that?

Samuel has reached the end of his rope. The people elected Saul king, but he's no longer qualified. What are they to do? Israel is surrounded by enemies, and they need someone to carry the scepter. But who? Samuel didn't know and couldn't imagine. The people didn't know and had no suggestions. No one knew . . . except God.

What Samuel didn't realize—what we often don't realize—is that behind the scenes, before He ever flung the stars into space, God had today in mind. He had this very week in mind. In fact, He had you in mind. And He knew exactly what He was going to do. God is never at a loss to know what He's going to do in our situations. He knows perfectly well what is best for us. Our problem is, *we* don't know. And we say to Him, "Lord, if You just tell me, then I'll be in great shape. Just reveal it to me. Explain Your plan to me, and I'll count on You." But that's not faith. Faith is counting on Him when we do *not* know what tomorrow holds.

When a man or a woman of God fails, nothing of God fails. When a man or woman of God changes, nothing of God changes. When someone dies, nothing of God dies. When our lives are altered by the unexpected, nothing of God is altered or unexpected. It was the prophet Isaiah who wrote: "Before they call, I will answer; and while they are still speaking, I will hear" (Isa. 65:24).

"Before you even utter a word," God promises, "I'm involved in answering. In fact, while you're speaking, I'm involved in bringing to pass the very thing I have planned from the get go."

God knows *exactly* what He's going to do, and nothing can restrain His bringing it to pass.

# GOOD DIRECTIONS

### ❧ *Read 1 Samuel 16:1–5* ❧

hat was Samuel's problem? He was panic-stricken. He was just plain scared. Where were Samuel's eyes? Well, they certainly weren't on the Lord. They were riveted on Saul.

From a human viewpoint, of course, Samuel was right. King Saul was murderous. But God was completely aware of the situation. After all, Saul was the one God was going to use to shape David's life in the in-between years, between the sheep and the throne. God knew Saul very well.

By the way, do you have a Saul in your life? Is there somebody who irritates and rubs and files and scrapes and irritates you? God knows all about it. That person is all part of His plan, strange as that may seem. The Lord doesn't answer Samuel's remark about Saul. Instead, He says, "Take a heifer with you, and say, 'I have come to sacrifice to the LORD.' And you shall invite Jesse to the sacrifice, and I will show you what you shall do; and you shall anoint for Me the one whom I designate to you" (1 Samuel 16:2–3).

Follow the Leader! That's what God is saying. You don't have to be smart to be obedient. You don't have to be creative or clever. All you have to do is obey. We think we have to sort of outwit God on the horizontal. But God says, "I know your situation. I'm telling you exactly what you ought to do, so go do it. Take a heifer, go to Jesse, offer the sacrifice, and look around. I'll tell you the man I've chosen for the job." Isn't that simple?

God has some extremely exciting things in mind for His children. For some it may happen tomorrow. For some it may happen next month or next year or five years down the road. We don't know when. For some, it could happen today. But the beautiful thing about this adventure called faith is that we can count on Him never to lead us astray. He knows exactly where He's taking us. Our job is to obey, to live in close fellowship with God as we walk our earthly path. In the process of that simple arrangement, God engages us in His eternal plan.

# NOBODIES INTO SOMEBODIES

### ✤ *Read 1 Samuel 16:1–11* ❧

*P*aul's whole thrust in his first letter to the believers at Corinth was, "I'm not coming to you with brilliance or human wisdom, and I'm certainly not coming to you with any kind of impressive physique or profound philosophy. Instead, I come in the power of God. And there's a good reason for that." Note carefully how Paul put it:

> For consider your calling, brethren, that there were not many wise according to the flesh, not many mighty, not many noble; but God has chosen the foolish things of the world to shame the wise, and God has chosen the weak things of the world to shame the things which are strong, and the base things of the world and the despised, God has chosen, the things that are not, that He might nullify the things that are, that no man should boast before God. (1 Corinthians 1:26–29)

Paul says, "Look around, Corinthians. You won't find many impressive people here." Why? So that no one can boast before God. That's a principle we tend to forget, because many of us are still a lot like the Greeks. When we look for people to admire as we choose our role models, our heroes, we are often swayed or impressed by things that are cause for boasting. We want the beautiful people, the brilliant people, the "successful" people. We want the best and the brightest. We are terribly enamored of the surface. The superficial still impresses us—much more than we'd like to admit. We even elect a president because he looks good on television! But God says, "That's not the way I make my choices. I choose the nobodies and turn them into somebodies."

And that, in a nutshell, is the story of how David was chosen to become a king.

# A Humble Servant

### ✤ *Read 1 Samuel 16:1—11* ✤

God saw in David the quality of *humility*. The Lord had gone to the home of Jesse in spirit form. Jesse didn't know God was there. Nobody did. God was on a secret surveillance mission in that home, and he spotted Jesse's youngest son and said, in effect, "That's My man!"

Why? Because, as we saw before, the Lord saw in David a heart that was completely his. The boy was faithfully keeping his father's sheep. God saw humility: He saw a servant's heart. If you want further confirmation of this, go to the Psalms: "I have found David My servant; With My holy oil I have anointed him" (Psalm 89:20).

It's as if God says, "I don't care about all that slick public image business. Show me a person who has the character, and I'll give him all the image he needs. I don't require some certain temperament, I don't care if he has a lot of charisma, I don't care about size, I don't care about an impressive education or résumé. I care about character! First, is the person deeply authentic in his or her spiritual walk or is he faking it? And second, is he or she a servant?"

When you have a servant's heart, you're humble. You do as you're told. You don't rebel. You respect those in charge. You serve faithfully and quietly without concern over who gets the credit.

That's David. God looked at David, out in the fields in the foothills surrounding Bethlehem, keeping his father's sheep, faithfully doing his father's bidding, and God passed His approval on him.

I repeat, a servant doesn't care who gets the glory. Remember that. A servant has one great goal, and that is to make the person he serves look better, to make that person even more successful. A servant does not want the person he serves to fail. A servant doesn't care who thinks what, just so the job gets done.

So while David's brothers were off in the army making rank and fighting big, impressive battles, David was all alone keeping the sheep. God loved his servant's heart.

# A MAN OF INTEGRITY

### *Read 1 Samuel 16:1–11*

God knew David had the quality of *integrity*. Today, we live in a world that says, in many ways, "If you make a good impression, that's really all that matters." But you will never be a man or woman of God if that's your philosophy. Never. You cannot fake it with the Almighty. He is not impressed with externals. He always focuses on the inward qualities, those things that take time and discipline to cultivate. God trained David for a leadership role with four disciplines.

First, God trained David in *solitude*. He needed to learn life's major lessons all alone before he could be trusted with responsibilities and rewards before the public. Solitude has nurturing qualities all its own. Anyone who must have superficial sounds to survive lacks depth. If you can't stand to be alone with yourself, you have deep, unresolved issues in your inner life. Solitude has a way bringing those issues to the surface.

Second, David grew up in *obscurity*. That's another way God trains His best personnel—in obscurity. Men and women of God, servant-leaders in the making, are first unknown, unseen, unappreciated, and unapplauded. In the quiet context of obscurity, character is built. Strange as it may seem, those who first accept the silence of obscurity are best qualified to handle the applause of popularity.

Which leads us to the third training ground, *monotony*. That's being faithful in the menial, insignificant, routine, unexciting, uneventful, daily tasks of life. Life without a break . . . without the wine and roses. Just dull, plain L-I-F-E. Just constant, unchanging, endless hours of tired monotony as you learn to be a man or woman of God . . . with nobody else around, when nobody else notices, when nobody else even cares. That's how we learn to "king it."

That brings us to the fourth discipline: *reality*. Up until now you might have the feeling that despite the solitude, obscurity, and monotony, David was just sitting out on some hilltop in a mystic haze, composing a great piece of music, or relaxing in the pastures of Judea and having a great time training those sheep to sit on their hind legs. That's not true.

# INNER QUALITIES

*Read 1 Samuel 16:11; 17:34–35*

T hink ahead with me to 1 Samuel 17. Here is David, standing by Saul, as a giant lumbers across the distant landscape.

Saul says, "Who are you?"

"I'm David."

Saul says, "Where have you been?"

"With my father's sheep."

Then Saul says, "You can't fight this Philistine. You're just a little kid."

Though only a teenager, David responds without hesitation:

"Your servant was tending his father's sheep [that's solitude, obscurity, monotony]. When a lion or a bear came and took a lamb from the flock [that's reality], I went out after him and attacked him, and rescued it from his mouth; and when he rose up against me, I seized him by his beard and struck him and killed him." (1 Samuel 17:34–35)

Where did David get such courage? He had learned it all alone before God. What kind of man is this David? A man of reality. He's a man who remained responsible when nobody was looking.

Goliath was no big deal. Why? Because David had been killing lions and bears while nobody was around. He'd been facing reality long before he squared off against Goliath. David may have lived many centuries ago, but the things we can learn from him are as current as this morning's sunrise. Two stand out in my mind.

First, *it's in the little things and in the lonely places that we prove ourselves capable of the big things.* If you want to be a person with a large vision, you must cultivate the habit of doing the little things well. That's when God puts iron in your bones!

Second, *when God develops our inner qualities, He's never in a hurry.* When God develops character, He works on it throughout a lifetime. He's not in a rush.

It is in the schoolroom of solitude and obscurity that we learn to become men and women of God. It is from the schoolmasters of monotony and reality that we learn to "king it." That's how we become—like David—men and women after God's own heart.

# HUMBLE APPOINTMENT

### ❦ *Read 1 Samuel 16:12–17* ❧

ere's our first good look at David. He walks into the house, still smelling like sheep, and all of a sudden an old man hobbles over and pours oil on his head. It drips down his hair and drops on to his neck. Josephus, the historian, writes, "Samuel the aged whispered in his ear the meaning of the symbol, 'You will be the next king.'"

What did David do? What *do* you do in a situation like that? I mean, it doesn't come along every other day. God's ways are so marvelous, aren't they? At the most surprising moment, the most magnificent things happen. "You're going to be the next king." What did he do? Well, I'm happy to report, he did not go down to the nearest department store and try on crowns. He didn't order a new set of business cards, telling the printer, "Change it from shepherd to king-elect." Didn't have a badge saying, "I'm the new man." Didn't shine up a chariot and race through the streets of Bethlehem, yelling, "I'm God's choice . . . you're looking at Saul's replacement!"

What did he do?

It made no difference that Samuel had anointed him with oil. He didn't bronze that horn and hang it up in his tent. He didn't expect special treatment from others. No, he simply went back to the sheep. And when the king said, "Come on over here and play music for me," David went over and played a little. And when he got through, he thought, *Hey, I gotta get back with my sheep; that's my job.*

David was sensitive enough to hear the whisper of God's voice, "You will be the next king." But as soon as the big moment was over and they turned out the lights, he was humbly back with his sheep. People had to actually pull him from the sheep to get him to do anything that was related to the limelight. In fact, I think that's one of the reasons he was a man after God's heart. He was always approachable, always believable, always authentic . . . and always faithful in the little things.

# PERMANENT DWELLING

### *Read 1 Samuel 16:14–15*

*I* think it's important that we notice that the Spirit of the Lord departed from Saul before an evil spirit came. Christians read those words about "an evil spirit from God" and they fear that could happen today. I've heard evangelists use that as a tool to shock Christians. "You continue to walk in the flesh," they say, "and God will lift His Spirit from you, and you won't have God's presence within you as you once had." Then they'll quote this verse or the one in Judges 16 where Samson is in Delilah's lap, and it says, "He knew not that the LORD had departed from him." Or the one in Psalm 51:11 that says, "Take not Thy Holy Spirit from me." That's a fearful thought, that God could lift His Spirit from us and we'd be lost, having once been saved.

So let's go on record right now with a good dose of theology. Before the Holy Spirit came at Pentecost (Acts 2), the Spirit of God never permanently rested on any believer except David and John the Baptizer. Those are the only two. It was not uncommon for the Spirit of God to come for a temporary period of strengthening or insight or whatever was the need of the moment and then to depart, only to return again for another surge of the need of the moment, then to depart, once again.

However, at Pentecost and from that time on, all the way through our present era, when the Spirit of God comes into the believing sinner at salvation, He never leaves. He comes and baptizes us into the body of Christ. That happens at salvation. We remain sealed by the Spirit from that time on. We're never exhorted to *be* baptized by the Spirit. We *are* baptized into the body of Christ, placed there by the Spirit, sealed until the day of redemption (Ephesians 4:30). That's the day we die. So He's there, and He never leaves. Furthermore, our bodies are the temple of the Holy Spirit in which the Spirit of God dwells. He permanently resides within us and will never, ever depart. So, rest easy, Christian friend. The Lord has come to stay.

# GOD SPEAKS . . . WE RESPOND

### ❧ *Read 1 Samuel 16:14–23* ❧

hree timeless lessons ring through my head as I look at these significant scenes in David's life.

First, *God's solutions are often strange and simple, so be open.* We try to make God complex and complicated. He isn't. Amid all the complications with Saul and the throne, God simply said to Samuel, "Go where I tell you to go. I've got a simple answer. A new man. You just follow Me, and I'll show you." Don't make the carrying out of God's will complicated. It isn't. Stay open to His strange yet simple solutions.

Second, *God's promotions are usually sudden and surprising, so be ready.* At the time you least expect it, it'll come. Just like His Son's return from heaven. Suddenly and surprisingly He will split the clouds and be with us. Just when we expect Him the least He'll be there, like a thief in the night. And that's the way His promotions are. He watches you as you faithfully carry out your tasks, and He says to you, "I know what I'm doing. In a sudden and surprising moment, you be ready. I know where you are, and I know how to find you. You just stay ready as you carry out your job."

Finally, *God's selections are always sovereign and sure, so be sensitive.* That applies to choosing a mate as well as losing a mate. It applies to our being moved from one place to another, even though we thought we'd remain there ten more years. It also applies to those God appoints to fill the shoes of another. How easy to second-guess God's selections! How necessary, when tempted to do that, to remind ourselves that His selections are sovereign and sure.

God is looking at your town, your city, your neighborhood, and He's looking for His people to whom He can say, "You are Mine. I want to use you there because you proved yourself faithful there." The only difference is our geography. Our calling is to be faithful in the demanding tasks, whether that is our education, our marriage, our occupation, or just the daily grind of life. That's the kind of men and women God wants to use.

# David's Unique Ability

### ❧ *Read 1 Samuel 16:16—18* ❧

N ow that's not a bad resume, is it? He's a skilled musician; he's a man of valor; he's a warrior; he has control of his tongue; he's handsome; and the Lord is with him.

One important thing this says to me is that you should never discount anything in your past. God can pick it up and use it in the most incredible ways. You never know when something that happened years ago will open a door of opportunity into the future.

That's precisely what happened to David. There he was all along, plucking away on his instrument, out in the fields of Judea. He'd never even met Saul, yet he's ultimately to be Saul's replacement. Get that! So God works out a way to bring them together—music! Soon David receives a message that says, "Saul wants to see you." It's incredible how it all falls together. I never cease to be amazed at how perfectly God weaves His will together without our help!

Even though Samuel had anointed David earlier, Jesse let him go back with the sheep. And now a runner comes from the king, saying, "Saul wants to see your youngest son." So Jesse releases David, but first he loads him down with gifts for the king. Now David trudges along with a donkey loaded with bread and a jug of wine and a goat, and his stringed instrument slung over his shoulder!

David didn't know it, but he was getting ready to enter boot camp on the road to becoming a king. That's the way God's program works. You may think some skill you learned or used years ago is lost, or that you've wasted all that time doing whatever, but don't you believe it. God can use what may seem to be a most insignificant part of your past and put you in exactly the right place to use that particular gift or skill.

That's the way it was with David. He never once said to Saul, "I'm gonna take your place, pal." Never once did he pull rank on Saul. He was never jealous of or pushing for the king's position. He wasn't presumptuous. He'd been anointed, but he continued to let the Lord open all the doors. Remember, David was a man after God's heart.

# MUSIC'S EFFECTIVE MINISTRY

### ✵ *Read 1 Samuel 16:21–23* ✵

God had His hand on this young man whose music not only would fill the heart of a depressed king overwhelmed by blackness, but also would someday fill His written Word. Thus, David, with his primitive stringed instrument, walked bravely into that dark place where Saul was living.

Saul was willing to try anything. "Provide a man," he says. "I don't care who it is. Bring him to me."

Somehow David's music unleashed the caged feelings inside this tormented man and then soothed the savage beast within. By the time David left him, Saul was relieved. The evil presence had departed.

God used the gift of music to put David into the very presence of the king's chamber. And the king not only found relief from his inner torturings, he found love in his heart for the young shepherd boy whose music touched his soul.

The Spirit-filled saint is a song-filled saint. And your melody is broadcast right into heaven—live—where God's antenna is always receptive, where the soothing strains of your song are always appreciated.

Never mind how beautiful or how pitiful you may sound. Sing loud enough to drown out those defeating thoughts that normally clamor for attention. Release yourself from that cage of introspective reluctance. SING OUT! SING OUT! You're not auditioning for the church choir; you're making melody with your heart to the Lord your God! If you listen closely when you're through, you may hear the hosts of heaven answering back for joy.

Soft music for a hard heart, that's what David provided for Saul. That's the soul music that Christ the Savior provides, and that's the place we all must begin. He died for us. He rose from the dead to give us the desire and the power to live a positive, fulfilling life free from the clutches of human depression and despair. He is our shepherd, and we are his sheep, needing the music of his voice. We can rejoice and exult in God together. Let's do more of it!

# GOD VS. OUR GIANTS

### *Read 1 Samuel 17:1–16*

here's no reason for your entire army to be involved in this. Just send a fighter, and I'll take him on. I am the champion. I am the greatest." Goliath didn't issue this challenge one time and then leave. No. His challenge went on for *forty days* (17:16). Every morning and every evening for well over a month, he strutted out there, flaunting his size and his strength, daring someone to take him on.

How applicable to any "giant" we encounter! That's the way with the giants of fear and worry, for example. They don't come just once; they come morning and evening, day after day, relentlessly trying to intimidate. They come in the form of a person, a pressure, or a worry. Some of you have fear that hammers on your heart every morning and every night, day in and day out, yelling across the ravine in your own personal valley. Few things are more persistent and intimidating than our fears and our worries . . . especially when we face them in our own strength.

I want to look again at something that occurred prior to that battle, when the Lord said to Samuel, "Do not look at his appearance or at the height of his stature, because I have rejected him; for God sees not as man sees, for man looks at the outward appearance, but the LORD looks at the heart" (1 Samuel 16:7).

Literally, God said, "for man looks at the face, but the Lord looks at the heart."

We, being human, are subject to that same problem. We are impressed with, or not impressed with, individuals because we judge on the basis of surface appearance. We look at the externals, and we form opinions that are usually erroneous.

If God's statement ever applied, it applied in the story of this battle. Goliath had all the things that would normally impress and intimidate. In this instance, however, David had been given the ability to see as God always sees, and he was neither impressed nor intimidated. Because no matter how big the giant might be, God is greater. And no matter how powerful he might be, God is all-powerful.

# UNIQUE TECHNIQUES

### ❧ *Read 1 Samuel 17:17–39* ❧

*M*an is impressed with the externals; he doesn't see the heart. God is different. He doesn't judge by appearance or intelligence. King Saul hadn't learned that, however, so he looked at David and said, "You don't have the size for it. You're just a kid. Look over there at that giant!"

As I picture it, David was blinking and thinking, *What giant? The only giant in my life is God. That's a dwarf over there, Saul. God is not impressed with the externals; He looks on the heart. God is omnipotent! And if He's on my side, omnipotence can't lose.*

So often, when facing our own giants, we forget what we ought to remember, and we remember what we ought to forget. We remember our defeats, and we forget the victories. Most of us can recite the failures of our lives in vivid detail, but we're hard-pressed to name the specific, remarkable victories God has pulled off in our past.

Not so with David! He says, "You know why I can fight Goliath, Saul? Because the same God who gave me power over a lion and a bear will give me power over Goliath. It is God who will empower me . . . so just let me at him."

Well, that let Saul off the hook, so he says, "Go, and may the Lord be with you." Isn't it remarkable how people can use spiritual clichés to cover up their empty lives? They know all the right words to use . . . all the pious-sounding sayings. Saul sure did.

Then Saul said, "Now wait a minute, David. We have to fix you up for battle." Imagine it! You can't tell me the Bible doesn't have humor, because it says, "Saul clothed David with his garments." Here's Saul, a 52 long, and David is a 36 regular.

What works for one person will not necessarily work for someone else. We're always trying to put our armor on someone else or wear someone else's armor. But that's not the way to do battle. It was a great breakthrough in my own life when I finally discovered that I could be me and God would use me. I couldn't operate well, wearing another's armor. God provides unique techniques for unique people.

# "The Battle Is Mine"

### ✦ *Read 1 Samuel 17:40–47* ✦

*T*he beautiful thing about this story is that it's a perfect example of how God operates. He magnifies HIS name when we are weak. We don't have to be eloquent or strong or beautiful or physically fit or handsome. We don't have to be well-traveled or brilliant or have all the answers to be blessed of God. He honors our faith. All He asks is that we trust Him, that we stand before Him in integrity and faith, and He'll win the battle. God is just waiting for His moment, waiting for us to trust Him so He can empower us to battle our giants.

Remember, Goliath is still a giant . . . still an imposing presence. David had all the odds against him. There wasn't a guy in the Philistine camp—or probably the Israelite camp either—who would have bet on David. But David didn't need their backing. He needed God—none other. After picking up the stones, he approached the gigantic Philistine warrior.

The shepherd boy made the giant smile. What a joke!

Just imagine! David stood before this massive creature unintimidated!

Intimidation. That's our MAJOR battle when we face giants. When they intimidate us, we get tongue-tied. Our thoughts get confused. We forget how to pray. We focus on the odds against us. We forget whom we represent, and we stand there with our knees knocking. I wonder what God must think, when all the while He has promised us, "My power is available. There's no one on this earth greater. *You trust Me.*"

Be assured, David's eyes weren't on the giant. Intimidation played no part in his life. What a man! His eyes were fixed on God. With invincible confidence in his God, David responded, "that all this assembly may know the LORD does not deliver by sword or by spear; for the battle is the LORD's" (17:47). There it is. That's the secret of David's life. "The battle is the LORD's." Are you trying to do your own battle? Trying to do things your way? Trying to outsmart the enemy, outfox him? You can't. But God can. And He's saying to you, "You do it My way and I'll honor you. You do it your way and you're doomed to fail. The battle is Mine."

# "TRUST ME"

### ✤ *Read 1 Samuel 17:48–51* ❧

*A*ll David had was a sling and a stone as he took on a giant wearing two hundred pounds of armor. It may seem silly, but that's the way God operates. In the final analysis, there was a whoosh, whoosh, whoosh—one stone flew through the air, and that's all there was to it. Goliath fell like a sack full of sand. Got any more giants?

I don't know what your intimidating giant is today. It may relate to your job, your roommate, or your school. Maybe it is a person, a lawsuit, unemployment, a disaster . . . maybe even your own partner in life. Perhaps it is some fear that is lurking around the corner, sucking your energy and draining your faith. God is saying to you right now, "All I ask of you is five smooth stones and a sling of faith. I'll take it from there. You don't have to wear somebody else's armor. You just trust Me. And I'll strip you down to nothing but faith, and then I'll accomplish a victory where I'll get the glory. But as for you . . . you trust Me."

Perhaps you don't know what lies across the valley. Maybe you can't get a handle on what that giant is; but it's there, haunting you. That uncertainty alone is a giant. But look at that worry in comparison to the Lord God Himself, and say, by faith, "The battle is Yours, Lord. It is Your battle. I lean on You. I give You all my weapons, all my skills, and I stand before You, trusting You."

It is God's love for us that causes Him to bring us to an end of our own strength. He sees our need to trust Him, and His love is so great that He will not let us live another day without surrendering our arms to Him, giving Him our fears, our worries, even our confusion, so that nothing becomes more significant to us than our Father.

Never, ever forget it: the battle is the Lord's!

# A KINDRED SPIRIT

### ✤ *Read 1 Samuel 18:1–4* ✤

God knew that David needed an intimate friend to walk with him through the valley that was ahead of him. Intimate friends are rare in life. Often we have only one, occasionally two, usually not more than three in our entire lives. There's something about an intimate friend that causes your souls to be knit together. It's what we call a kindred spirit.

You don't have to beg a close friend for a favor, which was certainly the case with Jonathan. "And Jonathan stripped himself of the robe that was on him and gave it to David, with his armor, including his sword and his bow and his belt" (1 Samuel 18:4).

He wanted to give David something that belonged to him and was meaningful to him. Friends do that. They're never stingy with their possessions. Later, Jonathan says to David, "Whatever you say, I will do for you" (20:4). That's the promise of an intimate friend. You can hardly impose on an intimate friend. He doesn't keep score. An intimate friend is there to assist whenever and in whatever way is needed. Unselfishness prevails.

An intimate friend is a loyal defense before others. He's not a fair-weather friend. He won't talk against you when you're not around. It says, "Jonathan spoke well of David to Saul his father" (19:4). That was very significant, because Saul was not only the king and Jonathan's father, but also, by that time, Saul had determined to be David's enemy. Yet Jonathan stood up to his father and said, "Dad, you're wrong about David." In fact, he not only defended his friend, he also rebuked his father for his attitude toward David.

What a friend Jonathan was! No pettiness, no envy, no jealousy. After all, Jonathan, as Saul's son, might have been the heir apparent. He might have wanted the praise of the people, yet here was this kid from the hills of Bethlehem, garnering all of it. Still, Jonathan stood in defense of his friend against his own father, who was ready to take David's life. This is what we might call bottom-line theology. This is putting shoe leather to your belief, to your faith. He stood in his defense because he was his friend.

# A TEACHABLE SPIRIT

### ✣ *Read 1 Samuel 18:5—16* ✣

hey were singing and dancing in the streets, welcoming and honoring this young man who had defended the name of their God. If there is a single statement that best describes David at this time in his life, it would be this one: "And David was prospering in all his ways for the LORD was with him" (1 Samuel 18:14).

Four times in this one chapter we read that David "prospered." That interested me, so I looked up the Hebrew word *sakal* from which "prospered" is derived. I discovered two insightful things about that term. Proverbs 10:19 reveals the first: "When there are many words, transgression is unavoidable, but he who restrains his lips is wise *[sakal]*."

A person who is wise (who *prospers*), knows how to keep his mouth shut. He can keep confidences when people say, "Look, don't share that." That's another characteristic of a good friend, by the way. A good friend can be trusted with the details of your life; he keeps his mouth closed.

Furthermore, when he opens his mouth, he opens it with discretion. That's a sign of a *sakal* person. That was David.

And the second insight is in Proverbs 21:11: "When the scoffer is punished, the naive becomes wise; but when the wise is instructed *[sakal]*, he receives knowledge."

The *sakal* person is *teachable*. Again, that's the kind of man David was. He was wise because he guarded his lips, and he maintained a teachable spirit. No matter how fast the promotion or how high the exaltation may be, we are never to lose our teachability. We never reach a level where we are above criticism or we no longer need the input of others. And, frankly, there are times when our best lessons can be learned from our enemies.

# WALKING IN VICTORY

### ✣ *Read 1 Samuel 18:8–15* ✣

*A*s fear and worry intensified, Saul became paranoid. "What more can he have now but the kingdom?" His self-talk lost control. "Hey, I've got a problem on my hands. Here's a giant-killer who's about to become a king-killer. What can I do about that?" He's afraid of his own shadow.

That's Saul. Within a matter of hours, he "looked at David with suspicion from that day on." When imagination is fueled by jealously, suspicion takes over . . . and at that point, dangerous things occur.

David has done nothing to deserve that kind of treatment! He has served God, killed a giant, submitted himself to his superior, and behaved properly. In fact, verse 15 says, "When Saul saw that he was prospering greatly, he dreaded him."

Why? Because Saul saw that God was on David's side, and he realized that he, himself, didn't have that kind of power. The contrast was more than he could handle.

The Bible is so practical, isn't it? Jealousy is a deadly sin, and the suspicion of Saul shackled him in its prison. Because he operated in that tight radius of fear, worry, and paranoia, Saul's great goal in life became twisted. Instead of leading Israel onto bigger and better things, he focused on only one objective: making David's life miserable.

Being positive and wise is the best reaction to an enemy. When you see your enemy coming, don't roll up your mental sleeves, deciding which jab you will throw. Remember how David handled Saul. David just kept prospering—just kept behaving himself wisely. And when the heat rose, he fled the scene. He refused to fight back or get even.

So if you are rubbing shoulders with a jealous individual, whether it be a roommate, a boss, a friend, or even a partner, remember the model of David.

It boils down to this: walking in victory is the difference between what pleases us and what pleases God. Like David, we need to stand fast, to do what is right without tiring of it. Plain and simple, that's what pleases God. And in the final analysis, isn't that why we're left on earth?

# ·NEVER ALONE

*Read 1 Samuel 21:10–22:2; Psalm 142*

*D*avid had bottomed out. This was the lowest moment of David's life to date, and if you want to know how he really felt, just read the song he composed during those days, Psalm 142.

Can you feel the loneliness of that desolate spot? The dampness of that cave? Can you sense David's despair? The depths to which his life has sunk? There is no escape. There is nothing left. Nothing.

Yet in the midst of all this, David has not lost sight of God. He cries out for the Lord to deliver him. It's here we catch sight of the very heart of the man, that inward place that God alone truly sees, that unseen quality that God saw back when He chose and anointed the young shepherd boy from Bethlehem.

David has been brought to the place where God can truly begin to shape him and use him. When the sovereign God brings us to nothing, it is to reroute our life, not to end it. Human perspective says, "Aha, you've lost this, you've lost that. You've caused this, you've caused that. You've ruined this, you've ruined that. End your life!" But God says, "No. No. You're in the cave. But that doesn't mean it's curtains. That means it's time to reroute your life. Now's the time to start anew!" That's exactly what He does with David.

Here he is, broken, at the end, without crutches . . . crushed in spirit. And would you look who comes to him? Those same brothers and his father along with the rest of the household. Sometimes when you're in the cave, you don't want others around. Sometimes you just can't stand to be with people. You hate to admit it publicly; in fact, you usually don't. But it's true. Sometimes you just want to be alone. And I have a feeling that at that moment in his life, this cave dweller, David, wanted nobody around. Because if he wasn't worth anything to himself, he didn't see his worth to anybody else.

David didn't want his family, but they came. He didn't want them there, but God brought them anyway. I love it that they crawled right into that cave with him.

# DECLARATION OF DEPENDENCE

### ❧ *Read 1 Samuel 22:3–23; Psalm 34 and 57* ❧

*W*e looked at Psalm 142. Now let's look at two others David wrote, Psalms 57 and 34. We don't know in what order he wrote these, but looking at his life, they seem to fit in this backward order—Psalm 142 when he was at his lowest moment on his face, Psalm 57 when he's on his knees, and finally Psalm 34 when he's back on his feet.

At this point, David is on his knees. He's still down, but at least he's looking up.

See where David's eyes are now? "O God, You be exalted." In Psalm 142 he's saying, "I'm in the cave, I'm at the end, there's no one on the right hand or left. I have no one who cares." And now in Psalm 57 he says, "Now you be gracious to me, God. I'm stretched, I'm pulled beyond my limits. Please meet my needs."

He's crying out his declaration of dependence.

Why did such a major change take place in David's life and attitude?

First, *because David hurt enough to admit his need.* When you are hurting, you need to declare it to someone, and especially to the Lord. David hurt enough to admit his need.

Second, *he was honest enough to ask for help.* We have lived under such a veneer for so long in our generation that we hardly know how to ask for help. But God honors such vulnerability. He did then, and He does now.

And third, *he was humble enough to learn from God.* How tragic it is that we can live in one cave after another and not learn what God wants to teach us. Not David! I love the man's utter humility. If it is to be a cave, then let's not fight it. We'll turn it into a training ground for the future!

As I look at this time in David's life, I cannot help but reflect upon Jesus and His coming from the glories of heaven to accept a bunch of malcontents and sinners like us.

# CAVE DWELLERS

### ❧ *Read 1 Samuel 22:3–23; Psalm 34* ❧

N ow look at Psalm 34, which I believe is the third psalm he wrote while in the cave. What a difference. What a change has come over David! He says, "I will bless the LORD at all times, his praise shall continually be in my mouth" (v. 1).

Later we learn that David's men became acutely able with the sword and spear and with the bow and arrow. Obviously, they had training practices. They learned how to get their act together in battle. They developed discipline in the ranks. They might have been mavericks, but they are on the way to becoming skilled hunters and courageous fighters.

So David, seeing his men marching in step and using the sword and the spear and the bow with skill, says to them, "Magnify the Lord with me, let us exalt His name together." He's putting their eyes on the Lord. "I sought the Lord, and He answered me, and delivered me from all my fears."

To the distressed among the group he says, "O taste and see that the Lord is good; how blessed is the man who takes refuge in Him!"

To those in debt he says, "O fear the Lord, you His saints; for to those who fear Him, there is no want."

To the discontented he says, "The young lions do lack and suffer hunger; but they who seek the Lord shall not be in want of any good thing."

And finally, he gives sort of a wrap-up lesson to the entire group: "Many are the afflictions of the righteous [dark and lonely are the caves of the righteous]; but the Lord delivers him out of them all."

You may be living in an emotional cave, where it is dark and dismal, damp and disillusioning. Perhaps the hardest part of all is that you cannot declare the truth to anybody else because you feel so desperate . . . so alone.

I tire of hearing that the Christian life is just one silver-lined cloud after another—we're always soaring. Not so! Sometimes the Christian life includes a deep, dark cave.

Why not share David's shelter?

We know Him today by another name: Jesus. He's still available, even to cave dwellers and lonely people needing someone to care.

# A TRUE FRIEND

### ❧ *Read 1 Samuel 23:14–18* ❧

What a friend Jonathan was! No pettiness, no envy, no jealousy. Remember, as Saul's son, Jonathan would have been the heir apparent. He might have wanted the praise of the people, yet here was this kid from the hills of Bethlehem garnering all of it. Still, Jonathan stood in defense of his friend against his own father, who was ready to take David's life. This is what we might call theology at its most-basic level. This is putting shoe leather to your belief, to your faith. He stood in his defense because he was his friend. Here we are again—back to their great friendship.

Friends give each other complete freedom to be themselves. When you've got a friend that close, that knitted to your own soul, you don't have to explain why you do what you do. You just do it, and your friend understands.

When your heart is broken, you can bleed all over a friend like this, and he won't be offended. He won't confront you in your misery or quote three Bible verses, then tell you to straighten up.

When your good friend is hurting, let him hurt. If she feels like weeping, let her weep. If a good friend needs to complain, listen. An intimate friend doesn't bale; he's right there with you. You can be yourself, no matter what that self looks like.

True friends are a constant source of encouragement. "Now David became aware that Saul had come out to seek his life while David was in the wilderness of Ziph at Horesh. And Jonathan, Saul's son, arose and went to David at Horesh, and encouraged him in God" (1 Samuel 23:15–16).

Think of that. There was a hit man after David, and his name was Saul (Jonathan's father!). David was out in the wilderness, and at any moment, behind any bush or rock or hill, Saul and his men might have been lurking in the shadows, waiting to strike him down. The murderous hatred of Saul haunted David's life.

And what does the son of this hit man do? He encourages his friend. Wow! That's the kind of friend to have. He sees David at the lowest moment of his life, frightened, beleaguered, stumbling through the wilderness, and he brings him encouragement. "I understand how that feels. You have every right to have those feelings. There'll be a brighter day some day, but right now I'm here with you, no matter what."

# THE ART OF PERSUASION

### ✤ *Read 1 Samuel 24:1–7* ✤

*H*ere we see a guy who did the right thing and brought a whole group with him. He *persuaded* them with his words. The literal meaning here, strange as it may seem, is "tore apart." He tore them apart with his words. The same Hebrew word is used in Isaiah 53 where we read, "He was wounded for our transgressions." It means pierced through, torn apart, ripped up.

I have a feeling that David's men didn't just stand together and mildly say, "You think you should have done that?" No, their dialogue must have been heated.

"Don't be a fool, David!"

"DAVID, the guy's done everything but take your life."

"Look, I can't do it!"

Back and forth, back and forth they argued, but David stood for a righteous principle until their argument was torn apart. They were persuaded. Remember this when you are hanging in the balance somewhere. Maybe in your profession or business. Perhaps in the way you've done your studies or carried on your lifestyle. You've compromised and sort of waltzed along on very thin wires of rationalization, and you've begun to lean. And God says, "You have no business doing that. Get back where you belong."

Hey, who knows whom you could persuade if you walked with God? Few things are more infectious than a godly lifestyle. The people you rub shoulders with every day need that kind of challenge. Not prudish. Not preachy. Just spot-on clean living. Honest-to-goodness, bone-deep, nonhypocritical integrity. Authentic obedience to God.

David persuaded the men because, ultimately, he had absolute confidence in God. He wrestled with his guilt, hung his life on a righteous principle, and then stood fast in absolute confidence in God to make the situation right, even in the face of the opposition. "Vengeance is Mine, I will repay," says the Lord. David put his confidence in that.

David's son Solomon would later write in his Proverbs, "When a man's ways are pleasing to the LORD, he makes even his enemies to be at peace with him" (16:7). What a promise! The word "easy" is not in Proverbs 16:7, however. It's true, but it's not easy.

# A Clear Conscience

### ✤ *Read 1 Samuel 24:8–21* ✖

*D*avid told Saul the whole unvarnished truth; he told it to the person to whom it mattered most. Not to his comrades or to Saul's friends or to the people of Israel, but to Saul himself. He came to terms with the individual with whom there was the battle. Then he said, "May the LORD judge between you and me, and may the LORD avenge me on you; but my hand shall not be against you" (1 Samuel 24:12).

David wasn't dangling his righteousness before Saul. David wasn't built like that. He was a man of integrity. He said, "Saul, I could have taken your life, but I didn't. And here's the proof. When you were vulnerable, I didn't strike. I will let God judge between you and me."

Read Saul's response slowly and thoughtfully:

Saul called back, "Is it really you, my son David?" Then he began to cry.

And he said to David, "You are a better man than I am, for you have repaid me good for evil. Yes, you have been wonderfully kind to me today, for when the Lord delivered me into your hand, you didn't kill me.

"Who else in all the world would let his enemy get away when he had him in his power? May the Lord reward you well for the kindness you have shown me today."

(1 Samuel 24:16–19 TLB)

Talk about a living example of the proverb, "When a man's ways please the Lord, He makes even his enemies to be at peace with him."

Now wait a minute. Let's revisit reality. This is one case study. I wish I could promise you that when you do what is right, your enemy will always see the error of his ways this quickly and turn and repent and view you correctly, but I can't make that kind of promise.

You're responsible for telling a person the truth, but it is impossible to make him change his opinion. Frankly, that person may die believing the lie. But down inside your heart you will know the fulfillment of that sense of righteous dealings. Your conscience will be clear.

# REVENGE OR FORGIVENESS?

*Read 1 Samuel 24:8–22*

*A*ll this brings me to three helpful principles to live by when it comes to life's most subtle temptation. Each is worth remembering when we are mistreated.

First, *since man is depraved, expect to be mistreated.* The same nature that beat in the heart of Saul beats in the heart of every person, yourself included. When we are operating our lives in the flesh, we will respond like Saul. Or, if you are the person who's doing the mistreatment, the offense, come to terms with it. Call it sin.

Second, *since mistreatment is inevitable, anticipate feelings of revenge.* I'm not saying retaliate. I'm saying anticipate the feelings of revenge, because you can be sure they will come. It's the nature of the beast.

Handling mistreatment doesn't come naturally. Which is why Jesus' statement is so revolutionary: "Do unto others as you would have them do to you,"—*not as they do to you.* Rare is the individual who will not retaliate, or at least not want to.

Third, *since the desire for revenge is predictable, refuse to fight in the flesh.* That explains how David came out on top. His men said, "Go get him, David." He almost did, I'm convinced. But when he came near the king, he got cold feet and just cut off a piece of robe instead of plunging his knife in Saul's back. Then he made it right.

Let's leave the ancient scene and bring this truth home to rest today. If you are resentful of the way someone has treated you, if you are holding it against that person, hoping you can retaliate at least or get even, you need to ask God to free you from that bondage. The secret, plain and simple? Forgiveness! Claim God's power to forgive through Jesus Christ. Begin by asking His forgiveness for excusing and cultivating that deep root of bitterness within your own heart. Ask him to expose it in all its ugliness and put it to death. Jesus Christ, who went through hell for you, can give you the power you need to overcome the worst kind of condition in your life.

# WISE PROTECTION

### ❧ *Read 1 Samuel 25:1–19* ❧

our hundred men! That'll probably handle Nabal, don't you think? When you overdo something in our house, we have a saying, "You're killing a roach with a shotgun." You kill the roach all right, but you blow the wall out at the same time. Hey, nobody puts on a sword just to have a discussion, so we have a pretty good idea what's going through David's mind here. But talk about overkill! There's no need to take four hundred men to squash one tightwad. David has lost control.

Meanwhile, back at the ranch, put yourself in Abigail's sandals. Candidly, this could be her opportunity to get rid of an obnoxious loser of a husband! She gets word from the servants that David is going to finish him off. She could say something spiritual like, "Oh, I better pray about this." Those thundering hoofbeats are coming down the hill, and she's in there praying, "Lord, take him swiftly!" It's her chance! After all, Nabal has set himself up for this! It's time he learned a lesson.

That's the way a carnal wife, (or a carnal husband) thinks. That's the way a carnal employee thinks. "Now's my chance. He's vulnerable, and it's all his fault anyway. How great is this?" Depravity on parade. Instead, observe what happens.

> But one of the young men told Abigail, Nabal's wife, saying, "Behold, David sent messengers from the wilderness to greet our master, and he scorned them.
>
> "Yet the men were very good to us, and we were not insulted, nor did we miss anything as long as we went about with them, while we were in the fields.
>
> "They were a wall to us both by night and by day, all the time we were with them tending the sheep.
>
> "Now therefore know and consider what you should do, for evil is plotted against our master and against all his household; and he is such a worthless man that no one can speak to him." (1 Samuel 25:14–17)

Note that the messengers come to Abigail, not to Nabal.

Why? Because he wasn't approachable. That's another indication of Abigail's wisdom. She sees her husband for what he is. She knows his weaknesses. And in his weakest moment, Abigail did not fight, she protected. How gracious of her . . . how wise!

# CRITICAL DECISIONS

### ✦ *Read 1 Samuel 25:20—28* ✦

*A*bigail knew her husband, didn't she? Everyone knew what he was like, so why hide it? Why try to cover up what he had done? She didn't. And yet she took the responsibility upon herself. "When you sent those ten men and they had that interaction with my husband, I wasn't there to give another kind of response. But I'm here now as an advocate. I'd like to stand as a mediator between this man and all of your men who have been unjustly treated."

What faith she had. She says, "David, as I look at you, I'm looking at the next king. Don't ruin your record with a murder. You're bigger than that. You have been wronged, but murder isn't the answer. Wait! Wait, David. Take what I've provided and turn around and go back."

What a speech! What a plea!

When you're faced with critical decisions, sometimes you have to do something very creative. Apart from the Bible, there's no handbook that tells you what to do when those times come.

Often when we are faced with a crisis, the standard, garden-variety answer is to sort of tuck your tail between your legs, run into a corner, and let cobwebs form on you. But there is a better way. As long as you have breath in your lungs, you have a purpose for living. You have a reason to exist. No matter how bad that track record might have been, marked by disobedience and compromise through much of your life, you're alive, you're existing. And God says, "There's a reason. And I'm willing to do creative things through you to put you back on your feet. You can lick your wounds if that's your choice. But there's a better way." It will take creativity, it will take determination, it will take constant eyes on the Lord. But when He pulls it off, it's marvelous.

# PATIENTLY WAITING

### ✣ *Read 1 Samuel 25:29–34* ✣

*M*y, oh my, did David learn a lesson! "Blessed be God. He kept me from murdering this man—from doing evil. I don't have to fight that kind of battle, that's God's job. If vengeance is required, it is God's to do."

Three things strike me as I think about this incident in the life of David and our lives today.

*Whatever you do when conflicts arise, be wise.* If you're not careful, you will handle conflicts in the energy of the flesh. And then . . . you'll be sorry. What do I mean by being wise? Well, look at the whole picture. Fight against jumping to quick conclusions and seeing only your side. Look both ways. Weigh the differences. There are always two sides on the streets of conflict. Weigh the differences. The other part of being wise is to pray. Get God's perspective. He gives us the wisdom we need when we ask Him for it.

*Take each conflict as it comes . . . and handle it separately.* You may have won a battle yesterday, but that doesn't count when today's skirmish comes. You may have a great measure of patience today, but it makes no difference tomorrow when the attack comes again. God doesn't give you patience on credit. Every day is a new day.

*Whenever you realize that there's nothing you can do, wait.* Wait patiently. Impossible impasses call for a firm application of brakes. Don't keep going. Restrain yourself from anything hasty. Whenever possible, apply the brakes! Slow down. I've seldom made wise decisions in a hurry. Furthermore, I've seldom felt sorry for things I *didn't* say. David obviously learned this lesson well, for he writes in Psalm 40,

> I waited patiently for the LORD;
> And He inclined to me, and heard my cry.
> He brought me up out of the pit of destruction, out of the miry clay;
> And He set my feet upon a rock making my footsteps firm. (Psalm 40:1–2)

Psalm 40 never says that David's situation changed. It says David changed. When you wait, your situation may not change, but you will. In fact, you may discover that the reason for waiting was all for your benefit, because you're the one who needed to change.

# HE'LL HANDLE IT

### 🦋 *Read 1 Samuel 25:35–38* 🦋

*M*ission accomplished! Everybody wins. David and his men go back full of food and all the wiser. Fantastic! Abigail goes home, and her husband puts his arm around her and says, "Honey, thanks. You're a great lady . . . more precious than rubies." No. I wish it said that. On the contrary.

> Then Abigail came to Nabal, and behold, he was holding a feast in his house, like the feast of a king. And Nabal's heart was merry within him, for he was very drunk; so she did not tell him anything at all until the morning light.
>
> But it came about in the morning, when the wine had gone out of Nabal, that his wife told him these things, and his heart died within him so that he became as a stone. (1 Samuel 25:36–37)

She had stood between her husband and death, but the fool was so drunk she couldn't even tell him about it. So she crawled in bed, pulled up the covers, and went to sleep. I'm sure she poured out her heart to God and got things squared away between herself and the Lord, realizing she might never know what it was like to have a husband who appreciated her.

The next morning, after Nabal sobered up, she told him what had happened. And what was his reaction? The guy had a stroke. Literally. He listened to the story of how 401 guys were on the way to cut off his head, and he got really still, his eyes became glazed. I would imagine! Ten days later, "the LORD struck Nabal, and he died" (25:38).

Isn't it amazing! When you do what is right, without tiring of it, God takes care of the impossible things. As we've seen, "When a man's ways please the Lord, He makes even his enemies to be at peace with him." The same could be said of a woman, of course. There is no impossible situation that God cannot handle. He won't handle it necessarily your way, but He'll handle it.

# "A Very Present Help"

### ❧ *Read 1 Samuel 30:1—6* ❧

*D*avid had reached the point in life where some people think of taking their own lives. He was so far down the ladder of despair that he'd reached the bottom rung. The last stop. The place where you either jump off into oblivion or you cry out to God for His forgiveness. For rescue. The wonderful thing is that we do have that choice, because God never gives up on His children.

David made the right choice. "David was greatly distressed . . . But David strengthened himself in the LORD his God" (1 Samuel 30:6).

Now you're talking, David. That's the way to endure the Slough of Despond. The pits may seem bottomless, but there's hope above. Reach up! Help is there.

For the first time in months, David looks up, and he says, "Oh, God, help me." And He does. He always will. He is "a very present help" when needed.

Dark days call for right thinking and vertical focus. That's what David learns at this moment in his life. He finds that the test isn't designed to throw him on his back and suck him under, it's designed to bring him to his knees so he will look up.

Perhaps you have known the joys and ecstasies of walking with Christ, but in a moment of despondency, you've opted for the wrong fork in the road, and you're now living in the wrong camp . . . you're living in the "carnal corral." In the words of the prophet, you've been like those who "sow the wind, and . . . reap the whirlwind" (Hos. 8:7).

But, like David, you've gotten tired of feeling displaced. The disillusionment has bred distrust, and the depression is killing you.

Reach up. Come home. The Father is waiting at the door, ready to forgive and willing to restore. It's time to return and strengthen yourself, yet again, in the Lord your God.

# Your Epitaph

### ❧ *Read 1 Samuel 31:1–13* ❧

*W*hat do you think those who survive you will write as your epitaph? How will your obituary read? What words will be used in the eulogy to sum up your life? Saul's epitaph was a sad one, summing up the tragic life of this man who played such an important role in David's life. He was a king who could have been David's role model and mentor, but who instead almost became his murderer.

Like Saul and his sons, we are all going to die. There's no escaping it. That means that rather than denying death, we must come to terms with it.

Sometimes death is sudden. Sometimes it's long and drawn out. Occasionally, it is beautiful, sweet, and peaceful. At other times it is wrenching and hideous, bloody and ugly. There are times, from our viewpoint, it comes too early. On other occasions it seems the cold fingers of death linger too long as some dear soul endures pain and sadness, loneliness and senility. But however it comes . . . *it comes to us all.* There is no escape.

But here's the good news for Christians: We who know the Lord Jesus Christ carry within ourselves a renewed soul and spirit, that part of us which He invaded at the moment we were born from above—when we became Christians. He has taken up His residence there and has given us a new nature. Though our outer shell hurts and groans and is dying, our inner person is alive and vital, awaiting its home with the Lord. That connection occurs the moment—yes, the very moment—we die.

> Therefore we do not lose heart, but though our outer man is decaying, yet our inner man is being renewed day by day. For momentary, light affliction is producing for us an eternal weight of glory far beyond all comparison, while we look not at the things which are seen, but at the things which are not seen; for the things which are seen are temporal, but the things which are not seen are eternal. (2 Corinthians 4:16–18)

What role are you playing today? Is it authentic? Is it genuinely Christian? If so, let me return to the questions I asked as you began this reading for today. What do you think those who survive you will write as your epitaph? How will your obituary read? What words will sum up your life?

# TAKE CONTROL

### ❧ *Read 1 Samuel 31:1—13* ❧

*B*ehind the great tragedy of Saul's life is a very interesting analogy—an analogy between Saul's death and Christ's death. At first glance we might say, "What in the world would we find common to both Saul and Christ?" Actually, there are six analogies worth noting.

First, *Saul's death appeared to be the end of all national hope.* When Saul died, many people must have thought, *That's the end of Israel. The Philistines will surely conquer us now.* In a similar way, Christ's death appeared to be the end of all national *and* spiritual hope.

Second, *with Saul's death it seemed that the adversary had won the final victory.* When Christ died, it seemed as though the Adversary of our souls had won. He must have strutted all over the gates of hell declaring, "The victory is mine. I am the conqueror. The Messiah is dead."

Third, *Saul's death paved the way for an entirely new plan of operation and ushered in David's kingly line,* which led to the Messiah. When Jesus Christ died, a whole new operation moved into action and set in motion our great salvation.

Fourth, *Saul's death opened the opportunity for another who would not otherwise have been included in God's line of blessing,* namely David. Christ's death graciously opened the opportunity of salvation's blessing to the Gentile who would never have otherwise been able to enter and come boldly to the throne of grace.

Fifth, *Saul's death ended an era of dissatisfaction and failure.* Christ's death ended an era of law and guilt, introducing an entirely new arrangement based on grace.

Sixth, and finally, *Saul's death displayed the foolishness of man.* Christ's death displayed, in human terms, the foolishness of God. Through the "foolishness" of God's plan, He brings to pass the incredible. He takes the preached word and He changes lives because of His Son's death.

It is quite possible the Lord is saying to some Sauls who are in the process of living out that kind of regrettable life, "Now is the time to stop." It is time to say, "Lord, don't change sides, just take over." We do, indeed, come before our Lord like sheep, not asking Him to take sides, but just to take control.

# FROM FUGITIVE TO MONARCH

### ✦ *Read 2 Samuel 2:1–7* ✦

*B*ecause of David's many mighty acts and the legacy he left, it is easy to forget that for a dozen or more years he lived as a fugitive and spent many hours of discouragement and disillusionment in the wilderness. He was a broken, humbled man during those days as a fugitive. He learned much from those crushing years, but little good would come from his reliving the pain they brought into his life.

Finally, though, he becomes king, the second king of Israel, chosen and anointed by God Himself. How did he take the throne? Did he storm into the role and demand everyone to submit to his rule? No. David was a sensitive man. He had learned how to lead and how to rally others around him in the afflictions of his yesterday . . . especially while he was a cave dweller.

Often we're better at handling affliction than we are at handling promotions. As Thomas Carlyle, the Scottish essayist and historian, said, "But for one man who can stand prosperity, there are a hundred that will stand adversity." But David was a man faced with success. His predecessor was dead, by his own hand. If there was ever a chance for a person to take life by his own two fists and demand a following, it was now. But he didn't.

David remembered when Samuel anointed him and whispered, "You will be the next king." He remembered that from many years earlier when he was only a teenager, so he asked, "Lord, shall I go up to one of the cities?" He really wanted to know, "Is it time now, Lord?" He didn't rush to the throne and take charge. He waited patiently on God for further instruction. And God revealed His plan to him. He said, in effect, "Begin your reign in Hebron."

In those days the Lord spoke audibly to His servants. Today He speaks from His Word. You might be in a situation where you are wondering, "God has opened the door, and I'm about to walk through it. But is that what I should do?" Our tendency is to race in when there is some benefit that will come our way. Sometimes it's best to begin very quietly, to pace our first steps with great care.

# GOD CARES

### ❧ *Read 2 Samuel 6:1–9* ❧

e've got David standing here mad at the Lord, when, in fact, the Lord was angry at David. About now you might be thinking, *Well, I thought you said he was a man after God's heart?* I did—or, rather, God did. Does that mean he's perfect? It does not. Having a heart for God doesn't mean you're perfect, it means you're sensitive. It means every detail is important. And when you see you're wrong, you face it. You own up. You come to terms with it.

The problem was that David had not done his homework. We often get into trouble when we don't do our homework—when we think we see pretty clearly what the Lord's will is, and so in expediency or in convenience (usually in a hurry) we dash off to do it our way. And the Lord says, "Look, I've written a lot of things in My Book about that decision you just made, and I want you to take counsel from Me. That's why it's not working. If you want to have a heart for Me, then you check My Word, and you find either a precept or a principle then go according to that. When you do that, I'll give you joy like you can't believe. If you don't, I will make you miserable." In fact, in David's case, the Lord said, "I'll even take some lives."

Centuries later, Ananias and Sapphira did very much the same thing. They presumed on the Lord and didn't take Him seriously. We see Uzzah the same way, taken from the earth because he touched an ultra-holy article of furniture that was not to be touched, especially by a non-Levite. Who cares about Levites? God does. Who cares about little ringlets and little golden poles that go through ringlets? God does. If He didn't care, He wouldn't have said anything about it. And because He cares, we must also care.

That's the whole point here. When we begin to care about the things God cares about, we become people after His heart, and only then do we begin to have real freedom and real happiness.

# PRINCIPLES VS. PRECEPTS

*Read 1 Samuel 13:14; 2 Samuel 6:9–15; Acts 13:21–22*

What an epitaph! Not, "I found David to be a great warrior," or, "I found David to be a faithful shepherd," or, "I found David to be a brilliant king"—none of those things. It says, "I found David to care about the things I care about. He's a man whose heart beats in sync with Mine. When I look to the right, David looks to the right. When I look to the left, David looks to the left. And when I say, 'I care about that,' David says, 'I care about that too.'" As we've already seen, that's what it means to be a person after God's heart.

Some of us look upon life as, "Well, you win some, you lose some. You just pull it off the best you can. Nobody's perfect." Others say, "If God says it, I want to do it." Those are the ones who are "after God's heart."

Those in the first group spend a lot of time doing their own thing—a lot of time moaning and complaining and later recovering from journeys that are far from His plan and will. But the others don't get very far at all before they start taking account of where they are. They keep short accounts. They come back in line quickly because they're "after His heart." To those people, nothing in their relationship with God is considered insignificant. Those who live most of their lives in the second category are rare. There are not a great number of people whose hearts are hot after God, who obey God's precepts and honor His principles, regardless. But David was like that.

When you drive down the road and you see the sign, "Speed Limit 35 Miles an Hour," that's a precept; there's no give or take.

If the sign reads, "Drive Carefully," that's a principle.

When it comes to the spiritual life, those who are after God in their hearts care as much about the principles as they do about the precepts. And when they come across a precept that is clearly delineated, they say, "As I look at my life, I see where it's not like that precept. I need to bring my life in line with it." And they do just that. That's what David did, according to 2 Samuel, chapter 6 . . . a classic example of why he was "a man after God's heart."

# TRUE FREEDOM

### ✧ *Read 2 Samuel 6:16–23* ✧

hy in the world would they get so excited about it? Because they're free. When you obey, you're free. When you disobey, you're in bondage. All around us we see individuals in bondage because they're in sin, and all they talk about is freedom. *They're not free.* The obedient guy dancing is free.

I should warn you, when you're really free, the people who are not so free will have trouble with your being free. Look at David's wife in verse 16. Her husband is down there dancing and singing and shouting, and there's Michal up on in the second floor flat, frowning down on her husband. "Then it happened as the ark of the LORD came into the city of David that Michal the daughter of Saul looked out the window and saw King David leaping and dancing before the LORD; and she despised him in her heart" (2 Samuel 6:16).

Two things strike me here. Both have to do with the issue of focus; one is horizontal, and one is vertical. David's eyes were on the Lord; Michal's eyes were on other people.

First, *the better you know where you stand with the Lord, the freer you can be.* When you do the homework, you find out where you stand with your Lord, and you follow His plan, then you are free. I mean *really* free! Many won't understand, of course. To some, you will be seen as independent—a maverick. You'll be misunderstood. Like David with his own wife. But you won't care that much about public opinion either. You'll care mainly about the Lord's opinion. There is no freedom like the kind He provides. In a word, it's *grace.*

Second, *the freer you are before the Lord, the more confident you will become.* When you know where you stand, that is real security.

Knowing where you stand before the Lord leads to true freedom. Being free before the Lord, you will become confident, and that is genuine security.

# THE INTERLUDES OF LIFE

*Read 2 Samuel 7:1–3*

*D*avid brought the ark of God up to Jerusalem and back to the people of Israel. It had begun to bother him that the ark of God was in a tent while he lived in a beautiful house. So he got the idea in his mind to build a permanent residence for God in which to house all the sacred furniture. David said, "It isn't fitting that the king should live in this lovely cedar dwelling and the ark, the very presence of Jehovah himself, should be in a little tent out there. I will build a house for God. I want to build a temple in His honor." God had never dwelt in a permanent house, but David resolved to do something about that.

Now I want to emphasize, from everything we know about him, David had no ulterior motive here. He had no selfish ambition. He had no desire to make a name for himself or his family. As a matter of fact, he wanted to exalt no other name but God in building this house.

It is during the interludes of life that we have time to seize a dream or an ideal objective. Some of you, in a quiet moment of your life, realized the vocation into which God was calling you. Maybe it happened at a camp or a retreat, where you threw a branch of promise on the fire, having determined an objective to follow. Maybe it happened in the quietness of your own room after a church service one evening. Or maybe it was while you were a student in a dormitory. You couldn't go to sleep, so you turned through the Scriptures and landed on some thoughts that began to make sense. Before long, they stretched into a direct arrow toward some new and exciting objective. And you said, "That's it! That's my commitment; that's where God is leading." It's in the interludes of life that those things happen. You have to slow down and become quiet in those special times to hear His voice, to sense His leading.

But let me add this: sometimes the dream is from God; sometime it's not. Both are noble. Both are great resolves. Both are ideals. But when it's not of God, it won't come to fulfillment —nor should it.

# WHEN GOD SAYS "NO"

### ❧ *Read 2 Samuel 7:4–17* ❧

*D*avid, you will know the delight of having a son by whom this temple will be built. Not through *your* efforts, but through *your son* the dream will be fulfilled."

It is not a question of sin here. It is not God's judgment that is coming upon David as a consequence of wrong. It is simply God's redirecting David's plan and saying, "This is a great resolve, but I say 'no' to you and I say 'yes' to your son. Now accept that."

Well, was David wrong to begin with—wrong in thinking of building the temple?

It is not a question of being wrong. It's a question of accepting God's "no" and living with the mystery of His will. We people on this earth package everything. And we expect God to package His plan for us just like we would. We want the logic that we use to be His logic. And when it isn't, we wonder what's wrong because it's not working out like we would have worked it out.

When God says no it is not necessarily discipline or rejection. It may simply be re-direction. You have pursued His will; you have wanted to do His will. With all good intentions you said, "By God's grace I am going to pursue this." And here you are, thirty or forty years later, or maybe only five years later, and it hasn't materialized.

Now if you listen to some people, you'll be put on a guilt trip. "You see there," they say, "you set your heart on God, but you have run from Him. You're out of His will." I don't know how many couples I have talked with who, early in their lives, had their life's plan all mapped out, but it didn't transpire. Perhaps the very road they are traveling is God's will for them, and it took His saying "no" to get them on that right road. Others were of little help.

The thing we have to do in our walk with God is to listen carefully from day to day. Not just go back to some decision and say, "That's it forever, regardless." We need to look at it each day, keep it fresh, keep the fire hot, keep it on the back burner, saying, "Lord, is this Your arrangement? Is this Your plan? If it is not, make me sensitive to it. Maybe You're re-directing my life."

# Who Am I?

### ❧ *Read 2 Samuel 7:4–17* ❧

*od does not call everybody to build temples.* He calls some people to be soldiers. He calls some people to do the gutsy work in the trenches. He calls some people to compose and conduct music. God has all kinds of creative ways to use us—ways we can't even imagine and certainly can't see up there around the next bend in the road. One of the hardest things to hear is that God is going to use someone else to accomplish something you thought was your role to fill. That's what David had to hear. "It won't be you, David . . . it will be your son, Solomon."

> "Who am I, O Lord GOD, and what is my house, that Thou hast brought me this far? And yet this was insignificant in Thine eyes, O Lord GOD, for Thou hast spoken also of the house of Thy servant concerning the distant future . . . And again what more can David say to Thee? For Thou knowest Thy servant, O Lord GOD!" (2 Samuel 7:18–20)

Isn't that like a little child? When a child refers to himself, he often calls himself by name. Just like a little boy, David sat down before the Lord and said, in effect, "Dad, what is David, that You've blessed my house and You've blessed my life, and You've brought me from leading a little flock of sheep to giving me this magnificent throne? Who am I?"

It's important that every once in a while we sit down, take a long look at our short lives, and count our blessings. Who are we to have been protected from the rains that fell and the strong winds that destroyed regions, leaving hundreds homeless? Who are we that He has blessed our house and kept it safe? Warm in the winter . . . cool in the summer. Who am I, Lord, that You should give me health and strength to be able to hold a job or pursue this career or get this degree? Or to have parents who have encouraged me? Or to have these great kids and to see them grow? Who am I?

"Dream or no dream, I'm a blessed person," says David. Here is more evidence that David was a man after God's own heart.

# HELPFUL HOPE FOR BROKEN DREAMS

### *Read 2 Samuel 7:18–29; 1 Chronicles 22:1–6*

*W*hat a father! He may have been weak at other times, but at this moment, David stands tall. "Lord, I know You don't want me to fulfill the dream, but, Lord, I'm going to set apart as much as I can to support my son as he fulfills the dream that was on my heart." What an unselfish response.

I see two simple truths in all this. First, *when God says no, it means He has a better way, and He expects me to support it.*

*Second, my very best reaction is cooperation and humility.* He doesn't call everybody to build the temple, but He does call everyone to be faithful and obedient. Some of you who are reading this are living with broken dreams. Sometime in the past you had high hopes that your life would go in a certain direction. But the Lord, for some mysterious reason, has now said, "No." And you've moved along in life and now you're up in years, and you find yourself slowly becoming shelved, and the younger ones are taking charge and moving on. How quickly age takes over!

Just about the time we get our act together, we're too old to pull it off. And so we release it to the Solomon in our lives. It takes genuine humility to say to that person, "May God be with you. I'll do everything I can to support you in seeing that it gets accomplished."

Do you identify with David? Did you have your hands full of your dreams and your visions, ready to present them to God on the altar of sacrifice? Did you have your plans all prepared and thought through, only to see them crumble at your feet? And now you're standing there, empty-handed?

Know this: God is ready to fill your empty hands like you would never believe, if you will only lift them up to Him in obedience and praise, as David did. God is still alive and well, and He knows what He's doing. To some He says yes. To others, no. In either case, the answer is best. Why? Because God's answers, while surprising, are never wrong.

# THE CONSEQUENCES OF SIN

### ✤ *Read 2 Samuel 11:1–12:13* ❧

athan didn't come on his own; he was sent by God: "Then the Lord sent Nathan to David." I think the most important word in that sentence is the first one, "then." God's timing is absolutely incredible.

When was he sent? Right after the act of adultery? No. Right after Bathsheba said, "I am pregnant"? No. Right after he murdered Uriah? No. Right after he married Uriah's pregnant widow? No. Right after the birth of the baby? No. It's believed by some Old Testament scholars that there was at least a twelve-month interval that passed before Nathan paid the visit. God waited until just the right time. He let the grinding wheels of sin do their full work, and *then* He stepped in.

To be totally honest with you, there are times when I really question the timing of God. Times when I just don't know why He's so slow to carry out what I think He ought to do. But every time I have looked back in retrospect, I have seen how beautifully He worked out His plan, how perfectly it had come to pass. God not only does the right thing; He does the right thing at the right time.

In confronting someone in his sin, the timing is as important as the wording. Most importantly, you need to be sure that you're sent by God. Nathan was.

In his sin, David had despised the God he served. Now, as a result of that sin, in days and years to come, David would experience grief within his own household.

> Thus says the LORD, "Behold, I will raise up evil against you from your own household; I will even take your wives before your eyes, and give them to your companion, and he shall lie with your wives in broad daylight. Indeed you did it secretly, but I will do this thing before all Israel, and under the sun." (2 Samuel 12:11–12)

Whew! Talk about the consequences of sin. David sits there with his mouth still open, leaning back, perhaps staring at the ceiling, listening to the voice of God from Nathan.

David, realizing he was absolutely guilty, admitted without hesitation, "I have sinned. I've sinned against the LORD." With that admission, restoration began.

# RIDING OUT THE STORM

### ❧ *Read 2 Samuel 12:13–25* ❧

*D*avid refused to give up. When suffering the backwash of sin, our tendency is to say, "I am through. I am finished with living. Life isn't worth it any longer." But look at what David did: he "comforted his wife Bathsheba." It's easy to forget that she was also grieving. Both of them went through a period of grief. They wept. And then they went on living.

David is once more walking with the Lord as he did in days past. One of the most pathetic scenes on earth is a child of God who sits in the corner too long, licking his wounds in self-pity. It takes as much (often more) spiritual strength and purpose to recover and move on as it does to go through a crisis. "I will go on, I will pick up the pieces, I will get back on target, I will go back to work, I will begin to enjoy my friends again, I will carry on as I did before. In fact, by God's grace, I will be wiser and even more effective than I was before."

David, in riding out the storm, gives us some beautiful guidelines. He prayed, he faced the consequences realistically, he turned it all over to the Lord as he claimed the scriptural truth concerning death, and then he refused to give up. He moved on, relying on his God for strength.

Riding out the storm is a *lonely* experience. You will never be more alone emotionally than when you are in the whirlwind of consequences. You will wish others could help you, but they can't. They will want to be there, they will care, but for the most part, you have to ride out the storm alone.

Riding out the storm, thank God, is also a *temporary* experience. It may be the most difficult time in your life. You will be enduring your own whirlwind. On the other hand, you may be the innocent bystander caught in the consequential backwash of another's sin. You'll feel desperately alone, and it may seem that it will never, ever end. But believe me, the whirlwind is a temporary experience. Your faithful, caring Lord will see you through it.

# A Sheltering Tree

### ✦ *Read 2 Samuel 15:1—18* ✦

*T*he poet Samuel Taylor Coleridge once described friendship as "a sheltering tree." What a beautiful description of that special relationship. As I read those words, I think of my friends as great, leafy trees, who spread themselves over me, providing shade from the sun, whose presence is a stand against the blast of winter's lonely winds. A great, sheltering tree; that's a friend.

David was leaving the great city of Zion—the city named after him, the City of David. As he came to the edge, at the last house, he stopped and looked back over that golden metropolis he had watched God build over the past years. His heart must have been broken as he stood there looking back, his mind flooded with memories. All around him the people of his household scurried past, leading beasts of burden piled high with belongings, running for their lives.

He was at the last house, and he needed a tree to lean on. Somebody who would say, "David, I'm here with you. I don't have all the answers, but, man, I can assure you of this, my heart goes out to you." When the chips are down and there's nobody to affirm you and you run out of armor and you have no reputation to cling to, and all the lights are going out, and the crowd is following another voice, it's amazing how God sends a sheltering tree.

All of us need at least one person with whom we can be open and honest; all of us need at least one person who offers us the shelter of support and encouragement and, yes, even hard truths and confrontation. Sheltering trees, all!

Thankfully, David had a grove of such trees. As a result he made it through the toughest days and loneliest hours of his life.

*Do you?* If so, it is a good time to call them up and thank them for their shelter. If not, it's a good time to get a shovel and plant a few. You'll need every one.

Just ask David.

# DOWNWARD STEPS OF SIN

*Read 2 Samuel 13:1–30; 18:24–33*

racing the downward steps in David's eroding family relationships, we now have Absalom murdering Amnon, *a brother murdering a brother.* "The sword will never depart out of your household, David." Here he is groaning under the ache of that prediction.

Now if that's not bad enough, after Absalom kills David's son, he then flees: *rebellion.*

When Absalom fled, he went to Geshur. That's where his grandfather lived—his mother's father, who was a king in Geshur. He can't live at home, so he'll go stay with grand-dad while he licks his wounds and sets up his plan later on to lead a revolt against his daddy. And that's precisely what he does. Absalom *leads a conspiracy against his father.*

Later, *Joab murders Absalom.* The sword has still not departed from David's house.

David dearly regrets the day he ever even looked at Bathsheba and carried on a year of deception. And finally, in the backwash of rape, conspiracy, rebellion, hatred, and murder, he's sitting alone in the palace, no doubt perspiring to the point of exhaustion, and in comes a runner bearing bad news. Absalom has been killed.

David is a beaten man. He's strung out, sobbing as if he's lost his mind. Every crutch is removed. He's at the bitter end, broken and bruised, twisted and confused. The harvesting of his sins is almost more than he can bear.

If you have taken lightly the grace of God, if you have tip-toed through the corridors of the kingdom, picking and choosing sin or righteousness at will, thinking grace covers it all, you've missed it, my friend. You've missed it by a mile. As a matter of fact, it's quite likely that you are harvesting the bitter fruit of the seeds of sin planted in the past. Perhaps right now you are living in a compromising situation, or right on the edge of one. You are skimming along the surface, hoping it'll never catch up. But God is not mocked. It will. Trust me on this one . . . it will.

Turn to Him right now. Turn your life over to Him. Broken and bruised, twisted and confused, just lay it all out before Him. Ask Him to give you the grace and strength to face the consequences realistically and straight on.

# PENETRATING THE DARKNESS

### ❧ *Read 2 Samuel 22:1–51* ❧

*A*re times hard? Are days of trouble upon you? When times are tough, the Lord is our only security. David assures us in his song that the Lord delights in us; He sees and cares about what is happening in our lives, this very moment.

The Lord is our support. In tough times He is our most reliable security. He rescues us because He delights in us. What encouragement that brings as the battle endures and exhausts us. David's song of triumph begins on this easily forgotten theme. I am thankful he reminds us of it.

> For Thou art my lamp, O LORD;
> And the LORD illumines my darkness. (2 Samuel 22:29)

That reminds me of a scene from my boyhood days. When I was just a lad, my dad and I used to go floundering, a popular pastime on the Texas Gulf Coast. We'd carry a lantern in one hand and a two-pronged spear in the other (called a gig) as we walked along, knee-deep in the shallow water along the shore. As we walked, we'd swing the lantern back and forth as we searched the soft sand for the flounder that came up close to the shore in the evening to eat the shrimp and the mullet. The little lantern provided just enough light to reveal the fish down on the sand beneath the shallow water . . . and just enough so that we could see a few feet ahead as we waded through the water. Actually, it was all the light we needed. It penetrated just enough of the darkness so that we could see where to walk, but not much beyond that.

The same is true of the light we receive from God. At times we flounder along, trying to peer too far into the darkness ahead. Yet He gives us just enough light so that we can see to take the next step. That's all the light He gives and, in reality, that's all we need.

# THE BEST I CAN

### ❧ *Read 1 Chronicles 28:1–11* ❧

*D*avid was saying, "God did not give me a yes answer. When it came to my own dream, He gave me a no answer. But He did give me other things in place of that dream, and I'm making the very most I can of those other things." We can all glean much from David's mature response.

Do you have some cherished desire that you know you are going to have to relinquish? Usually it takes getting up in years to realize that's going to happen, because the younger we are, the greater our dreams, the broader our hopes, and the more determined we are to make them happen. But as we get older, many of us see that some of those great hopes and dreams are never going to be realized. Perhaps it is a dream of some great accomplishment through a unique kind of ministry. Maybe it is a desire for a an unusual career or personal recognition. Maybe it is a desire for romance and marriage. Maybe it's a longing for relief from something in your life that you've had to live with for years. Whatever it is, you may now recognize that it is never going to happen, and that's a hard pill to swallow. But, like David, it's an opportunity to find satisfaction in what God has allowed you to do. As he reflects on his life and his own unfulfilled desire, he says, "I want to turn my attention away from what wasn't to be and focus on the things God has done."

This is our challenge, isn't it? We can live the last years of our life swamped by guilt or overwhelmed by regrets from the past. We can either "eat our heart out," or we can say, "By the grace of God, I did the best I could with what I had. And I claim His promise that somehow He'll use what I did accomplish for His greater glory." What a wonderful attitude to have at the end of one's life!

# A LEGACY

### ✤ *Read 1 Chronicles 29:10–13* ✤

inally, and naturally, David falls on his knees and utters a beautiful prayer, an extemporaneous expression of his worship of the Lord God. The first verses are expressions of praise. Praise leaves humanity out of the picture and focuses fully on the exaltation of the living God.

David was surrounded by limitless riches. Yet they never captured his heart. He fought other battles within, but never greed. David was not trapped by materialism. He said, "Lord, everything we have is Yours—all these beautiful places where we gather for worship, the place where I live, the throne room—all of it is Yours, everything."

What an important investment it is to pass on to our children a proper scale of values, so that they know how to handle the good things of life, knowing that those good things are just a wisp—here today and gone tomorrow. Such an investment also teaches them how to handle it when things aren't easy. David held everything loosely, another admirable trait.

What lessons can we learn from such a man? We learn hope, in spite of his humanity. We learn courage, even in the midst of his own fear. We learn encouragement and praise in the songs that grew out of his hours of despair. We learn forgiveness in his dark moments of sin. And we learn the value of serving the purpose of God in our own generation, even though all our dreams may not be fulfilled.

Thank you, David, for being a good model, teaching us by your life such significant truths. And thank you, Father, for being our Master; using us though we are weak, forgiving us when we fail, and loving us through all the Sauls and Goliaths and Jonathans and Abigails and Bathshebas and Absaloms and Joabs and Solomons of our lives. Thank you for showing us that we can be people like David . . . people of passion and destiny.

*Elijah: A Man of Heroism & Humility*

# ALONE IN THE GAP

### ❧ *Read 1 Kings 16:29—17:1* ❧

*W*e're first introduced to him as "Elijah the Tishbite" (1 Kings 17:1). Talk about stepping out of nowhere! Elijah came out of this insignificant place—out of nowhere—to make such a significant contribution to God's plan for His people that he became one of Israel's most famous heroes. He became what we often call today, a legend.

The first thing that commands our attention is Elijah's name. The Hebrew word for "God" in the Old Testament is *Elohim,* which is occasionally abbreviated, *El.* The word *jah* is the word for "Jehovah." Thus, in Elijah's name we find the word for "God" and the word for "Jehovah." Between them is the small letter *I,* which in Hebrew has reference to the personal pronoun "my" or "mine." Putting the three together, then, we find that Elijah's name means "My God is Jehovah" or "The Lord is my God." No one had a reason to doubt that!

Ahab and Jezebel were in control of the northern kingdom of Israel, and Baal was the god they worshiped. But when Elijah burst on the scene, his very name proclaimed, "I have one God. His name is Jehovah. He is the One I serve, before whom I stand."

By now, the spiritual chasm between God and His people had reached its widest breadth. Elijah stood alone in that gap.

Today there are still those who stand alone in the gap, those who still strive to shake us awake. A handful of brave students at Columbine High School come immediately to mind. Loaded guns and the threat of death couldn't silence them. I think of them as modern-day Elijahs, whom God uses to deliver a life-changing message. Men and women of courage, ready to stand and deliver. Authentic heroes.

Our Lord is still searching for people who will make a difference. Christians dare not be mediocre. We dare not dissolve into the background or blend into the neutral scenery of this world. Sometimes you have to look awfully close and talk awfully long before an individual will declare his allegiance to God . . . someone with the courage to stand alone for God. Is that what we have created today in this age of tolerance and compromise?

Elijah's life teaches us what the Lord requires.

# SPECIAL PEOPLE FOR SPECIAL TIMES

### *Read 1 Kings 16:29—17:1*

God looks for special people at difficult times. God needed a special man to shine the light in the blackness of those days. But God didn't find him in the palace or the court. He didn't find him walking around with his head down in the school of the prophets. He didn't even find him in the homes of the ordinary people. God found him in Tishbeh, of all places. A man who would stand in the gap couldn't be suave or slick; he had to be rugged—soft-hearted with a tough hide.

God looked for somebody who had the backbone to stand alone. Someone who had the courage to say, "That's wrong!" Someone who could stand toe to toe with an idolatrous king and his wicked wife and proclaim, "God is God."

And I searched for a man among them who should build up the wall and stand in the gap before Me for the land, that I should not destroy it; but I found no one. (Ezekiel 22:30)

In our culture—our schools, our offices and factories, our lunchrooms and boardrooms, our halls of ivy and our halls of justice—we need men and women of God, including young people of God. We need respected professionals, athletes, homemakers, teachers, public figures, and private citizens who will promote the things of God, who will stand alone—stand tall, stand firm, stand strong!

How's your stature? How's your integrity? Have you corrupted your principles just to stay in business? To get a good grade? To make the team? To be with the "in" crowd? To earn the next rank or promotion? Have you winked at language or behavior that a few years ago would have horrified you? Are you, right now, compromising morally because you don't want to be considered a prude?

Those who find comfort in the court of Ahab can never bring themselves to stand in the gap with Elijah.

# A Unique Spokesperson

### ✤ *Read 1 Kings 16:29–17:1* ✤

God's methods are often surprising. God did not raise up an army to destroy Ahab and Jezebel. Neither did He send some scintillating prince to argue His case or try to impress their royal majesties. Instead, God did the unimaginable—He chose somebody like . . . well, like Elijah.

Are you thinking right now that somebody else is better qualified for that short-term mission assignment? For that leadership training group? For that community service?

Are you a wife and homemaker who feels that your contribution to God's service is not noteworthy? Do you see other people as special or called or talented?

You may be missing an opportunity that is right there in front of you. You may be in the very midst of a ministry and not even realize it. (What greater ministry can there be, for example, than that of a faithful wife and loving mother?) Your ministry may be to just two or three people. Don't discount that. God's methods are often surprising.

When we're standing alone in the gap, ultimately, we're standing before God. When the call comes, will God find us ready and willing to stand for Him? Will He find in us hearts that are completely His? Will He be able to say, "Ah, yes, there's a heart that is completely Mine. Yes, there's sufficient commitment there for Me to use that life with an Ahab. That's the kind of disciplined devotion I'm looking for."

No matter what role you fill in life, you're not unimportant when it comes to standing alone for truth.

What spot has God given you? Whatever it is, God says, "You're standing before *Me,* and I want to use you. I want to use you as My unique spokesperson in your day and age, at this moment and time."

Elijah, this gaunt, rugged figure striding out of nowhere, suddenly stepping into the pages of history, is a clear witness of the value of one life completely committed to God. An unknown man from a backwater place, he was called to stand against evil in the most turbulent and violent and decadent of times.

Look around. The need is still great, and God is still searching.

# His Word Is Final

### ❧ *Read 1 Kings 17:1* ❧

God keeps His promises. It's a major part of His immutable nature. He doesn't hold out hope with nice-sounding words, then renege on what He said He would do. God is neither fickle nor moody. And He never lies. As my own father used to say of people with integrity, "His word is His bond."

When you stop to think about it, it was because of a promise of God that Elijah came on the biblical scene in the first place. It was the prophet's unpopular task to announce God's message to the king. That message had to do with a terrible drought that was coming: the drought would last for years, and it would not end "except by my word" (1 Kings 17:1). That message was not only a wake-up call to get Ahab's attention, it was also a not-so-subtle reminder that, even though Ahab thought he was in charge, "the God of Israel lives," and He, alone, determines what will happen, and when.

Elijah's heroism in standing before the king of the land and telling him what he didn't want to hear came from the man of God's confidence in the word of his Lord. The Master of heaven had spoken, and that was the message Elijah brought to the attention of Ahab. God promised a drought, and nothing Ahab could do would keep it from arriving or diminish its devastating results. Furthermore, God had assured the prophet, who passed it on to the king, that the drought would not end until God determined it would end. Period. End of announcement. Exit Elijah. Bring on the drought.

The very thing that God had communicated through His prophet came to pass. Exactly as God promised, there was not a drop of rain to relieve the scorched earth. The land became parched and barren as months passed, turning into years. Rivers no longer flowed, streams dried up, wells ran dry, crops burned to a brown crisp, animals died, and the king found himself totally helpless to interfere with God's act of judgment.

God keeps His promises. Agree with it or not, His word is final.

He never forgets anything He promises. That's right . . . never.

# CUT DOWN TO SIZE

### *Read 1 Kings 17:2—6*

*I* am going to cut you down to size!" If I heard that once during the ten weeks I spent in a U.S. Marine Corps boot camp more than forty-five years ago, I must have heard it a dozen times. As I recall, those words formed the theme of the opening speech, delivered with passion, by a man I quickly learned to obey. Those words still play back to me in my mind, and the shrill tone of my drill instructor's voice remains a vivid memory. He meant every word he said, and he kept his promise.

There we stood, an unorganized, ragtag bunch of seventy or so young men of every conceivable size and background, thrown together in a strange place, having no idea (thankfully) what was ahead of us. During the months that followed, every shred of self-sufficient arrogance, every hint of independent spirit, and all thought of rebellion was scraped away. Any indifference toward authority was replaced by a firm commitment to do only as we were told, regardless. We learned to survive in the crucible of intense, extreme training that has characterized the Marine Corps throughout its proud and proven history.

The disciplined regimen of boot camp—day after day, week after week—brought about remarkable changes in each one of us. As a result, we left that place completely different than we were when we arrived. The isolation of our location, the absence of all creature comforts, the relentless, monotonous drills and demanding repetition of inspections, the tests that forced us to encounter the unknown without showing fear (all mixed with the maddening determination and constant harassment of our drill instructor), yielded powerful dividends. Almost without realizing it, while learning to submit ourselves to the commands of our leader, we ultimately found ourselves physically fit, emotionally stirred, and mentally ready for whatever conflict might come our way, even the harsh reality of facing the enemy in combat.

That kind of raw recruit training is precisely what the Lord had in mind when He sent His servant Elijah from the court of King Ahab to the brook Cherith. Little did the prophet know that his being hidden away at Cherith would prove to be *his* boot camp experience. There, he would be trained to trust his Leader so that he might ultimately do battle with a treacherous enemy.

# From Hurt to Usefulness

### ✣ *Read 1 Kings 17:2–6* ✤

*A*s we read those words and try to imagine the original setting, we begin to see the surprising nature of God's plan. The most logical arrangement, seemingly, would be to keep Elijah in the king's face—to use the prophet as a persistent goad, pressing the godless monarch into submission, forcing him to surrender his will to the One who had created him. After all, none of King Ahab's advisors and counselors had Elijah's integrity. There was no one nearby to confront the king's idolatrous ways or his cruel and unfair acts against the people of Israel. It only made good sense to leave Elijah there in the court of the king.

So much for human logic.

God's plan is always full of surprise and mystery. While *we* might have chosen to leave Elijah there, confronting Ahab, such was not the Father's plan. He had things He wished to accomplish deep within His servant's inner life, things that would prepare Elijah for encounters that might destroy a less-obedient, less-committed, and less-prepared servant. Hence, God immediately sent him away to a place of isolation, hidden from everyone, where he would not only be protected from physical danger but would also be better prepared for a greater mission.

For the godly hero to be useful as an instrument of significance in the Lord's hand, he must be humbled and forced to trust. He must, in other words, be "cut down to size." Or, as A. W. Tozer loved to say, "It's doubtful that God can bless a man greatly until He has hurt him deeply."[5] It has been my observation over the years that the deeper the hurt, the greater the usefulness.

# INTO THE SHADOWS

### ❧ *Read 1 Kings 17:2–6* ❧

*A*ny recruit who has been through boot camp can tell you that every hour of the day someone is ordering you where to go, when to be there, what to do, and how to survive. That's a vital part of basic training. And God did the same for His prophet. He told Elijah exactly where he was to go, what he was to do when he got there, and how he would manage to survive. How strange the plan must have seemed to Elijah.

The first thing he was to do was *hide.*

"Hide myself? I'm a prophet! I'm a palace man. I'm out there in public proclaiming your Word. You seem to forget, Lord, I'm called to preach."

No, God told Elijah. Not this time. "Hide yourself," God said.

The Hebrew word here suggests the idea of concealment, of being absent on purpose. "Conceal yourself, Elijah," God said. "Absent yourself in secrecy."

One of the most difficult commands to hear, and one of the hardest commands to obey, is the command to hide. The admonition to go off and be alone, to get away from the public spotlight, to drop back and deliberately remain hidden. This is especially true if you are comfortable in the limelight, an up-front kind of person, one who is obviously gifted with leadership abilities. It's also true if you are a doer. A get-the-job-done kind of person.

You may be a capable woman, whether homemaker or career woman. Then, suddenly, you are snatched from your world of endless activity and effective involvement. God says, in no uncertain terms, "Hide yourself. Get alone. Get out of the limelight. Get away from all those things that satisfy your human pride and ego, and go live by the brook."

Sometimes sickness forces such a change. Sometimes we reach the peak of our energy output and begin to burn out, or we are about to do so. Sometimes God, without explaining Himself, simply removes us from one place and reshapes us for another.

God had two reasons for commanding Elijah to hide himself. First, He wanted to protect Elijah from Ahab; and second, He wanted to train him to become a man of God. When God says to us, almost out of the blue, "Hide yourself," He usually has both purposes in mind: protection and training.

# A STEP AT A TIME

### ✦ *Read 1 Kings 17:4* ✦

od's direction includes God's provision. God says, "Go to the brook. I will provide." Vance Havner, in his book, *It Is Toward Evening*, tells the story of a group of farmers who were raising cotton in the Deep South when the devastating boll weevil invaded the crops. These men had put all of their savings, dedicated all of their fields, set all of their hopes in cotton. Then the boll weevil came. Before long, it looked as if they were headed for the poorhouse.

But farmers, being the determined and ingenious people they are, decided, "Well, we can't plant cotton, so let's plant peanuts." Amazingly, those peanuts brought them more money than they would have ever made raising cotton. When the farmers realized that what had seemed like a disaster had actually proved to be a boon, they erected a large and impressive monument to the boll weevil—a monument to the very thing they once thought would destroy them.

"Sometimes we settle into a humdrum routine as monotonous as growing cotton year after year," says Havner, himself a seasoned old saint of God at the time he wrote these words. "Then God sends the boll weevil; He jolts us out of our groove, and we must find new ways to live. Financial reverses, great bereavement, physical infirmity, loss of position—how many have been driven by trouble to be better husbandmen and to bring forth far finer fruit from their souls! The best thing that ever happened to some of us was the coming of our 'boll weevil.'"[6]

When God directs, God provides. That's what sustained Elijah during his boot camp experience.

We have to learn to trust God one day at a time. Did you notice that God never told Elijah what the second step would be until he had taken the first step? God told His prophet to go to Ahab. When Elijah got to the palace, God told him what to say. After he said it, God told him, "Now, go to the brook." He didn't tell Elijah what was going to happen at Cherith; He just said, "Go to the brook and hide yourself." Elijah didn't know the future, but he did have God's promise: "I'll provide for you there." And God didn't tell him the next step until the brook had dried up.

# GOD'S PROVISIONS

#### ❧ *Read 1 Kings 17:4–6* ❧

*T*he ravens were God's catering service, delivering provisions to His prophet. "The ravens will bring in your food, Elijah." Isn't that incredible? God makes provision for Elijah's physical welfare during this time of seclusion. But He also provides for his spiritual welfare. God knew what Elijah needed; therefore, the silence and solitude were to be essential parts of his boot camp experience.

In essence, God said to Elijah, "You need to get out of the spotlight. You need to come up in the mountains, alone with Me, where you can hear my voice clearly. We need more time together, Elijah, and you need more training."

The good news is this: without one moment's hesitation, Elijah obeyed. He didn't even ask why.

So he went and did according to the word of the LORD, for he went and lived by the brook Cherith, which is east of the Jordan (1 Kings 17:5).

Notice the wording here. He went and *lived* by the brook Cherith. It's one thing to take a day trip off the beaten track, to go camping for a weekend, or even to spend two or three weeks backpacking in the wilderness. Such adventures offer all the delights of being away from the cares of the real world for a time, even as you have the comfort of knowing that your lifeline to civilization is still there. It's quite another thing to *live* in the wilderness, alone, for an extended time. But that's exactly what Elijah did for months, possibly the better part of a year. God said, "Go there. Settle there. Live there." That's exactly what Elijah did.

Would you accept such an assignment from God? Would you respond with such immediate obedience? How many of us would say nothing except, "Yes, Sir. I trust You completely. I don't need the spotlight to survive." Very few! We much prefer only comfortable and active Christianity.

While there is certainly nothing wrong with being a leader or fulfilling the role of spokesman for God, how easy it is to become addicted to the public forum, feeling that we are indispensable to God's plan. How easy to neglect, ignore, or overlook those occasions when we need to pull back, be quiet, regroup, rethink, and renew our souls.

# The Brook Has Dried Up

*Read 1 Kings 17:5–7*

One morning Elijah noticed that the brook wasn't gushing over the rocks or running as freely as it had in days past. Since that single stream of water was his lifeline, he checked it carefully. Over the next few days he watched it dwindle and shrink, until it was only a trickle. Then one morning, there was no water, only wet sand. The hot winds soon siphoned even that dampness, and the sand hardened. Before long, cracks appeared in the parched bed of the brook. No more water. The brook had dried up.

Does that kind of experience sound familiar to you? At one time you knew the joy of a full bank account, a booming business, an exciting, ever-expanding career, a magnificent and exciting ministry. But the brook has dried up.

At one time you knew the joy of using your voice to sing the Lord's praises. Then a growth developed on your vocal chords, requiring surgery. But the surgery removed more than the growth; it also took your lovely singing voice. The brook has dried up.

Your partner in life has grown indifferent and has recently asked for a divorce. There's no longer any affection and no promise of change. The brook has dried up.

I've had my own times when the brook has dried up, and I've found myself wondering about the things I've believed and preached for years. What happened? Had God died? No. My vision just got a little blurry. My circumstances caused my thinking to get a little foggy. I looked up, and I couldn't see Him as clearly. To exacerbate the problem, I felt as though He wasn't hearing me. The heavens were brass. I would speak to Him and heard nothing. My brook dried up.

That's what happened to John Bunyan in seventeenth-century England. He preached against the godlessness of his day, and the authorities shoved him into prison. His brook of opportunity and freedom dried up. But because Bunyan firmly believed God was still alive and at work, he turned that prison into a place of praise, service, and creativity as he began to write *Pilgrim's Progress*, the most famous allegory in the history of the English language. Dried-up brooks in no way cancel out God's providential plan. Often, they cause it to emerge.

# TOUGH SPOTS

### Read 1 Kings 17:5–7

*E*lijah was in a tough spot. A life-threatening spot. The brook had dried up. Had God forgotten His faithful servant? Has God forgotten you? Has He left you all alone?

The God who gives water can also withhold water. That's His sovereign right.

Our human feelings tell us that once our faithful heavenly Father gives water, He should never take it away. It just wouldn't be fair. Once God gives a mate, He should never take a mate. Once God gives a child, He should never take a child. Once He gives a good business, He has no right to take that business. Once He provides a pastor, He must never call him elsewhere. Once He gives us rapid growth and great delight in a ministry, He has no right to step in and say, "Wait a minute. There's no need to grow larger. Let Me take you deeper instead." On the contrary, He has *every* right!

When we hit a tough spot, our tendency is to feel abandoned, to become resentful, to think, *How could God forget me?* In fact, just the opposite is true. In times of testing, we are more than ever the object of His concern.

But God says, in the midst of your dried-up brook, "You are written on the palms of My hands. You are continually before me." Then He uses that wonderful image of a young mother with her new baby, and He surprises us with a realistic reminder: "Can a woman forget her nursing child?" You wouldn't think so, would you? But look at the stories in the news, and you know how many women do exactly that. Babies left in garbage dumpsters. Tiny babies abandoned—sometimes even abused or tortured or murdered. Yes, as unimaginable as it seems, even a mother *can* forget her nursing child. But here's the clincher: Not God. Not God! He will *never* forget us. We are permanently inscribed on the palms of His hands. Pause, and let that sink in.

# LAYING THE FOUNDATION OF COURAGE

*Read 1 Kings 17:1—7; James 5:17—18*

Elijah had prayed that it would not rain, and ultimately, it did not rain for three and a half years. So the dried-up brook was just an indication that the very thing he had prayed for was beginning to take place. He was living in the result of his own prayer. Have you ever had that happen? "Lord, make me a godly man. Lord, mold me into a woman after your own heart." Meanwhile, in your heart you're thinking, *but don't let it hurt too much.* "Lord, make me stable, long-suffering, and gracious," *but don't remove too many of my creature comforts.* "Lord, teach me faith, make me strong," *but don't let me suffer.* Have you ever bargained with God like that? We want instant maturity, not the kind that requires sacrifice or emotional pain or hardship. "Lord, give me patience . . . and I want it right now!"

God's spiritual boot camp doesn't work that way. It is designed for our development toward maturity, not for our comfort. But self-denial is not a popular virtue in today's culture.

A short time before Robert E. Lee passed into his Lord's presence, a young mother brought her tiny infant to him. With tenderness, Lee took the child and held him in his arms, looking deeply into the baby's eyes. He then looked up at the mother and said, "Teach him he must deny himself."

The seasoned veteran knew whereof he spoke. As Douglas Southall Freeman writes, "Had his [Lee's] life been epitomized in one sentence of the Book he read so often, it would have been in the words, 'If any man will come after Me, let him deny himself, and take up his cross daily, and follow Me.'"[7]

Our God is relentless. He never ceases His training regimens. He shaves off our hair, He takes away our comfortable and secure lifestyle, He moves us into cramped and unfamiliar quarters, and He changes our circle of friends—it's like we're in a spiritual boot camp!

In the process, He strips us of *all* our pride! And then He begins to lay the foundation blocks of heroic courage, and a new kind of confidence, if you will—the kind that no longer defends us but defends Him. What a magnificent change that is. And how essential in our journey toward maturity! Again, it's all part of being cut down to size.

# OUR OBSTACLE COURSE

*Read 1 Kings 17:5–7*

*P*art of every boot camp experience is the grueling, grinding, and sometimes daunting obstacle course. It is neither fun nor easy, but its demanding discipline prepares the recruit for whatever situations he or she may face in the future, particularly under enemy fire. In the spiritual life, before we can truly benefit from "the hidden life" that God uses to prepare us for whatever future He has planned for us, we must overcome at least four major obstacles. I think of them as four tough membranes of the flesh: pride, fear, resentment, and long-standing habits. Conquering these layers of resistance will prepare us for the future and harden us for combat with the adversary.

In a very real sense, God has designed a boot camp for His children, but it doesn't last just eight weeks or ten weeks. Nor is it a weekend seminar we can take or a day-long workshop we can attend. God's training course takes place periodically throughout the Christian life. And there, in the very center of obstacles and pain and solitude, we come to realize how alive God is in our lives—how alive and in charge. He will invade us, reduce us, break us, and crush us, so that we will become the people He intends us to be.

No matter how many years we walk with the Lord, we must still, at times, pass through our own Gethsemane. It happens every time He sends us to the brook to live the hidden life. It happens every time He disorients us as He displaces us; every time He pulls out all the props; every time He takes away more of the comforts; every time He removes most of the "rights" we once enjoyed. And He does all this so that He can mold us into the person that we otherwise never would be. He knows what He's about.

Elijah went to Cherith as an energetic spokesman for God—a prophet. He emerged from Cherith as a deeper man of God. All this happened because he was left beside a brook that dried up. Alone, but not forgotten. Tested, but not abandoned.

# CRUCIBLE FOR CHRIST

*Read 1 Kings 17:8–9*

*A*s we did earlier, let's first examine the significance of the name of this place where the prophet was told to go. Zarephath comes from a Hebrew verb that means "to melt, to smelt." Interestingly, in noun form it means "crucible." The place may have gotten its name because there was a smelting plant located somewhere near there; we don't know for sure. But whatever the source of its name, Zarephath would prove to be a "crucible" for Elijah—a place designed by God to further refine the prophet and make a major difference in the remainder of his life.

It was almost as if the Lord were saying to His servant, "I first took you to Cherith to wean you away from the bright lights and the public platform, where I could cut you down to size and reduce you to a man who would trust Me, regardless. It was there I began to renovate your inner man through the disciplines of solitude, silence, and obscurity. But now it's time to do an even deeper work. Now, Elijah, I will turn up the heat in the furnace and melt you so that I might mold you far more exactly into the kind of man I need to fulfill the purposes I have in mind."

If you walk with the Lord long enough, you will discover that His tests often come back-to-back. Or perhaps it would be even more accurate to say back to back to back to back to back. Usually, His preparatory tests don't stop with one or two. They multiply. And as soon as you climb out of one crucible thinking, "Okay, I made it through that one," you're plunged into another, where the flame is even hotter.

Crucibles create Christlikeness. This is precisely what the hymn writer had in mind when he wrote:

> *The flame shall not hurt thee; I only design,*
> *Thy dross to consume and thy gold to refine.*[8]

That's what a crucible does. That's what a furnace does. It brings all the impurities to the surface so that they can be skimmed off, leaving greater purity.

# INCREDIBLE ASSOCIATIONS

### ⚜ *Read 1 Kings 17:10–16* ⚜

*E*lijah had walked into a situation that was, from all human perspective, impossible. But the good news is that he saw beyond the difficulty. He handled the problem with faith, not fear.

Elijah was determined that those initial first-impression blues were not going to get him down. The widow had her eyes on the impossibilities: a handful of flour, a tiny amount of oil, a few sticks. Elijah rolled up his sleeves and focused only on the possibilities.

How could he do that? Because he was an emerging man of God.

He had been to Cherith. He had seen the proof of God's faithfulness. He had survived the dried-up brook. He had obeyed God, and, without hesitation, he had walked to Zarephath.

You can't talk the talk if you've never walked the walk. You can't encourage somebody else to believe the improbable if you haven't believed the impossible. You can't light another's candle of hope if your own torch of faith isn't burning.

When Elijah saw the near-empty flour bin and oil jug, he said, almost with a shrug, "That's no problem for God. Get in there and fix those biscuits. And fix some for you and your son too." Then he told her why. Listen to these confident words of faith: "The bowl of flour shall not be exhausted, nor the jar of oil be empty, until the day that the Lord sends rain on the face of this earth."

What a promise! That woman must have looked at Elijah, this tired, dusty stranger, with wonder and bewilderment, as she heard words like she'd never heard before.

Have you ever spent time in the presence of a person of faith? Ever rubbed shoulders with men and women of God who don't have the word "impossible" in their vocabulary? If not, locate a few strong-hearted souls. You need them in your life. These are the kind of incredible associations God uses to build up our faith!

# CONFIDENT IN THE LORD'S POWER

*Read 1 Kings 17:17–19*

She stands there, tears streaming down her face, holding the body of her son in her arms. And at that precise moment, Elijah holds out his arms and says, "Give him to me."

And he said to her, "Give me your son." Then he took him from her bosom and carried him up to the upper room where he was living, and laid him on his own bed (1 Kings 17:19).

There the woman stands, holding the limp, lifeless body of her only child. Her world has come crashing down, suddenly and unexpectedly. And Elijah simply says, "Give him to me."

Do you know what really impresses me here? It's the silence of Elijah. Somehow he knows that nothing he can say at this moment will satisfy this grieving mother. No words from him can soothe her stricken spirit. So he does not argue with her. He does not rebuke her. He does not try to reason with her. He doesn't remind her of all she owes him or of how ashamed she should be for blaming him. He simply asks her to place her burden in his arms.

Pause for a moment to realize that Elijah is again in a situation that, at least from a human point of view, he doesn't deserve. He has obeyed God by going to Ahab then hiding at Cherith. He has walked with God from Cherith to Zarephath. He has done *exactly* as the Lord instructed. He's trusted God, and now he's receiving the brunt of this woman's blame.

God sometimes seems to put us in the vise, and then He tightens it and tightens it more, until we think, in the pain of His sovereign squeeze, "What's He trying to do to me?" We walk closer to Him and even closer to Him. We don't see how we could walk any closer, but still more tests come, one on top of another.

That's where Elijah is, but he doesn't waver. He stands tall and silent in the shadow of God, grounded in faith, confident of his Lord's power. That's humility at its best.

He doesn't question God. He doesn't fall apart at the seams. He doesn't lose control. He doesn't argue with the woman. He simply says, with quiet compassion, "Give me the boy."

# WHEN TRAGEDY STRIKES

### ❧ *Read 1 Kings 17:17–19* ❧

*I*'m deeply impressed by the man's gentleness. Though Elijah deserved none of the woman's blame, he stood silent under her blast. That's gentleness. Someone, somewhere, has called this fruit of the Spirit "the mint-mark of heaven." When it is present in a highly-charged setting such as this, it becomes a testimony of the Spirit of God at work in the one who could lash back, but doesn't. It is His life, at that gentle and tender moment, being made evident.

I am also impressed with this grieving mother. She, without question or hesitation, places her precious, lifeless son into Elijah's arms. Perhaps the prophet's gentleness suddenly melted her and prompted her, once again, to trust him.

Then, Elijah, the man of God, silently climbed the stairway to the room where he had been doing battle before God on a regular basis. I say this because I believe that Elijah had spent hours, even days, on his knees in that room. He had formed that habit while alone with his God at Cherith.

Do you have a room like that—a place where you meet with God? Do you have a quiet retreat where you and the Lord do regular business together? If you don't, I strongly urge you to provide yourself just such a place—your own prophet's chamber where you and God can meet together. It will be there that you will prepare yourself for life's contingencies. Without it, you'll lack the necessary steel in your foundation of faith.

What do you do when tragedy strikes? What do you do when a test comes? What's your first response? Is it to complain? To be angry? To blame? To try to reason your way out of it? Or have you formed the habit of doing what Elijah did? Do you go to your special place and get alone with God? Elijah provides a wonderful example for us. No panic. No fear. No rush. No doubt.

# ALONE WITH GOD

### ✤ *Read 1 Kings 17:20–22* ✤

ow wait a minute. What is going on here? Up to this point in Scripture, there has been no account of anyone ever being raised from the dead. The closest to that would be Enoch, but he was not resurrected or resuscitated, because he didn't die. God simply took him to glory. "And Enoch walked with God; and he was not, for God took him" (Genesis 5:24).

So what is Elijah thinking here? How does he dare ask God to do such an unprecedented thing?

Elijah could not go back through the record like some spiritual attorney and try to find another case he could point to and say, "Ah! Precedence recorded in the Scriptures—there's a case like mine. God did it there. He will do it here." But God never claimed to provide a written record of *absolutely everything* He has ever done. And I believe He has left the record incomplete, so to speak, so that we will not trust in the past but in the God who is fresh and alive and creative and real, able to meet today's need *today*.

Elijah had no this-is-how-God-always-does-it manual to follow. Instead, he relied solely on one thing: faith. He had only his faith in the living God.

Don't you wish at times that you had a book where you could look up "impatience"? Okay. "What to do when I'm impatient in the face of testing": here are steps one, two, three, four, and five. And in case of severe emergency: six, seven, and eight. You've got the answer! Or, what to do when death comes: one, two, three, four. If it is the dearest friend you've ever known: five and six. If it is your own child: seven and eight. But there's no such manual. Thankfully, in His Word God does include principles to follow in most crises, but not a precise procedure in all difficult or impossible situations. God leaves us on the cutting edge of today so that we will trust in Him and the principles in His great and gracious Word. That's all we have. That's enough.

# ALL YOUR HEART

### ❧ *Read 1 Kings 17:20–22* ❧

hat was some prayer. Elijah was not able to say, "Let this child's life return to him, as it happened to Enoch, as it happened to Isaac, as it happened to Moses," because there was no precedence for this particular miracle. So Elijah said, "Lord, I'm trusting You for a miracle. I'm asking You to perform the impossible." He then waited. Everything, at that epochal moment of faith, rested in the Lord's hands.

You may be in the process of placing your own life before the Lord in this way. Things are critical, and only a miracle can breathe new life into your situation. Circumstances are totally out of your control. So you take it to your special place, and, standing in the shadow of your God, you lay it out before Him, prostrating yourself before Him, pleading for His intervention, trusting completely in His miraculous power, refusing to lean on your own understanding.

Dr. Raymond Edman, in his little book, *In Quietness and Confidence,* writes about a godly man who faced just such a trial.

*This is how he met it: He was quiet for a while with his Lord, then he wrote these words for himself:*

*First, He brought me here, it is by His will I am in this strait place: in that fact I will rest.*

*Next, He will keep me here in His love, and give me grace to behave as His child.*

*Then, He will make the trial a blessing, teaching me the lessons He intends me to learn, and working in me the grace He means to bestow.*

*Last, in His time He can bring me out again—how and when He knows.*[9]

Can you make these four statements? If you can … *will* you?

1. I am here by God's appointment.

2. I am in His keeping.

3. I am under His training.

4. He will show me His purposes in His time.

By God's appointment, in God's keeping, under His training, for His time. What an outstanding summary of what it means to trust in the Lord with *all* your heart!

# A HUMBLE SERVANT

*Read 1 Kings 17:22–23*

No words can describe what happened in that little upstairs bedroom when the corpse began to stir and Elijah saw life returning to the boy's body. No words can describe being in the midst of such a trial and then watching God, in a miraculous moment or period of time, work it out. Only you who have been there can nod, smile, and say, "Amen. I know exactly what you're describing; I've seen God do it."

Elijah saw that kind of miracle. It happened before his eyes.

Now, look at what he did.

And Elijah took the child, and brought him down from the upper room into the house and gave him to his mother; and Elijah said, "See, your son is alive" (1 Kings 17:23).

Elijah did not say, "See what I did!" No! That's what *we* might have done, or perhaps that's what some televangelist might do, but that's not what Elijah did. Elijah quietly walked downstairs with the boy by his side and said, "See, your son is alive."

Once again, words fail to describe the feelings of the mother, or the experience between mother and child, at that moment.

In years past, Cynthia and I had a close, personal friend who was a dear woman of God and, therefore, a faithful woman of prayer. She prayed for us for many years. Periodically, she would ask, "What's the Lord doing in your life?" When we told her about various things that were happening, her response invariably was, "Isn't that just like the Lord." Or, "Isn't the Lord wonderful! That's just like Him to do this." Rather than being surprised, she was always humbly affirming and grateful. Her God never disappointed. His miraculous powers only strengthened her faith . . . and ours!

That's what Elijah wanted this woman to see. He stepped back into the shadows so that she would see the Lord.

Elijah wanted her to see what God had done and be impressed with Him, not His servant.

# FAITH PERSONIFIED

### *Read 1 Kings 17:24*

When the woman saw that her son was alive, she didn't see Elijah. She saw the Lord. "Elijah, I've heard you talk about the God of heaven. I've heard you refer to Him in various ways. But now, when I look at this miracle, I know that you speak the truth."

If you wish to be a man or woman of God, it is essential that you face the impossible situations of life with faith, as Elijah did. If you are a young person who desires to live a godly life that will leave its mark upon this world, you must learn early to stand in the shadow of your Savior, trusting Him to work through the trials you encounter, through the extreme circumstances you cannot handle. The God of Elijah is your God. He is still the God of impossible situations. He still does what no earthly individual can do. Trust Him to do that!

Elijah approached the impossible with calmness and contentment, with gentleness and self-control, with faith and humility. As I've mentioned from the beginning, Elijah was heroic in exploits of faith, but he remained a model of humility.

Examine your own life for these character traits and take them one by one before God. You might say to the Lord, for example, "Lord, today I want to do what You say regarding contentment; I want to have a calm and gentle spirit. I don't simply want to call myself a Christian. I want to be known as a genuine servant of God because my life demonstrates the truth I say I believe. Help me this day to face everything and deal with everyone with a gentle and quiet spirit. Help me to be content, even though things don't go my way.

"Help me today with diligence, Lord. I tend to lose sight of the goal as the day wears on. I'm a good starter, but I don't finish well. Help me to do a quality piece of work and not to give in to the mood of the moment.

"And, Lord, help me, when You begin to bring to pass these qualities in my life, not to call attention to them, but just to let them flow out my life in glory to You. Help me to become Your servant, Your man, Your woman."

That is how we personify a life of faith.

# THE GOD OF IMPOSSIBILITIES

### ✣ *Read 1 Kings 17:24* ✣

*A*ll over this world, around us every day, are people who are looking for the truth to be lived out in the lives of those who claim it. Just as the widow watched Elijah, there are people watching you. They hear what you say you believe, but they are watching to see what you do.

Remember, you are here by God's appointment, you are in His keeping, you are under His training, for His time. Give Him the corpse of your life, and ask Him to revive those lifeless areas that need to be revived. If the situation calls for it, trust Him for a miracle, in His time, if it be His will, for your life.

On the bed of your life place the remains of your broken and scarred past; the emptiness of your poor character traits; the habits, even the addictions that have so long controlled you; the limited vision that continues to characterize you; the slight irritation that nags or the large one that looms; the anger or violence or lust or greed or discontentment or selfishness or the ugliness of pride. Lay all these before the Father, and stretch yourself out under His shadow as you ask Him to bring about remarkable, even miraculous changes in your life.

Is He able? Get serious! I'm referring to "the God of impossibilities," the One who has limitless power, who has never—and *will* never—meet an intimidating obstacle He cannot overcome, an aggressive enemy He cannot overwhelm, a final decision He cannot override, or a powerful person He cannot overshadow.

Because Elijah believed in "the God of impossibilities," not even death caused him to doubt. He learned his theology of faith in the secret hiding place at Cherith. He was given the opportunity to develop it during his advance training at Zarephath. But it was not until he stared death in the face, literally, that he personified it. And he did it all standing in the shadow of God.

And so must I.

And so must you.

# No Doubt

### ❧ *Read 1 Kings 18:1—15* ❧

*I*n the first verse in 1 Kings 18, there is an eloquent phrase: "The word of the LORD came to Elijah in the third year." Three years! That's an incredibly long time to go without rain. We can't imagine it, can we? But God was up to something. By now, not even those false prophets could garner much credibility. All repetitious prayers and rituals and voodoo tactics had proven useless. Is it any wonder that Elijah had the people's attention when he challenged the prophets of Baal and Asherah to a public showdown with Jehovah God? By now, they were willing to try anything. Elijah didn't have to plead for their cooperation.

And is it any wonder that, when God proved Himself to them, the people "fell on their faces" and immediately acknowledged, "The Lord, He is God; the Lord, He is God" (18:39)? And when Elijah told those same people to seize the prophets and not let one of them escape, he didn't have to beg them; the people of Israel had had enough of those idolatrous fools! The fire from heaven may have convinced them, but the never-ending drought had already sucked dry most of the confidence they'd had in the pagan leaders they had once followed. God's delay worked wonders when the choice between who was worthy of worship needed to be made. Natural calamities normally turn hearts toward God, not from Him.

But look again at that first verse in 1 Kings 18, and you will find another promise of God. Elijah was more than ready to hear this one! "I will send rain on the face of the earth," God said.

Finally. What relief that promise must have brought. I find it interesting that God's prophet had never once complained about the drought, even though the very brook from which his water supply came had dried up, and even though it must have been as dreadfully difficult for him as it was for the others in the land of Israel. But the difference between Elijah and the others was simple: he knew God would one day fulfill His promise and bring rain. Until then, Elijah would wait, never doubting, because he was fully persuaded of something most of us, at one time or another, doubt: God keeps His promises.

# DIVIDED ALLEGIANCE

### *Read 1 Kings 18:16—21*

*D*ivided allegiance is as wrong as open idolatry. "How long will you hesitate between two opinions?" Elijah asks the people of Israel. The easiest thing to do when you are outnumbered or overwhelmed is to remain in that mediocre state of noncommitment. That was where the people of Israel lived, but Elijah never went there. He told them, "You cannot continue in this period of divided allegiance any longer."

The strongest words that were given to the seven churches mentioned in the Book of Revelation, chapters 2 and 3, were given to the church at Laodicea. And the reason is clear: They were uncommitted. They existed in neutrality. "'I know your deeds, that you are neither cold nor hot; I would that you were cold or hot. So because you are lukewarm, and neither hot nor cold, I will spit you out of My mouth'" (Rev. 3:15–16).

Get off the fence of indecision, Elijah told the people of Israel. Either you are for God or against Him.

Perhaps you have known God for many years but have never truly been committed to Him. Now is the time to change that. Stop hiding your love for and commitment to Christ. Let the word out! Tactfully yet fearlessly speak devotedly of your faith. Start now. There are so many strategic ways God can use you in your business, your profession, your school, your neighborhood. You don't agree with the ungodly cultural drift that's happening around you? Say so! You sense an erosion of spirituality at your church, and you're serving in a leadership capacity? Address it! Neutrality in the hour of decision is a curse that invariably leads to tragic consequences.

Our most effective tool is the prayer of faith.

When it came down to the wire, when Baal had failed and God was about to do His work, the one instrument that Elijah employed was prayer.

# PRAYER OF FAITH

### ❧ *Read 1 Kings 18:22—40* ❧

*I*sn't it amazing how often people try everything but prayer? It's like the old saying: "When everything else fails, read the instructions." The same with prayer. When everything else fails, try prayer. "Okay, okay . . . maybe we should pray about it." But Elijah didn't use prayer as a last resort. Prayer was his first and only resort. A simple prayer of faith was his major contact with the living Lord. It set everything in motion.

Let me ask you a straight-out question: Do you, personally, pray? Now notice that I didn't say, "Do you listen when the preacher prays or when your parents pray?" I didn't say, "Do you know a good Bible study on prayer?" I didn't even say, "Have you taught on prayer?" I asked, "Do *you*, personally, pray?" Can you look back over the last seven days and pinpoint times you deliberately set aside for prayer? Even just a solid ten or fifteen minutes of uninterrupted time with God?

This entire incident revolves around one dedicated life—the life of Elijah. He was a man all alone, overwhelmingly outnumbered by a hostile king, the king's wicked and powerful wife, eight hundred fifty pagan prophets and priests of Baal, and countless numbers of unbelieving Israelites. Yet all of them were silenced and intimidated by this one dedicated man of God.

*Never underestimate the power of one totally dedicated life.*

How exciting it would be if, through your own dedication to Jesus Christ, you could influence one person this next week, either by leading him to Jesus or by building her up in the faith. Sound impossible? You know it's not. The Bible and the history of the church are filled with stories of the difference one person's dedication to God has made.

Elijah staged a magnificent showdown with the prophets of Baal. But the greatest showdown of all time was at Calvary, where the enemy of God was defeated by the sacrifice of God's own Son. Why? Because God had one dedicated life He could count on: His own dear Son, Jesus. In fact, the difference He made changed all of history.

I urge you: step up!

# INVINCIBLE

### ✤ *Read 1 Kings 18:22–40* ✤

G od answered Elijah's prayer. This not only brought fire, but far more importantly, it turned the hearts of the people back to God. It also rid the land of the prophets of Baal.

Then Elijah said to them, "Seize the prophets of Baal; do not let one of them escape." So they seized them; and Elijah brought them down to the brook Kishon, and slew them there (1 Kings 18:40).

Some read that last verse and say, "What an extreme response!" Is it? What would you think of a physician who found a mass of rapidly growing malignant cells in your abdomen and said to you, "I think we'd better remove *some* of those cells"? Or, "I'd like to do just a little *minor* surgery"? No. A good physician would see that deadly mass and would say, "We have to get *all* of those cells out of there, along with any surrounding areas that might be contaminated." That's not extreme. That's essential. That's wise.

The prophets of Baal were an immoral, hostile, and anti-God malignancy in the land of Israel. Elijah knew he had to cut away all evidence of such a godless menace.

Nothing makes us more uncertain and insecure than not being sure we are in the will of God. And nothing is more encouraging than knowing for sure that we are. Then, no matter what the circumstances, no matter what happens, we can stand fast.

We can be out of a job but know that we are in the will of God. We can face a threatening situation but know that we are in the will of God. We can have the odds stacked against us but know that we are in the will of God. Nothing intimidates those who know that what they believe is based on what God has said. The equation is never eight hundred fifty against one. It is eight hundred fifty against one plus God.

When we know we're in the will of God, we're invincible.

Never once was Elijah intimidated. In this passage, Elijah spoke eight times, and every time he *commanded*. Yes, every time. He didn't shift, he didn't stutter, he didn't suggest; he leveled a command. He wasn't on the defense; he was on the offense. He knew where he stood. The word to describe that? Invincible.

# LIVING EXPECTANTLY

*Read 1 Kings 18:41—46*

*E*lijah was expectant. "And it came about at the seventh time, that he said, 'Behold, a cloud as small as a man's hand is coming up from the sea.'" All that Elijah had to go on was a tiny cloud, no bigger than a man's hand, in the midst of that vast expanse of sea and sky. But that was enough! He had such faith in God's promise that he acted upon what he expected to happen.

And he said, "Go up, say to Ahab, 'Prepare your chariot and go down, so that the heavy shower does not stop you'" (1 Kings 18:44b).

All Elijah saw was a tiny cloud, but he said, in effect, "Ahab, put the rain tires on your chariot. The deluge is coming!" The human eye saw only a little cloud, but the eye of faith saw the promise of God. Ahab would have shrugged, "So, what's the big deal?" But Elijah shouted within himself, "Finally, God is keeping His word!"

Do you live expectantly? Do the little things excite you? Do you imagine the improbable and expect the impossible? Life is full and running over with opportunities to see God's hand in little things. Only the most sensitive of His servants see them, smile, and live on tiptoe.

Children can teach us a lot about this kind of expectancy. Did you ever listen to a child pray? Their faith knows no bounds. And who are the least surprised people when God answers prayer? The children.

As we get older we grow too sophisticated for that. We use phrases like, "Let's be realistic about this." We lose that expectancy, that urgency of hope, that delightful, childlike, wide-eyed joy of faith that keeps us full of anticipation and excitement. May God deliver us from a grim, stoic, stale shrug of the shoulders! "Look, I haven't changed," He says. "I still delight in doing impossible things. I love to surprise you!"

Elijah's God was the God who kept His promises. He was the God of impossible things. So, in childlike faith, Elijah said to Ahab, "Get ready. The rain's coming. I know, because there's a tiny little cloud out there that's getting ready to unload God's abundance."

# THE BIG LEAGUES

### ✤ *Read 1 Kings 18:41–46* ❧

*T*he fervent prayer of a righteous man can accomplish much. "Elijah was a man with a nature like ours, and he prayed earnestly that it might not rain; and it did not rain on the earth for three years and six months. And he prayed again, and the sky poured rain, and the earth produced its fruit" (James 5:16b–18).

We read about Elijah and we say, "Wow, he's in the big leagues. He's a spiritual giant. I'm a pygmy in comparison to him. He's in another world entirely." Not true. Look again.

James doesn't say, "Elijah was a mighty prophet of God." He doesn't say, "Elijah was a powerful worker of miracles." He doesn't say, "Elijah was a model no man can match."

James says, "Elijah was a man with a nature like ours."

That means he was flesh and blood, muscle and bone. As we're about to see, he got really discouraged, and he had some huge disappointments. He had faults and failures and doubts. He was just a man, with a nature like yours and mine. He may have been a man of heroism and humility, but let's not forget his humanity. Elijah was our kind of man!

So, what kind of man was Elijah?

Well, he wasn't afraid to square off with the king of the land or take on the prophets of Baal. The guy had guts, no question. But he wasn't too powerful to pray or too confident to wait or too sophisticated to see rain in the tiny cloud or too proud to pull up his robe and run like a spotted ape down the mountain in the rain and mud, like the road-runner, thinking, *"C'mon, Ahab . . . catch me if you can!"*

No wonder Elijah is the kind of man we admire. Isn't it exciting to know we serve the same God he served? Isn't it thrilling to think we can trust the same God he trusted?

And what kind of God is that? He's the God who makes promises and keeps them.

# THE BLUES

### ✤ *Read 1 Kings 19:1–9* ✤

*E*lijah was an heroic prophet, without question. He was also a man of great humility, as we have seen. But let's keep in mind that he was just a man—a human being, subject to the human condition, as we all are. He suffered discouragement, despondency, and depression. On one occasion, he couldn't shake it.

It is not surprising that at this point in Elijah's life the great prophet hit bottom. For several years he had stood strong amidst and against almost insurmountable odds and circumstances. But now, after a great victory, he dropped into the throes of discouragement and total despair.

He's a man, he's human, just like us, remember. Since this is true, we shouldn't be shocked to read that he was afraid and arose and ran for his life and came to Beersheba, which belongs to Judah, and left his servant there.

But he himself went a day's journey into the wilderness, and came and sat down under a juniper tree; and he requested for himself that he might die, and said, "It is enough; now, O Lord, take my life, for I am not better than my fathers" (1 Kings 19:3–4).

I'm glad that this chapter has been included in Scripture. I'm glad that when God paints the portraits of His men and women, He paints them warts and all. He doesn't ignore their weaknesses or hide their failures.

Elijah *had* to get his eyes back on the Lord. That was absolutely essential. He had been used mightily, but it was *the Lord* who made him mighty. He stood strong against the enemy, but it was *the Lord* who had given him the strength.

Often we are more enamored with the gifts God gives us than with the Giver himself. When the Lord brings rest and refreshment, we become more grateful for the rest and refreshment than for the God who allows it. When God gives us a good friend, we become absorbed in that friendship and so preoccupied with the friend that we forget it was our gracious God who gave us the friend. How easy to focus on the wrong things.

# WHEN THE DARKNESS HITS

### *Read 1 Kings 19:1—9*

hy did Elijah fear Jezebel's intimidating threats? Why did he run away from his longstanding priority of serving God and hide in fear under the shadow of that solitary tree, deep in the wilderness?

First, *Elijah was not thinking realistically or clearly.* He was so shortsighted that he failed to consider the source of this threat. Think about it. The threat hadn't come from God; it had come from an unbelieving, carnal human being who lived her godless life light-years from God. If Elijah had been thinking clearly and realistically, he would have realized this.

Second, *Elijah separated himself from strengthening relationships.*

Third, *Elijah was caught in the backwash of a great victory.* Our most vulnerable moments usually come after a great victory, especially if that victory is a mountaintop experience with God. That's when we need to set up a defense against the enemy

Fourth, *Elijah was physically exhausted and emotionally spent.* For years Elijah had lived on the edge. He was a wanted, hunted man, considered by the king to be Public Enemy Number One. There is little doubt that Elijah had come to the end of his rope physically and, for sure, emotionally—all of which couldn't help but weaken him spiritually. I don't know if Elijah was disgusted, but I can tell you he was exhausted. You can hear it in his weary words: "It is enough; now, O Lord, take my life, for I am not better than my fathers."

Fifth, *Elijah got lost in self-pity.* Self-pity is a pathetic emotion. It will lie to you. Exaggerate. Drive you to tears. It will cultivate a victim mentality in your head. And in the worst-case scenario, it can bring you to the point of wishing to die, which is exactly where Elijah was.

We open the door for that pathetic liar, self-pity, when we establish an unrealistic standard and then can't live up to it. Self-pity mauls its way inside our minds like a beast and claws us to shreds.

# COME OUT

### ❧ *Read 1 Kings 19:10—18* ❧

God met his servant Elijah in his desperate moment of discouragement and despair. This is mercy at its best, beautifully portrayed by the Master Himself.

First, *God allowed Elijah a time of rest and refreshment.* No sermon. No rebuke. No blame. No shame. No lightning bolt from heaven, saying, "Look at you! Get up, you worthless ingrate! Get on your feet! Quickly, back on the job!"

Instead, God said, "Take it easy, my son. Relax. You haven't had a good meal in a long time." Then He catered a meal of freshly baked bread and cool, refreshing water. That must have brought back sweet memories of those simple days by the brook at Cherith. How gracious of God!

Fatigue can lead to all sorts of strange imaginations. It'll make you believe a lie. Elijah was believing a lie, partly because he was exhausted. So God gave him rest and refreshment, and afterward Elijah went on for forty days and nights in the strength of it.

Second, *God communicated wisely with Elijah.* God said, "Elijah! Get up and walk out of this cave. Man, it's dark in here. Go out there and stand in the light. Stand on the mountain before Me. That's the place to be encouraged. Forget Jezebel. I want you to get your eyes on Me. Come on, I'm here for you. I always will be."

God's presence was not in wind or earthquake or fire. His voice came in the gentle breeze. Those sweet zephyrs were like windswept, invisible magnets, drawing Elijah out of the cave. Do you see what God did? He drew Elijah out of the cave of self-pity and depression. And once Elijah was out of that cave, God asked him again, "What are you doing here, Elijah?"

God showed Elijah that he still had a job to do—that there was still a place for him. Disillusioned and exhausted though he was, he was still God's man and God's choice for "such a time as this" (Esther 4:14). And as far as this I'm-all-alone stuff went, "Elijah, let Me set the record straight," said God. "There are seven thousand faithful out there who have not bowed to Baal. You're really not alone. At any given moment, with the snap of My divine fingers, I can bring to the forefront a whole fresh battalion of My troops." What reassurance that brought.

# LOOK UP

### ✤ *Read 1 Kings 19:10–21* ❧

hanks to God's kind and gentle dealing, Elijah crawled out of the cave. "He departed from there." God graciously nurtured him through rest and refreshment, gave him some wise counsel, and made him feel significant again. Talk about compassion!

Then God allowed Elijah to pass his mantle to Elisha, his successor. But God did more than that, abundantly more. For Elisha "arose and followed Elijah and ministered to him." God not only gave Elijah a successor; He also raised up a close, personal friend—someone who loved Elijah and understood him well enough to help and encourage him.

God has not designed us to live like hermits in a cave. He has designed us to live in friendship, fellowship, and community with others. That's why the church, the body of Christ, is so very important, for it is there that we are drawn together in love and mutual encouragement. We're meant to be a part of one another's lives. Otherwise, we pull back, focusing on ourselves—thinking how hard we have it or how unfair others are.

Elijah reminds us to look up:

*Let's look up* after the Lord graciously delivers us from depression.

*Let's look up* when He allows us rest and refreshment following an exhausting schedule that has taken its toll on us.

*Let's look up* and thank Him when He gently and patiently speaks to us from His Word after we've climbed out of a pit of self-pity.

*Let's look up* and praise Him when He faithfully provides the companionship and affirmation of a friend who understands and encourages us.

*Let's look up* and acknowledge the Giver more than the gift.

Let's say, "Thank You, Lord, for telling us all about Elijah," who is an unforgettable example that there is nowhere to look but up.

# Two Solemn Reminders

### ✤ *Read 1 Kings 21:1–29* ✤

*A*fter recording these dire predictions, spoken by the Lord through Elijah, the writer of 1 Kings gives this commentary on the lives of Ahab and Jezebel: "Surely there was no one like Ahab who sold himself to do evil in the sight of the LORD, because Jezebel his wife incited him" (1 Kings 21:25). What a partnership! They were partners in unparalleled evil, until God finally said, "That's enough."

Here are two sobering and solemn reminders for us to consider:

First, *there is an end to God's patience*. No one knows it. God's wheels of justice grind slowly but exceedingly fine. God, in gracious patience and mercy, he waits for us to hear His voice and obey. People hear the Gospel of salvation and do not respond. Yet God waits. Some claim His name, but live in a way that says otherwise. Still God waits.

God's patience sometimes even frustrates us, particularly when evil persists, and He doesn't step in and stop it. At times like that, it's easy to convince ourselves that evil goes perpetually unnoticed.

You and I don't know at what point God reaches His divine limit and says, "That's enough! That's all! I will tolerate this no longer." But I know from this passage and others in Scripture, and I know from His dealings with Sodom and Gomorrah, Herod Agrippa, Ahab and Jezebel that God's patience can, and does, finally run out. Don't be fooled into thinking that His longsuffering is everlasting suffering.

Second, *God keeps His word*. No one stops it. Never forget what you've read in this section. Ahab and Jezebel were so powerful, so intimidating, so wicked. They thought they were in charge of everything—invincible. But when God stepped in, it was curtains for them. They were helpless to stop His judgment.

If you are a child of God, He will not cast you out of His family. But if you are stubbornly refusing to obey Him, continuing to walk your own way, He will bring severe discipline upon you. He loves you too much to ignore your actions.

God is good and just. And when His justice finally kicks in, there's no escaping it. If you think otherwise, you've bought into "a deadly opiate."

# CONSISTENT HEROISM

### ❧ *Read 2 Kings 1:1—18* ❧

*W*e cannot help but admire Elijah's consistent heroism. The man is alone, standing before the king and, surely, surrounded by armed warriors, faithful to Ahaziah, who could have finished him off with one thrust of a spear. Yet God's man never gave the risk a second thought. He was so convinced, so committed to his Lord, that the thought of self-protection never entered his mind.

The heroism of godly men and women is demonstrated in their willingness to face unpleasant conditions, even threatening circumstances, with remarkable calm. They act with firm resolve, even though it means incurring personal unpopularity. Nothing deters their passion to obey their God . . . regardless. *His* message is paramount. Period.

Few in the history of the church possessed this quality of passionate heroism in greater measure than Martin Luther. It's been asserted that he was, perhaps, as fearless a man as ever lived. "You can expect from me everything save fear or recantation. I shall not flee, much less recant," said Luther on his momentous journey to Worms.

Luther's friends were concerned for his safety. Focusing on the grave dangers ahead, they sought to dissuade him. But the mere thought of not going disgusted him. "Not go to Worms!" he said. "I shall go to Worms though there were as many devils as tiles on the roofs."

On a later occasion, while awaiting an audience before all the prelates of the church, Luther was asked if he were now afraid. "Afraid? Greater than the pope and all his cardinals, I fear most that great pope, *self*."

Elijah rose above his enemies, his king, even himself as he heroically stood his ground, delivered God's message, and refused to dull its edge. May his tribe increase in this day of shallow, feel-good theology, so popular among superficial, backslapping ministries.

And may you find the spirit of heroism in your own heart.

# STRAIGHT TALK

### ❧ *Read 2 Kings 1:1–18* ❧

*T*oday, countless people seek to know the future. Newspapers and magazines carry horoscope columns. Television networks advertise psychic hotlines. Bus stop benches boast ads for palm readers. Magazine racks beside grocery store check-out counters offer paperback books on astrology, numerology, and other occult subjects.

To many, this hype may sound like sheer silliness; it may appear to be nothing more than harmless fun. After all, what's so bad about reading your daily horoscope? But listen up—this is enemy territory! It is anything but silliness or harmless fun. Like the wood and stone idols of Ekron, these present-day seers are substitutes for putting our trust in the living God.

*God is displeased with any occult involvement.* No matter what the motive, no matter how great the need, dabbling with the occult is sin. God's Word is crystal clear on this subject. Far back in the book of Leviticus, God gives His people this direct command: "Do not turn to mediums or spiritists; do not seek them out to be defiled by them. I am the LORD your God" (Leviticus 19:31).

Beyond that, *God is dishonored by any specific pursuit of the future that does not find its source in His Word.* I realize that most people who begin dabbling in astrology, fortune-telling, or Ouija boards don't take it all that seriously. Astrology, for example, has a captivating appeal. Most do it for fun or out of curiosity. But these simple, harmless-looking games begin a process that many cannot handle; and they open doors that should remain closed. Then it's only a matter of time before the dark powers of demonic forces suck them in, and they find themselves ensnared.

But let me reassure you, *God is delighted when we trust Him only.* The Lord strengthens those who put their trust in Him. If we are not grounded in the Word of God and seeking Him daily as our source of strength and knowledge for the future, we, too, can easily fall prey to the lure of the occult.

Learn a lasting lesson from Elijah. As you stand strong for the truth, watch out for the enemy. He not only plays dirty; he plays for keeps. And he's playing for your soul.

# TIMES OF SEARCHING

### ✨ *Read 2 Kings 2:1–14* ✨

Self-denial does not come naturally. It is a learned virtue (often hard-learned), encouraged by few and modeled by even fewer, especially among those who are what we've come to know as Type A personalities. Prophets are notorious for exhibiting this temperament, which makes Elijah all the more remarkable. Without hedging in heroism, he was as soft clay in his Master's hands. As we saw earlier, he did his best work "under the shadow of the Almighty." His was a life of power, because he had come to the place where he welcomed the death of his own desires, even if it meant the greatest display of God's glory.

The place of beginning, the place of the prayer, the place of battle, the place of death. We, too, have such places in our lives.

First, there's a place of beginning. That's home base—the very beginning of our Christian experience when we are born anew. That's our place of new beginning. At our own Gilgal, we become brand new.

For some of us, that place of beginning, that home base, is far in the past. Search your memory. Can you remember when you took your first few baby steps? You tottered a little, and those who loved and mentored you helped steady you on your feet. And you learned the basics of life: how to get into the Word; how to pray; how to have time with God; how to share your faith.

And then comes the place of prayer. Remember? You first began to learn what it was to sacrifice, to surrender things dear and precious to you. For some it was a miscarriage or the loss of a child. For some it was the loss of a husband or wife. Perhaps for you it was the loss of a job, your own business, or a lifelong dream never to be realized. Coming all alone to your own Bethel, you learned to pray.

God did a real work in your life as He carried you from that place of communion to the next stage He planned for you. And because you'd learned the value of prayer, you built your altar, and you learned even more at His feet. Search back in time. Remember?

Self-denial is hard to learn, but it's worth the effort.

# MANTLE OF POWER

### ✣ *Read 2 Kings 2:12–15* ✣

*E*lijah's no-death contract suddenly went into effect. Elijah, prophet of power—gone. Elisha, prophet of double power—here, ready, and about to be used greatly by his God.

When a man or woman of God dies, nothing of God dies. We tend to forget that. We get so caught up in the lives of certain individuals that we begin to think we cannot do without them. What limited thinking! When even a mighty servant is gone, God has seven thousand who have never bowed the knee to Baal. He has them ready, waiting in the wings. Classic case in point: Elisha. God always has a back-up plan.

Think about it. Through the ages He has had His men and women in every era to carry on His work. Never once has God been frustrated, wondering, *What will My people do now that he's gone? Now that she's no longer with them?* Our Creator-God is omnipotent. He is never caught shorthanded.

Elisha may have been momentarily surprised and stunned, but that didn't last long. Remembering Elijah's words, he reached down and picked up the prophet's cloak. Claiming the power that now was his, he crossed back over the Jordan and began his own prophetic ministry. God's plan never missed a beat. Exit Elijah. Enter Elisha.

We can't help but wonder if, in the years to come, Elisha didn't stop and study that old mantle, calling to mind those great days of the past when his mentor and friend stood alone, representing God's presence and proclaiming God's message. The memory of the older Elijah—a man of heroism and humility—served to strengthen the younger Elisha, whom God destined to serve in even greater ways.

There are times, to this day, when I call to mind my granddaddy, L. O. Lundy. His wise words of counsel still linger. His life of quiet, deep character sometimes seems so close to me I can almost feel his warm breath on the back of my neck. Yes, to this day I miss him, but the mantle of his memory spurs me on to greater heights and deeper devotion.

The good news is this: I will one day see him. And we, together, will worship the same Lord face to face, " . . . and thus we shall always be with the Lord."

Whose mantle have you received? And what will you do with its inherited influence?

# REDIRECTING OUR GAZE

### ✤ *Read 2 Kings 2:12—15; Matthew 17:1—13* ✤

The Christian's greatest goal is to be like Christ. We want to emulate His exemplary life, model His method of teaching, resist temptation as He resisted it, handle conflicts as He did, focus on the mission God calls us to accomplish as Christ focused on His. And certainly it is our desire to commune with the Father as the Son did throughout His ministry and suffering. No greater compliment can be given than this one: "When I am with that person, it's as if I'm in the presence of Jesus Himself."

Throughout this study of Elijah, I have often thought of how closely the great prophet's life resembled the Messiah, who was yet to come: the way he spent time alone; the courage he showed as he stood in the presence of his enemy and delivered God's message; the power he exhibited when it took a miracle to convince his audience that he was a man with a message from God—the one true God; the compassion he demonstrated when he cared about the widow's grief and brought her son back to life; even the anguish he felt in his own Gethsemane as he wrestled in his soul. And finally, how much like Christ was his departure. As others stood staring, he was taken up to heaven out of their sight.

Is it any surprise, then, that when our Savior asked His disciples, "Who do people say that the Son of Man is?" the answer from some was, "Elijah." Why, of course! Small wonder, for in many ways their lives paralleled. And when the two men appeared before Jesus and three of His disciples on the Mount of Transfiguration, one was Moses, and the other was none other than Elijah (Matthew 17:3).

Elijah's heroic and humble life urges us to be like Christ—to lift our eyes from the grit and grind of today's woes and to turn our attention to the glory and hope of another land. Immanuel's land! And in that frame of mind, we'll redirect our gaze from who gets the glory to who gives the grace. Then, while fully focused on Him—our King of grace, the gentle Lamb of God—the deepest longings of our souls will be satisfied.

If you compare your life to Christ, how long would your list be of matching characteristics?

*Esther: A Woman of Strength & Dignity*

# GOD AT WORK

### ❦ *Read Esther 1:1–22* ❧

*T*emucan wanted an edict prohibiting Queen Vashti from ever entering King Xerxes' presence again written into the law of the Medes and the Persians—the law which can never be changed. In that way, his suggestion would affect far more than Vashti; it would have a direct effect on everyone's marriage. But if it was an attempt to get the women of Persia to have greater respect for their husbands, it was a strange way to make that happen!

What you have to keep in mind is that Esther doesn't have the foggiest idea that any of this is going on; she knows nothing of the events transpiring in the royal palace. She also knows nothing yet about this "royal edict," which will set events in motion that will totally change her own life. Esther is going about her no-big-deal business, living her everyday life, greeting the sunrise of each ordinary morning, carrying out her day-to-day responsibilities. Is she in for a surprise!

This is the wonder of God's sovereignty. Working behind the scenes, He is moving and pushing and rearranging events and changing minds until He brings out of even the most carnal and secular of settings a decision that will set His perfect plan in place. We see that here, and we'll see it throughout the story of Esther.

Don't fall into the trap of thinking that God is asleep when it comes to nations, or that He is out of touch when it comes to carnal banquets, or that He sits in heaven wringing His hands when it comes to godless rulers (even today) who make unfair, rash, or stupid decisions. Mark it down in permanent ink: God is *always* at work. But His ways are so different from ours, we quickly jump to fallacious conclusions and either react rashly or get paralyzed in panic.

Know this: God holds the future in His omnipotent hands. So you can rest assured.

# NOT FORGOTTEN

*❧ Read Esther 2:1–7 ❧*

G od's presence is not as intriguing as His absence. His voice is not as eloquent as His silence. Who of us has not longed for a word from God, searched for a glimpse of His power, or yearned for the reassurance of His presence, only to feel that He seems absent for the moment? Distant. Preoccupied. Maybe even unconcerned. Yet later, we realize how very present He was all along.

Though God may at times seem distant, and though He is invisible to us, He is always invincible. This is the main lesson of the book of Esther. Though absent by name from the pages of this particular book of Jewish history, God is present in every scene and in the movement of every event, until He ultimately and finally brings everything to a marvelous climax as He proves Himself Lord of His people, the Jews.

Mordecai was a descendant of one of those exiled Jews. He was a godly man, and his most significant role was his relationship to Esther.

Esther, which is this young woman's Persian name, means "star." This seems appropriate, since she is truly the star of the show, the heroine of the story. The immortal, invisible, all-wise hand of God is working behind the scenes, hidden from human eyes. Only such a gracious and all-knowing Being would have His hand on some forgotten orphan, a little girl who had lost her mother and father and was left to be raised by her cousin Mordecai.

There is a beautiful message here for anyone who has ever experienced brokenness, for anyone who has ever been crushed by life, for anyone who has ever felt that his past is so discolored, so disjointed, so fractured that there is no way in the world God can make reason and meaning out of it. We are going to learn some unforgettable lessons from Esther. Here was a little girl who must have cried her heart out at the death of her parents, bereft and orphaned, yet who, years later, would become key to the very survival of her people, the Jews. God and God *alone* can do such things—He, in fact, does do such things, working silently and invisibly behind the events of history.

And he is working quietly behind the scenes of your life too.

# MUNDANE AND MIRACULOUS

*Read Esther 2:1–7*

oven through the tapestry of this wonderful story we find at least three time-less lessons thus far. The first has to do with God's plan. The second has to do with God's purposes. And the third has to do with God's people.

First, *God's plans are not hindered when the events of this world are carnal or secular.* God is at work. He's moving. He's touching lives. He's shaping kingdoms. He's never surprised by what humanity may do. Just because actions or motives happen to be secular or carnal or unfair, it doesn't mean He's not present. Those involved may not be glorifying Him, but never doubt it, He's present. He's at work.

Second, *God's purposes are not frustrated by moral or marital failures.* How do I know that? Because He is a God who applies grace to the long view of life. Wrong grieves Him, and serious consequences follow, but no amount of wrong frustrates His sovereign purposes! He is a God of *great* grace.

Third, *God's people are not excluded from high places because of handicap or hardship.* Esther was a Jew exiled in a foreign land. She was an orphan. She was light-years removed from Persian nobility. Yet none of that kept God from exalting her to the position in which He wanted her.

God's hand is not so short that it cannot save, nor is His ear so heavy that He cannot hear. Whether you see Him or not, He is at work in your life this very moment. God specializes in turning the mundane into the meaningful. God not only moves in unusual ways, He also moves on uneventful days. He is just as involved in the mundane as He is in the miraculous.

He is a sovereign God at work amid the vast scenes of state and empires in our world. And we, even in the midst of our usual days, must remain pure and committed to the things of God and His work in our lives, even as we remain sensitive to His hand moving in carnal, secular, even drunken places. Only then can we bring to our broken world the hope it so desperately needs.

# STRENGTH AND DIGNITY

### ❧ *Read Esther 2:8—11* ❧

*E*sther exhibited a *grace-filled charm and elegance*. In this verse, the literal translation of the original language says, "She lifted up grace before his face." Isn't that a beautiful expression? Though she was brought to the harem and participated in these things reluctantly, Esther did not display a sour attitude. I'm convinced she sensed God's hand in her situation. Why else would she have been there? Finding herself unable to say no, Esther modeled grace before the face of the king's influential servant, Hegai. What a difference between Esther and all the other women around her. Her inner qualities could not be ignored. They, in fact, captured the attention of the king's servant.

Esther exhibited *an unusual restraint and control*. She told no one she was Jewish. Why? Because that is what Mordecai instructed her to do. Not even the head-spinning, Himalayan heights of the harem could tempt her to break her covenant with Mordecai.

God has given women an air of mystery. This is something, quite candidly, men don't have. We are a pretty predictable bunch. Yet how often I have heard a man say, "I just don't know how to figure her out. I just don't understand." For example, a woman will say, "What I need is a good cry." My friend, in all of my life I have never experienced a *good cry*. My wife knows them. Other women in our family know them. But it's a mystery to men. I'm honest, I've never been able to figure out how you can feel good after crying.

There is an unexplainable air of mystery about a woman, an unpredictability that men find intriguing. Esther's ability to restrain herself only heightens the mystery—especially her verbal restraint. She knew much more than she told. She could keep a secret.

Verbal restraint is fast becoming a forgotten virtue. Thanks to tell-all tabloids and hide-nothing television talk shows, nothing is restrained. When was the last time anyone in the media blushed? Yet restraint and control always work in your favor. Learn to keep confidences. Come to be known for keeping secrets! It's part of having character marked by strength and dignity.

Then, perhaps, you too can lift up grace before His face.

# SERVANT-HEARTED LEADERS

*Read Esther 2:10–20*

*E*sther sustained a continually teachable spirit. Mordecai had instructed her that she should not make them known. Esther had not yet made known her kindred or her people, even as Mordecai had commanded her, for Esther did what Mordecai told her as she had done when under his care. (Esther 2:10, 20)

Even becoming a finalist in this frenzied competition, or later, becoming queen, didn't cause Esther to flaunt her independence and strut her stuff. Not this lady! This lovely, dignified, wise woman was still willing to listen and learn.

She remains a sterling example for women today. Some of you are wonderfully gifted teachers. You have the ability to stand before a group and to open the Scriptures or some other area of expertise and hold an audience in rapt attention with your insight and creativity. Others of you have distinguished yourself in public service. You have played prestigious roles and offices in the community. You may be well-traveled and rather confidently move in exclusive circles with powerful men and women whom you know on a first-name basis. There is nothing wrong with any of that. But let me ask, has that changed your teachability? Do you now see yourself as the consummate authority? Or has it simply made you aware of how vast your ignorance really is? I hope it is the latter.

Someone has said, "Education is going from an unconscious to conscious awareness of one's ignorance." I agree. No one has a corner on wisdom. All the name-dropping in the world doesn't heighten the significance of your character. If anything, it reduces it. Our acute need is to cultivate a willingness to learn and to remain teachable. Learning from your children. Learning from your friends. Learning even from our enemies. How beautiful it is to find a servant-hearted, teachable spirit among those who occupy high-profile positions of authority.

Are you, like Esther, still willing to listen and learn?

# MODESTY AND AUTHENTICITY

### ⚜ *Read Esther 2:12—14* ⚜

*E*sther exhibited *an unselfish modesty and authenticity.* Think of it: no job, no respon-sibility, no cooking, no clean-up, no washing, no ironing, no errands, no budget-watching, no holding back in any area. Imagine! Pampered and indulged, in this self-centered harem of Persia, all of the emphasis rests upon her becoming a woman of greater physical beauty. Jewelry, clothing, perfumes, cosmetics, whatever she wishes, from coiffure to pedicure, are hers. The only thing on everyone's mind is to win this contest—to please the king and gain his favor.

Remember, at this time Esther cannot be more than twenty years old or so, and she could have been even younger. This is a chance of a lifetime for her to have whatever she wishes. Instead, she remains true to what she has been taught and abides by the counsel of Mordecai, believing that he knows what's best for her. She does not succumb to the tempta-tion around her—the superficiality, the selfishness, the seduction, the self-centeredness. She displays an unselfish modesty, an authenticity, amid unparalleled extravagance.

As ironic as that may sound, I think that most Christian women do not use cosmetics to appear false or become other than who they are. The women we admire use cosmetics to subtly enhance the natural beauty that is already there. I'm sure that was true of Esther.

Frankly, I'm convinced that Esther went in to the king without fear because she had no driving ambition to be queen. Her life didn't revolve around her physical appearance or making a king happy. She was there for one reason: because she knew that the hand of God was on her life, and through circumstances and Mordecai's wisdom, she had been brought to this place for a reason. To use one of my favorite expressions, she had her stuff together. She knew where she was coming from. She knew who she was. She knew what she believed. And she knew that God's hand was on her life. If it was His pleasure that she be here, if it was part of His plan, then she would willingly accept it. If not, she would willingly relin-quish it. She was modest about her own person, and she was authentic.

Can you say the same thing about yourself? After all, God's hand is on your life too.

# A Charming and Graceful Spirit

*Read Esther 2:15–17*

*E*sther modeled a kind winsomeness, regardless of her surroundings.

And Esther found favor in the eyes of all who saw her. So Esther was taken to King Ahasuerus to his royal palace in the tenth month which is the month Tebeth, in the seventh year of his reign. And the king loved Esther more than all the women, and she found favor and kindness with him more than all the virgins, so that he set the royal crown on her head and made her queen instead of Vashti. (Esther 2:15, 16–17)

Clearly, Esther had something about her that caused everyone to "favor" her, from the king to the women in the harem who were competing against her for his attention and affections. I think she must have had a winsomeness about her. Webster says winsomeness is "being pleasant, delightful, attractive in a sweet, engaging way." A person who is winsome draws you to him or to her. We are intrigued by that person's charming and gracious spirit.

In the past, I have shared the traits of Esther with my own beloved daughters, hoping that they will not only think about them but cultivate them. And it's with the same sense of care that I share these things with you, because I personally believe they are more needed than ever in our environment of insecurity and sensuality.

# ASK AND TRUST

### *Read Esther 2:12—18*

God does not mock us with the things He includes in His Word. He isn't in the business of making His people squirm under some unrealistic expectation that they can never attain—something that is totally unique to one person but remains for everyone else a frustrating and unreachable challenge. But I must quickly add, you cannot become these things by taking your cues from the world. That only brings defeat and frustration. You, as an individual, have your own pressures, your own difficulties, your own unique circumstances, but God offers ways to handle them and become His special person. The question is how?

First, *ask God.* Ask him to cultivate character within you. Ask Him to give you a discontent for the superficial and a deeper desire for the spiritual. Make yourself available to His strength, His reproofs. Seek His counsel for the things you lack. Allow him to help you set reasonable goals. Record them in your journal so you will have a written account of your prayer to Him.

Ask God to give you that kind of authenticity. To place more emphasis on what's happening deep within your heart and less emphasis on the externals, the superficial, the temporary.

Second, *trust God.* Trust Him to control the circumstances around you—those very circumstances that you perhaps are using as an excuse for not being the woman you want to be. Don't wait for your circumstances to be perfect. Remember Esther. At the height of competition, surrounded by sensual, greedy, superficial women, Esther stood alone. And, amazingly, God gave her favor in others' eyes!

Ask God. Trust God. We are completely dependent on Him for eternal life, for forgiveness, for character, for security. His light in our lives gives us a growing disgust for things that merely satisfy the flesh. It shows us the importance of character, the incredible change that can come by standing alone on the things of God. He alone can give us grace and winsomeness and keep us from becoming squint-eyed, cranky Christians. It is His working in our lives that uses us even in the harems of life to make a difference and to model a charm and a beauty, a dignity and an elegance that cannot help but cause people's attention to be drawn to Him and His power. Ask. Trust.

# MAKE A DIFFERENCE

### ❧ *Read Esther 2:19–3:15* ❧

*O*nly one missionary invests his whole life in a remote area, and an entire tribe is ultimately evangelized. Only one statesman stands for right, and a country is saved. Only one strong-willed and determined citizen says, "I stand against this evil," and a community ramps-up morally and changes its direction.

And only one woman decided it was worth the risk to break with protocol and speak her mind, and a nation was preserved.

The Jews have been threatened with extermination. Wicked Haman has influenced King Ahasuerus with his promises: "Because of this plan I have set up, it is possible for me to pour money into your treasuries and for us to rid the land of these people who will not bow down and worship you as the king." Though it pandered to the king's pride, that plan had the makings of the worse kind of holocaust. "The Jews will no longer be in our land. We'll be rid of these people."

In case you wonder what impact it had on the community, return to the last phrase in chapter 3: "the city of Susa was in confusion." That had to be a major understatement!

While Haman and Ahasuerus sat over their drinks in the palace, the general public wandered in bewilderment and confusion, especially the Jews, not unlike those in the ghetto at Warsaw and other European scenes of horror in the late '30s and early '40s. "What's going on here?" "Why have those in authority ordered this?" "How much worse can things get?"

What terror this struck in their hearts, what fear in their minds! "How can we continue?" "How can we fight this?" This was the law of the Medes and the Persians. When an edict was issued in that era, it was final. Nobody could change this plan, even the king, but certainly no Jew. Helplessness quickly eroded into hopelessness.

Yet, in the midst of all this, God was not sleeping. In His sovereign plan, He determined that one person would make the difference. One individual would stand in the gap. Her name is Esther.

# WATCH YOUR WORDS

*Read Esther 4:1—8*

ave you noticed how suffering brings people together? Have you watched how people join forces to respond to disasters? Hardship forces us to grab hands with one another and pull up closer together. Suffering never ruined a nation! Hardship doesn't fracture families. Affluence does! But not suffering. Not hardship. It pushes everybody to the same level with the same goal: *survival*.

And so we're not surprised to find the Jews weeping and wailing and fasting together.

Mordecai not only informs Esther, through her servant, of all that has happened, even down to the specifics regarding the exact amount of money in the deal; he also sends along official evidence—a copy of the text of the edict. "Have your queen read this," he says. "This was signed with the king's signet ring." He didn't lose control of his emotions; he didn't exaggerate. He was careful with the information he communicated.

Why do I make such a point of this? Because we live in a day of hearsay, when few people pass along information that is precise and reliable. Do you? Are you careful about what you say? Do you have the facts? Do you offer proof that the information you are conveying is correct? While there are occasions when it's appropriate to pass along needed and serious information to the right sources, there's a growing preoccupation with rumor and slander. Half truths and innuendos become juicy morsels in the mouths of unreliable gossips. There is no way to measure the number of people who have been hurt by rumor, exaggeration, and hearsay. Perhaps you have suffered this yourself.

Be careful what you say. Be careful how you say it. Be careful that you send the right message, that you send it to the right person, and that you do so with the right motive.

# Cultivating Character

### ❧ *Read Esther 4:9–14* ❧

N ow, before you frown and entertain thoughts of self-righteousness, thinking that you would never have responded like that, remember, you're sur-rounded by friends in a safe and unthreatened environment where there are no armed soldiers outside and governmental protocol to obey. Furthermore, chances are good you don't live under a cloud because of the race into which you were born, and there's no king sitting on a throne at whose whim you live or die. It's easy to be brave when we're protected and secure, when we have nothing to risk.

If Esther obeyed Mordecai, she stood to risk everything, including her life. Although the king was her husband, she couldn't just stroll into his office and casually unload what was on her mind. Things didn't work like that in ancient Persia. He had to send for her. And at that time, he hadn't sent for her for a month. If she went to him without being summoned, he could have her put to death. On top of all that, she was Jewish. Who knows how that Gentile monarch would respond when he found that out?

It was a huge dilemma. But Mordecai knew Esther. He had taken care of her. He had trained her. He knew how far he could push. Most of all, he knew her character. He knew the stuff of which she was made.

Encouraging the cultivation of character is exactly what wise parents do, nudging, urg-ing their children toward maturity. As a parent, you have occasions in your life, brief vignettes, little windows of time, where you can step forward and help your children to understand the value of being brave. As they grow up and those hands-on occasions change to a more distant relationship, you must call upon your children to stand for what they believe, even if they must stand alone—and then trust them to do it without you alongside.

Mordecai faces that moment. So when Hathach comes to him with Esther's answer, Mordecai tightens the sash around his sackcloth and says the hard thing. He appeals to her character.

In that same situation, what do you think *you* would have said to the queen?

# I'm Available

### ✣ *Read Esther 2:19—4:14* ✣

*L*et's look at Haman. This guy hates Mordecai not just because he's a Jew, but because Mordecai will not bow down to him. So Haman talks the king into a game plan. "If you follow my rules, I will pour money into your treasury. All I ask is that you give me the right to rid the land of all these Jews." And so King Ahasuerus, believing Haman and ignoring the brutal genocide he is plotting, passes it off with a wave of his hand, "Go ahead, do whatever you need to do."

When Mordecai gets word of what Haman is planning, he makes a crucial but dangerous decision. He must tell his adopted daughter, Esther; she must know about Haman's evil plan. Because, you see, by now Esther had become queen, but nobody knew she was a Jew. When she was chosen as the king's consort, Mordecai had advised her not to tell anybody about her ethnic origins. Obediently, she hadn't (Esther 2:10).

Mordecai entertained no doubt that the Jews would survive this holocaust. He was convinced that God would not let His people be wiped from the face of the earth. He and Esther might be killed, but ultimately someone would deliver the Jews. However, what if God's plan was already in process? What if the means to that deliverance had already been put in place by the hand of God? What if it included Esther's getting involved? She was, after all, the queen.

"Esther, listen!" says Mordecai. "God's hand was on my getting the message from Haman that the Jews will be killed. And God's hand was on your being appointed queen. Perhaps you were put into this position just for this altogether unique hour in our history. Don't be silent. This is your greatest hour. *Speak!* Plead with the king. Stop this plot against our people!"

I've heard some people claim that they can't believe in the sovereignty of God because doing so makes you passive. Frankly, I don't see it. Not if it stays balanced *and* biblically oriented. If anything, the sovereignty of God makes me active. It drives me before Him as I plead, "Lord, involve me in the process, if it pleases You. Activate me in Your action plan. I'm available. Speak through me. Use me."

# RISK IT!

### *Read Esther 4:12–14*

*hat does it matter if I get involved or not?* It matters greatly—it matters to your character! Yes, it's true that God has other ways to accomplish His objectives. He has other people He can use. He isn't frustrated or restrained because you and I may be indifferent. But when that happens, we are the losers. When we have been called "for such a time as this," how tragic it is if we are don't stand up in that hour.

There will be no celestial shout urging you to take a stand. Nor will a flash of lightning awaken you in the midst of your slumber. It doesn't work like that, so don't sit around waiting passively. Numerous needs and issues surround us. They summon us to stand up and be counted. While we will not be able to respond to all of them, the solution is not to respond to *none* of them! So let me ask you: What are you doing to stand up, to stand alone, to answer the call of God in this hour? Allow me to spell out a few issues and needs worth considering.

Are you involved in helping dysfunctional families? How about those who are homeless and hungry? Or those who are addicted to drugs and/or alcohol? What do you do for the orphans and widows? In "such a time as this," what do you stand against and stand for? Do you take a stand against pornography? Do you support any part of the cause of the pro-life movement against abortion? Where do you stand as it relates to the absence of masculinity, the whole extreme feminist movement? What about the horror of sexual abuse that has become so rampant in our society? Or prejudice against other races or nationalities? What about the developmentally disabled? This is an urgent hour of need. Are you there, ready to be salt and light, in this hour?

*Not until you believe one person can make a difference will you be willing to take a risk.* Quit being so careful about protecting your own back. Stop worrying about what others will think. You don't answer to them. You answer to Him. He will help. He will give you wisdom and courage. You may be only one, but you are one. So, take a risk!

# THE CAUSE

*Read Esther 4:12—16*

*I*s that a great answer or what? Is this a great woman? She's had only a few moments to consider what Mordecai had told her, a brief slice of time to weigh his counsel. It was all she needed. She is determined to make a difference, no matter what the consequences to her personally: "If I perish, I perish. If a guard drives a sword through my body, I die doing the right thing." She has changed from fear to abandonment and faith, from hesitation to confidence and determination, from concern for her own safety to concern for her people's survival. She has reached her own personal hour of decision and has not been found wanting.

Do you recall when young David was asked by his father to leave the sheep and take some food and supplies to his brothers who were fighting the Philistines at the valley of Elah? When he got there, he found the giant Goliath roaming the battlefield, taunting and blaspheming the God of Israel. When he learns what is going on, he says, in effect, "Let's do something about it." And his older brother, Eliab, laughs and says sarcastic stuff like, "Oh, so you're going to be the big-time hero, huh? How are all those little woollies doing while you're out here on the battlefield with us?" Remember young David's answer? "Is there not a cause?" (1 Samuel 17:29 KJV). Shortly thereafter he whips out his slingshot and downs Goliath with one smooth stone.

"Of course there is a cause!" David implies, if not in words, at least in his actions: "What are you doing sitting around in your tents with your knees knocking? There is a giant out there who hates the cause of the living God! What are you men doing standing here? Our God will fight for me. And if I perish, I perish."

Esther realized the same thing. She realized there was an enemy out there, not only of her people, but more importantly, of the living God. And as soon as that realization seized her awareness, the softness of the palace became uncomfortable.

"Enough of the easy life," said Esther. "It's time to put my name on the line. I am Jewish, and I believe in the living God. I'm ready to stand alone for my people. And if I perish, I perish."

"Is there not a cause" in your heart and mind?

# I WILL STAND

### ✦ *Read Esther 4:12—16* ✦

*W*hen it comes to touching the heart, few things do it as well as a song or a story. We all know occasions where the right music combined with the right lyrics wooed us or someone we know back to God. Sometimes it is a song that our mother taught us, or some moving hymn we learned years ago in church. Nostalgia serves us best when it's a magnet, drawing our hearts back to God.

A story will do the same, softening the soil of our souls. When you have the right characters who carry out life's issues in a plot that is mixed with adventure, surprise, and some humor, along with purpose and an ultimate moral, there's something about that story that sweeps us into a right state of mind. Esther is just such a story. It has adventure and suspense mixed with courage and hope, plus a touch of humor and certainly a twist of surprise.

What a great film or play *Esther* would make. Can't you just hear the words of Mordecai ringing with passion as he says, "If you remain silent at this time, relief and deliverance will arise for the Jews from another place, and you and your father's house will perish. And who knows whether you have attained royalty for just such a time as this?"

And then, with incredible courage, Esther herself replies, "Go and assemble all the Jews who are found in Susa, and fast for me; do not eat or drink for three days, night or day. I and my maidens also will fast in the same way. And thus I will go to the king, which is not according to law; and if I perish, I perish."

I can hear the applause as the curtain closes on this act with this grand speech that prepares our leading lady to take her place in history.

It reminds me of something C. S. Lewis said about the importance of being loyal to a cause that is greater than ourselves. He likened that quality to a person's chest. "What we need are people with *chests*." The old American word for this is "guts." We need people with guts who will say, "I will stand for this, and if I must die for it, then I die."

Will you be one of those people?

# A Silent Interlude

### ❧ *Read Esther 4:12—17* ❧

*B*etween chapters four and five of this ancient book of Esther, there's a break in time. It's a space of suspense when we don't know what is happening. Nothing is recorded for us to read. At the end of chapter four, we left Esther just as she had sent word to Mordecai that she was going to enter the king's presence uninvited, which could mean her instant death. Then there is a grand pause, and we pick up the story again in chapter five, three days later, when Esther is preparing to walk into the presence of the king, not knowing what the future holds. She literally breaks the law of the land by voluntarily interrupting the king.

This space represents a silent yet powerful interlude during which Esther draws on the source of her strength. How easy it is for us to forget that source. How easy for us to believe that she was born with a Mother Teresa conscience and a Joan of Arc courage. Yet just as no one is born prejudiced, so no one is born courageous.

Allow me a moment to pause here and ask you a couple of very personal questions. Do you teach your children to stand up for what they believe? Are you teaching your grandchildren how to be people of character, regardless? That's the way they will learn it. Let me probe one question deeper. Are you modeling authentic character? That leaves the message permanently etched in their minds.

You see, Esther didn't come onto this earth with a sensitive conscience and a courageous heart. She learned it from her cousin, who became her mentor and adoptive father, Mordecai. He knew how far he could stretch her with his challenge. And she rose to the challenge and said, "I'll do exactly as you have taught me to do."

Proverbs 22:6 says, "Train a child in the way he should go, and when he is old he will not turn from it" (NIV).

# RESULTS OF WAITING

*Read Esther 4:12–17; Isaiah 40:31*

Now, even though what happened in the three days between chapters 4 and 5 is not recorded, don't think for a moment that God is whiling away His time, busy with other things. Remember, He may be invisible, but He is at work. That's the beauty of His invisibility. He can be moving in a thousand places at the same time, working in circumstances that are beyond our control. During a waiting period, God is not only working in our hearts, He's working in others' hearts. And all the while He is giving added strength. Remember Isaiah's words about waiting?

> Yet those who wait for the LORD
> Will gain new strength;
> They will mount up with wings like eagles,
> They will run and not get tired,
> They will walk and not become weary. (Isaiah 40:31)

Even though the prophet's pen put these words on the sacred page centuries ago, that verse of Scripture is as pertinent and relevant as what you read in the paper this morning—and far more trustworthy. From this verse we learn that four things happen when we wait.

First, *we gain new strength*. We may feel weak, even intimidated, when we turn to our Lord. While waiting, amazingly we exchange our weakness for His strength.

Second, *we get a better perspective*. It says we "will mount up with wings like eagles." Eagles can spot fish in a lake several miles away on a clear day. By soaring like eagles while waiting, we gain perspective on our situation.

Third, *we store up extra energy*. "We will run and not get tired." Notice, it's future tense. When we do encounter the thing we have been dreading, we will encounter it with new strength—extra energy will be ours to use.

Fourth, *we will deepen our determination to persevere*. We "will walk and not become weary." The Lord whispers reassurance to us. He puts steel in our bones, so to speak. We begin to feel increasingly more invincible.

We'll gain new strength. We'll get better perspective. We'll store up extra energy. We'll deepen our determination to persevere. All that happens when we . . . wait.

# WAIT . . . AND LISTEN

### ✦ *Read Esther 4:12–17; Isaiah 41:10,13* ✦

*D*uring the three days of waiting, there is a "white space" when nothing is happening—at least nothing visible. You could easily tell yourself at the time, "I'm waiting in vain. Nothing's going to change." That's what the adversary wants you to think: "Waiting's a waste." Don't you believe it! When the enemy's message roams into your mind, you need to kick it out. Reject it. Look at another verse in Isaiah, just a few verses after the "eagle" verse.

Do not fear, for I am with you;
Do not anxiously look about you, for I am your God.
I will strengthen you, surely I will help you,
Surely I will uphold you with My righteous right hand.

For I am the LORD your God, who upholds your right hand,
Who says to you, "Do not fear, I will help you." (Isaiah 41:10,13)

It's those kinds of thoughts that surely strengthened Esther while she was waiting, praying, and fasting for those three days. Mordecai did the same, as Esther had commanded. But now their roles were reversed. He was no longer in charge; she was. Or, better still, the Lord was. And as the Lord gripped her heart, she became unafraid of what she faced.

This may be one of those "white spaces" in your own life. Maybe it's time for you to pray and fast and to call upon a few close friends to fast and pray with you. Maybe it's time for you to say, "I'm not going to rush into this unpredictable and unprecedented situation. I can't find the path to walk. So I'm going to wait. In the meantime, I'm going to give it to God. I'm going to listen with a sensitive ear and watch the Lord's leading with a sensitive eye."

God counsels us with His eye. The eye makes no sound when it moves. It requires a sensitive, earthly eye to watch the movement of the eye of God—God's directions. All He may do is turn your attention in another direction. But that may be all you need. As you wait, listen. Pore over a favorite passage in His Word. Quietly give attention to His presence, and He gives you direction.

# CALM, WISE, AND CONFIDENT

### 🦎 *Read Esther 5:1–3* 🦎

No king has ever intimidated God, no matter how wealthy his treasury, how extensive his kingdom, or how powerful his armies. God can handle anyone. Anyone! He can handle your husband. He can handle your wife. He can handle your kids. He can handle your pastor. He can handle the person who gives you grief. He can handle your ex-mate, that person who made you all those promises and broke most of them. He can even handle your enemy. He can handle the most intimidating situation, because in the hand of the Lord, any heart is like water.

Esther walks in that confidence. Look at her. She doesn't cringe and cower; she *stands*. "Esther *stood* in front of the king's rooms. The king saw Esther the queen *standing*." (emphasis mine) She's not trembling. Though she's doing what's never been done before, she is standing tall, confident in the Lord.

And when the king saw her standing in the court, she obtained favor in his sight, and he extended his golden scepter to her. Remember, without that gesture from the king, she would die. And now, confident, she touches the top of the scepter, making a connection with the king. "Then the king said to her, 'What is troubling you, Queen Esther? And what is your request? Even to half of the kingdom it will be given you'" (Esther 5:3).

I love that. Esther doesn't know what to expect, and the king says simply, "What's on your mind? What's troubling you?" In fact, he goes further. He says, "What can I do for you? Name it. There's no limit; it's yours."

Now this is her moment to bring down the roof on Haman—but she doesn't. Not now. This is a wise woman who understands the value of timing. She isn't in a hurry, nor is she revengeful. You know why? She has been *waiting* on the Lord.

We get in a hurry when we don't wait on the Lord. We jump ahead and do rash things. We shoot from the hip. We run off at the mouth, saying things that we later regret. But when we have sufficiently waited on the Lord, He gets full control of our spirit. At such moments, we're like a glove, and His hand is moving us wherever He pleases. Having known that experience, I can testify, there's nothing to compare it to. It's marvelous!

Wait on the Lord.

# FULL OF SURPRISES

### ✤ *Read Esther 5:4–14* ✤

God was at work in the waiting, filling her thoughts with a plan. When you wait on the Lord, you don't have to sit in a corner contemplating your navel, or walk around in a daze humming "Sweet Hour of Prayer." You don't have to go out on a hillside, eat birdseed, and strum a guitar. You don't have to wear a robe and live in a hut in Tibet for the winter. Sometimes, of course, you need to sit down quietly, by yourself, alone with the Lord for a time of quietness. Solitude and silence are wonderful when nourishing our souls. But mostly you go right on with your business. You press on with your regular activities. You just focus more fully on the Lord in the midst of it. You stay preoccupied with Him. You try to think His thoughts. You recall words from His Book that you've memorized. You feed your soul His manna.

"Great idea," the king says. "Banquets are my thing." (She knew that.) "Then the king said, 'Bring Haman quickly that we may do as Esther desires.' So the king and Haman came to the banquet which Esther had prepared" (Esther 5:5).

The king may rule the kingdom of Persia, and Haman may sign edicts with the king's official seal, but it is the Lord who is in control of this entire situation. And in the nucleus of His divine plan, Esther becomes invincible.

Esther must have been sitting there thinking, *Isn't God great? I could have lost my head. Instead, here they are at this banquet I've prepared. The plan is working beautifully. What a surprise!*

God is full of surprises. But it takes a sensitive spirit to see them, to be jolted by them. Too many Christians are lulled into languor. Some can warble all the Christian songs, recite all the right Bible verses, and quote this preacher and that teacher, but their Christian lives, down deep inside, are jaded. Are you in that condition? When that happens, you become calloused and insensitive, and you're in for a life of boredom and mediocrity. How tragic for that to happen! The walk of faith is designed to be a walk of adventure, filled with periodic and delightful surprises.

Watch for the surprises!

# GOD'S SILENCE

### ⚜ *Read Esther 5:5–7* ⚜

Since we are trapped in this earthbound cage, this little space where light is often diffused and God is sometimes silent, how can we be sensitive to His interventions? What do we do when we, like Job, struggle in the fog with God's silence, when we're convinced that His silence means absence?

Please be assured, He is not absent. He may be silent, but He's not absent.

The fog on your lake is neither accidental nor fatal. So while swimming, listen very carefully and patiently for His voice. Some days you will be seized with panic and dog-paddle like mad. You'll try various approaches: breaststroke, butterfly, backstroke, float. But all the time, you want to be listening for His voice. I urge you to listen with great sensitivity, because His message will come in various ways.

I get nervous around some people and the way they talk about hearing God or seeing Him at work. Sometimes I freely admit that I want to recommend a good therapist. Especially when I hear people say things like, "The Lord spoke to me in my kitchen at 2:15 this morning." Or, "God found me a parking space today." I consider these folks "bumper-sticker Christians." They're often scary folks, almost spooky. Miracles are everyday occurrences to them. They see skywriting in the clouds, and they hear voices in the night. Hear me well, that's not the kind of "voice" I'm talking about.

God gave you a mind. God gave you reason. God gave you a unique sensitivity; it's built into your spiritual system, and each person's system is tuned differently. God wants to reveal His will to you and to teach you while you are waiting. So while you are waiting, don't start searching for spooky stuff. We walk by faith, not by sight (2 Corinthians 5:7). Get into His Word. Get on your knees. Accept counsel from those who are maturing and balanced believers, solidly biblical in their theology and in their own lives. And wait.

However, there are tangible things to connect with. Passages of Scripture that bring comfort and insight. Messages that enlighten and enliven. Certain people you respect. Tap into those, wait, and listen with a sensitive ear. Like Esther, don't rush into big decisions. And may I be painfully direct? Don't talk so much! Believers who are maturing not only respect God's silence, they model it as well.

# GOD NOTICES

*Read Esther 6:1–14*

N ever fails, does it? Things are not as they seem. And about the time you think they cannot get worse, they do. This was certainly true for Mordecai at a pivotal point in the story of Esther.

*When all seems lost, it isn't.* Mordecai could have despaired at the situation in Persia. The king was a Gentile. He had no interest in the Jews. Furthermore, his closest confidant was Haman, who shamelessly hated the Jews. Esther was in the palace, but when the king found out she was a Jew, her life might be over in an instant. When all seems lost, it isn't.

*When no one seems to notice, they do.* Remember Mordecai's courageous decision earlier when he heard of a conspiracy between two of the doorkeepers of the palace, who were plotting to kill the king? When Mordecai heard of that conspiracy, he told his adopted daughter Esther about it. And she, being the queen, alerted the king.

Esther had told the king that the information had come from Mordecai, yet no one ever rewarded him for his great act. It seemed as though no one noticed or remembered. So Mordecai went on living his life unnoticed, unrewarded, and unappreciated—until this pivotal night.

I love the first three words of 6:1, "During *that* night." That's the way it is with God. At the eleventh hour, He steps in and does the unexpected. When no one seems to notice and no one seems to care, He notices and He cares "during *that* night."

Learn a lesson from Mordecai today, will you? Through all that happens to him, Mordecai never becomes a man of vengeance. He never tries to get back at Haman, even when he has the opportunity, even when he has Haman in a very vulnerable spot. He doesn't kick him in the face when he has a chance to. He doesn't even speak against the man. Let me challenge you to guard your heart as Mordecai did.

> For God is not unjust so as to forget your work and the love which you have shown toward His name, in having ministered and still ministering to the saints. (Hebrews 6:10)

I love those words, "God is not unjust so as to forget." When no one else notices, mark it down, *God notices.* When no one else remembers, God records it so it won't be forgotten.

# GENUINELY HUMBLE

### 🐾 *Read Esther 6:1–14* 🐾

*W*hat goes around comes around." That popular saying has never been truer than it is here. Things have gone around for Haman—yet they finally come around for Mordecai. Sitting on that horse in regal attire, he was the most surprised man in the kingdom. That's the beauty of the story. He was not a proud man. He was not a vengeful man. He was not whispering, "Say it a little louder. Eat your heart out, Haman." According to what is written here, Mordecai didn't utter a word.

I think that's what I appreciate most in this whole episode: the silence of Mordecai. How rare are the people who can be promoted to a place of highly visible significance and not live for their own clippings or crave the spotlight or demand center stage. Soft-spoken, genuinely humble celebrities are extremely rare. Not convinced? Check the rank and file of today's pro athletes. How refreshing (and unusual!) to find a modern-day Mordecai!

In fact, the next thing we read is that "Mordecai returned to the king's gate." A brief phrase, it's easy to overlook. But isn't it wonderful? "Mordecai returned to the king's gate," it says, rather than, "Mordecai accepted a major promotion." And do you know why it's significant? Because that's where he's been all the time. His honor has not gone to his head. He just went back to work.

Have you recently been promoted? Has God's providence smiled on you so that your name is now honored in circles where you were once not even known? Have you come to a place of popularity and prosperity? Are you now esteemed in the eyes of others? If so, the real question is: Are you still comfortable at the king's gate, or must you now live in the palace? Must you now be treated with special care and be given kid-glove treatment and not be bothered with everyday problems? Mordecai shrugged, "Just drop me off where all this started—at the king's gate."

No matter what happens to you, remember "the pit from which you've been dug." You'll find the best place on earth is still pretty close to your roots. Like the country song reminds us, "Look how far I had to come, to get back where I started from."

# WHEN GOD SEEMS ABSENT

### ❧ *Read Esther 6:12—14* ❧

*I*f you're like me, you're often waiting for the other shoe to drop. In this instance, we're waiting for—and wanting—Haman to get what he deserves. Everything within us craves justice. Especially with a loser like Haman, who has strutted his stuff long enough.

Never once in all of Haman's peacock strutting and evil plotting had God ignored him or his plan to murder Mordecai and the Jews. God had not missed his statements, the pride of his heart, the violent and prejudicial motives behind his decisions. God was invisible, but He was not out of touch or passive. He had not forgotten His people or His promises to them—and to their enemies.

A knock came at the door. And before he could even get his thoughts together, Haman was swept out of the house and escorted to the palace for the banquet that would spell his doom. I can't help but wonder if on the way to the palace Haman glanced again at the gallows he had built for Mordecai, shook his head, and regretted what he had done.

A magnificent theological principle underscored again and again in the Scriptures is this: *When God seems absent, He's present.* Even when you think you have lost *all*, God uses it as an opportunity to awaken you to the realization that He is still in charge, as well as to bring you to your knees.

Do you feel that God has been absent or on hold in your life, distant in some way? I want to remind you of this: He may have *seemed* absent from you, but He has been present all along. Furthermore, He knows your heart. He knows the true condition of your soul. He knows the hidden impurities of your motives. He knows the deep depravity of your sin. But He's heard your cry, and He will not turn you away.

# THE FOG IS LIFTING

### ✍ *Read Esther 7:1–2* ✍

*I*magine swimming in a vast lake and getting three or four hundred yards offshore when suddenly a freak fog rolls in and surrounds you. You're trapped in this tiny circle of diffused light, but you can't see beyond your arm's reach.

You and I are locked in a tiny space on this foggy lake of life called the present. Because our entire perspective is based on this moment in which we find ourselves, we speak of the present, the past, and the future. If we want to know the hour or minute or second, we merely look at our watches. If we want to know the day or the month, the year or the century, we look at the calendar. Time. Easily marked, carefully measured. It is all very objective: measurable, understandable, and conscious.

God is not like that at all. As a matter of fact, He lives and moves outside the realm of earthly time. In His time and only in His time, He begins to move in subtle ways until, suddenly, as His surprising sovereignty unfolds, a change occurs. It's God's way of lifting the fog, which always happens when He decides and when He pleases!

"What is your petition?" the king asks Esther. "What is your request?"

He's already asked that two other times: when she first approached him and he held out his scepter, and then at the first banquet. But Esther never answered him, because the time wasn't right. Esther had a sensitive ear, a wise heart; she sensed something wasn't quite right. So, she didn't push it. She knew when to act—and she knew when to wait.

Are you as sensitive as that? Do you know when to listen? Do you know when to speak up and when to keep quiet? Do you know how much to say and when to say it? Do you have the wisdom to hold back until exactly the right moment in order to achieve maximum results? Those things make a difference, you know. The question is: Are you sufficiently in tune with God to read His subtle signals? It's easy to jump at the first sighting of the fog's lifting.

As Solomon once wrote, "There is a time for every event under heaven . . . a time to be silent, and a time to speak" (Ecclesiastes 3:1, 7).

# THE RIDE OF YOUR LIFE

### *Read Esther 7:3–5*

*T*alk about the power of a woman! Can you believe Esther's diplomacy and sensitivity, even in the midst of pleading for her life and the lives of her people? "If we were only being sold into slavery, I wouldn't have troubled you with this matter. You have so many important matters to worry about, I wouldn't have bothered you. But he wants to annihilate us!" Esther beautifully portrays in this moment the character qualities of greatness. Her husband is all ears!

Then King Ahasuerus asked Queen Esther, "Who is he, and where is he, who would presume to do thus?" (Esther 7:5).

At this point, I confess that my response might have been something like, "What do you mean, 'Who is he'? You were there when Haman proposed this heinous thing. You gave him your seal to sign the edict. What do you mean, 'Who is he?' Open your eyes!" Thankfully, I wasn't there to blow it.

We live in a world of preoccupied people. They, too, live in a fog—the fog of busyness, stress, and obligations. Who knows how many edicts Ahasuerus signed that day? Who knows how many pressing matters of government were on his mind? The king had countless decisions to make. And Haman, a trusted official, had proposed it in such a way that he seemed to be solving a problem that directly affected the good of the kingdom. So the king probably signed it without giving it a great deal of attention, believing that Haman, a man he trusted, knew what he was doing.

Suddenly, however, things changed. Never try to convince me that some situations in this life are absolutely permanent. God can move in the heart of a king. He can move an entire nation. He can bring down the once-impenetrable Iron Curtain. He can change the mind of your stubborn mate. He can move in the affairs of your community. He can alter decisions of presidents, prime ministers, present-day kings, and national dictators. No barrier is too high, no chasm is too wide for Him, because He's not limited by space or time, by the visible or the invisible. Remember, He lives in a realm that transcends all that. He is all-powerful. When God is ready to move, He moves. And when He does, hang on. You're in for the ride of your life!

# WHEN GOD CALLS THE SHOTS

### ✣ *Read Esther 7:3–10* ✣

*T*he plot thickens as the excitement builds. Esther plans a banquet for the king and Haman. Blinded by his own conceit, Haman thinks the queen wants to honor him. But when the king asks Esther what request she might have that he can grant, she says, "I want both of you to come to another banquet tomorrow. Then I will tell you what I want."

Haman was thrilled! The queen was going to honor him *twice* with a feast in the presence of King Ahasuerus. *She must really think I'm something,* he thought.

On the way back home, he saw Mordecai, that Jew who would not give him the homage and deference he felt he had coming. Haman was infuriated at the sight of his nemesis.

You see, when God calls the shots, nobody can stop the action! The most powerful man in the land next to the king gets his hands tied and his mouth silenced. God and God alone can do such things.

When I come to this book that never mentions God, I see Him all the more profoundly and eloquently portrayed throughout it. It's there in invisible ink. Just like life. I've never seen skywriting that says, "I'm here, Chuck. You can count on Me." I've never heard an audible voice in the middle of the night reassuring me, "I'm here, My son." But by faith I see Him, and inaudibly I hear Him on a regular basis, reading Him written in the events of my life—whether it be the crushing blows that drive me to my knees or the joyous triumphs that send my heart winging. When I pause long enough to look back, I realize it is the unsearchable mind, the unfathomable will, the sovereign control, the irresistible providence of God at work, because He, though invisible, remains invincible.

Are you letting God call the shots in your life?

# SURPRISING SOVEREIGNTY

### ❦ *Read Esther 7:6–10* ❦

*A*ll the time Haman was having the gallows built, he could see—enthusiastically anticipate—Mordecai impaled there. Now, he is condemned to die there himself. We call this irony. Theologians call it sovereignty. I call it God's surprising sovereignty!

I can remember a time early on in my ministerial training when the sovereignty of God was frightening to me. Not understanding its implications as fully as I do now some thirty-five years later, I felt it would make me passive and virtually irresponsible. Furthermore, I feared what it would do to my theology of evangelism. If I really threw myself into this doctrine, God could become a distant deity, sort of a celestial brute, pushing and maneuvering His way through nameless humanity, as He did what He pleased to get what He wanted. I could see my zeal waning and my passion for souls drained to the point of indifference.

Through a series of events far too numerous and complicated to describe, I've come to realize that, rather than being frightened by God's sovereignty, I'm comforted in it. Since He alone is God, and since He, being God, "does all things well" and in doing them has only good as His goal, how could I do anything but embrace it?

Does that mean I can explain it? No, only rarely, when hindsight yields insight. Does that mean I always anticipate it? No, like you, I occasionally rush to judgment or respond in panic, wondering why He is so silent, allowing wrong to run its course so long. But looking back in more reasonable moments, with my emotions under better control (*His* control!), I can see what He was about. I can even see why He delayed, or why He acted when He did. Usually, I freely admit, I think He is awfully slow (I can't number the times I've pleaded, "O, God, please *hurry up!*"), and I am usually surprised, though I shouldn't be, at how beautifully things work out, right on time.

In the final analysis, God is God, and He will have His way when He pleases and for His glory. What could be better than that? In all the mystery of His waiting and working, and in all the wrong of our doing and undoing, He can still be trusted. The main thing is that you and I remain sensitive to those moments when He finally breaks the silence and suddenly intervenes on our behalf. At least to us it seems sudden. To Him, it happened exactly as He had planned it all along.

# THE WORKINGS OF GOD

### ❧ *Read Esther 7:6–10* ❧

*T*he workings of God are not related to our clocks; they are related to our crises. That's why God doesn't care if this is the last day you can buy that car on sale. It doesn't bother God that it is the first day of summer or high noon or a quarter after seven or ten minutes to one in the morning. His timing is unrelated to Planet Earth's clock time. So while waiting, look beyond the present.

The best way to do that is to *pray!* Make your life a life of prayer. Tell Him, in anguish if necessary, the pain of waiting. Express your panic. Tell Him you're trapped. (Ask Him to hurry up, if that helps. He can handle it!) You don't know how you can stay afloat much longer. In those moments, ask Him to help you see beyond the frustration and fear of the present.

The surprises in store are not merely ironic or coincidental; they are sovereignly designed. While anticipating, trust Him for justice. You may not live to see that justice, but it will come. He is a just God; you know He is. So trust Him for it.

I have found while in the fog that my great temptation is either to doubt or to deny—maybe they're the same thing—to doubt or to deny that He is even at work. But, more often than not, when something looks like it's the absolute *end,* it's really just the *beginning.* I can see this later, when I look back.

Esther, our heroine, is a lovely model to follow. And her story is certainly one to remember. But the best focus of all? God Himself. How perfectly He works, how sovereignly He controls, and how remarkably He changes the face of things once He moves in. A queen who was passive is actively in charge. A king who was duped is now fully informed. An enemy who was only moments away from exterminating a nation is now an object of scorn. And those ghastly gallows, built for a Jew named Mordecai, will soon suffocate the body of a Gentile named Haman.

When will we ever learn? At the precise moment when it will have its greatest impact, God ceases His silence and sovereignly makes His move. And when He does, life is full of surprises.

# TAKE HEART

### ✦ *Read Esther 8:1–8* ✦

The king's heart is like mush, like soft putty, or we could say like Play-Doh in the hands of the Lord. Just for a moment imagine another name in that proverb in place of "the king." Someone who is giving you grief perhaps. It may be one of your own grown, wayward children. Maybe it's someone who represents a formidable presence. Someone who haunts you and maybe wishes to bring you down. Stubborn person, right? Strong-hearted individual, correct? Imagine that heart that is so hard, so granitelike, changing into soft putty in the hands of the Lord. It's possible! There is no heart so stubborn that it cannot become breakable in the hands of the Lord.

Many years ago, in another place and at another time in my life, I went through a dreadful experience with a person who decided to make me his enemy. I still don't know why. It remains a mystery. Nevertheless, it occurred. This individual decided to make my life miserable. He watched my every move. He questioned my decisions. He cast doubts on my ministry. This person applied pressure, sometimes to the point where I thought I would scream. I don't know how much he said to others. I never asked. But he said enough to me and was bullying and intimidating enough that I became frightened, especially when I realized he carried a gun. Eventually, on one occasion, he threatened me with it.

One bitterly cold Sunday after church, I went home and fell across our bed, not even taking off my overcoat. I cried out to the Lord. I wept audibly until I could not cry another tear. I had come to my wit's end. I was exhausted, trying everything I knew to do to bring about a change. *Nothing* changed! This man had a heart like King Ahasuerus.

There is no wall so strong that Almighty God is not stronger still. There is no will so stubborn that He is not able to soften it. If God can change the heart of an Ahasuerus, He can change any heart—*any heart!* Read that again. You who live your days intimidated and threatened, anxious over the falling of the next shoe, listen to this counsel! God is able to take the heart of anyone and change it, just as He did with the heart of this king.

Yes, *anyone.*

# HE'S IN CHARGE

### ❧ *Read Esther 8:9—14* ❧

*T*he law of the Medes and Persians couldn't be changed. The law Haman had written had to stay on the books. But because the heart of the king had been softened by the pleas of Esther, he provided a way by which that law might never come into affect—or would at least be neutralized.

The Jews could protect themselves. In fact, they could do more than that. They could take the lives of anyone who might attack them, including women and children, and they had a right to plunder and take ownership of their possessions. So at least it was an even playing field. The Jews now had their own defense, established of all things, by the Persian law. "The couriers, hastened and impelled by the king's command, went out, riding on the royal steeds; and the decree was given out in Susa the capital" (Esther 8:14).

Amazing! And to think these rights provided for all the Jews were granted by the same man who earlier had virtually sealed their doom.

You may have some person after you. You may have some document, something that's been written that seems irrevocable—some magazine article, some newspaper article, some transcript, some occupational report, some lawsuit, whatever. Because it's in writing, it looks so intimidating, so unerasable, so legal. And you're reading these words, thinking, *Yeah, but if you only knew who's behind that.* That's my whole point here! Who is *anybody* compared to the living Lord? I don't care who's behind that document. We serve a sovereign God who has yet to go "Ahh!" when He finds anything on this earth. Nothing frightens Him. Nothing causes Him to do a neck jerk. He's in charge! We live "in the shelter of the Most High." We "abide in the shadow of the Almighty" (Psalm 91:1). Nothing is too hard for Him! Nothing!

# BREAKING DOWN WALLS

### ✣ *Read Esther 8:15—17* ✣

*I*t was like Thanksgiving, Christmas, and New Year's all rolled into one. It was like Berlin on the ninth of November 1989! It was like nothing they had ever seen before. They would sing all night and all the next day because the gloom was lifted! The darkness wasn't impenetrable after all. It had just seemed so.

Do you live in a place of gloom and darkness, where laughter doesn't echo off the walls? Has your life become grim or even borderline tragic? While others go home to the love and warmth of a family, do you go home alone to the awful memory of broken relationships, remorse, and guilt?

Perhaps your last sounds of the day are the clanging of a cell door and some guard yelling, "Lights out!" Do you look with longing at a scene like this one in Esther?

Esther's story is no irrelevant slice of history tucked away in the folds of an ancient scroll. These principles are still at work today. This is life, as relevant today as when it was first recorded. This is written to people who face intimidating, stubborn souls. Perhaps they live with them, are married to them, or have grown children like that. This is written to people whose lives have been scarred by documents and lawsuits, bad reports, or rumors. This is written to people whose lives are lived within the thick, stone walls of depression and doom. And this chapter announces in bold letters: *There is hope!*

Walls fall every day. But we cannot predict when yours will fall. God is in the business of breaking down walls. Take hope! Take heart! This will pass. The truth will become known. Every day walls of depression and gloom are penetrated by the wonderful presence of the living God.

Weeping may last for the night,
But a shout of joy comes in the morning. (Psalm 30:5)

# UNEXPECTED WITNESSES

### ✣ *Read Esther 9:1–10:3* ✤

*A*t the end of Esther's story, we have the same king as at the beginning, King Ahasuerus. We have the same kingdom, where he reigns from India to Ethiopia, more than 127 provinces. We have the same country, Persia, and the same capital city, Susa. But some things have changed. Vashti is no longer queen; Esther is queen. And she is a queen who has won her husband's overwhelming respect and loyalty. Haman was once second in command, but he is gone forever. Mordecai is alive and well. Wicked plans have been thwarted. Corruption has been rooted out. Evil has been fully dealt with. To make matters even better, Mordecai has been promoted by the king, and he is now in Haman's old position—"second only to King Ahasuerus."

When God wins, the people He uses are often unexpected. Or consider another unexpected choice. If you wanted to lead an exodus of two million people out of Egypt, who would you choose to confront Pharaoh—a Jew or a fellow Egyptian? Be honest, now. And if you chose a Jew, would you choose a man with murder on his record? And would he be eighty years old? And would you select a leather-skinned shepherd who hadn't been in a big city for forty years? See, the further you look, the more surprising it gets. Moses' resumé was pretty unimpressive: "Worked for father-in-law as shepherd for past forty years." He was an over-the-hill Bedouin.

Would you have chosen a harlot to hide the spies? Would you have chosen a defecting, rebellious prophet to lead the Greater Nineveh Evangelistic Crusade? Would you have chosen a former Christian-hating Pharisee to model grace and to write most of the New Testament? Would you have chosen a man who denied Jesus (three times!) as the major spokesman for the early church?

But, you see, God does surprising things. That's why He lifts a no-name Jew from the gate of the king and makes him a prime minister. God delights in lifting up nobodies and using them as somebodies. As Paul writes to the Corinthians, "not many mighty, not many noble"—in other words, not many bluebloods are chosen. He has chosen the despised and many of the losers of the world to follow the One who died on a cross and bring ultimate victory for us all. So, as you have seen so clearly in the book of Esther, the God who seems not to be present, is, in fact, ever-present, omnipotent, and in complete control. And so He is in your life too.

*Job: A Man of Heroic Endurance*

# LIFE IS DIFFICULT

### *Read Job 1:1–12*

*L*ife is difficult. That blunt, three-word statement is an accurate appraisal of our existence on this earth. When the writer of the biblical book named Job picked up his stylus to write his story, he could have begun with a similar-sounding and equally blunt sentence, "Life is unfair."

No one could argue the point that life is punctuated with hardship, heartaches, and headaches. Most of us have learned to face the reality that life is difficult. But unfair? Something kicks in, deep within most of us, making it almost intolerable for us to accept and cope with what's unfair. Our drive for justice overrides our patience with pain.

Life is not just difficult, it's downright unfair. Welcome to Job's world.

Job was a man of unparalleled and genuine piety. He was also a man of well-deserved prosperity. He was a godly gentleman, extremely wealthy, a fine husband, and a faithful father. In a quick and brutal sweep of back-to-back calamities, Job was reduced to a twisted mass of brokenness and grief. The extraordinary accumulation of disasters that hit him would have been enough to finish off any one of us today.

Job is left bankrupt, homeless, helpless, and childless. He's left standing beside the ten fresh graves of his now-dead children in a windswept valley. His wife is heaving deep sobs of grief as she kneels beside him, having just heard him say, "Whether our God gives to us or takes everything from us, we will follow Him." She leans over and secretly whispers, "Why don't you just curse God and die?"

His misery turns to mystery with God's silence. If the words of his so-called friends are hard to hear, the silence of God becomes downright intolerable. Not until the thirty-eighth chapter of the book does God finally break the silence, however long that took. Even if it were just a few months, try to imagine. You've become the object of your alleged friends' accusations, and the heavens are brass as you plead for answers from the Almighty, who remains mysteriously mute. Nothing comes to you by way of comfort. It's all so unfair; you've done nothing to deserve such anguish.

Pause and ponder their grief—and remember that Job had done nothing to deserve such unbearable pain. If it had been you, how would you have responded?

# THE ACCUSER

### ✒ *Read Job 1:1–12* ❧

*V*erses 1 to 5 are full of good news, wonderful blessing, business integrity, purity of heart, faithfulness of life. The man is spiritually mature, domestically diligent, and professionally respected.

As he sleeps, another scene opens to us that Job doesn't see. Similar things happen in our lives as well. When we're not aware of it, God is carrying out a plan that would amaze us and, on occasion, shock us. He is permitting things to get underway that we would have never expected. Without Job's knowledge, something is happening in the heavenlies. We are transported from Planet Earth to the third heaven to witness its occurrence.

As the Lord God looks about, He sees His angelic servants who have come to present themselves before Him. And why not? They're accountable to Him. They do His bidding as they carry out His divine will.

Suddenly the Accuser appears among the other angels. He is the evil one who accuses God's people day and night.

Pause and remember that Satan is not a little imp with a red body, carrying a pitchfork, and sitting on one of your shoulders whispering ugly little nothings in your ear. That's a medieval caricature that Satan would love for you to believe. Instead, he is the most attractive, brilliant, powerful archangel that God ever created. He has not lost his brilliance. He has not lost his power. He has certainly not lost his appealing beauty. He is also insidious. Satan's favorite method of working is behind the scenes. Because he is invisible does not mean he is not real. As we will see a little later, he has personality. And he is engaged in a relentless commitment to destroying God's people and opposing God's plan. It is this insidious Adversary we find standing in the heavenlies among the group of faithful angelic servants.

Look at the permission slip He hands Satan. "All that he has is yours to deal with." He adds a caveat, "only do not put forth your hand on him" (Job 1:12). "Don't you touch his life. Don't touch his body or his soul or his mind. You can remove his possessions, and you can attack his family, but leave the man, himself, alone."

Satan departed from the presence of the Lord with a sinister grin. Keep in mind, Job knew nothing of that dialogue and the evil that would soon befall him. And remember this: we don't know what wicked schemes Satan is planning against us either.

# THE UNSEEN ENEMY

### *Read Job 1:1–12*

*J*ob does not deserve even the suggestion of mistreatment. He has walked faithfully with God, certainly in his adult years. He is now the best of the best, "greatest of all the men of the east." On top of all that, he is an humble servant of God. But none of that impresses Satan. Evil suspicions prompt his insidious plot: "You want to know what he's really made of, remove all that indulged treatment and pervasive protection. Strip away the veneer of the man's comfort, and You'll see right away, he'll turn on You. 'He will surely curse You to Your face'" (Job 1:11). His point is clear: Job is worshiping God because of what he gets out of it, not because the Lord is truly first in his life.

There is an enemy who we encounter that we cannot see, but he is real. We have a supernatural enemy, and we encounter him or one of his emissaries regularly. And never doubt it—all of that is real. He hopes that his deceptive strategy will play tricks on your mind and will weaken you and ultimately bring you down. The Accuser's desire is to ruin your testimony as he destroys your life. In the process, if it means ruining your family relationships, he'll go there. If it takes tempting you to secretly cut a few corners in your business, which you would not have done in earlier days, he'll go there. Whatever it takes to bring you down, he will try. Because we have an enemy we cannot see does not mean he is not real.

There are trials we endure that we don't deserve, but they are permitted. You read that correctly. Life includes trials that we do not deserve, but they must, nevertheless, be endured. In the mystery of God's unfathomable will, there are elements we can never explain or fully understand. Don't try to grasp each thread of His profound plan. If you resist my counsel here, you'll become increasingly more confused, ultimately resentful, and finally bitter. At that point, Satan will have won the day. Accept it. Endure the trial that has been permitted by God. Nothing touches your life that has not first passed through the hands of God. He is in full control, and because He is, He has the sovereign right to permit trials that we don't deserve.

We do have an unseen enemy, but we have an even more powerful, unseen Defender.

# WALK BY FAITH, NOT BY SIGHT

### ❦ *Read Job 1:1–12* ❧

ithout Job's knowing it, a dialogue took place in the invisible world. As the Lord and Satan had their strange encounter, the subject quickly turned to this well-known earthly man. The Lord calls Satan's attention to Job's exemplary life, and Satan responds with a sinister sneer. "Of course, who wouldn't serve You the way You've prospered and protected him. Take away all the perks and watch what happens; the man will turn on You in a flash." God agrees to let the Adversary unload on Job.

And so, in today's terms, the Lord bet Satan that Job would never turn on Him. Philip Yancey refers to that agreement as the "divine wager." Satan instigates a sudden and hostile removal of all the man's possessions, leaving him bankrupt. Within a matter of minutes, everything he owned was gone.

This brings us to the first lesson worth remembering: *we never know ahead of time the plans God has for us.* Job had no prior knowledge or warning. That morning dawned like every other morning. The night had passed like any other night. There was no great angelic manifestation— not even a tap on his window or a note left on the kitchen table.

In one calamity after another, all the buildings on his land are gone, and nothing but lumber and bodies litter the landscape. It occurred so fast, Job's mind swirled in disbelief. Everything hit broadside . . . his world instantly changed.

You and I must learn from this! We never know what a day will bring, whether good or ill. Our heavenly Father's plan unfolds apart from our awareness. Ours is a walk of faith, not sight. Trust, not touch. Leaning long and hard, not running away. No one knows ahead of time what the Father's plan includes. It's best that way. It may be a treasured blessing; it could be a test that drops us to our knees. He knows ahead of time, but He is not obligated to warn us about it or to remind us it's on the horizon. We can be certain of this: our God knows what is best.

# Necessary Consequences

### ✦ *Read Job 1:13–22* ✦

*T*here is a plan that we explore which we will not understand, but it is best. Though each segment of it may not seem fair or pleasant, it works together for good. The disease Job endured wasn't good in and of itself. Hardly! But it worked together for good. Our perspective is dreadfully limited. We see only a pinpoint of time, but God's view is panoramic. God's big-picture, cosmic plan is at work now, and He doesn't feel the need (nor is He obligated) to explain it to us. If He tried, our answer would be like the confused teenager listening to his calculus teacher, "What?" You wouldn't get it, nor would I. Just remember, the Father knows what is best for His children. Rest in that realization.

There are consequences we experience that we could not anticipate, but they are necessary. I don't know where you find yourself today, but I would be willing to wager that most of you reading this book are going through something that is unfair. Chances are good that you simply don't deserve what's happening. The consequences may have started to get to you. You didn't anticipate any of this. You didn't think it would come to this, but it has. Trust me here. What has happened is a necessary part of your spiritual growth. Yes, necessary. I've finally begun to accept that reality after all these years of my life.

I want to address you who have moved onto Job's turf. If nothing else, it has prepared you to pay closer attention to the message of Job. You've seen only a glimpse of how things started. The story doesn't end with Satan's departing from the presence of the Lord. There's a whole lot more to Job's story. And the more it unfolds, the more you will realize that life is not only difficult, it's unfair.

The silence of God's voice will make you wonder if He is even there. And the absence of God's presence will make you wonder if He even cares. He is there. And He does care.

# HUMBLE SUBMISSION

### ✒ *Read Job 1:20* ✒

*P*erhaps Job lay under the stars until he was wet from the dew. Finally, he spoke. And when he did, what a remarkable response! Verse 20 comprises nine words in the Hebrew text. These words describe what Job did before the text goes on to tell us what Job said. Five of the nine words are verbs. When you read your Bible, always pay close attention to the verbs, because they move you through the action of a narrative, helping you vicariously to enter the event.

First, Job peeled himself off the ground. He "arose."

The next verb tells us something strange. He "tore his robe." The word translated "robe" is a term describing a garment that fits over the body loosely, like an outer gown that reaches below the knees. This is not the undertunic; it's the outer robe that kept him warm at night. Job reached to his neck and, not finding a seam, he seized a worn part of the fabric and ripped it. In the ripping of the robe he is announcing his horrible grief. It was the action of a man in anguish. It's used several times in the Old Testament to portray utter grief.

And then we read the third verb. He "shaved his head." The hair is always pictured in the Scriptures as the glory of an individual, an expression of his worth. The shaving of the head, therefore, is symbolic of the loss of personal glory. And to carry his grief to its lowest depth, his fourth action is to fall to the ground. But, let's understand, this was not a collapse of grief, but for another purpose entirely. It's this that portrays the heroism of Job's endurance. He doesn't wallow and wail, he worships. The Hebrew verb means "to fall prostrate in utter submission and worship." I dare say most of us have never worshiped like that! I mean with your face on the ground, lying down, full-length. This was considered in ancient days the sincerest expression of obedience and submission to the Creator-God.

Before moving on, I'd like to suggest you try this sometime. Palms down, facedown, knees and toes touching the ground, body fully extended, as you pour out your heart in worship. It's the position Job deliberately took. Complete and humble submission.

# ON LOAN

### ✑ *Read Job 1:21* ✑

ith Job facedown in worship to God, the only one cursing is Satan. He hated
it! He resented Job's response! Of all things, the man still worships his God—
the One who would allow these catastrophes to happen. There wouldn't be
one in millions on this earth who would do so, but Job did exactly that. The wicked spirits sat with their mouths wide open as it were, as they watched a man who responded to
all of his adversities with adoration; who concluded all of his woes with worship. No
blame. No bitterness. No cursing. No clinched fist raised to the heavens screaming, "How
dare you do this to me after I've walked with you all these years!" None of that.

Instead he said, "Naked I came from my mother's womb, and naked I shall return there.
Blessed be the Name of the Lord." That says it all. At birth we all arrived naked. At death we
will all leave naked, as we're prepared for burial. We have nothing as we are birthed; we have
nothing as we depart. So everything we have in between is provided for us by the Giver
of Life.

Get that clearly in your mind. Get it, affluent Americans as we are. Get it when you stroll
through your house and see all those wonderful belongings. Get it when you open the door
and slip behind the steering wheel of your car. It's all on loan, every bit of it. Get it when the
business falls and fails. It, too, was on loan. When the stocks rise, all that profit is on loan.

Face it squarely. You and I arrived in a tiny, naked body (and a not a great looking one
at that!). And what will we have when we depart? A naked body plus a lot of wrinkles. You
take nothing because you brought nothing! You own nothing. What a grand revelation. Are
you ready to accept it? You don't even own your children. They're God's children, on loan for
you to take care of, rear, nurture, love, discipline, encourage, affirm, and then release.

Praise God for "every good and perfect gift is from above, coming down from the Father
of the heavenly lights (James 1:17 NIV).

# HOLD EVERYTHING LOOSELY

### ✥ *Read Job 1:22* ✥

*W*ithout realizing it, by worshiping God during his woes, Job is saying, "In your face, Lucifer! I never set my affections on these things in the first place. And when it came to the kids, I've understood from the day we had our first child until we had our last, they're all God's. He is the One who gave them, and He is the One who has the right to take them whenever He wants them back."

That explains how Job could say in all sincerity, "Blessed be the name of the Lord." And why the biblical narrative adds, "Through all this Job did not sin nor did he blame God" (Job 2:21–22). Since he never considered himself sole owner, Job had little struggle releasing the Lord's property. When you understand that everything you have is on loan, you are better prepared to release it when the owner wants it back.

We enter the world with our tiny fists clenched, screaming, but we always leave the world with hands open on our silent chests. Naked in, naked out. And in the interlude, "Lord God, blessed be Your name for loaning me everything I'm able to enjoy."

"Through all this Job did not sin." Isn't that wonderful? "Nor did he blame God." Why blame God?

As one man has written, "God has given him a rehearsal for death. All things belong to God, absolutely, to be given as a gift, not claim, to be taken back without wrong. There is no talk of human 'rights.' The Lord is the sovereign owner of all, and Job rejoices in this wonderful fact."

With 20/20 perspective, Job lifted himself off the ground, looked around at all that had changed, then put his arm around his grieving wife, held her close, and whispered, "God gave, and for some unrevealed reason, He chose to take back. He owns it all, sweetheart."

This entire chapter could have been written in three words. I believe they represent the reason Job became a man of heroic endurance: *hold everything loosely.*

Are you doing that?

# ROUND ONE

### ✣ *Read Job 2:1–9* ✣

hen bad things happen, they often happen to the wrong person. And when that occurs, we're always left with that haunting question, "Why?" Somewhere in all of this, there is room for the story of Job. For, as we have learned, a better man never lived in his day. He was not only a good man, he was a godly man. He was not only a faithful husband, he was a loving and devoted father. He was a good employer. With plenty of land, an abundance of food, and sufficient livestock and camels to fund Job's dreams, it looked as though his entire future would be a downhill slide.

I imagine that in the struggle of that first fitful night, trying to sleep after burying all ten children with his own hands, laying alongside his grieving wife who had also endured the loss, much of what had happened was still a blur. And there was more to come, much more. He couldn't have imagined it any more than those in the Pentagon who were already busily engaged in dealing with the details of the Northeastern Atlantic shoreline and the New York Harbor, where the terrorists had struck. Our military personnel had no idea they were next. A third plane on another evil mission would soon plunge into the very side of the building in Washington where some were already working on the atrocity that had just happened in New York.

I have spoken to some of those officers who were in the building at that time. One admitted to his own embarrassment, "It never dawned on most of us that the Pentagon was next." We may never know for sure if the third plane was seeking to locate the White House, and because of the foliage of mid-September, couldn't do so. The pilot, in his maddening plan to crash the plane, spotted this five-sided building and tore a hole 200 feet wide due to a double explosion—first from the plane itself crashing into the building and then the igniting of the fuel that sent fire down the wide hallway.

As with Job, it just wasn't fair! At least, it wasn't fair from our perspective. The man had modeled genuine integrity. He had blest his Father; in fact, he had worshiped Him, and Satan couldn't stand it.

The Adversary lost round one.

# A Plea for Understanding

### ❧ *Read Job 2:1–9* ❧

*I* want to confess that for too long in my ministry I took unfair advantage of Job's wife, especially since she was not present to defend herself. I think it was probably due to immaturity on my part. Furthermore, I hadn't been married long enough to know better than to say those things. I cannot leave this one snapshot of Mrs. Job in the story without clarifying the record in her defense.

Now that you've seen the incredible disaster they shared, isn't it a little easier to understand how she could suggest, "Job, darling, let's just pull the plug? Don't go on. You can't keep living like this, I can't stand it. Curse God, and let Him take you home to be with Him." I think so. She's reached her limit and is willing to let him go. I'm not justifying the woman's reasoning as much as trying to understand it.

Always guard your words when your husband is going through terribly hard times. I want to confess something about us men. Mainly, I want you to remember: going through sustained hard times weakens most men. For some reason, hardship seems to strengthen women; we admire you for that. But we men are weakened when times of affliction hit and stay. In our weakened condition we lose our objectivity, sometimes our stability. Our discernment is also skewed. Our determination lags. We become vulnerable, and most men don't know how to handle themselves in a vulnerable state of mind. So in light of all of this—hear me—we need your clear perspective, wisdom, and spiritual strength. Most of all, we need you to pray for us as you've never prayed. We need not only your prayers, we need your emotional support. We need you to take the initiative and step up.

We need your words of confidence and encouragement. We even find it hard to say, "I need you right now." My wife could tell you that she lived with me for our first ten years of marriage before she ever thought I needed her. I finally admitted it and learned how to say it. In the lonely hours of a man's great trial, nobody's words mean more to him than his wife's words. That is one of the God-given reasons you and your partner were called to be together. When we husbands lose our way, you wives help us find our way back.

# WAIT AND WATCH

### ❧ *Read Job 2:10* ❧

*J*ob's response to his wife's suggestion that he curse God and die is magnificent. "You speak as one of the foolish women speaks" (Job 2:10). Hats off to the old patriarch! In his weakened condition, sitting there in the misery of all those sores, not knowing if any of that would ever change, he stood firm—he even reproved her. He said, in effect, "I need to correct the course of this conversation. We're not going there."

He went further than stating a reproof; he asked an excellent question. "Shall we indeed accept good from God and not accept adversity?" (Job 2:10). His insight was rare, not only back then, but today. What magnificent theology! How seldom such a statement emerges from our secular system.

Job is thinking these thoughts: *Doesn't He have the right? Isn't He the Potter? Aren't we the clay? Isn't He the Shepherd and we the sheep? Isn't He the Master and we the servant? Isn't that the way it works?*

Somehow he already knew that the clay does not ask the potter, "What are you making?" And so he says, in effect, "No, no, no, sweetheart. Let's not do that. We serve a God who has the right to do whatever He does and is never obligated to explain it or ask permission. Stop and consider—should we think that good things are all we receive? Is that the kind of God we serve? He's no heavenly servant of ours who waits for the snap of our fingers, is He? He is our Lord and our Master! We need to remember that the God we serve has a game plan that is beyond our comprehension, including hard times like this."

And I love this last line, "In all this Job did not sin with his lips"(v. 10). There's absolute trust there. And faith. "Sweetheart, we can't explain any of this, so let's wait and watch God work. We would never have expected what happened. Both our hearts are broken over the loss. We've lost everything. Well—not *everything*. We've still got each other. Our God has a plan that is unfolding, even though we cannot understand it right now. Let's wait and watch to see what He will do next."

# TRUTH SPOKEN IN LOVE

### ❧ *Read Job 2:10* ❧

*I*'m impressed that Job listened to the words of his wife. He pondered them, he considered them, he turned them over in his mind. He neither misunderstood nor ignored her. He heard what she said, and he didn't interrupt her as she said it. That places Job in a unique category among husbands, quite frankly.

Men, I've found that most of us are not hard of hearing; we're hard of listening. Our wives frequently have the most important things to say that we will hear that day, but for some strange reason, we have formed the habit of mentally turning off their counsel.

Let me add here, when you do respond, always tell her the truth. If what she says is wise and squares with what you know to be truth—if it is helpful—then say so. And thank her. If it is not, say that. Job disagreed and said so. His response after hearing her was, "You speak as one of the foolish women speaks."

Job detected in his wife a snag of bitterness, some disillusionment; so he said to her, in effect, "This is advice I cannot and will not act on. It isn't wise. It's wrong counsel, and I can't accept it."

In the four decades I've been dealing with folks who are married, I find one of the most difficult things to get couples to do is say the truth to each other. Admit when we've done wrong rather than skirt it or rationalize around it or excuse it—just say, "I was wrong." Or if we hear our mates say something we know is not wise, or we detect a questionable motive, we tend not to say the hard thing. How much better to respond, "You know, honey, I realize you've got my good at heart, but I honestly have to say that I don't agree with it. I think it is unwise for you to suggest that." In the long haul, your marriage will be healthier if you will allow truth to prevail, especially if it's truth spoken in love. Listen well, and always speak the truth wrapped in loving care.

# COMPLETE ACCEPTANCE

### ❧ *Read Job 2:10* ❧

*B*ecause we've lived with our wives over the years and have become extremely comfortable around them, we tend to be unguarded in our words. Wives usually get the brunt of our worst words. Since this is true, let's agree today that we will restrain ourselves from verbal impurity. Job didn't make a blasphemous statement. He didn't curse God. Furthermore, he didn't curse her. As we read earlier, Job didn't call her "wicked," but "foolish."

Job may have been a public figure, but he didn't throw his weight around. It makes no difference how well known or how important you are, how long you've been married, how much money you make, or how big your company is—or your church is; no man has the right to talk down to his wife. She is your partner—your equal. Furthermore, she knows a lot of stuff on you. Someday she may write your long-awaited, unauthorized biography!

Accept her completely; love her unconditionally. A wife thrives in a context of love and acceptance. She is who she is. God has made her into the woman she has become. And may I remind you, she is the wife you chose. She has become the woman God is making her into, and that calls for complete acceptance and unconditional love on your part.

Ideally, that combination results in a deep commitment. Both of you are in this relationship for the long haul. You're there to stay. And no amount of hardship, difficulty, test, or trial will separate you. In fact, it can pull you closer.

Tragically, many a marriage is bound together by very thin, fragile threads. As tests come—from the in-laws or the children, perhaps a difficulty at birth that leads to birth defects in a child, or trials and tests in the business or financial realm . . . whatever—deliberately pull together and determine to hang in there. Tell her how much she means to you. Talk to her about her value in your life—how much she represents to you. When the crucible heats up, too many guys look for ways to get out.

Don't get out. Get tough with yourself and stay, no matter what.

# RAISING FAITH TO NEW HEIGHTS

### ✦ *Read Job 2:11–13* ✦

Since our lives are full of trials, we need to remember there are always more to come. Job admits, "For man is born for trouble, as sparks fly upward" (Job 5:7). He is absolutely correct. Trials are inevitable, so don't be surprised. Be aware that our Adversary, Satan, is on the loose.

Since our world is fallen, we need to understand that those who love us may give us wrong advice. During the many years of my life, I have received wrong advice on several occasions from people who truly love me. They were sincere, but wrong. They didn't mean to be wrong, but they were.

Since our God is sovereign, we must prepare ourselves for both blessing and adversity. Because He is God, He's unpredictable. My advice here? Don't be disillusioned. Because our God is sovereign, we must prepare ourselves for blessing *and adversity*.

Our God has no obligation to explain Himself. He doesn't have to step into a hospital room and say, "Now let me offer five reasons this has happened to your son." Understand, God is full of compassion, but His long-term, divine plan is beyond our short-term, human comprehension.

So we say, with Job: "O God, I trust You. I don't know why I'm going through this. If there's something I can learn, wonderful. If there's something someone else can learn, great. Just get me through it. Just hold me close. Sustain me. Deepen me. Change me."

"It is easier to lower your view of God than to raise your faith to such a height," writes a perceptive author. He then adds, "We shall watch the struggle as Job's faith is strained every way by temptations to see the cause of his misfortune in something less than God." God is totally, completely, and absolutely in charge. Please accept and submit to that teaching. How magnificent it is to find those who trust Him to the very end of this vale of suffering saying, "And may His name be praised. I don't understand it. Can't explain it. Nevertheless, may His name be praised." That is worship at its highest level.

May God enable you to raise your faith to such heights rather than lower your view of Him.

# WITHOUT ASKING

*Read Job 2:11–13*

F riends care enough to come without being asked to come. No one sent a message saying to Eliphaz and Bildad and Zophar, "Would you please come and bring a little sympathy and comfort for Job? The man is dying in this crucible of anguish and pain." That wasn't necessary, because real friends show up when someone they love is really hurting. Friends don't need an official invitation. Spontaneously, they come.

Friends respond with sympathy and comfort. Sympathy includes identifying with the sufferer. Friends do that. They enter into his or her crucible, for the purpose of feeling the anguish and being personally touched by the pain. Comfort is attempting to ease the pain by helping to make the sorrow lighter. You run errands for them. You take care of the kids. You provide a meal. You assist wherever you can assist because you want to comfort them.

Friends openly express the depth of their feelings. They have ways of doing that, don't they? It's not uncommon to see a friend standing nearby in the hospital room fighting back the tears. It's not unusual for the friend to express deep feelings. Casual acquaintances don't usually do that; genuine friends make their feelings known.

Friends aren't turned off by distasteful sights. On the contrary, they come alongside and they get as close as possible. Friends are not offended because the room has a foul smell. Friends don't turn away because the one they've come to be with has been reduced to the shell of his former self, weighing half of what he used to weigh.

Friends see beyond all of that. They don't walk away because the bottom has dropped out of your life and you're at wits' end. On the contrary, that draws them in. These men literally tore their robes, sprinkled dust on their heads, and raised their voices and sobbed as they sat down on the ground with Job. They demonstrated the depth of their anguish by staying seven days and seven nights without uttering a word.

Friends understand, so they say very little. Words are not always what they need. What they need is you.

# GOD'S PRESENCE IN SUFFERING

### ❧ *Read Job 2:11–13* ❧

*T*he book of Job is not only a witness to the dignity of suffering and God's presence in our suffering, but it's also our primary biblical protest against religion that has been reduced to explanations or "answers." Many of the answers that Job's so-called friends give him are technically true. But it is the "technical" part that ruins them. They are answers without personal relationship, intellect without intimacy. The answers are slapped onto Job's ravaged life like labels on a specimen bottle. In response, Job rages against this secularized wisdom that has lost touch with the living realities of God.

The late (and I might add great) Joe Bayly and his wife, Mary Lou, lost three of their children. They lost one son following surgery when he was only eighteen days old. They also lost the second boy at age five because of leukemia. They then lost a third son at eighteen years after a sledding accident, because of complications related to his hemophilia.

Joe writes in a wonderful book, *The Last Thing We Talk About*:

I was sitting, torn by grief. Someone came and talked to me of God's dealings, of why it happened, of hope beyond the grave. He talked constantly; he said things I knew were true.

I was unmoved, except I wished he'd go away. He finally did.

Another came and sat beside me. He didn't talk. He didn't ask leading questions. He just sat beside me for an hour and more, listened when I said something, answered briefly, prayed simply, left.

I was moved. I was comforted. I hated to see him go.

You have done it right when those in agony hate to see you go.

We must leave Job in his misery for now. We're mere onlookers. Had we lived in his day, there is no way we could say, "I know how you feel." We don't. We can't even imagine. But we do care. Our presence and our tears say much more than our words.

Words have a hollow ring in a crucible.

# RAW REALITY

*Read Job 3:1–26*

*I*f Job's story were made into a movie and your family had rented it for tonight, when you came to this part of the story you'd fast-forward; you wouldn't want your children to watch. It's not only unedited, it's raw and borderline heretical! Some of it is downright offensive. We don't want to think a man as great as Job in chapters 1 and 2 is the same man you meet in chapter 3. We just don't want to believe it. Why? Partly because we have this skewed idea that anybody who walks this closely with God lives happily ever after. After all, "God loves you and has a wonderful plan for your life." Right? If you didn't know better, you could think you might sprout wings before your conversion is a week old and start to soar through life.

We need to understand that God's "wonderful plan" is wonderful from His perspective, not yours and mine. To us, "wonderful" means comfortable, healthy, all bills paid, no debt, never sick, happily married with two well-behaved children, a fulfilling, well-paying job, and the anticipation of nothing but blessing and success and prosperity forever. That's "wonderful" to us. But God's wonderful plan is not like that.

Job brings us back to raw reality—God's kind of reality. Remember his question, the one he asked his wife? "Shall we accept good from God and not accept adversity?" And remember that closing line? "In all this Job did not sin with his lips" (Job 2:10).

The same man soon steps into a whole new frame of reference. That's why Job 3 makes us uneasy. We don't want our hero to think or talk as he does here. He doesn't seem as if he's a man of God anymore. He even has the audacity to say at the end, "I am not at ease. I am not quiet. I am not at rest. I am in turmoil." What has happened? We're given entrance into a dark side of Job's life that is as real as any of our lives today, but the difference is, Job lets it all out. Thankfully, he reminds us that even the godly can be depressed.

Have you ever been seriously depressed? God is still there.

# WORDS OF COMFORT

*Read Job 3:1–26*

In the early 1960s when a Christian suffered from a depression that resulted in Job's kind of thinking and candid admission, you never said so publicly. You swallowed your sorrow. The first book I read on this subject, covering emotional turmoil and mental illness among Christians, was considered heresy by most of my evangelical friends.

The pervasive opinion then was simple: Christians didn't have breakdowns. Furthermore, you certainly didn't stay depressed! You know what term was used to describe those who struggled with deep depression in the early and midsixties? "Nervous." "He's got a nervous problem." Or simply, "She's nervous." And if you ever, God help you, had to be hospitalized due to your "nervous" disorder, there just wasn't a Christian word for it. I repeat, you didn't tell a soul. Shame upon shame that you didn't trust the Lord through your struggle and find Him faithful to help you "get over" your depression.

I remember being told by a seminary prof, who talked to us about assisting families with funerals, that if you did funerals for those who had committed suicide and the deceased who took his/her own life, and the deceased was a Christian, we were never to mention that fact. Frankly, it didn't sound right then, and it doesn't sound right today. Shame-based counsel never sounds right because it *isn't* right! And I didn't know enough to know that Job 3 was in the book back then. Had I known, I would have said, "Hey, what about Job?"

I want to write to you who are reading these lines who may be in the pit, struggling to find your way back. It's possible that things have gotten so dark that you need a competent Christian psychologist (or psychiatrist) to help you find your way. The most intelligent thing you can do is locate one and go. In fact, go as long as you need to go. Make sure that the counselor really does know the Lord Jesus and is truly competent, able to provide the direction you need so you can work your way through your maze of misery. And, I would add, "God bless you for every hour you spend finding your way out of the hole that you have been in. There is hope. Our faithful God will see you through."

# EXPRESSING GRIEF

### ❧ *Read Job 3:1–26* ❧

T here are days too dark for the sufferer to see light. That's where Job is as we end this chapter. Unfortunately, his so-called friends will not bring him any relief. Like Job, you may not have seen light for a long time either.

There are experiences too extreme for the hurting to maintain hope. When a person drops so low due to inner pain, it's as if all hope is lost. That's why Job admits his lack of ease, his absence of peace, and his deep unrest.

There are valleys too deep for the anguished to find relief. It seems, at that point, there is no reason to go on. We run out of places to look to find relief. It's then that our minds play tricks on us, making us think that not even God cares. Wrong! Do you remember the line that Corrie ten Boom used to quote? I often call it to mind: "There is no pit so deep but that He is not deeper still." I know, I know. Those who are deeply depressed don't remember that and can't reason with it. They would deny such a statement because they feel a vast distance between them and God, and it's confusing—it's frightening. But the good news is that God is not only there . . . He cares.

It is noteworthy that there is no blast against Job at the end of chapter 3. God doesn't say, "Shame on you, Job." God could handle Job's words. He understood why he said what he said. He understands you too. Unfortunately, Job has his words on record for preachers to talk about for centuries. Yours and mine, thankfully, will hopefully remain a secret inside our cars, or in the back part of our bedrooms, or along the crashing surf, or perhaps under tall trees in a forest. God can handle it all; so let it all out. Tell Him all that's in your heart. You never get over grief completely until you express it fully. Job didn't hold back. And I admire him more now than when I first began the book.

Look up to find the Light.

# GOOD AND BAD ADVICE

*Read Job 3:1—26*

*E*very person reading this chapter has been the recipient of bad advice. You listened as someone gave it to you. You followed the counsel you received and then suffered the consequences. We have all benefited from someone's good advice too. We were unsure and confused, so we reached out to somebody we trusted. We received good counsel, followed the advice, and enjoyed the benefits.

Take for example Proverbs 12:15: "The way of a fool is right in his own eyes, but a wise man is he who listens to counsel." You and I have experienced those very words. We have been foolish, thinking we were right, and along came a parent or teacher, perhaps a friend who talked some sense into our heads, thankfully. As a result we benefited from wise counsel.

"As in water face reflects face, so the heart of man reflects man" (Proverbs 27:19). I'm sure you have known such occasions. You've had something deep in the well of your heart you've not been able to pull up. Along comes someone who loves you and has the ability to drop a bucket in that deep well of yours, pull it out, then splash the contents around for both of you to see it clearly.

I need to add that wise counsel is not always easy to hear. "Faithful are the wounds of a friend, but deceitful are the kisses of an enemy" (Proverbs 27:6). The Hebrew uses an interesting verb stem here. It's known as the "causative stem," which allows us to render the statement: "Trustworthy are the bruises caused by the wounding of one who loves you." The bruise that comes after the verbal blow of one who loves you is a trustworthy bruise. In genuine love, your friend confronts you with the truth—you're alone, in private, and you hear the hard thing that needs to be confronted. That bruise stays with you, and you're a better person for it. Such bruising is much more helpful and reliable than a phony embrace, the "kiss" of a flatterer whom Solomon calls our "enemy." Good counsel is a good thing, even if it hurts to hear it, whether you are the receiver or the giver of that counsel.

# NOW I KNOW

### ✣ *Read Job 3:1—26* ✣

*T*here are times when others' words only make our troubles worse. That may seem too elementary to mention, so why would I? Well, have you learned it? Are you still listening to everybody? If so, it's small wonder that you're confused.

There are times when God's ways only make us more confused. There, I've said it. I've been wanting to say that all through this chapter, and I finally worked up the courage. My point? Don't expect to understand everything that happens when it occurs.

I don't care if you have a Ph.D. you earned at Yale or in Scotland. Just stand in front of the mirror, all alone, nobody around, shrug, and say, "I don't know . . . I really don't know." You can add, "I can't tell you why that happened. I don't know." Repeat the words several times: "I don't know."

The great news is that God never shrugs. He never says that. With acute perception He says, "I know exactly why this happened. I know the way you take. I know why. I know how long you'll be there, and I know what will be the end result." Shrugging and deity are incompatible.

While you're shrugging in genuine humility, saying, "I don't know," He's saying, "Good for you. Rely on Me in the mystery. Trust Me." God never promised He would inform us all about His plan ahead of time; He's just promised He has one. Ultimately, it's for our good and His glory. He knows—we don't. That's why we shrug and admit, "I don't know." So, if you and I meet someday and you ask me a deep, difficult question, don't be surprised if I shrug and say, "I don't know."

But I do know this: *The death of His Son was not in vain; Christ died for you; and if you believe in Him, He will forgive your sins, and you will go to live with Him forever. You'll have heaven and all the blessings of it,* I do know that.

It's a tough journey, getting there. Full of confusion, struggle, shrugs, followed by a lot of "I don't knows." But when the heavens open and we're there, hey, there will be no more shrugs, and you'll be able to say, "Now I know!"

# AN ARBITRATOR

### ✺ *Read Job 9:1–35* ✺

*J*ob longs for an arbitrator who could serve as his go-between, communicating with this mighty and holy God. He's wishing for one who could argue his case. Job would love to present his case in God's court, but he doesn't have a mediator. He is saying, in effect, "I would love to come and stand before the holy Judge, this God of mine, but I can't do it. He's not a man to come to me, and I don't have in myself what it takes to come before Him. I need a mediator, a go-between. Is there an arbitrator available?"

Would that Job had lived many centuries later! "There is One Mediator," Paul writes to his younger friend Timothy, referring to Him who represents us before God the Father. He is none other than Christ Jesus the Lord.

> This is good and acceptable in the sight of God our Savior, who desires all men
> to be saved and to come to the knowledge of the truth. For there is one God, and
> one mediator also between God and men, the man Christ Jesus, who gave
> Himself as a ransom for all, the testimony borne at the proper time. (1 Timothy
> 2:3–6)

Paul writes of our mediator, our arbitrator, "there is one mediator between God and men," and He is specifically identified as "the man Christ Jesus." When it comes to eternal life, there are not many mediators. There is only one, Christ Jesus. Don't be afraid to be that specific. Jesus wasn't. During His earthly ministry, Jesus spoke of Himself as "the Way, the Truth and the Life; no one comes to the Father but through Me" (John 14:6).

When it comes to the Person of Christ, He is the one and only mediator between God and humanity. He is the one and only Savior! We find ourselves responding, "Oh, Job, there is a mediator. You just haven't met Him, but someday, Job, the world will hear of Him."

And what about you, friend? Have you met my Savior?

# FUTILE SEARCHES

### ✧ *Read Job 10:1–22* ✧

*J*ob is still struggling. Eliphaz left him cold. He has received neither comfort nor insight from Bildad. He has no mediator to present his case; therefore, he is very candid. Matter of fact, he's returning to questions he asked earlier. He has every right to ask them. He's confused. He still doesn't get it. So, understandably, he asks:

> Why then have You brought me out of the womb?
> Would that I had died and no eye had seen me!
> I should have been as though I had not been,
> Carried from womb to tomb.
> Would he not let my few days alone?
> Withdraw from me that I may have a little cheer. (Job 10:18–20)

"Why didn't He just take me from the womb and carry me to the tomb?" Oh, Job, you're back where you started. In fact, as he ends his response, he is back in the doldrums. He writes of his own "gloom" and "deep shadow" and "darkness." Out of respect for Job's private struggle, I suggest we draw all this to a close. This ends sadly, but so it is with Job as Bildad frowns, then walks away. And God stays silent. We end sadly, but not without lessons to remember.

First, *when misery breaks our spirit, philosophical words don't help us cope.* All Job's so-called comforting companions had to offer were hollow words in the form of philosophical meanderings and theoretical concepts. That brought him no relief, no break in his misery. Philosophical words fall flat when they're mouthed to those in misery.

*Second, when a mediator can't be found, futile searches won't give us hope.* We're surrounded by people today on a search for hope to go on . . . to make it through the maze of their misery. Many of them long for a mediator, someone who can represent their cause and plead their case. You may be that person. If so, you can know what Job didn't know. The mediator he longed for is not only alive, He is available and ready to hear your story. Unlike Job's friends, He's no philosopher. He's the Redeemer. His name is Jesus. Anyone who comes to Him for comfort will find it. He has more mercy than you have misery.

# SKIMMING THE SURFACE

### ⚓ *Read Job 11:1–20* ⚓

*A*re you seeking to know the depths of God, or are you just skimming the surface?

> Can you discover the depths of God?
> Can you discover the limits of the Almighty?
> They are high as the heavens, what can you do?
> Deeper than Sheol, what can you know? (Job 11:7–8)

Let me repeat the question: Are you seeking to know the depths of God, or are you just skimming the surface? Only you know the answer. Our current culture is so busy we can become proficient at faking it. We can look like we're going to the depths when, in fact, we're just skating. So you must answer for yourself. Are you seeking to know the depths of God? Or do you find that you're just attending a lot of religious meetings, reading a few religious books, and learning all the religious-sounding language.

One of Larry Crabb's latest books is titled *The Pressure's Off.* In it he writes,

> As a culture, present-day Christianity has redefined spiritual maturity. The reformers knew we were saved to glorify God. We moderns live to be blessed. The mature among us are now thought to be the successful, the happy, the effective people on top of things and doing well . . . We're more attracted to sermons, books, and conferences that reveal the secrets to fulfillment . . . than to spiritual direction that leads us through affliction into the presence of the Father.[10]

*We seem more interested in managing life into a comfortable existence than in letting God spiritually transform us through life's hardships.*

That cuts to the quick, doesn't it? Don't run from the hardship. Don't seek a friend who'll help you get out from under it quickly. Stay there. Stay in it. The Lord God will get you through it. As a result you'll stop skating.

This question is for you to answer: personally, introspectively, truly. Are you seeking to know the depths of God, or are you just skimming the surface?

# GOD IS IN CONTROL

### *Read Job 12:1–25*

*F*rankly, I admire Job's guts. I'm pleased he doesn't cave in and say, "Well, maybe you're right, Zophar. You sound like those other two guys, so I'm not going to disagree and fight you on this." No way! The strong rebuke of Zophar is met by an even stronger resistance from Job. This, by the way, is the only way to deal with a legalist. They, too, are like roaches! You leave them alone and let them have their way, they proliferate. They attract others. And before you know it, the legalists take over. Bullying their way into leadership is their favorite approach. And if they can't bully, they take their ball and bat and go elsewhere (thank the Lord). They leave.

There was a time in my life when I allowed legalists to take more control of me than they should have been allowed. I'm making up for lost time now. Age has its benefits. I've learned the hard way, you need to fight fire with fire when bullies are determined to take charge. Job would have nothing to do with that! He put the stop to Zophar like Paul resisted the legalistic Judaizers and "did not yield in subjection to them for even an hour" (Galatians 2:5).

When Job finally does speak, he says, in effect, "Okay. That's enough." He stood up to them. I, for one, greatly admire Job for not sitting there any longer taking it on the chin.

Job declares, "It is all about our God! It is the inscrutable, Almighty God who is in charge of all things. Don't you think I know that?" And what a creative way to say it! "The God I serve takes delight in undoing human activities and in dismantling human enterprises, and in the process, executing His miraculous undertakings. He alone is in full control."

Job is making it clear that God alone is the One before whom he bows, and in doing so he implies, "I'm not sure you've ever met Him. Don't bully me. While I don't know why I'm suffering like this, I can tell you that somehow and in some way the God of heaven, the silent God, the One who seems to be absent from my perspective, is still in control."

Would you be able to say the same thing if you were in Job's situation?

# A DISAPPOINTING DISCOVERY

### ✣ *Read Job 14:1–22* ✤

*W*ill it be well when God examines your life, or will it be a disappointing discovery? I can't speak for you because I have no idea. But I do know "we must all appear before the judgment seat of Christ, so that each one may be recompensed for his deeds in the body, according to what he has done, whether good or bad" (2 Corinthians 5:10). Is that going to be a disappointing discovery, or will it be well with you? Probing thought, which is why I've urged you to give these questions such serious consideration.

Look at Job 14:14: "If a man dies, will he live again? All the days of my struggle I will wait, until my change comes."

Here's what I'd like you to think about: When you die, where will you live again? Will it be with the Lord or away from His presence forever? The choices are heaven or hell. Will it be eternal bliss filled with joy and relief and the rewards awaiting God's people? Or eternal judgment, away from God and all those things you hold dear? Only you can determine which.

C. S. Lewis wrote this:

> There's no doctrine which I would more willingly remove from Christianity than the doctrine of hell, if it lay in my power. But it has the full support of Scripture and especially of our Lord's own words; it has always been held by Christendom and it has the support of reason.[11]

C. S. Lewis was no intellectual pushover. His words deserve serious consideration. Problems have a way of multiplying. The good news is—that's true only in this life—"How frail . . . how few our years . . . how full of trouble." But once we're in our Lord's presence, all that changes.

However, should you choose to ignore this opportunity to secure such hope, the alternative results will be dreadful beyond imagination. Come to think of it, that kind of future would make Job's trials seem like a piece of cake. Who wants a destiny like that? Don't go there!

# NEEDED GRACE

### ✤ Read Job 15:1—35 ✤

*T*hat's it, Job! It's your arrogance!" Eliphaz backs away and stares at him with that glare, saying, again, "You are getting exactly what you deserve!" The style of communication Eliphaz employs is not that unusual to those who lack grace. It may not always be this brutal, but haven't you noticed this tone when you're around people who evidence no grace? When you're down, they kick you. When you're drowning, they pull you under. When you're confused, they complicate your life. And when you're almost finished, they write you off. Other than that, they're pretty good folks.

It is easy to forget the grief Job was trying to get past—the shocking loss of his adult children. Releasing the vise grip of grief that comes from a sudden death takes an enormous toll.

I can't help but think of that when I see Job, as he sits there enduring this, awash in his grief, trying his best to believe his ears—that this man who was once a friend is saying such graceless words. I'm left with one thought: "Lord, if you are teaching us anything through Job's endurance, teach us the value of *grace*. Teach us about demonstrating *grace*. Show us again that grace is *always* appropriate. *Always* needed. Not just by a student in Missouri taking a final exam. Not only by a grieving family in Dallas. *All* of us need it!"

The person sitting near you in church next Sunday, the lady pushing that cart in the grocery store, the one who's putting gas in his car at the next pump, the man behind you at the movies, waiting to buy his ticket, the student across from you at school. You have no idea what that person is going through. If you did, chances are you'd be prompted to show grace or to say a few encouraging words even quicker. Remember this please: grace is *always* appropriate, *always* needed!

"Amazing grace—how sweet the sound!"

# A LOT OF GRACE

### ❧ *Read Job 17:1—16* ❧

*Y*ou know why I love the Bible? Because it's so real. There's a lot of fog rolling into Job's life, just as in our lives. On this earth nobody "lives happily ever after." That line is a huge fairy tale. You're living in a dream world if you're waiting for things to be "happy ever after." That's why we need grace. Marriage doesn't get easier, it gets harder. So we need grace to keep it together. Work doesn't get easier, it gets more complicated, so we need grace to stay on the job. Childrearing doesn't get easier. You who have babies one, two, three years old—you think you've got it tough. Wait until they're fourteen. Or eighteen. Talk about needing grace!

I'll be painfully honest here. If I called the shots, I would have relieved Job five minutes after he lost everything. I'd have brought all his kids back to life the very next day. I would have immediately re-created everything he lost, and I would really deal with those sorry comforters! I'd have cut the lips off of Eliphaz after about three sentences. And if that didn't stop him, I'd take the neck. I mean, who needs that clod? But you know what? You would never mature under my kind of treatment. You'd just enjoy the comfort. We'd all go to picnics then on a motorcycle ride and have tons of fun. That's my style. Which explains why Cynthia says to me, "Honey, if everybody handled things like you wanted, all we'd bring to the party is *balloons*. Nobody would think to bring the food." As usual, she's right.

So, the fog's rolled in. As all hell breaks loose, grace takes a hike. Welcome to the human race, Job. But the wonderful old song says,

Thru many dangers, toils and snares,
I have already come;
'Tis grace hath brought me safe thus far,
And grace will lead me home.[12]

That's the ticket. Even in the fog, grace will lead us home.

# JOB'S LONGING

### ✣ *Read Job 19:1–29* ✣

*J*ob longed for his words of woe to be etched into granite so that people through time could enter into all the things he was enduring. He thought his words would be forgotten. He had no idea that his words would survive him. Yet, think of it, God chose to include them in His eternal Word! Along with scriptures like Genesis 1, Psalm 23, Romans 8, 1 Corinthians 13, and Revelation 22, we call to mind Job 19:25–27 to this day!

As for me, I know that my redeemer lives, and at the last He will take His stand on the earth. Even after my skin is destroyed, Yet from my flesh I shall see God; whom I myself shall behold, and whom my eyes shall see and not another. My heart faints within me.

Thanks to Handel's *Magnum Opus*, every Christmas season we hear that message over and over again. Little did Job realize in his dreadful anguish that his Lord would honor his name by preserving his words for all the world to hear *and sing!*

I need to pause right here and speak to you whose God is distant and silent. And, perhaps (like Job), your friends have begun to turn against you. There is a future that is brighter than your wildest dreams! As Job will one day experience, justice will win out, God will replace evil, and right will eclipse wrong. In the end, God wins. And so will we. Job will be vindicated and remembered and respected. And all the Zophars, Bildads, and Eliphazes will be judged, silenced, and forgotten. "Then be afraid of the sword for yourselves, for wrath brings the punishment of the sword, so that you may know there is judgment" (Job 19:29).

In all his misery, Job had not lost sight of who was right and who was wrong. He reminded all three men that "judgment and punishment are not coming my way; they're coming *yours*."

Focus on the future!

# A Context of Pain

### ❧ *Read Job 19:1–29* ❧

here is nothing like hope in the truth to clarify perspective and keep you going. Enduring a painful journey can be done a lot more easily if you embrace truth as your traveling companion. Not only will it give you hope, it will clarify your perspective. Truth reminds us that God is alive and just and good. I say again, wrong will ultimately be judged. Today may seem dark and terribly long, but there will be a bright tomorrow.

There is nothing like a lack of assurance to haunt your steps and make you afraid. Let me put it to you straight: If you are without the Lord Jesus Christ in your life, your steps are marked by uncertainty. And deep into the night when the lights are out and your head is sunk into the pillow, thoughts of your ultimate future will haunt you. Few thoughts are more frightening than not knowing where you will be when you die. If you die without Christ, you're facing a fearful judgment. "It is appointed for man to die once and after this comes judgment" (Hebrews 9:27). To have inner peace you need to know without a doubt where you're going.

My wife and I have a commitment regarding giving our money while we're alive. I like the old saying, "Do your givin' while you're livin', then you're knowin' where it's goin'." With that in mind, be sure you're believing right while you're living, then you'll be knowing where you're going. It's scary not knowing where you're going.

Do you really know where you're going? Is your eternal destination guaranteed? Amazingly, Bildad talked to the wrong man and with the wrong motive. He had a strong message, but it was for some other person. Could that person be you? If so, there is reason to be concerned.

# SILENCING LIES

### *Read Job 20:1–29*

*L*et's fast-forward momentarily and face the music. Some of you who are reading these words have awfully sharp tongues. You say things that cut, but you couch your words in phrases that sound pious and even eloquent. They can sound superreligious at times, but they're hurtful and damaging. They imply much more than is actually said. It is here that self-control plays such a vital role. How valuable it is to think before we speak and then, even after giving our words careful thought, to measure their tone, their possible impact, their truthfulness. Zophar did none of the above. With reckless abandon he dropped his harsh words like depth charges. Though Job was a seasoned and mature man of God, they must have hurt as they exploded in his mind. Even for the strong, false accusations hurt.

Forming habits of self-restraint is an essential discipline. When receiving information about another, it's best to ask the source: "How do you know that? Who told you? Is this information credible?" Those questions have a way of silencing people who tend to pass along damaging and exaggerated information. They assist in getting to the bottom of rumors. Furthermore, truth is given the opportunity to flourish, replacing lies. But you need to know that this kind of truth-talking comes with a price.

Throughout Zophar's lecture, Job has been listening to what my mother used to call "a lot of palaver." Just a lot of lip flapping—he's been talking nonsense. What he's saying against Job isn't true, even though Zophar delivers his words poetically and eloquently. Job has patiently endured, but he refuses to let those words slide by.

I've heard it said that, no matter what, when false accusations are made, you just sit quietly and say nothing; God will defend you. There are some occasions when that may be appropriate. Not always. I often call to mind a motto from the American Revolution: "Trust in God but keep your powder dry." Wise counsel! If your reputation is being ruined by lies, if your company is going down the tubes because of false accusations, if your church is being destroyed and demoralized because of wrong information from lying lips, there are times it is necessary to step up and set the record straight. Truth has a way of silencing lies.

# STAY WITH THE TRUTH

### ✦ *Read Job 21:1–34* ✦

C hances are good that many of you who are reading these lines are currently the target of someone's lying accusations. That can be an anguishing cross to bear. I've been there, so I speak from painful experience. Since this is an ongoing issue for many of us, it should be helpful to draw a few guidelines to follow based on the way Job handled his accuser.

Listen to what is being said, considering the character of the critic. *Stay calm!* You will be tempted to jump in and rashly react in the flesh, saying things you will later regret. Do your best to listen to what is being said. While doing so, keep in mind the character of the person who is the source of the accusation. Calmly take it all in. Job did that, which prepared him for his further response.

Respond with true facts and accurate information, knowing the nature of your accuser. *Speak truth!* Stay on the side of accuracy, regardless. The other person may be a former husband or former wife. He or she could be your previous or current boss, an employee, a neighbor, a pastor, or a friend. It doesn't matter who the individual is. If you are being accused, you need to focus only on facts. Don't *react* or ponder ways to *retaliate*. If you yield to either temptation, you'll come off sounding like the accuser. God honors integrity. Maybe not immediately, but ultimately you'll be vindicated. Remember David's prayer: "Vindicate me, O LORD, for I have walked in my integrity" (Psalm 26:1). Truth will prevail among people who traffic in it and make their decisions based on it.

Abraham Lincoln was told that he needed to fire his postmaster general. All kinds of accusations were being leveled against the man. Lincoln weighed rumor against hard evidence, and on July 18, 1864, he wrote Secretary Stanton a letter saying he was not going to do that because the information was based on hearsay, not accurate facts. In that letter he correctly concluded, "Truth is generally the best vindication against slander." Wise response.

Stay with the truth. Don't exaggerate it, don't deny it, and don't hesitate to say it.

# HARSH BUT REALISTIC

### ✦ *Read Job 21:23–34* ✦

*W*hile speaking the truth Job left the defense of his own character in the Lord's hands. He was firm and deliberate, but he remained in control. I repeat, I understand what it's like to be unjustly maligned. I have been accused of things, and that rumor has kept me awake. It has made my stomach churn. It has taken away my appetite. I have determined not to pay any attention to it, yet found that I was unable to turn it off in my mind. Not until I decided to leave things in the Lord's hands and rest in His sovereign control, did I find inner peace. Without exception (please hear this!), not until I deliberately stepped back and leaned hard on my God, did my mind begin to relax, my emotions settle down, and my inner peace return. I say again, the truth will win out. And God will be glorified.

Refuse to let the accusations discourage and derail you, remembering they are nonsense and lies. *Get tough!* Returning to that one-liner from the Revolutionary War, "Trust in God but keep your powder dry," is essential to keeping your balance. You may be trusting the Lord for safety, but you still lock your doors every night, hopefully, and turn on your alarm. When you get in your car, you lock your doors, don't you? You roll up your windows, don't you? If you don't, you are playing with fire. Trusting God is not naive presumption. Wisdom must be applied to a life of faith. Going through hard times requires a get-tough mind-set. Go there. That may seem harsh, but it's realistic. And realism is a powerful message.

To you who are going through a time of false accusation, may God strengthen you in it. May He hold you close through it. May He give you wisdom and grace in responding to it. May He become real and personal to you, even giving you songs in the night and quiet rest with the assurance that He is defending your integrity. And may He toughen your hide so you don't cave in while awaiting vindication.

# DEMONSTRATING CLASS

### ❧ *Read Job 23:1–17* ❧

As we get to chapters 23 and 24 of Job, we observe three calm, vulnerable responses from him. Take the time to read through these two chapters—they're magnificent! Job's first theme seems to be, *"I am unable to locate the presence of God, but I trust You, Lord."* I find that coming through loud and clear in the first twelve verses of chapter 23.

It seems that Job has a courtroom in mind. "I wish I knew the bench on which Almighty God sits. I wish I knew where I could locate Him. Some place—anyplace—on this earth that I could get to Him."

Hidden within these passionate words is found one of the great things about our God. When we come to Him as we are, we never hear Him shout, "Shame on you!" God hears our pleading, our feelings of need, and He is quick to respond, "I forgive you. I love you. I understand you. I'm here; I commend you for facing the truth."

Notice how Job refers to the Lord's response:

Would He contend with me by the greatness of His power?
No, surely He would pay attention to me.
There the upright would reason with Him;
And I would be delivered forever from my Judge. (Job 23:6–7)

All of God's people find here a valuable truth we can learn from our God. When people come, open and vulnerable with their confession, there is one appropriate three-word response: *I forgive you.* They don't need to be put on the spot or shamed because they failed. They need the assurance of forgiveness.

Job asks, "Would He contend with me?"

Then he answers himself, "He would not contend with me, even though He's much more powerful. He would pay attention to me. I could reason with Him, and I would be delivered forever from my Judge."

How wonderful is that?

# HIS PURPOSE

### *Read Job 23:1–17*

*J*ob struggles, finally admitting his frustration: he cannot find God. Ever been there? Of course. All of us have! There are days we search in vain for some visible evidence of the living God. I'm thinking, *Wouldn't it be great to wake up in the middle of a full-moon sky tonight, peek out my bedroom window, and see some skywriting, "Dear Chuck, I hear you. I'm right here. I'm in charge. Love, God."* I would love for that to happen! I'd love to get into my pickup after a tough day at the church, turn the radio on, and have God interrupt, saying, "Before you listen to this station, Chuck, I want to talk to you for a few minutes." Let's face it, all of us would love to hear an audible voice or read a visible message from God. But that's not the way it works. Our walk with Him is a walk of faith, not sight.

Job is a great and godly man. He is a mature saint, no doubt about it. Nevertheless, he longs to witness God's presence. "Oh, that I could know where He is. But I cannot see Him, behold Him, or perceive Him."

Though unable to locate the presence of God, Job states his trust in Him: "Eliphaz, Bildad, and Zophar, you can say whatever you wish against me. God knows which way I go. He knows the truth. He is my Justifier. He and I are on speaking terms. I trust Him. I believe in Him. Furthermore, after the trial is over, and He has accomplished His purpose within me, 'I shall come forth as gold.'"

You can count on that, my friend. When the trial has passed, you will be deeper and richer for it. Gold will replace alloy. I want you to allow those words to burn their way into your brain so deeply that they become like a divine filter for everything that happens in your life from this day forward. God knows which way you're going. And His Word will be "a lamp for your path" (Psalm 119:105).

# GOD WILL REWARD

### ❧ *Job 23:1–17* ❧

*B*ack when Job's body was covered with sores, when his friends were still against him, when he was bankrupt and sitting in a garbage dump at the outskirts of the city, Job had the temerity to say, "But He knows the way I take; when He has tried me, I shall come forth as gold" (Job 23:10).

Job makes three statements based on faith in the midst of his suffering. All three are about his God.

First: *I know that God knows my situation.* "He knows the way I take."

Second: *I believe it is God who is testing me.* "When He has tried me."

Third: *I believe that after the trials have ended, He will bless me in a unique way.* He doesn't deny the trials, but there's hope beyond them. God knows. God will reward. That's what we find when we get to the last chapter of Job's life.

Wouldn't it be great if we could be in Job's position at the *end* of the book without going through what he did *through* the book? How good would it be to gain his knowledge without all the suffering? Impossible! Stay realistic and realize that cannot happen. It takes fire to refine gold.

Just as we are different in our appearance, our background, and our levels of maturity and chronological age, so we experience different tests. For all you know, the person living in your neighborhood is going through one of the deepest times of her or his life.

I hope these two words will not seem hollow or pious when I write them: *take hope*. Take hope that this is not going on without God's awareness. The Lord God knows the way you take, and it's not without purpose. After the fiery trial you, too, will come forth as gold. You're being refined by the test He's allowed, and you're being reshaped in the process— purified and humbled. Better times are coming. If not soon, and if not later on this earth, they will surely come when you stand before Him and He distributes the "gold, silver, and precious stones." It will then be worth it all. Many of Job's rewards came while he was still alive on planet Earth. Yours may await you in glory. Either way, God knows. God always remembers. God will reward.

# GRACE UNDER PRESSURE

### 🌿 *Read Job 24:1—25* 🌿

W e could go all the way through this list to the end. There are wrongs, there are failures, and there are injustices. There were robberies and sexual sins and hidden wrongs done in the dark. And where is God? He is permitting it. Why? "I don't know," says Job. "I think His point here is that these things are allowed for purposes unknown to us. God has permitted it all!" Those who do wrong often get away with it. Those who take advantage of others get away with that too. Unexplainable suffering falls into the same category.

You and I could mention events in our lifetime that the Lord could have stopped, but He didn't. This isn't just about the Jewish Holocaust. This isn't simply about the wrongs of the Crusade Era. This isn't only about the priests in the Roman Catholic Church who have molested young boys. This is also about all kinds of things that we could name, and God could have stopped each one—but He didn't. *It's a mystery!* That's the point. "I can't justify the permissions of God, but I trust Him."

Refuse to believe that life is based on blind fate or random chance. Everything that happens, including the things you cannot explain or justify, is being woven together like an enormous, beautiful piece of tapestry. From this earthly side it seems blurred and knotted, strange and twisted. But from heaven's perspective it forms an incredible picture. Best of all, it is for His greater glory. Right now, it seems so confusing, but someday the details will come together and make good sense.

There it is—part of God's perfect plan unfolding. You can't explain it. You couldn't piece it all together if you tried. You aren't able to understand it, and there will be times you won't like it. But, as we're learning from Job, God's not going to ask your permission. And so? We trust Him anyway. I'll write it once more: Those who do that discover without trying to make it happen that they have begun to demonstrate grace under pressure. To settle for less is a miserable existence.

Do you trust God anyway?

# ACCEPTING GOD'S PLAN

### ✦ *Read Job 24:1—25* ✦

*D*avid, in Psalm 139, makes the appropriate comment, "Such knowledge is too wonderful for me; it is too high, I cannot attain to it" (v. 6). If David lived today, he would write, "This blows my mind." The vastness of God's inscrutability has a way of doing that to us—and so it should.

If nothing else, the study of Job reveals that we don't fully understand God's ways. We cannot explain the inexplicable. We cannot fathom the unfathomable. So let's not try to unscrew the inscrutable.

If only the men who considered themselves Job's friends had acknowledged that. It would have been so much more comforting to Job, sitting in such enormous misery, longing for an arm around his shoulder and someone honest enough to say, "We're here, but we don't understand why this is happening any more than you do. God knows, but we're here to be with you through it. God is doing something deep and mysterious, but it is so beyond us we cannot understand it either."

May I go one step further? God doesn't have a "wonderful plan" for everybody's life. Not here on earth, for sure. For some lives His plan is Lou Gehrig's disease. For some lives (like Job's) His plan is a life of pain. For others, heartbreak and brokenness, blindness or paralysis, or congenital complications. For many, His plan is to answer no to their requests for healing. But we don't like that. Some won't accept it. In fact, they go so far as to say, "If you believe that, you lack faith." On the contrary, I say if you believe that, you believe the Bible!

The God of the Bible includes the lives of people who don't get well, who don't quickly get over their problems, who don't easily overcome accidents or illnesses. God's Word pictures its heroes, warts and all. They hurt. They fall. They fail, and on occasion, by His grace, they succeed.

How well do you accept the unfolding plan of God for your life?

# No Surprise

### *Read Job 26:1–14*

What Job lacked here in tact, he made up for in total honesty. Frankly, this was no time for tact. Bildad has been brutal. It's doubtful he would even hear if Job had been soft and diplomatic. Job gets tough!

Sores will do that to you. Any nurse will tell you, especially those who work at the bedside of patients in great pain, that tact fades as pain progresses. There's something about the continuation of anguish that finally wears a soul down to raw, red reality.

Many years ago I came across this statement: "Pain plants the flag of reality in the fortress of a rebel heart." Even among those who have been stubborn and rebellious, when pain hits and persists, reality comes in full measure. So it was with Job. He took off the gloves, looked into Bildad's eyes, and said it straight. The man needed that kind of response.

There's a little prayer I'd suggest you repeat each morning.

Lord, help me today not to add to anybody's burden. Help me to bring encouragement to others. Where I can, enable me to comfort. And when I don't know, help me to admit it. When I feel sorrow and sympathy for someone, help me to say that. Help me to lift the load of the hurting, not to add to their burden.

If others are going through an agonizing experience, they need us to be supportive and strong. Bildad never learned that principle; he never prayed that prayer. Too bad.

An intriguing change of roles now occurs. Instead of Bildad teaching Job, Job becomes the teacher. It's almost as if he decides, "Since you don't have any answers, let me tell you about the infinite, incomprehensible God, who hasn't revealed all the whys and wherefores of His activities."

From verse 5 through verse 13 of chapter 26, Job takes Bildad through the paces. He communicates what we would call a fascinating, cosmological explanation. Amazingly, Job starts with the departed spirits of the dead then goes all the way to the top of the universe. In a simple, straight-forward manner, Job is saying, "God is in control of every bit of it. He knows about it, He understands it, He is in the midst of it, and He takes full responsibility for all of it. None of it is a surprise to the living God."

# WHO CAN UNDERSTAND?

### ✦ *Read Job 26:1–14* ✦

hat a thrilling thought! "Bildad, as magnificent as all of these things are, what I've mentioned represents only the fringes of His ways." Isn't "fringes" a great word? The fringes, the outer edges of His ways; only the quiet whispers of His mighty voice, the hushed tones of omnipotence. Bildad—listen to me! Who can fully understand? And to think that this Creator-God pierces through all the millions of galaxies of "the heavens" and gives His attention to this tiny green-pea planet called Earth, reaching down to folks like us, knowing even the number of hairs on our heads.

Perspective like that is needed when the sores on my body are running with pus and the fever won't go down. Job ends where Bildad should have begun. "Who can understand?"

Indeed, how unsearchable are His judgments and unfathomable are His ways. Now, be careful here. That does not mean He's not in touch, out of control, and He doesn't have a plan. It just means He isn't obligated to explain Himself. And because He doesn't reveal everything, we're left with three very honest words, which are helpful coming from the lips of otherwise proud people. And what are those three words? *I don't know.*

In the final analysis, God knows, and He does all things well. He is in charge. I am the clay; He is the Potter. I am the disciple; He is the Lord. I am the sheep; He is the Shepherd. I am the servant; He is the Master. That means I am to submit myself. I am to humble myself under His mighty hand. I must be willing to adjust my life to His choices for me, to listen, to learn, to adapt to His leading wherever it may go whether I'm comfortable, happy, or healthy. That is obedience. Job, by now, is beginning to see it, and when he reaches the end of his brief explanation, he wisely asks, "Who can understand?"

Train yourself to think theologically. Make it your determined purpose to think God's thoughts after Him, acknowledging His lofty magnificence. Teach yourself to be at ease saying the words, "I don't know." Because Job thought correctly about God, he was able to endure, even while not understanding why. May his tribe increase. And may it include you.

# LOOK UP

### ❧ *Read Job 26:1–14* ❧

*I*'ve lived long enough to be convinced that suffering is not an enemy. It seems strange to put it this way, but the truth is, suffering is a friend. Not until we acknowledge that will we glean its benefits. Job is living in the crucible. His misery in that difficult arena has forced him to focus on things that really matter.

I have finally come to realize that one of the benefits of going through times of suffering is that my focus turns vertical. Charles Spurgeon, the great pulpiteer of London for so many years, was a flashpoint of controversy. The media of his day relished taking him on. They took advantage of a target that big. Normally he could hold his own, but there was one occasion when it began to get the best of him. All of us have our breaking points.

His wife noticed a depression that was lingering. She became concerned for him that he not lose his zeal and not miss the opportunities that were his while going through such hard times. That led her to do an unusual thing. She turned in her Bible to the Sermon on the Mount where Jesus said:

> Blessed are you when people insult you and persecute you, and falsely say all kinds of evil against you because of me. Rejoice and be glad, for your reward in heaven is great; for in the same way they persecuted the prophets who were before you. (Matthew 5:11–12)

In her own handwriting she wrote those words on a large piece of paper. She then taped it on the ceiling above their bed. When the preacher turned over the next morning, he awoke, blinked his eyes, and as he lay there he read those words. He read them again, aloud. He focused vertically on what God was saying, and it renewed him within. He pressed on with new passion. What a wonderful, creative idea Mrs. Spurgeon had!

Here's the point: when flat on your back, the only way to look is up. Focus on god, rather than your pain. Become totally absorbed with thoughts of Him.

# THINGS THAT MATTER

### ❧ *Read Job 27:1–23* ❧

*T*hinking God's thoughts is our highest goal. That's one of the reasons I'm such a proponent of the discipline of Scripture memorization. You cannot think God's thoughts more acutely than when you quote God's very words back to life's situations.

What comes into our minds when we think about God is the most important thing about us. So what comes to mind when *you* think about God? I remember as a little boy thinking of God as a very old man with a long white beard, cheeks puffed out, blowing strong winds from the north. I had seen His face portrayed this way at school on old map of the world.

What comes to your mind when you think about God? Do you see Him as the One who gives you breath and keeps your heart beating? Do you see Him as the One who will call everyone into judgment someday? Do you see Him as the One who watches over your children and your business? Do you acknowledge His power as greater than any power you could ever witness on this earth? Or, honestly now, is He a little remote, sort of out of touch with today's hi-tech society to you? Your view of God makes all the difference in how you view life.

Think of Job's situation—he is now bankrupt, childless, friendless, and diseased. Covered with boils, he is living with a high fever and constant pain. On top of that he is misunderstood, being blamed for secret sins, and is now rejected by those who once respected him. How in the world does he go on? There's only one answer: his view of God keeps him going, not what others are saying. And in light of that, he recommits himself to things that matter. In a swirl of humanistic thinking, coming from Eliphaz, Bildad, and Zophar, whom Job has mentally turned off, he is now focused fully on the things of God.

What thoughts are distracting you from mentally dwelling on the glory of God? You can overcome them by spending more time in God's Word on the things that really matter.

# BIBLICALLY CORRECT

### ❧ *Read Job 27:1–23* ❧

*I*sn't that closing comment a great line? The wicked man may have more clothes in his closet, but he'll wind up leaving them to us. Remember the materialistic line that is framed around license plates?" "He who dies with the most toys wins." The truth is, he who dies with the most toys passes them off to the righteous, and the righteous get to enjoy them! Job has come to realize this priority: wrong will occur, but it will not ultimately triumph. That brings a sense of justice.

There go those great riches! How often have we witnessed or heard about individuals who are loaded financially, but it isn't too many years before it is gone. Those riches were like an eagle—they made themselves wings. Rest assured, God keeps accurate records. He knows what He's about. Furthermore, He knows who is righteous and who is wicked.

It's easy to become confused if you watch too much of the evening news on television. Be very discerning about what you watch and what you read. If the source is not reliable, the information will be skewed. Thankfully, there are still some in our day who think straight and aren't afraid to say so. Their words remind us that evil is evil, that wrong actions will be judged, that even though the wicked may seem to be winning, they will ultimately lose! The nineteenth century American poet and essayist, James Russell Lowell, put it well:

> Truth forever on the scaffold
> Wrong forever on the throne—
> Yet that scaffold sways the future
> And, behind the dim unknown,
> Standeth God within the shadow,
> Keeping watch above His own.

Stay on the scaffold. Keep thinking straight. Refuse to tolerate wrong! Like Job, keep forming your priorities from the Word of God. Spend less time in the papers or watching TV and more time in the Scriptures. Let God dictate your agenda and help you interpret the events of our times. Become biblically correct rather than politically correct.

# TRUE CONVICTIONS

### *Read Job 27:1–23*

*R*eflecting on past blessings gives us reasons to rejoice. Let me urge you who are parents still rearing young children to teach them how to do this by practicing it often. Suppertime is a great opportunity to reflect. It's an ideal time to look back over the day and to count the blessings.

*Rehearsing* present trials forces us to swallow our pride. I suggest that we rehearse the present trials we're going through and allow them appropriately to cut us down to size. Being "leveled" has its benefits.

*Reaffirming* our commitment to integrity strengthens us with confidence and courage. This is what I love most about Job: even when he is discouraged and disappointed, he is not defeated.

Cynthia and I recently returned from a life-changing tour of the sites made famous by a small group of strong-hearted, straight-thinking men. We know them today as Reformers. They were the leaders of the Great Reformation that swept across Central Europe in the sixteenth century.

Jon Huss of Czechoslovakia, Martin Luther and Philip Melanchthon of Germany, Ulrich Zwingli and John Calvin of Switzerland, and John Knox of Scotland (to name only a few) were not supermen in stature or strength. Nor were they anywhere near perfect. But they were men of integrity, which included character qualities that kept them faithful. It also resulted in their being unintimidated in the face of opposition that was not only vocal but life-threatening. To borrow from Luther's now-famous line, each one said, in effect, "Here I stand, I can do no other," as they refused to weaken or recant. Like Job, they were misunderstood, maligned, falsely accused, and openly insulted by their critics. They represented lonely voices of truth while standing true to their convictions.

While on our tour, I often lingered at a bronze statue or stood in the pulpit where one of them once preached, wondering if, perhaps, they were strengthened to stand alone by the example left by Job in the Scriptures. Long before they lived, he testified, "Till I die I will not put away my integrity from me. I hold fast my righteousness and will not let it go" (Job 27:5–6).

I also asked myself, "Would I have the courage to do what they did?" Would you?

# GOD AND GOD ALONE

*Read Job 28:1–28*

*A*llow me to offer a simple definition of *wisdom*. Wisdom is looking at life from God's point of view. When we employ wisdom we are viewing life as God sees it. That's why it's so valuable to think God's thoughts. You look at difficulties and tests as God looks at them. You look at family life and child rearing as God looks at them. You interpret current events as God would interpret them. You focus on the long view. You see the truth even though all around you are deception and lies.

Let's go a step further and define another scriptural term: *understanding*. What does it mean? Understanding is responding to life's struggles and challenges as God would have us respond. Not in panic and confusion. Not forfeiting those things that are valuable to us, and not by compromising our integrity. Instead, when we have understanding, we respond to life's challenges as God would have us respond. We trust Him. We believe in Him. We refuse to be afraid. We don't operate our lives according to human impulses or in step with today's politically correct culture.

How terribly important it is that we stand firm in wisdom, responding in understanding. Neither can be found by our own effort or as a result of our searching. God graciously provides both. Verse 20 asks two great questions:

*Where then does wisdom come from?*

And *where is the hiding place of understanding?*

Not, where can we get advice? Not, where does opinion come from? I could name a dozen sources, but most of them aren't worth listening to. Then where does this *wisdom* come from? Where can we find true *understanding*?

You can earn four Ph.D. degrees and never gain wisdom or understanding. You'll certainly not get a grasp of the fear of the Lord from higher learning. Even in the finest of universities, there's no course offered on the fear of the Lord. The source? God and God alone. By "fear of the Lord" I'm referring to an awesome respect for God accompanied by a personal hatred for sin. Now we can see why Solomon wrote, "The fear of the LORD is the beginning of wisdom, and the knowledge of the Holy One is understanding" (Proverbs 9:10).

# LEARN FROM SUFFERING

### ✦ *Read Job 28:1—28* ✦

There is a man in our congregation who recently underwent brain surgery. The tumor in the frontal section within his cranium was pushing his brain back and slowly eroding his memory. Each week the growth of the tumor became more pronounced and debilitating for him. Brain surgery was the only option.

I visited him in the hospital following successful surgery. A scar on his scalp stretched from his left ear across the top of his head down to his right ear. Stainless steel staples held the incision closed. He was lying there on the bed, smiling when I walked in. It wasn't long before I realized that my visiting him was for a different reason than I had planned. In going I received a fresh load of wisdom. He didn't get any from me; I got it from him.

He spoke of the Lord from the moment we started our conversation until I left. He mentioned insights the Lord had given him. He talked about lessons he'd begun to learn. He spoke of an overwhelming sense of peace he had enjoyed from the git-go. I mean, if ever a man was fully focused on the Lord, this man was. His words flowed with a gentle tone. There was a calm pace in our conversation as he responded. He was saying, in effect, "Please don't feel sorry for me. This brain surgery has become my opportunity to trust in the Lord with my whole heart, to have Him show me some things I would have otherwise missed." He was, literally, rejoicing, as was his wife. Wisdom and understanding had completely eclipsed pain and panic.

How true! My friend in the hospital didn't need pity, he needed respect, and he got it from me that day! He has a head start on wisdom beyond many of us. So when he speaks, it is with new insight about life. He is still responding to life's challenges with joy. Both have come to him from God through the experience of suffering. The major benefit has been the rearrangement of his priorities.

Job teaches us a valuable lesson: the greater the suffering, the better we determine what really matters. Now we come back to where we started: suffering helps us clarify our priorities and focus on right objectives.

What wisdom have you gained through suffering?

# NOTHING COMPARES

### ✦ *Read Job 38:1–41* ✦

G od is prominent and preeminent. He is majestic in His power, magnificent in His person, and marvelous in His purposes. How refreshing to step back into the shadows of our own insignificance and give full attention to the greatness of our God! *It's all about Him!*

How unlike the little girl walking beside her mother in a pouring rain and loud thunderstorm. Every time the lightning flashed, her mother noticed she turned and smiled. They'd walk a little further, then lightning, and she'd turn and smile. The mother finally said, "Sweetheart, what's going on? Why do you always turn and smile after the flash of lightning?"

"Well," she said, "Since God is taking my picture, I want to be sure and smile for Him."

We take a major step toward maturity when we finally realize it's not about us and our significance. It is all about God's magnificence. His holiness. His greatness. His glory.

In whirlwind and storm is His way,
And clouds are the dust beneath His feet.

The LORD is good,
A stronghold in the day of trouble,
And He knows those who take refuge in Him. (Nahum 1:3,7)

God is transcendent. He is magnificent. He is mighty. He alone is awesome! He is all around us, above us, and within us. Without Him there is no righteousness. Without Him there is no holiness. Without Him there is no promise of forgiveness, no source of absolute truth, no reason to endure, no hope beyond the grave. Nothing compares to Him. As in that grand hymn:

O worship the King, all glorious above,
And gratefully sing His wonderful love;
Our Shield and Defender, the Ancient of Days,
Pavilioned in splendor, and girded with praise.[13]

# HOW BIG IS YOUR GOD?

### ❧ *Read Job 38:1–41* ❧

When God finally does speak, He answers Job out of a whirlwind. Suddenly, there He is! Wouldn't it have been great for us to have been there? Whoosh! Lightning, loud thunder, mighty winds blowing dark clouds across the heavens, and out of nowhere God bursts on the scene. It must have taken Job's breath away when the Lord "answered Job out of the whirlwind" (Job 38:1).

Many years ago (I was no more than ten years old) on a still and silent morning, long before dawn, I was fishing with my father. Our little fourteen-foot fishing boat was sitting on a slick, in a small body of water just this side of Matagorda Bay. We both had our lines in the water, and neither of us was saying a word. My dad was at the stern by the old twenty-five-horsepower Evinrude, and I was up near the bow of the boat. It was one of those mornings you could flip a penny onto the surface of the water and then count the ripples. It was silent as a tomb—almost eerie.

Suddenly, from the depths of the bay near the hull of our boat, comes this huge tarpon in full strength, bursting out of the water. He does a big-time flip in the air, then plunges with an enormous crash back into the bay. I must have jumped a foot off my wooden seat, shaking with fear. My dad didn't even turn around. Still watching his line, he said quietly, "I told you the big ones were down there."

That's Elihu's message. He is here, Job! Our awesome God—all glorious above. "Job, listen. He's here. He isn't always silent. When He speaks there is no voice like His." Job's view of God may have been enlarged, thanks to his friend's final remarks.

When your God is too small, your problems are too big and you retreat in fear and insecurity. But when your God is great, your problems pale into insignificance and you stand in awe as you worship the King.

How big is your God? Big enough to intervene? Big enough to be trusted? Big enough to be held in awe and ultimate respect? Big enough to erase your worries and replace them with peace?

Remember: the more you know God, the bigger He becomes.

# I Am Insignificant

### ✤ *Read Job 40:1–5* ✤

*I*f you take the time to analyze those words, you'll see that Job has three responses. The first is a response of *humility.* The second is a response of *relief.* And the third is a response of *surrender.* That's all God wanted to hear. And what an important change for Job! Without realizing it, he had become this independent, determined, self-assured apologist defending himself. Without saying so, he'd begun to appear as if he had his arms around the providence of God.

His first response is verse 4, *"I am insignificant."* Many of those who have been schooled in the fine points of psychology will reject this response. They will say we should be encouraged to realize how important we are, how valuable we are to God, what a significant place we fill in this world. They would counsel, "Don't think or say, 'I am insignificant.'" Before we're tempted to go there, take note that God doesn't reprove Job for saying he is insignificant or unworthy.

We'd put it this way: "I'm a lightweight." Frankly, it's true. It is an appropriate term for Job to use after being asked so many things he couldn't answer and shown so much he didn't understand. In unguarded humility the man admits, "I'm insignificant."

His second statement is, *"What can I reply to You?"* I see that as an expression of *relief.* God didn't want answers, He *knew* the answers. He knows all of them! He wanted Job to acknowledge, "I don't know any of the answers. And if I don't know about those things, as objective as they are, how could I ever fully understand the profound mysteries surrounding my world?" By acknowledging that, quiet relief replaced troubling resistance.

My point here—and this is terribly important: When we are broken and brought to the end of ourselves, it is not for the purpose of gaining more answers to spout off to others. It's to help us acknowledge that the Lord is God, and His plans and reasons are deeper and higher and broader than we can comprehend. Therefore, we are relieved from having to give answers or defend them.

Job's third response is a statement of *surrender: "I lay my hand on my mouth,"* verse 4 concludes. "I dare not say more. I've said enough—actually too much—already."

Can you make these three admissions to God? If not, work on it!

# FOLLOW IN OBEDIENCE

### ✦ *Read Job 40:1–5* ✦

*J*ob's response prompts me to think of what this says to our twenty-first-century world. What needed messages it offers to our times!

The first: *If God's ways are higher than mine, then I bow before Him in submission.* The result of that attitude is *true humility.* Submission to the Father's will is the mark of genuine humility. And all of us could use a huge dose of that. How unusual to find a humble spirit in our day, especially among the competent, the highly intelligent, the successful.

Here's the second: *If God is in full control, then however He directs my steps, I follow in obedience.* What *relief* that brings! Finally, I can relax, since I'm not in charge.

I was speaking at a pastors' conference at Moody Bible Institute in Chicago not long ago. The most vivid memory of that conference was the large sign up front. It was hung above the platform for all in attendance to read each time we came together. In big, bold letters it read:

**Relax Everybody, for Once You're Not in Charge.**

The auditorium was full of pastors—fifteen hundred in all! And each one of us is usually in charge (we think), only to show up at this conference and be reminded to relax—we're *not* in charge. It was an encouraging relief for everybody in attendance.

That's the sign God stretched in front of Job. "You're not in charge of anything, Job; this is My responsibility. You're my servant; I'm your Master. I know what I'm doing." Since God knows what He's doing, however He directs my steps, I simply follow. What an encouraging relief that should bring!

What do you feel about letting God control your life—relief, frustration, panic? What can you do to help yourself relax in His control?

# TURN AROUND

### ✨ *Read Job 42:1–6* ✨

*I*'ve come to the end of my understanding, and I leave it at that. My very existence is Yours, O God. It's Yours to unravel the mystery, to track the labyrinthine ways, to handle the profound, to know the reasons behind the inexplicable events of my life." In full surrender Job backs off and bows down.

This is Job's way of acknowledging his inability to understand why, with no further argument, harboring no bitterness. There is no thought of *How dare you do this to me?* What do we see in Job instead? A broken and contrite spirit. Do you know what Job finally realized? It's all about God, not me. Job got it! And what does that mean?

God's purpose is unfolding, and I cannot hinder it.

God's plan is incredible, and I will not comprehend it.

God's reproof is reliable, and I dare not ignore it.

God's way is best, and I must not resist it.

Have you learned those things yet? Have you come to realize that your business is about your God? Your family is about your God. Everything you claim to possess, He owns. Every privilege you enjoy is granted by His grace. None of it is deserved. Job got all that. The question is, have you? Tragically, many don't get it until faced with impossible moments. God has ways of leveling His own.

How satisfying a submissive life can be. The blend is beautiful: a strong-hearted person, surrendered and humbled with a "broken and contrite spirit"—entertaining no grudges, making no demands, having no expectations, offering no conditions, anticipating no favors, fully repentant before the Lord God. And the marvelous result? The Lord begins to use us in amazing ways. Why? Because the world doesn't see that unique combination very often.

Job finally sees God for who He really is, and he fully repents. The result is one blessing after another. In fact, double blessing upon double blessing comes his way. Once God placed His mighty hands on the man's shoulders, Job finally got it. Have you?

# A PROFOUND PLAN

*❧ Read Job 42:1–6 ❧*

That's what makes the climax of Job's life so satisfying. This dear man, who never deserved the suffering he endured, is dealt with justly. And those who made his life so miserable weren't overlooked either. The God of Justice finally steps up, bringing great rewards and restoration to the righteous, and strong discipline on the unrighteous.

Job finally realized that God's plan is profound, that His reasoning is right, and that His ways are higher than he could ever understand. With that, Job waves the white flag of surrender and says in complete sincerity, "I retract and I repent. I've said things I shouldn't have been saying, I talked about things I knew nothing about, I became self-righteous in my own defense. Lord, please know that my heart is Yours. I humble myself before You. I place myself at Your disposal. Your purpose is right; Your plan is incredible; Your reproofs are reliable; Your way is best."

That did it. When the Lord heard the deepest feelings of Job's contrite heart, when the Lord witnessed the humility of his broken spirit and the openness and teachability of Job's soul, mercy kicked in, and justice rolled down. There is even poetic justice as the Lord decides to use Job in the process of bringing the other men to justice. This is a good place to insert an insight worth remembering.

You will be amazed at how the Lord will use you in others' lives once you adjust your life to His ways. You will be many things for them: a reproof, a refuge, a point of hope, a reason to go on, a source of strength, a calming influence, and so much more. It's wonderful to realize (to your surprise) how He chooses to use you as a vehicle to help restore those who've strayed so far. This often includes those who hurt *you* in their straying.

I'm reminded of the destraught father in *Les Misérables* whose only plea comes in a powerful song about his son as he cries, "Bring him home!" Our Father, too, pleads with us to help guide His straying children back home to Him: "Bring them home!"

# SET FREE

### ❧ *Read Job 42:1–11* ❧

*D*id you miss something? If you take the time to read the biblical account, you'll see that God gives Job the same title four times: "My servant" (Job 42:7–8). What an honorable title. He had it before the suffering began (Job 1:8), and he has it still. Job's heroic endurance resulted in his keeping the same title in God's estimation. Talk about justice rolling down, Job must have been deeply gratified to hear these words spoken in the ears of those who had spent so many days putting him down: "My servant Job has spoken what is right."

Here are these men who earlier stood over Job as judges, now getting the required animals and bowing before the Lord with their offerings, waiting for Job to pray for them. Isn't this a great scene? We've been waiting *so* long to see it! And how healthy it was for those three to make it right, not only before God, but with Job! It is good for us to confess our wrongdoing to those we have offended. It is right for us to say by our actions that we have done what is wrong as we seek forgiveness.

Job obeys the Lord once these men have done their part. Eliphaz and Bildad and Zophar "went and did as the LORD told them; and the LORD accepted Job" (Job 42:9). They did it rather quickly. There was no arguing, no wrestling, no reluctance. Furthermore, they did *exactly* as the Lord required. And so did Job. Graciously, he prayed for each one. There's no bitterness on his part. He doesn't say, "Okay, kneel down. You guys have put me through hell. I'm gonna see what you look like when you're humbled. Kneel down there—get on your faces!" There's none of that. Remember? *A contrite heart makes no demands of others.*

Yes, it's a grand scene! You know why it's happening? Sins are being forgiven. Guilt is being removed. That's what happens when justice and mercy are blended.

How beautifully this portrays what happened at the cross. That's why the death of Christ is called "efficacious." It is *effective*, because God's justice against sin was once and for all satisfied in the *death* of the Lamb. And as a result, God's mercy is released in the *forgiveness* of those who trust in the Lamb. And we are then set free. Free at last!

# INCAPABLE OF COMPREHENDING

### ✤ *Read Job 42:1–11* ✤

God's plans are beyond our understanding and too deep to explain. Perhaps God doesn't explain Himself because knowing and understanding His way may not help us all that much. Stop and ask yourself: Does knowing why really help? Is the pain removed by knowing the cause? Ours is a world filled with devastating catastrophes, random shootings by hidden snipers, jets crashing into tall buildings, deliberately poisoning elderly people at rest homes, serial rapists and murderers, mothers who kill all of their own children, droughts and famines, wives in automobiles who run over their husbands, preachers who are fraudulent and phony, CEOs who take unfair advantage of their employees. The list doesn't end. How could God permit such things? Would it really help to know why? In a fallen world full of depraved people who act out their worst thoughts, would it change the wrong?

I'll go a step further. Maybe God doesn't explain Himself because we're incapable of comprehending His answers. Since He lives in an existence that is completely unlike ours and in a realm far beyond our comprehension, ours being tactile and limited by space and time, within the rigid boundaries of all the physical laws, how could we possibly understand? None of our limitations apply to Him, so what would enable us to grasp His plan?

What bothers us is that He doesn't act as we think He ought to act. He doesn't do what our earthly dads would have done in similar circumstances. While I'm at it, where was He when His own Son was crucified? To the surprise of many, He was there all the time working out His divine plan for our salvation. As the process was running its course, Jesus' own disciples didn't get it—they were the most disillusioned people on the planet. Do you remember what they were thinking? They were wondering how in the world they could have believed in a hoax. From their perspective, their Master's death didn't make any sense.

Do you know what Job finally sees? Job sees God, and that is enough. He doesn't see answers. He is to the place where he doesn't need answers. He has gotten a glimpse of the Almighty, and that is sufficient. Have you had glimpses of His glory?

# HUMBLE YOURSELF NOW

### ❧ *Read Job 42:1–11* ❧

*T*ake special notice of Job's words. He does not reply, "I've got an argument here." On the contrary, He says, "I retract and repent." There's no divine force. There's no threatening rebuke from God. "Job, if you don't get down on your knees and beg for mercy from Me, I'm going to finish you off!"

No. In gentle, resigned submission Job rests his case in the Father's will. He says, "You instruct me, and as a result of Your instruction, I will willingly submit and accept it." Do you know what I love about Job's attitude? There is an absence of talk about "my rights." There is not a hint of personal entitlement. There is no expectation or demand. There's not even a plea for God to understand or to defend him before his argumentative friends. Furthermore, there's no self-pity, no moody, depressed spirit. He is completely at rest. His innermost being, at last, is at peace.

You may say, "Well, if God had blessed me as He blessed Job, I'd say that too." Wait. He hasn't yet brought relief or reward. The man is still covered with boils. He still doesn't have any family. He's still homeless. He's still bankrupt. With nothing external changed, Job says quietly, "Lord, I'm Yours."

Focus on the timing. Humble yourself not after He exalts you, but humble yourself now. Don't wait. Pull back, stop the arguing, and rest in Him. It is remarkable how He will quiet your spirit and transport you to a realm of contentment you've never known before, even with most of the answers missing. The philosophers of this world demand answers. The believer who has now learned through this kind of cataclysmic experience to trust, regardless, demands nothing. And the worries slowly fade away, one after another.

"Humble yourself in the sight of the Lord, and He will exalt you" (James 4:10).

# GOD HEARS

### ❧ *Read Job 42:1–11* ❧

When the day of reckoning arrives, God is always fair. He blesses those who have walked with Him. He forgives those who bring their offerings and humble themselves before Him. God restores. God rewards. God heals. God honors Job who prayed for his friends with an open heart. God noticed it all. I suggest you underscore Hebrews 6:10 in your Bible: "For God is not unjust so as to forget your work and the love which you have shown toward His name, in having ministered and in still ministering to the saints." Eugene Peterson, in *The Message,* renders those first words "God doesn't miss anything."

Some who read my words have been terribly abused. You have been victims of the worst kind of mistreatment. You have been taken advantage of by someone you trusted. You have been abandoned by your mate, treated unfairly, ripped off. You've lost a fortune through a fraudulent scheme. Every one of us could give Hell stories of abuse and neglect, misrepresentation and unfair treatment that have never been made right. So, please return to this great truth: God does not forget. He just doesn't adjust His plan to our timetable. His Accounts Settlement desk doesn't operate on a nine-to-five schedule. He doesn't handle our cases when we want them handled. I wanted God to zap Eliphaz the very moment he said that first insulting word to Job. He's waited through all the sarcastic speeches, stayed silent through all the insults. Finally, He says, "Eliphaz, Bildad, Zophar, you have been *wrong.*"

God heard! Yes, He heard! He didn't say anything at the time, but He heard it all. He is not unjust to forget one idle word. And I can assure you, He didn't overlook one wrong act committed against you. He has a perfect plan. His plan is unfolding. When His timetable says, "Now," justice will roll down, and His Accounts Settlement desk will take swift action.

God's arrangement of things is not a frustrated plan. God is not sitting on the edge of heaven, biting His nails, wondering what He's going to do about our world. He knows exactly what He's going to do and when He's going to do it. Job sees that clearly . . . now. He realizes, finally, that God doesn't miss anything.

He hasn't missed anything in your life either.

# GOD'S JUSTICE

### ✍ *Read Job 42:1–17* ✍

*I* find at least two enduring truths for us as I think through these closing scenes in Job's story.

First, *forgiveness is worth asking for.* If there's something that has come between you and your heavenly Father, why wait at a distance? Come. Talk openly with Him. He loves to hear the unguarded confessions of His children. He takes delight in our humble admission of wrong. Just tell Him. As we have seen, He will never turn you away. Forgiveness is worth the asking.

Second, *justice is worth waiting for.* God is a God of justice. He will faithfully bring it to pass—if not now, later. If not later, in eternity. God will make it right. His fairness is part of His veracity. God, who patiently allowed Satan's dastardly experiment with Job to run its course, has now brought it to completion. His servant has been rewarded. These friends have been brought to their knees. Best of all, Satan has been silenced and proven wrong (again!). And the Lord is still enthroned, in charge, and fully glorified.

I have no way of knowing what your situation is right now. I don't know what you're wrestling with or who has wronged you. Nor do I know how severe life has been for you. But I do know this: life has not been easy. Your tests have probably not been as severe as Job's, but I'm sure they have been difficult, maybe the worst you've ever known in your lifetime. You may find yourself in prison. You've been wronged, and it's never been made right, and justice is on hold.

There's a reason for the delay. Perhaps it's to give you time to examine your own life. Is there a wrong you need to confess, an offense you've caused but never attempted to reconcile? I urge you to set aside your pride and step back into that unfinished business and take care of things now. You will be amazed how relieving it will be to draw in that anchor so you can get moving in the right direction.

It might very well be that your willingness to forgive and move on is all that is necessary to prompt the Lord to let His justice roll down. So, what are you waiting for?

# FOUND FAITHFUL

### *Read Job 42:1–17*

*I*f you return to Job 1:3, you can read what Job originally owned. He had 7,000 sheep, and he winds up with 14,000. So his flocks grow as he feeds them and breeds them. Their numbers increase to twice the original flock. There's plenty to eat. And there's also plenty of land to graze, so the sheep grow in number to 14,000.

He must have been able to see from every window of his home luscious, green, and colorful plants and the growth of all his crops. He's even got 1,000 female donkeys. So the man has twice as much as he had before. Not instantaneously, but over the passing of a few years, his possessions grew. Candidly, Job had more than enough. Much more. He was rich before; now he is enormously wealthy!

There are times when the Lord chooses to bless certain individuals with much more than is enough. What we must learn is to let it be. If envy is your besetting sin, I urge you to break yourself from one of the ugliest habits among Christian people! I'll be completely honest with you, I hear it frequently. The great temptation is to remind the Lord of how faithful *you* have been when you see a neighbor or a friend whose business grows when yours doesn't. Please stop trying to outguess the Lord in such matters.

It is both unfair and inaccurate to assume that most wealthy individuals have not earned their riches or did not receive them from the hand of God. Some of God's dearest saints are eminently wealthy. So? I say again—let it be. If you are one of them, you hardly need the reminder that you didn't create it yourself. It came because of His grace. Use it appropriately. Give generously. Walk in humility. And if He chooses not to bless you as He has blessed another, respect and appreciate His choice rather than resent it. Let's applaud Job for being a recipient of God's prosperous favor. He has "come forth as gold," having been tested and found faithful.

"Rejoice with those who rejoice!"

# STAYING YOUNG

### ✤ *Read Job 42:10–17* ✤

*I*'d like to offer several tips on how to stay young.

Number one: *Your mind isn't old, keep developing it.* Watch less television and read more. Spend time with people who talk about events and ideas rather than sitting around a shop talking about people and how sorry this young generation has become. Nobody wants to be around a crotchety old person who sees only the clouds and talks only about bad weather.

Number two: *Your humor isn't over, keep enjoying it.* I love being around older people who still see the sunny side of life. They see funny things happening. They can tell a great story. They enjoy a loud belly laugh. You look *fabulous* when you laugh. And it takes years off your face.

Number three: *Your strength isn't gone, keep using it.* Don't let yourself get out of shape. Stay active. Eat right. Watch your weight. Guard against becoming isolated and immobile. And while I'm at it, quit addressing every ache and pain. Quit talking about how weak you're getting and how others will have to do this or that for you. Jump in there. *You* keep doing it.

Here's a fourth: *Your opportunities haven't vanished, keep pursuing them.* There are people all around you who could use an encouraging word, an affirming note, a phone call that says, "I love you and believe in you, and I'm praying for you." So go there. Opportunities to help others have not vanished.

Fifth is obvious: *Your God is not dead, keep serving and seeking Him.* The living God is ageless. The Lord Jesus Christ is timeless and ever relevant. Continue to enjoy some time alone with your Lord. It's so important!

You have lived long enough to know that there is no one more trustworthy than the Lord Himself. Continue cultivating a meaningful relationship with Him. Seek Him diligently and often.

I wish for you a full life, like Job's, marked not by living happily ever after (an impossibility), but by being truly satisfied, fulfilled, challenged, useful, godly, balanced, and *joyful*.

Yes, for sure, joyful! And don't forget—reasonably sweet.

# CHOOSE GOD'S WILL

### ❧ *Read Job 42:10—17* ❧

*A* major goal of wholesome, healthy Christians is the hope of reaching maturity before death overtakes us. I will tell you without hesitation that one of my major goals in life is to grow up as I grow older. A commendable etching on a gravestone would be: "Here lies a man who kept growing as he kept aging." Growing up and growing old need to walk hand in hand. Never doubt it: maturing is a slow, arduous process. Job accomplished it; he reached that goal. Small wonder we read that he died an old man and full of days. He lived the rest of his years (140 more) full of enthusiasm and passion. What an enviable way to finish life.

When trouble comes we have two options. We can view it as an intrusion, an outrage, or we can see it as an opportunity to respond in specific obedience to God's will—that rugged virtue James calls "endurance."

Endurance is not jaw-clenched resignation, nor is it passive acquiescence. It's "a long obedience in the same direction." It's staying on the path of obedience despite counter-indications. It's a dogged determination to pursue holiness when the conditions of holiness are not favorable. It's a choice in the midst of our suffering to do what God has asked us to do, whatever it is, and for as long He asks us to do it. As Oswald Chambers wrote, "To choose suffering makes no sense at all; to choose God's will in the midst of our suffering makes all the sense in the world."

Where are you today? Where is your journey leading you? More importantly, which option have you chosen? Are you viewing your trial as an outrage or an opportunity? Try hard not to forget the lessons Job teaches us about ourselves. It will make an enormous difference. As you grow older, keep growing up. And, instead of simply reading about the life of Job, begin *living* that kind of life.

That makes all the sense in the world, doesn't it?

# BLESSED

### ✤ *Read Job 42:9–15* ✤

*D*id you read that too quickly? The end of verse 9? Mark it. "The LORD accepted." And then, "The LORD restored." End of verse 10, "The LORD increased." Beginning of verse 12, "The LORD blessed." Those are words of grace—statements of divine favor. Let them hit with full impact:

Accepted.

Restored.

Increased.

Blessed.

Because of the fallout of our cynical society, you and I are being programmed to rush by words of grace and blessing and to hurry on to words that are negative. They bring us down. Killings in the workplace. Mold in your house. Weather disasters. Fractured families. Forest fires. High rate of divorce. Economic woes. Acts of terrorism. The homeless. Fallen ministers. Broken hearts. Mistreatment of children. Spouse abuse. Chemical dependence. Deadbeat dads. Premature deaths. Fraudulent builders. Rising unemployment. Scandals among CEOs and famous athletes. On and on. That's what fills the evening news.

We never hear: "Now, tomorrow night we'll report only good news." Instead, it's "Stay tuned if you think *that* report was bad; in a moment we'll have a full exposé."

I mean, even the weatherman predicts "partly cloudy." He never says, "Mainly sunny tomorrow." It's always a 20 percent chance of rain. He never says, "There's an 80 percent probability of sunshine." And furthermore, he's usually wrong (talk about job security). Enough of all that!

Who does God bless? Job! This is *great* news! You haven't forgotten that Job cursed the day he was born, have you? Or that he resented the fact he didn't die when he was placed on his mother's breast? He was also the one who said, "I am not at ease. I am not quiet." In other words, "I resent what has happened." That's the same Job who is wonderfully blessed at the end of the book. Why? Grace, grace, grace, grace, grace!

*Paul: A Man of Grace & Grit*

# A BRUTAL BEGINNING

### *Read Acts 5:29–32; 8:1–3*

*W*e must not forget that as we study the life of the man they called Paul. We must also brace ourselves for some rather gruesome surprises. The first pen portrait of Paul (whom we first meet as Saul of Tarsus) is both brutal and bloody. If an artist were to render it with brush and oils, not one of us would want it hung framed in our living room. The man looks more like a terrorist than a devout follower of Judaism. To our horror, the blood of the first martyr splattered across Saul's clothes while he stood nodding in agreement, an accomplice to a vicious crime.

Throughout our lives we've naturally adopted a Christianized mental image of the apostle Paul. After all, he's the one who gave us both letters to the Corinthians. He wrote Romans, the *Magna Carta* of the Christian life. He penned that liberating letter to the Galatians exhorting them and us to live in the freedom God's grace provides. And he wrote the Prison Epistles and the Pastoral letters so full of wisdom, so rich with relevance. Based on all that, you'd think the man loved the Savior from birth. Not even close.

He hated the name of Jesus. So much so, he became a self-avowed, violent aggressor, persecuting and killing Christians in allegiance to the God of heaven. Shocking though it may seem, we must never forget the pit from which he came. The better we understand the darkness of his past, the more we will understand his deep gratitude for grace.

The first portrait of Paul's life painted in Holy Scripture is not of a little baby being lovingly cradled in his mother's arms. Nor does it depict a Jewish lad leaping and bounding with neighborhood buddies through the narrow streets of Tarsus. The original portrait is not even of a brilliant, young law student sitting faithfully at the feet of Gamaliel. Those images would only mislead us into thinking he enjoyed a storybook past. Instead, we first meet him as simply a "young man named Saul," party to Stephen's brutal murder, standing "in hearty agreement with putting him to death" (Acts 7:58; 8:1).

That's the realistic Saul we need to see in order to truly appreciate the glorious truths of the New Testament letters he wrote. No wonder he later came to be known as the "apostle of grace."

# AN UNEXPECTED ALLY

### *Read Acts 5:33–38*

*W*illiam Barclay calls Gamaliel an "unexpected ally." In the midst of flaring tempers and irrational thinking, this wise, seasoned teacher calmly rose to his feet and warned, "Take care here. Don't rush to judgment." In his words: "Stay away from these men and let them alone, for if this plan or action should be of men, it will be overthrown; but if it is of God, you will not be able to overthrow them; or else you may even be found fighting against God" (Acts 5:38–39).

The young Pharisee shook his head in disbelief. "This man was supposed to be a spokesman for Judaism. He taught me much of what I know about Judaism and the Law. He schooled me in how to do precisely what I'm doing. Master Gamaliel, you've lost your mind!"

Saul, of course, had no way of knowing that it would be this sort of calm reasoning that would hold him together when he later carried the torch for Christ. He would remind himself that those who fight against him were really fighting God. But at this moment he knew none of that. All he saw was red. Blood red. He couldn't believe the Sanhedrin would heed such calm counsel and consider going soft on these infidels. But that's exactly what they did.

If you would allow me a moment of digression here, I think Peter remained alive then and in the years that followed because of Gamaliel's wise intervention. I think this "unexpected ally" saved his life. Saul and the rest of them would have stoned the whole bunch. But God graciously intervened through Gamaliel. He used the words of a wise professor to preserve the lives of those who would later play strategic roles in the formation of his Christian church. Keep that in mind when you feel your circumstances have become hopeless. No matter what you face, God is still in control, silently and sovereignly working all things out according to His perfect plan. He has His Gamaliels waiting in the wings. At the precise moment when their words will have the greatest impact, they will step out of the shadows and onto the stage to deliver their life-saving words.

# ROADSIDE CONVERSION

*Read Acts 9:1–4*

*T*he ninth chapter of Acts begins abruptly. Saul's blood is boiling. He's on a murderous rampage toward Damascus. He charged north out of Jerusalem with the fury of Alexander the Great sweeping across Persia, and the determined resolve of William Tecumseh Sherman in his scorching march across Georgia. Saul was borderline out of control. His fury had intensified almost to the point of no return. Such bloodthirsty determination and blind hatred for the followers of Christ drove him hard toward his distant destination: Damascus. If you were a follower of Jesus living anywhere near Jerusalem, you wouldn't have wanted to hear Saul's knock at your door.

We read this: "And it came about that as he journeyed, he was approaching Damascus, and suddenly a light from heaven flashed around him; and he fell to the ground, and he heard a voice saying to him, "Saul, Saul, why are you persecuting Me?" (Acts 9:3–4). You can almost hear the screeching of brakes. At that moment, Saul's murderous journey was brought to a divine halt.

Suddenly. Isn't that just like the Lord? No announcement ahead of time. No heavenly calligraphy scrolled across the skies with the warning, "Watch out tomorrow, Saul, God's gonna getcha." God remained silent and restrained as Saul proceeded with his murderous plan to invade Damascus. Surely he discussed the details with his companions. God didn't interrupt . . . until. At the hour it would have its greatest impact, God stepped in. Without warning, the course of Saul's life changed dramatically.

That still happens, even in our day. Without warning, life takes its sudden turns. Maybe it's a tragic auto accident that claims the life of your mate. Suddenly, God steps onto the scene and arrests your attention. Or it may come through the death of a child. In the hour of deepest grief, your life and the lives of your family are impacted forever. Occasionally, life's unexpected turns come in the horrible crash of an airplane, causing a calamity that wipes out half a neighborhood. Or in the halting words of your physician as she admits, "You have cancer." Like a rogue wave, adversity crashes onto the peaceful shores of our lives and knocks us flat. Amazingly, the jolt awakens our senses, and we suddenly remember that God is in control, no matter what.

# No Surprises

### ❧ *Read Acts 9:1–4* ❧

For more than three decades, Saul controlled his own life. His record in Judaism ranked second to none. On his way to make an even greater name for himself, the laser of God's presence stopped him in his tracks, striking him blind. Like that group of shepherds faithfully watching their sheep years earlier on another significant night outside Jerusalem, Saul and his companions fell to the ground, stunned.

That's what still happens today when calamity strikes. You get the news in the middle of the night on the telephone, and you can't move. As the policeman describes the head-on collision, you stand frozen in disbelief. After hearing the word "cancer," you're so shocked you can hardly walk out the doctor's office doors. A friend once admitted to me that, after hearing his dreaded diagnosis, he stumbled to the men's room, vomited, dropped to his knees, and sobbed uncontrollably. Life's unexpected jolts grip us with such fear we can scarcely go on.

For the first time in his proud, self-sustained life, Saul found himself a desperate dependent. Not only was he pinned to the ground, he was blind. His other senses were on alert, and to his amazement, he heard a voice from heaven say, "Saul, Saul, why are you persecuting Me?" (Acts 9:4). Saul was convinced he had been persecuting people—cultic followers of a false Messiah. Instead, he discovered that the true object of his vile brutality was Christ Himself.

We live in a culture that regularly confuses humanity with deity. The lines get blurred. It's the kind of sloppy theology that suggests God sits on the edge of heaven thinking, *Wonder what they'll do next?* How absurd! God is omniscient—all-knowing. This implies, clearly, that God never learns anything, our sinful decisions and evil deeds notwithstanding. Nothing ever surprises Him. From the moment we're conceived to the moment we die, we remain safely within the frame of His watchful gaze and His sovereign plan for us.

# A QUICK TURNAROUND

### ✍ *Read Acts 9:1–4* 🐦

*T*he essence of genuine repentance is that the mind does a turnaround. The Greek word is *metanoia*, meaning, literally, "to change one's mind." That's precisely what happened to the once-proud Pharisee on the road to Damascus. So many things within Saul's thinking changed—and changed completely. He changed his mind about God, about Jesus, about the Resurrection, about those who followed Christ. He must have shaken his head for days. He thought Christ was dead. Now he was convinced Jesus was alive. This One who knew his name also knew what he'd been doing. The raging rebel had finally met his match, and there was no place or way to hide.

Now let me pause to clarify something important. Some Christians try to impose their rigid system of dos and don'ts on the issue of conversion. I want to caution against that sort of exercise. It's impossible to find any single place in Scripture that reveals the one-and-only way every sinner comes to Christ. While the message of the Gospel is the same, methods differ. We are so conditioned by denominational backgrounds, religious traditionalism, and narrow-thinking prejudice, we miss the point of God's grace. We tend to require more than God does! Be careful about exacting requirements on someone who genuinely turns to the Savior.

Lost people are saved while listening to a great song about Christ or while hearing a preacher or Bible teacher explaining God's Word from a pulpit or over television or on the radio. Others are saved during a small-group Bible study. Many come to Him on their own, while praying in the privacy of their homes. Day or night a sinner can call on the Lord Jesus Christ in faith and be saved. Let's stop making it so complicated. As it happened with Saul, grace abounds.

Regardless of exactly when Saul was converted, he realized that the living Jesus, whom he had hated and denied his entire life, was now his Savior and Lord.

Is He your Savior and Lord too?

# GOD'S GOADS

### ❧ *Read Acts 9:5–9* ❧

*A*pparently, "to kick against the goads" was a common expression found in both Greek and Latin literature—a rural image, which rose from the practice of farmers goading their oxen in the fields. Though unfamiliar to us, everyone in that day understood its meaning.

Goads were typically made from slender pieces of timber, blunt on one end and pointed on the other. Farmers used the pointed end to urge a stubborn ox into motion. Occasionally, the beast would kick at the goad. The more the ox kicked, the more likely the goad would stab into the flesh of its leg, causing greater pain.

Saul's conversion could appear to us as having been a sudden encounter with Christ. But based on the Lord's expression regarding his kicking back, I believe He'd been working on him for years, prodding and goading him.

I believe the words and works of Jesus haunted the zealous Pharisee. Quite likely, Saul had heard Jesus teach and preach in public places. Similar in age, they would have been contemporaries in a city Saul knew well and Jesus frequently visited.

Imagine Saul (the name *Paul* means "small," suggesting he may have been shorter than average), standing on tiptoe, straining to watch Jesus, all the while grudgingly wondering how this false prophet could be gaining popularity. Nonsense. He has to be of Satan! Pharisees loved to think that. Nevertheless, Jesus's ministry stuck in Saul's mind. The more it goaded him, the more he resisted God's proddings.

Once you've seriously encountered Jesus, as Saul did, there's no escaping Him. His words and works follow you deep within your conscience. That's why I encourage people who are intensifying their efforts to resist the Gospel's claims to study the life of Christ—to examine carefully His captivating words. Most people who sincerely pursue them can't leave Him without at least reevaluating their lives.

# GOD WINS

### ❧ *Read Acts 9:5–9* ❧

God goaded and prodded the stubborn pride of Saul—that Pharisaic ox. Day after day he kicked against those goads, until finally he got the message. There would be no more running. No more hiding. The fight was over. As always, God won.

C. S. Lewis likened God's conquering work of Saul's rebel will to a divine chess player: systematically, patiently maneuvering his opponent into a corner until finally he concedes. "Checkmate."

Like Saul, we're no match for God. Checkmate is inevitable. It's no game either. God will do whatever it takes to bring us to a point of absolute dependence on Him. He will relentlessly, patiently, faithfully goad until we finally and willingly submit to Him.

You're probably not a notorious criminal. I know that. More importantly, God knows that. Your life may be morally clean. Let's face it, you may qualify as the finest person on your block. You don't cheat on your taxes or deliberately lie to your partner. You may have never committed what we would call a scandalous act, to say nothing of seriously hurting someone you love. You're living a life that's impressive to others, but you are light years from being righteous before God. Until you've surrendered your life to Christ, you're as lost as Saul was on the Damascus road.

If you've never made that decision, what a great moment this would be if you'd set this book aside, bow your heart before the living Christ at this tender moment, and receive Him as your Savior.

You may have been a Christian for some time, but you're clinging to the reigns of your own rebel will. You need to know that God will goad you too. Sooner or later He'll get your attention. No matter what it takes. He'll bring you to a place in your life where you realize there's no point in continuing to kick against the goads.

Don't wait for a storm. By then it may be too late. Settle it today on your knees. Give God complete control. Stop your own Damascus Road journey today. Like Saul, surrender. And like Saul, you'll never regret it.

# A Chosen Instrument

### ❧ *Read Acts 9:10–16* ❧

*I*f you haven't yet done so, stand for a few moments in Ananias's sandals. Understand how difficult it would have been to see how God's plan could possibly work. How in the world could God take a man known for such vicious, merciless, and murderous treatment of innocent Christians and turn him into an ambassador for Christ? Perhaps Ananias failed to hear the answer in the Lord's Word to him: "But the Lord said to him, 'Go, for he is a chosen instrument of Mine, to bear My name before the Gentiles and kings and the sons of Israel; for I will show him how much he must suffer for My name's sake'" (Acts 9:15–16).

God's answer to Ananias's question is clear: "I will show him how much he must suffer for My name's sake."

Suffering. Down through the centuries it has been God's taming ground for raging bulls. The crucible of pain and hardship is God's schoolroom where Christians learn humility, compassion, character, patience, and grace. It's true for you and for me, and it would soon be true for Saul. Years later, with scars to prove it and under the pile of heavy ministry responsibilities, he gave testimony that suffering had been his companion.

I don't understand all the reasons we suffer for the Name. But I'm convinced of this: it is part of God's sovereign plan to prepare us to be His instruments of grace to a harsh and desperate world. Clearly, that was God's plan for Saul. On his body would be the enduring stripes of his suffering—imprisonment, severe beatings, stonings, shipwreck, near-drowning, ambushes, robberies, insomnia, starvation, loneliness, disease, dehydration, extreme hypothermia. Beyond all that, he faced the stressful, inescapable responsibilities of church leadership. Each painful, awful ordeal brought him to his knees, turning him into a deeper man of grace, humbly committed to following his Savior's lead.

What have you suffered for the name of Christ?

# A New Beginning

### ✒ *Read Acts 9:10–19* ✒

egardless of what you have done, no one is beyond hope. That's the great hope of the Christian message. No amount or depth of sin in your past can trump the grace of God. If you question that, remember Saul, the brash Pharisee of Tarsus. When the Lord saved him, He didn't put him on probation. The other disciples did that. No, God gave Saul a new name, and in the process, made him a new creation. That's what makes grace so amazing!

Even though your past is soiled, anyone can find a new beginning with God. I've made the same statement throughout my ministry: It's never too late to start doing what is right. When Saul knelt before the living God, he finally faced the reality of his sin. Deep within the man, Christ transformed his life, and he started doing what was right. Grace provides that sort of new beginning.

Don't get stuck on where you *were*. Don't waste your time focusing on *what you used to be*. Remember, the hope we have in Christ means there's a brighter tomorrow. Sins are forgiven. Shame is cancelled out. We're no longer chained to a deep, dark pit of the past. Grace gives us wings to soar beyond it.

Could it be that you are stuck because of something from your past? Perhaps it has pinned you to the ground with embarrassment, shame, and fear. You're crippled by it. The best you can do is to limp through each day, hoping for a painless end. That way of thinking is the enemy, Satan. He loves to push your nose in the dirt, hoping to make you miss the marvelous claims of grace.

Don't allow him that power in your life today. Around you are people who have no greater claim on grace than you do, and the Lord mercifully brought them out of their pit of sin. If He could turn a Saul of Tarsus, who was engaged in a murderous rampage, into a Paul the apostle, who preached and lived the message of grace, He can change your life too.

# SURPRISING ELEMENTS

### ✯ *Read Acts 9:10–21* ✯

urprises are always part of God's leading. In Saul's case, the surprise came in the form of a light from heaven, marking a life-changing transformation. For Ananias, it was a seemingly unreasonable and illogical command from the Lord, delivered in a vision.

If you're waiting on God to fill in all the shading in your picture, you will never take the first step in obeying His will. You must be prepared to trust His plan, knowing it will be full of surprises. Surprises are always a part of God's leading.

Surprises always intensify our need for faith. When you encounter the surprising element of God's will, your faith must engage full throttle. Otherwise, you'll turn and run in the opposite direction. At times God's plan will frighten you. Or you'll be intimidated by its demands. Other times you'll be disappointed. For instance, when God tells you no, to wait, or to sit tight, you'll want to argue. You may decide to fight. You might attempt to negotiate. You may become angry. But when your faith kicks in to gear, none of those impulses will control you. Faith says, "I can do this. I trust you, Lord. I don't understand everything, but I trust you completely. Let's do it."

Quite possibly God has a major move in store for you in the near future. After almost seventy years on this earth, and having spent fifty of those years studying and learning more about the ways of God, I can tell you His will for our lives is full of surprises. He has more moves in mind for us than we could possibly anticipate. And they're not all geographical.

Many are attitude adjustments. Some mean moving us out of our comfort zones to touch the lives of people we've never met. Or we might be in for a cross-country or cross-cultural journey that requires a level of faith we've not exercised in the past. Be careful about feeling too settled where you are—physically, emotionally, spiritually, or geographically. If the Lord wants you to move, I strongly suggest you cooperate, regardless of the risks. If He leads you to change, then change, even if it's difficult. Surprises from God always intensify our need for faith.

# STEPPING OUT

### ❧ *Read Acts 9:10–21* ❧

S tepping out in faith always brings clarification of God's plan. When Ananias went to see Saul, he received additional information. As Saul submitted himself to the ministry of Ananias, he found out more about God's plan for his life. "You're a chosen vessel of Mine. I'm going to use you to bear My name." Saul hadn't known that before. (He had never read the book of Acts!) He knew nothing of what was in store for him until Ananias took that initial step of faith. Both men discovered that God Himself chose Saul to be His instrument and that intense suffering would mark his ministry. That's the way God operates.

When Cynthia and I first sensed God's directing us to leave California and relocate our ministry, we could hardly believe it. We had planned to stay in the same place for the rest of our lives—serving Christ at the First Evangelical Free Church in Fullerton and continuing to lead the ministry of Insight for Living. Neither space nor time allow me to describe the things God has shown us since we made the decision to move. Initially, very few people could grasp God's plan for us. It came as a surprise to everyone. In fact, some firmly rejected it. But now as God continues to put the finishing touches on His magnificent portrait, what we see is absolutely beautiful. Until we took that initial step of obedience, all we had was, "It's time to go." It's amazing to me even as I write these words! Surprises always bring about clarification of God's plan.

Obedience always stimulates growth. By the way, the Swindolls have grown deeper in our relationship with the Lord, having trusted Him without first knowing all the details. Obeying God drives the roots of your faith much deeper. And that obedience stimulates growth in every area of life. We're stretched emotionally, often physically, but most importantly, spiritually.

Ananias's compliance with God's surprising plan allowed him to witness supernatural power. No one else in Scripture witnessed the scales miraculously falling from the contrite Pharisee's eyes. Only Ananias. When Saul's sight returned, Ananias's own eyes were also opened to the amazing power of God to transform a life. Obedience always stimulates growth.

Step out on faith, and you'll always find solid ground.

# A Forgotten Hero

### ❧ *Read Acts 9:20—25* ❧

*T*he transformation is stunning. Saul, no doubt with blood stains still on his garment from Christians he had tortured, now stood with arms outstretched announcing, "I'm here to testify to you that Jesus is the Messiah, God's Son." And the people who heard it were amazed. The Greek text uses the term from which we get the word *ecstatic*. They responded with nothing short of ecstatic astonishment at the swift reversal of Saul's life.

Imagine sitting in the synagogue. In front of you, preaching Jesus as the Messiah, is the very man responsible for condemning innocent Christians to death. Others he had taken into prisons, perhaps, some of them relatives and friends. The room was full of jaw-dropped stares. The next statement assures us he didn't slow down: "But Saul kept increasing in strength and confounding the Jews who lived at Damascus by proving that this Jesus is the Christ" (Acts 9:22).

It gets better. Not only did Saul preach about Christ, he preached with remarkable skill. The word translated *proving* comes from a Greek verb, which means, "to knit together from several different strands." Saul's sermons were skillfully woven together, seamlessly delivered with compelling logic—all signs of a gifted expositor.

Word by word, sentence by sentence, point by point, Saul walked his listeners through the powerful passages of the Old Testament Scriptures, including the writings of the prophets, presenting an air-tight case for believing in Christ as their promised Messiah. Until Saul made his case, most had never made that connection. What a convincing communicator!

Before we go on, let's pause and remind ourselves, none of these remarkable events could have been witnessed, or even recorded for that matter, had it not been for Ananias's courageous faith. You may have never thought of that until now. Saul would have remained blind and trembling had the disciple of Damascus refused to obey and go to Straight Street. All this was set in motion because God used the memorable faith of a little-known but faithful hero. His trembling but faithful obedience changed the destiny of millions, including you and me.

# DESERT RETREAT

*Read Acts 9:20–25; Galatians 1:11–17*

*I*'m convinced it was there, in that barren place of obscurity, that Paul developed his theology. He met God, intimately and deeply. Silently and alone, he plumbed the unfathomable mysteries of sovereignty, election, depravity, the deity of Christ, the miraculous power of the Resurrection, the Church, and future things. It became a three-year crash course in sound doctrine from which would flow a lifetime of preaching, teaching, and writing. More than that, it's where Paul tossed aside his polished trophies and traded his resumé of religious credentials for a vibrant relationship with the risen Christ. Everything changed.

It was there, no doubt, he concluded "whatever things were gain to me, those things I have counted as loss for the sake of Christ. More than that, I count all things to be loss in view of the surpassing value of knowing Christ Jesus my Lord, for whom I have suffered the loss of all things, and count them but rubbish in order that I may gain Christ" (Philippians 3:7–8).

He had been so busy, active, engaged, advancing, and zealous. The same words describe many Christians sitting in churches today. And therein lies our problem. We're not busy doing all the wrong things or even a few terrible things. We're certainly not persecutors or destroyers. But if the truth were known, we'll go for miles on fumes, all the while choking the life-giving spirit within.

Not long ago academy-award-winning actor Tom Hanks starred in *Castaway*. It was one of those films with few words but an enormous amount of emotion. How he escapes is fascinating, but the good news is he is picked up by a ship and is, at last, returned safely to the now-unfamiliar world of life as it used to be. And he doesn't fit in at all anymore. The changes that transpired within him are so radical, so all-consuming, he finds himself a different man— much deeper, much more observing, much less demanding—all because of the lessons learned in solitude, quietness, and obscurity.

And so it was with Saul. He changed. How greatly he changed! And the change within him led to a change in the lives of millions of people down through the ages.

# SLOW DOWN!

### ✦ *Read Galatians 1:11—17* ✦

*P*art of the solution is to pursue the benefits of solitude and silence found in times of obscurity. For the first time in seven years, I took six weeks off one summer. No preaching, no writing, no counseling, no speaking engagements . . . no nothing. I focused on slowing down and refilling my soul with the deep things of the Lord. I prayed, I sang, I studied, I walked, I fished, I stayed quiet, and I sat thinking about and reevaluating my life. It was magnificent!

You may not have that much time available. You may have only three days, or perhaps two weeks. If you're not careful, you'll quickly fill those days with things to do, places to go, and people to see. Resist that temptation to crowd out the Lord. What a perfect opportunity to carve out time to be alone, just you, the family, and the Lord. Computer off. Fax unplugged. Cell phone tossed in the ocean.

*Instead of speeding up, slow down and rethink.* I don't want you to miss any of these words. I've thought about them for years. Instead of speeding up, let's find ways to slow down and rethink. Taking time to discover what really matters is essential if we're going to lift the curse of superficiality that shadows our lives. Don't wait for the doctor to tell you that you have six months to live. Long before anything that tragic becomes a reality, you should be growing roots deep into the soil of those things that truly matter.

Once Saul left Damascus and slipped into Arabia, he began taking inventory. There was no "To Do Before Sundown" lists. No "Six Fast Steps to Success" or other self-help scrolls clumped under his arms. He was alone. He walked slower. He watched sand swirl over the stones. He thought deeply about his past. He relived what he had done. He returned to what he had experienced on the road to Damascus. He considered each new dawn a gift from the Lord, the perfect opportunity to rework his priorities and rethink his motives. It takes time, of course . . . lots of time. But time spent in solitude prepares us for the inevitable challenges that come at us from the splintered age in which we live.

Slow down. Sit still. Be quiet. Rethink.

# A LESSER KNOWN

### ❧ *Read Acts 9:26–30* ❧

*A*ct two of the drama opens with, "And when he had come to Jerusalem . . ." (v. 26). Jerusalem! Saul owned Jerusalem. He went to graduate school in that great town. I mean, the man knew that old city like the back of his hand— every alleyway, every narrow passage, every escape route. He knew virtually everyone of any significance. What a venue to restart his public ministry. "Get the microphones. Turn the lights up bright. Pharisee-turned-evangelist now appearing at the central Jerusalem Auditorium. Come and hear! Come listen to this man preach!" Forget it. It was nothing like that.

Instead, we read this: "He was trying to associate with the disciples; and they were all afraid of him, not believing that he was a disciple" (v. 26). Rejected again, only this time by those he most wanted to meet. Fear stood between them and the zealous, gifted preacher.

That's understandable; who wouldn't be afraid of him? He killed their fellow Christians, some of whom may have been relatives. They thought Saul was a spy—part of an elaborate hoax designed to trap them and drag them to trial. "Saul? No way. Don't let him in our ranks!"

Ever felt the sting of that kind of rejection? Have you ever had such a bad track record that people didn't want to associate with you or welcome you into their fellowship? (Or welcome you back?) It happens all the time. People are rejected because of their pasts. The load of baggage they drag behind them as they enter the Christian life keeps them from enjoying what should be instant acceptance. The rejection at times is unbearable. You may say, "Yes. I've been there. And I'm trying to forget those memories, thank you very much." No, don't forget those times. Those painful memories are part of God's gracious plan to break your strong spirit of independence. They've become an essential segment of your story—your testimony of God's grace.

Thankfully, in the midst of those times, God faithfully provides lesser-known individuals who come alongside and say, "Hey, I'm on your team. Let me walk through this with you." That's exactly what happened to Saul in Jerusalem. Someone stepped up, voluntarily. He didn't have to, he wanted to. His name . . . Barnabas, the encourager.

# SON OF ENCOURAGEMENT

### ✤ *Read Acts 9:26–30* ❧

The disciples feared Saul. They couldn't bring themselves to believe he was a disciple. "*But Barnabas . . .*" Isn't that a great opening? Out of nowhere comes Barnabas to encourage Saul and be his personal advocate. How did Barnabas know Saul needed his help? We don't know. Yet we do know that God is sovereign and has his Barnabases in every town, every church, on every college and seminary campus, and even on the mission field. Each Barnabas stands ready at a moment's notice to come to the aid of someone in need of encouragement.

So rather than operating out of fear and prejudice, Barnabas stepped up and "took hold of Saul." Saul was willing to accept his assistance. That's a healthy dependence. Barnabas took Saul under his wing and said, "Come with me, I'll set this thing straight with these men. They trust me." So off they went, and the sacred narrative says that Barnabas "brought him to the disciples and described to them how he had seen the Lord on the road, and that He had talked to him, and how at Damascus he had spoken out boldly in the name of Jesus." That's what I call divine intervention through a lesser-known saint! Barnabas basically said, "I've checked this guy out—he's the genuine item. He saw the risen Christ, just like all of you. The man is on our team. Make room . . . relax!"

The next statement describes the result of Barnabas's action on behalf of Saul: "And he was with them moving about freely in Jerusalem, speaking boldly in the name of Jesus." For the first time in his ministry, Saul spoke freely about Christ in Jerusalem, in the company of respected disciples—set free to be himself for the glory of God. What made the difference? *Barnabas!*

You may be a Barnabas today. Do you know someone who has been kicked in the teeth because he has a bad track record? Someone who can't get a hearing, yet she's turned her life around and nobody wants to believe it? I urge you to step up like Barnabas did for Saul. Look for those individuals who need a second chance—a large dose of grace to help them start over in the Christian life. Everybody needs a Barnabas at one time or another.

304

# THE VALUE OF OTHERS

### ❧ *Read Acts 9:28–31* ❧

*T*he Message, Eugene Peterson's paraphrase, wraps up this part of the narrative nicely: "Things calmed down after that and the church had smooth sailing for a while. All over the country—Judaea, Samaria, Galilee—the church grew. They were permeated with a deep sense of reverence for God. The Holy Spirit was with them, strengthening them. They prospered wonderfully."

They didn't need Saul. In Tarsus he had the time to learn that he needed them. It wasn't about independence. It was about his discovering the value of dependence. Tragically, some never learn.

This is a good time to pause and make a twenty-century jump to today. Learn to appreciate and embrace the value of other people. Don't try to go out there on your own. Rather than viewing others around you as hindrances, become aware of their value. Remind yourself that they play a strategic role in your survival and your success. God rarely asks us to fly solo. When He leads us to soar the heights, there is safety in others soaring with us.

God has designed His family to be that sort of support network for all of us. Nobody can handle all the pressure over the long haul. Companionship and accountability are essential!

You may be resisting becoming an active member of a church or enrolling in a small-group fellowship at your church. You think you can go it alone, and so far your plan has worked. But it's only a matter of time before a gust of adversity knocks you off your feet, and you'll need someone to pick you up. Don't let a stubborn spirit of independence rob you of the joy of sharing your life, your weaknesses, your failures, and your dreams with others. You and I are not indispensable. You and I are not irreplaceable. God is both. It's His church. He's looking for broken vessels, wounded hearts, and humble servants, even those with bad track records who have some scars, who have learned not to hide them or deny them—people who understand and appreciate the value of others. Is that you?

# HUMBLE RELIANCE

### ❧ *Read Acts 9:28–31* ❧

asn't it a waste of great talent for God to put Saul on hold? Not at all. Wasn't Tarsus a strange assignment? Not if He wanted him to be prepared to write the letter to the Romans. Not if he would have any lasting impact on the backsliding believers at Corinth. Not if He wanted Saul to mentor Timothy for a lifetime of strategic ministry in Ephesus. Those projects (and dozens of others) called for a depth of character, forged through the lessons that taught him dependence—both on God and on others.

Humble yourself. Rather than racing into the limelight, we need to accept our role in the shadows. I'm serious here. Don't promote yourself. Don't push yourself to the front. Don't drop hints. Let someone else do that. Better yet, let God do that.

If you're great, trust me, the word will get out. You'll be found . . . in God's time. If you're necessary for the plan, God will put you in the right place at just the precise time. God's work is not about us; it's His production, start to finish. So back off. Let Him pull the curtains and turn on the stage lights. He'll lay hold of an Ananias or Barnabas, who'll come and find you at your most vulnerable point and lift you over the wall. Or He may choose you to be one of the nameless, lesser-known individuals who make the difference for someone else. Your part, pure and simple: humble yourself.

This would be a good time for you to resist going through life trying to live according to your own understanding—thinking if you can just climb up one or two more rungs on the ladder, you'll be there. You'll have what you need. Your family will be (what's that word we like to use?) . . . "comfortable." You know what your family needs more than extra money in the bank or a more impressive address or a TV in each room? They need you to be right with the Lord. That means that you walk humbly with Him. They need your gentle touch, acknowledging that He's the Lord of your home, not you. That takes humility. Go there, my friend, go there.

# STUBBORN INDEPENDENCE

*Read Acts 9:28–31*

*R*ather than considering yourself (even secretly) indispensable, remind yourself often, *It's the Lord's work to be done the Lord's way.* I first heard that principle from Francis Schaeffer while attending one of his lectures. There he stood in knickers and a turtleneck sweater, delivering this very message to a group of young, idealistic listeners—many of us struggling to find our way. I heard him say this again and again: "The Lord's work must be done the Lord's way. The Lord's work must be done the Lord's way. The Lord's work must be done the Lord's way."

If you're in a hurry, you can make it work your way. It may have all the marks of promotion, but it won't be the Lord's way. Stop and realize that. It may be time for you to be let down off your wall in a basket to learn that in your life.

John Pollock, in his splendid book *The Apostle*, states, "The irony was not lost on him that the mighty Paul, who had originally approached Damascus with all the panoply of the high priest's representative, should make his last exit in a fish basket, helped by the very people he had come to hurt."

That about says it all, doesn't it?

Just to set the record straight, our lives are not caught "in the fell clutch of circumstance." Our heads are not to be "bloodied, but unbowed." You and I are neither the "masters of our fate" nor are we the "captains of our souls." We are to be wholly, continually, and completely dependent on the mercy of God, if we want to do the Lord's work the Lord's way. Paul had to learn that. My question is: Are *you* learning that? If not, today would be a good day to start. Now is the time to humble yourself under His mighty hand. If you don't, eventually, He will do it for you. And it will hurt. In His time, in His way, He will conquer your stubborn independence.

God is never pleased with a spiritually independent spirit.

# OUT OF THE SHADOWS

### ✣ *Read Acts 11:19–26* ✣

Some of you who read these words today could use a little extra hope, especially if you find yourself in a waiting mode. You were once engaged in the action, doing top-priority work on the front lines. No longer. All that has changed. Now, for some reason, you're on the shelf. It's tough to stay encouraged perched on a shelf. Your mind starts playing tricks on you.

Though you are well educated, experienced, and fairly gifted in your particular field, you are now waiting. You're wondering, and maybe you're getting worried, that this waiting period might be permanent. Admittedly, your response may not be all that great. You can't see any light at the end of the tunnel. It just doesn't seem fair. After all, you've trained hard, you've jumped through hoops, and you've even made the necessary sacrifices. Discouragement crouches at the door, ready to pounce on any thought or hope, so you sit wondering why God has chosen to pass you by.

I want to offer you some encouragement, but I need to start with a realistic comment: it may be a long time before God moves you into a place of significant impact. He may choose not to reveal His plan for weeks, maybe months. Are you ready for this? It could be years. I have found that one of God's favorite methods of preparing us for something great is to send us into the shadows to wait.

But that doesn't mean you're doomed to terminal darkness. Take heart from the words of British author James Stalker who wrote, "Waiting is a common instrument of providential discipline for those to whom exceptional work has been appointed." Pause and let that sink in. Read the statement again, slower this time.

Waiting is one of God's preferred methods of preparing special people for significant projects. The Bible makes that principle plain from cover to cover.

As Psalm 27:14 says, "Wait for the LORD; be strong and take heart and wait for the LORD."

# GOD'S WAITING ROOM

*Read Acts 11:25; 2 Corinthians 12:2—6*

*I*f you go back fourteen years, from the time Paul wrote the second letter to the believers at Corinth, that places him at the time he was waiting in Tarsus. Quite possibly, during one of his numerous floggings he received in Tarsus, or in an agonizing battle to survive being stoned, he lapsed into a semi-conscious state—something of a trance. Possibly, while in that state of mind, the Lord transported him to Paradise and revealed inexpressible, profound truths to him.

The point I want to make is, even in all that, he refused to boast in his giftedness. Instead, he confessed, "I will rather boast about my weaknesses, that the power of Christ may dwell in me . . . for when I am weak, then I am strong" (2 Corinthians 12:9–10). That's true humility. Incredible perspective. He learned *to boast* in nothing but his own weakness. And, remember, he learned that in the shadows. But nobody knew about it. His transformation never made the headlines.

Your time of God-ordained waiting will never be all that significant in other people's minds. All they may know is that you dropped out of sight. You're gone from the scene. It may begin with a bankruptcy. It may start with a horrible experience you go through, such as a tragic accident or a devastating illness. You may endure the pain of a torn reputation caused by someone who didn't tell the truth. All that devastation has a way of breaking you. The Lord uses the disappointment to lead you to your own Tarsus—otherwise known as His waiting room. There He begins to work deep within your soul until you, like Saul, gain such a renewed perspective, you can honestly confess, "When I am weak, *He* is strong." When that happens, as it did with Saul, you will be ready to come out of the shadows.

Saul was now ready. Not surprisingly, God moved.

# TRUSTING GOD IN THE SHADOWS

*✒ Read Acts 11:25; 2 Corinthians 12:2–6 ✒*

*I* want to dispense a fresh supply of hope. To help accomplish that, let me suggest four principles. They may mean more to you later than now—in a time when God leads you to wait in the shadows.

First, *when God prepares us for effective ministry, He includes what we would rather omit—a period of waiting. That cultivates patience.* As I write these words, it occurs to me that I've never met anyone young and patient. (To be honest, I've not met many *old* and patient folks either.) We're all in a hurry. We don't like to miss one panel of a revolving door. Patience comes hard in a hurry-up society. Yet, it's an essential quality, cultivated only in extended periods of waiting.

Second, *as God makes us wait, hiding us in His shadow, He shows us we're not indispensable. That makes us humble.* One major reason the Lord removes us and has us wait in His shadow is to remind us we're not the star attraction. We're not indispensable. That realization cultivates genuine humility. I'm convinced Saul never once questioned God for having His hand on Peter and Barnabas, rather than on him. In a time when most gifted individuals would have been volunteering at the revival headquarters, Saul willingly remained behind the scenes. All the while waiting for his time—correction, God's time.

Third, *while God hides us away, He reveals new dimensions of Himself and new insights regarding ministry. That makes us deep.* What we need today is not smarter people or busier people. A far greater need is deeper people. Deep people will always have a ministry. Always. God deepens us through time spent waiting on Him.

Fourth, *when God finally chooses to use us, it comes at a time least expected, when we feel the least qualified. That makes us effective.* The perfect set-up for a long-lasting, effective ministry begins with surprise. "Me? You sure You don't want that other person? She's got great qualifications and obvious gifts. You may want to talk to her." That's the idea. It's refreshing, in this highly efficient age, to find a few who are still amazed at the way God is using them.

# FROM GOD'S PERSPECTIVE

### ✑ *Read Romans 8:22–23* ✑

*A*ny study of the life of the apostle Paul requires a serious look at the subject of pain. Suffering is not a pleasant subject to explore. Explaining Paul's words to the Romans, John Stott writes, "It is not only our fragile body which makes me groan; it is also our fallen nature, which hinders us from behaving as we should. Our groans express both present pain and future longing. Some Christians, however, grin too much (they seem to have no place in their theology for pain) and groan too little."

The man has grown weary of the perpetual Christian grin—frankly, so have I. If you groan and allow your countenance to reflect any measure of inner turmoil, people frown at you judgmentally, as if to suggest you're not walking in the Spirit. Don't get me wrong. I find nothing offensive about Christians laughing. I wrote an entire book affirming that God's people need to laugh more. Laughter demonstrates authenticity in our lives. I simply believe there's no need to glue a permanent Cheshire grin to our faces, lest we look like we're not living a victorious Christian life. If a fellow believer tells you he's going through a particularly tough time, I urge you not to insist he smile. (I tell the folks at the church not to ask me to listen to one of my tapes on joy when they notice I'm feeling down.) Don't urge people to sing along with you on some tune you think they should be singing. Sometimes we just don't feel like singing or smiling. After all, God gave us more than one emotion on purpose.

My desire is to help equip you for what life will inevitably sling across your path. I understand you may be bearing a burden or heartache, the likes of which I've never known. You may be living with pressures or some debilitating physical disease or emotional pain I couldn't even begin to imagine. In almost four decades of pastoral ministry, I've often seen the evidence of inner turmoil surface on the faces of God's people. In those times, when I feel at a loss to offer encouragement, I am most thankful for the Scriptures. In God's Word we not only discover His will for our lives, we find words of genuine comfort for those times when life comes unglued.

So be careful not to grin too much and groan too little.

# A THORN IN THE FLESH

*Read 2 Corinthians 12:2—10*

Sailors on the high seas understand the importance of securing themselves to something sturdy in a fierce gale. You learn to cling to what's secure in a storm. Saul learned to cling to what he knew to be true about himself and the Lord who held him in His grip.

I see an interesting tension here. While Satan punched and pounded the apostle's resolve, the Lord's purpose was to humble him, to keep him from exalting himself. Pride doesn't reside in the hearts of the broken, the split-apart, the wounded, or the anguished of soul.

Many years ago I read these words: "Pain plants the flag of reality in the fortress of a rebel heart." Mothers and fathers keeping vigil in the leukemia ward of a children's hospital do not wrestle with issues of pride. They are humbled to the point of despair.

I'm not qualified to give you the intimate details of how Saul's thorn affected him. However, he does confess that he begged the Lord on three separate occasions to remove it from him (v. 8). And you know what? We would have done the same. You and I would have prayed and prayed and begged for relief. "Father, please take away the *thorn*. Lord, I beg of You, remove it. Take this pain away from me." That was Saul's response.

I see amazing transparency written in those lines. The world needs more followers of Christ who embrace pain and hardship rather than deny them. How helpful for us to see all this as God's plan to keep us humble. That can't be taught in Bible colleges or seminaries. Those lessons are learned in the trenches of life. What people of prayer we would become! How often we would turn to Him. How fully we would lean on Him. And what insights we would glean.

That is precisely what happened as Saul turned again and again to his Lord. And God gave an answer he never expected.

# GRACE THAT WON'T LET GO

### *Read 2 Corinthians 12:2–10*

*T*his is a good time to correct faulty thinking. It is not always God's will that you be healed. It is not always the Father's plan to relieve the pressure. Our happiness is not God's chief aim. He doesn't have a wonderful (meaning "comfortable") plan for everybody's life—not from a human perspective. Often His plan is nowhere near wonderful. As with Saul, His answer is not what we prayed and hoped for. But, remembering that He is forming us more and more into the image of His Son, it helps us understand His answer is based on His long-range plan, not our immediate relief.

Thankfully, in the midst of that suffering, He gently whispers, "My grace is sufficient for you" (v. 9). As with Saul, His grace supplies more than we need to endure whatever it is that threatens to undo us. Let me amplify that thought. His grace is more sufficient than your strength. His grace is more sufficient than the advice of any trained counselor or close friend (though God uses both). His grace is sufficient to carry you through whatever your own unique "thorn" may be. His grace—that's the ticket.

Would you like to know why? Because God's power is perfected in weakness (v. 9). What an amazing statement from the Lord! And all this time we thought power was perfected in success. We've been taught all our lives that it is achievement that makes us strong. No. A thousand times, no! Those things make us proud and self-sufficient and independent. Painful thorns make us weak. But the good news is this: when we are weak, He pours His strength into us, which gives an entirely new perspective on pain and suffering, hardship and pressure. Those stresses and strains drive us to our knees. It's at *that* point our God comes through, takes us by the hand, and by His grace lifts us up.

His grace is sufficient for you too.

# IT'S NOT ABOUT YOU!

### ✦ *Read 2 Corinthians 12:2—10* ✦

*I* need to underscore a foundational fact: God's goal is not to make sure you're happy. No matter how hard it is for you to believe this, it's time to do so. Life is not about your being comfortable and happy and successful and pain free. It's about becoming the man or woman God has called you to be. Unfortunately, we will rarely hear that message proclaimed today. All the more reason for me to say it again: Life is not about *you*! It's about *God*.

How can I say that with assurance? Because of Saul's response: "Most gladly, therefore, I will rather boast about my weaknesses, that the power of Christ may dwell in me. Therefore I am well content with weaknesses, with insults, with distresses, with persecutions, with difficulties, for Christ's sake; for when I am weak, then I am strong" (vv. 9–10). That's it! He got it too. And he went with it for the rest of his days.

When you and I boast of our strengths, we get the credit, and we keep going under our own head of steam. But when we boast in what He is doing in the midst of our brokenness, inability, and inadequacy, Christ comes to the front. His strength comes to our rescue. He is honored.

Don't miss that point. The very things we dread and run from in our lives are precisely what brought contentment to Saul. Look at the list: I am content when I lose. I am content when I am weak. I am content with insults. I am content when I'm slandered. I am content in distresses. I am content with persecutions. I am content with difficulties and pressures that are so tight I can hardly turn around. Why? "Because when I am weak then I'm strong" (v. 10). Knowing that brought the apostle, ablaze with the flaming oracles of heaven, to his knees. What a way to live your life—content in everything—knowing that divine strength comes when human weakness is evident.

That's what gave the man of grace true grit. It will do the same for us.

# NOTHING NEW

*Read 2 Corinthians 12:2—10*

*R*emember that suffering is not now. In what is probably the oldest book in the Bible, the book of Job, we read, "For man is born for trouble, as sparks fly upward" (Job 5:7). Now, there's a statement we need to teach our children and grandchildren, starting today. The message they consistently hear is that God has nothing but happiness and success in store for them if they'll entrust their lives to Him. The Bible never promises that! Amazingly, while scraping sores from his diseased and pain-racked body, Job asked, "Shall we indeed accept good from God and not adversity?" He made that statement in response to his wife's advice to "curse God and die." She too was broken from the loss of her children and the misery of watching her husband suffer so terribly. (As a young preacher, I came down too hard on Job's wife. Now I go easier on her. She was grieving, not blaming. She needed God's perspective on her pain.) It was when her husband witnessed how deep her grief was that he responded as he did. He wanted her to realize that God is not a heavenly bellboy, delivering only pleasurable and comforting things to our door. He doesn't exist to make us happy. We exist to bring Him glory.

We life in superficial, skeptical times. When hard times occur you will find scores of newly released titles questioning how a loving God could be so unfair and unjust. It is easy to be confused in one's understanding of God. But He has not changed. His ways have not been altered. As with Job and Saul, He continues to allow suffering to mold us into humble, useful servants. . . .

Throw one of us in a dungeon and we want to talk to our lawyer! Throw those guys in prison, and the world ends up with Pilgrim's Progress, or some other magnificent literary work that endures for centuries, putting our suffering back into perspective. Resist the temptation to rethink God just because hard times come. Look deeper. Cling to Him tighter. Refuse to question His motives. He's doing something great within you. Suffering is nothing new.

# SUFFICIENT GRACE

### ✦ *Read 2 Corinthians 12:2–10* ✦

*R*elease the idea that contentment requires comfort. Contentment is possible no matter how dire your circumstances. While under house arrest, Paul wrote, "I have learned to be content in whatever circumstances I am. I know how to get along with humble means, and I also know how to live in prosperity; in any and every circumstance I have learned the secret of being filled and going hungry, both of having abundance and suffering need. I can do all things through Him who strengthens me" (Philippians 4:11–13). There it is again. Did you see it? The secret to Saul's contentment was knowing Christ's strength was perfected in his weakness. He really got it . . . and what a liberating concept it became!

Suffering is a delicate subject. It's not easy to address because I realize I'm writing to people who have known a depth of suffering to which I have never gone. In no way do I wish to give the impression that I am a model of how to go through it. To be honest with you, I fail in my responses to adversity more than I succeed. It's a lot easier to write a chapter on it than it is to model those things that look good in print. Along with the occasional pity parties I throw for myself, my heart is occasionally broken, and my spirit takes a tumble. So if that is your experience today, I can identify with that.

My desire is for you and me, together, to claim grace and cultivate grit in the midst of our suffering—like Saul. And in the process to wean ourselves from the rabid pursuit of happiness so prevalent in our culture. Happiness is a byproduct of contentment. Once Saul discovered that, he lived it. I'm not fully there yet. Most likely, neither are you. And so, we press on together, growing and learning, reminding ourselves that He must increase, and we must decrease.

Next time you hear a knock at the back door, before you open it, repeat these words to yourself: "His grace is sufficient for me."

# THE POWER OF TWO

### ✣ *Read Acts 11:19–26* ✣

o you recall what David did after he killed Goliath? God had already appointed the young shepherd as the next king of Israel. Most young conquerors would have located the nearest Macy's and tried on crowns. Not David. He went right back to the Judean hills to keep his father's sheep—a true shepherd with a servant's heart.

Saul kept a similar vigil in Tarsus. He waited patiently until Barnabas tapped him on the shoulder. Only then did he step into that critical, highly visible role of leadership. I find nothing more attractive in a gifted and competent leader than authentic humility. Saul's giftedness was framed in the crucible of solitude where he had been honed and retooled by the living Christ.

The evangelist Dwight L. Moody, although unschooled, was a gifted man of God preaching in Birmingham, England, far back in 1875. A noted congregational minister and well-respected theologian, Dr. R. W. Dale, cooperated in that enormously successful campaign. After watching and listening to Moody preach and witnessing the incredible results of the ministry of that simple man, Dr. Dale wrote in his denominational magazine, "I told Mr. Moody that the work was most plainly of God, for I could see no real relation between him and what he had done. Moody laughed cheerily and said, 'I should be very sorry if it were otherwise.'" No defensiveness, no feeling of being put upon, no embarrassing uneasiness. Moody was the most surprised of anyone that God chose to use him so mightily.

That was Saul. No wonder Barnabas wanted Saul to lead the program in Antioch. What a duet they sang! For an entire year these two men served side by side, and God was greatly glorified.

I love Warren Wiersbe's succinct definition of ministry: "Ministry takes place when divine resources meet human needs through loving channels to the glory of God." Saul and Barnabas could have sat for that portrait. Why did Saul and Barnabas experience such pleasure in serving together? No competition. No battle of egos. No one threatened by the other's gifts. No hidden agendas. No unresolved conflicts. Their single-minded goal was to magnify Christ. It didn't matter if the crowds multiplied to thousands or shrank to only a few. All that mattered was that Christ be proclaimed and worshiped.

Praise God for the power of two!

# MINISTERING TOGETHER

### ❧ *Read Acts 11:19–26* ❧

*I*n every ministry there are at least three essentials that produce an atmosphere of joyous cooperation. They are objectives, people, and places.

First, *whatever God plans, He pursues*. That has to do with the ministry essential of objectives. There's nothing wrong with having a clearly defined mission statement that gives direction and purpose to the vision of a ministry. In fact, there's everything right about it as long as it is the Lord who provides the direction. God's plan unfolds in ways that confounds human wisdom and sometimes defy common sense. But it is His plan. Objectives are essential when they are *His* objectives, not ours.

Second, *whomever God chooses, He uses*. That has to do with the ministry essential of people. And I must quickly add, the people God chooses are never perfect. That includes me. That includes you. In fact, we prove more useful to the Lord when we accept that reality and trust Him with our imperfections.

Third, *wherever God selects, He sends*. That has to do with the ministry essential of places. I wish He would send all of the great ones to Stonebriar Community Church. And I wish He would never let any of them leave. That's desire based on my limited human perspective. I never prayed this prayer, but I've been tempted to pray, "Lord, send us only the great ones and keep them here forever. Don't ever take them anywhere else." (Being imperfect, I'm not above a few selfish prayers!)

God's plan, however, includes removing some very gifted people among us and sending them elsewhere. His ways are not our ways. His places are not the places we would choose to go on our own. None of that matters. What matters is this: God sends people of His choosing to places of His choosing. The sooner we accept and embrace that truth, the more contented we will be.

Ministering together is always an adventure. It's about embracing change. It's about maintaining flexibility. It's about walking with God through the surprising events He has designed. Barnabas needed help. The work was too much for one gifted but limited man. Saul stepped into the gap. And together they turned Antioch upside down for Christ.

# GENTLE NUDGING

### ❧ *Read Acts 12:25—13:3* ❧

*W*hile they were ministering to the Lord—fasting, singing, teaching, witnessing, and praying—the Holy Spirit said, "Okay, hitch up the wagons, fellas . . . westward, ho! I need Barnabas and Saul for the work to which I have called them."

Can you imagine how some would react today? "You can't be serious. You're gonna take two of the five chefs and send them to another joint? We'll starve! You're gonna reach down in our ranks and pull two of the best adult fellowship teachers we've got and move them to some distant mission field? That's two-fifths of our leadership. We can't let these guys slip through our fingers!"

But none of that occurred in Antioch. As soon as those folks realized it was the Spirit of God who was sending them on, they released them. And the change occurred (don't miss this!) "while they were ministering." It didn't happen in a lull, when giving was way down, or during a period of leadership transition. God lifted these men from that exciting setting while the church was at its zenith, steaming ahead full-bore. People were coming by the cartload, deep needs were being met, souls were being saved, lives were being transformed, families were getting healthy, the place was electric! Still, the Spirit said, "It's time for change." Who would've ever imagined? But God is full of surprises, since He sees the big picture while we focus mainly on the here and now.

It was God's way of telling Barnabas and Saul it was time to move. By the way, the Lord did the speaking. In those days the Lord revealed Himself in a number of ways. Today, I believe He speaks to us through His Word, through the gentle nudging of the Spirit, and through the collective witness of His people. Then it may have been in a night vision, or during a time while the disciples were praying, meditating on the Scriptures, or while fasting. A couple of the leaders sensed the Lord's leading in a new direction. Others verified the voice. The Lord said, in effect, "I have work for two of you to do elsewhere. Not all of you, only two, and My plan is best. Release Barnabas and Saul. They are the two I'm calling elsewhere."

Westward, ho!

# PEOPLE PLEASING

*Read Acts 12:25—13:3*

*I* need to make a couple of observations about the nature of ministry. The way God chooses to lead His ministry is often difficult to get our arms around. Finding direction in the corporate world comes somewhat easier. There's a clearly stated bottom line, shareholders to report to, and defined markets that guide company decisions.

Ministry matters are rarely that obvious and objective. We serve a Head we cannot see, and we listen to a voice we cannot literally hear. Often we feel as if we're being asked to follow a plan we do not understand. And I need to repeat here, during the process of discovering God's leading, we are subject to enormous changes. These are changes we must embrace in the power of the Spirit if we are to obey our Lord's lead. Though we are accountable to the churches we serve, ultimately, each one of God's servants answers to God. Without that sort of single-minded devotion to the Lord, we run the risk of becoming people-pleasers. Christian leaders who become pawns as they focus on pleasing people are pathetic wimps.

Honestly, there have been times in my younger life when I stumbled onto that slippery slide. I look back on those few occasions with only regret. Nothing good ever comes from a ministry devoted to pleasing people.

Rather than being a warrior for the King, it is easy to become an insecure wimp, relying on human opinions and longing for human approval. By His grace I won't go there again. My responsibility is to deliver what God's people *need*, not what they *want*. As I do, that truth hits me with the same authority as it does the folks with whom I communicate. May God deliver every honest pastor, every truth-seeking church leader, and every Christian from the bondage of pleasing people.

# LIKE CLAY

## ✨ *Read Acts 12:25—13:5* ✨

K eeping the clay of your will supple and flexible calls for constant attention along the way. Once you grow hard and brittle to God's leading, you're less usable to Him. I want to take the truths we've wrestled with here and make them into a softening ointment you can regularly apply when a change is on the horizon. The ingredients in the ointment you need to apply include a pinch of the negative and a smidgen of the positive.

First negative: *Do not remove any possibility.* Stay open to whatever it is God may have for you by removing all the limitations. Tell the Lord you're willing to cooperate. But don't forget, you may be the next Barnabas or Saul the Lord decides to move. Remember, we're dealing with change—changing so we might obey.

Second negative: *Do not allow a lot of activity to dull your sensitivity.* Remember, God spoke *while* they were ministering. You can be so busy in church activities you can't figure out what the Lord's saying.

First positive: *Let God be God.* He is selective when He moves people. He picked two and left three. That was His prerogative. He could have chosen all five or only one. It's His call. Our sovereign Lord does as He pleases, and when it's clear, our response is to obey.

Second positive: *Be ready to say yes.* Don't wait for all the details to be ironed out before you agree to release and obey. Sure, there will be hardships, some uphill stretches in the road. So what? Be ready to say yes, and trust Him to take care of the rest.

Only you and the Lord know the condition of your heart. Is it soft and pliable clay, ready to be molded and shaped by the Master sculptor? Or has it hardened into brittle and fragile pottery from years of faithless living? You know exactly what God is asking you to do. It may be well beyond the boundaries of logic and far outside your comfort zone. You may even have a few friends telling you that what you believe He's asking you to do is wrong, completely wrong. Still, His leading is clear. Only one thing is needed: say yes, Lord, yes.

# A PHONY PROPHET

### ✦ *Read Acts 13:6—12* ✦

his was no time for Paul to be tolerant or passive. We live in a culture that virtually deifies tolerance. One lady recently said to me with a broad grin, "I love everybody; I even love the devil." I call that "tolerance gone to seed." Make no mistake, we're not to love the devil, nor are we to love everything everybody does. Christ commands us to love people, even our enemies, but that doesn't mean we shrink from standing up for righteousness.

Paul didn't back off an inch. I can see the hair stiffening on the back of his neck as he showed his spiritual teeth and growled,

"You who are full of all deceit and fraud, you son of the devil, you enemy of all righteousness, will you not cease to make crooked the straight ways of the Lord? And now, behold, the hand of the Lord is upon you, and you will be blind and not see the sun for a time." And immediately a mist and a darkness fell upon him, and he went about seeking those who would lead him by the hand." (Acts 13:10–11)

When he had to be firm, he stepped up. The result was magnificent. Stunned by the obvious display of God's power and Paul's emboldened response, the pagan official believed, and we can almost see the door to the Gentiles opened wider.

You may face similar opportunities to confront enemies of truth. They come in a number of different forms. Some are more insidious than others. My advice, when the opposition against the truth is this severe, based on Paul's model, is that you confront it. Leave the results with God. Step up and speak out in the name of the Lord. Be certain of His protection. Don't rush in. Pray for wisdom in the choice of your words before saying anything, and then speak boldly. The results may not be as dramatic as what happened in Cyprus, but the Lord will honor your faith. The few times I've had to stand this firmly against wrong, the Lord gave me a sense of near-invincible courage.

When you stand *for* God, you stand *with* God. He's got your back. So you can stand with confidence.

# Press On!

❧ *Read Acts 12:25; 13:5, 13—15* ☙

*P*aul, Barnabas, and John Mark left Cyprus and sailed to the southern coast of Turkey—a land then known as Pamphylia, whose rugged coastline ascended sharply into the towering heights of a mountain range steeper and fiercer than the eastern Tauras near Tarsus, and more terrible than any hills known to the Cypriot Barnabas or the Judean John Mark.

That sight alone may have initiated the storm surge of doubt that would eventually flood young John Mark's soul. In this region Paul became gravely ill with Malaria or some other serious coastal fever. That may have been the last straw for the inexperienced traveler to endure. Without any explanation, Luke simply writes, "John left them and returned to Jerusalem." But going on from Perga, they pressed on. Without even as much as a hiccup, the journey continued. Paul and Barnabas were undeterred by John Mark's desertion.

Here's an important observation: all the way through ministry, people leave. In every church there will be individuals who, for whatever reason, move on to other things. This includes those in leadership. They leave, but the church presses on. Regardless of the circumstances surrounding their departure, the journey continued. For Paul and Barnabas there was neither time nor need for a long, drawn-out farewell. They pressed ahead, keeping their eyes focused on the goal.

It's hard to press on when you feel abandoned. It's easy to give in to discouragement and allow that to siphon your tank dry, but Paul and Barnabas had no such luxury. Emotions in check, they had a job to do. So they moved forward with an even stronger determination.

One of the marks of maturity is the ability to press ahead regardless of who walks off the scene. The alternative isn't an option. Once you've said goodbye, it's time for everyone to move on. That's exactly what Paul and Barnabas did. As Paul wrote in his letter to the Philippians: "I press on toward the goal to win the prize for which God has called me heavenward in Christ Jesus" (3:14).

# UNEXPECTED OPPORTUNITIES

### ✣ *Read Acts 13:14–52* ❧

*P*aul and Barnabas arrived at Pisidian Antioch, weary and aching from their perilous march through the mountains. Still, they wasted no time in making their way to the synagogue early enough to find a good seat to listen to the reading of God's Word. They made their destination by the Sabbath.

They said to Paul, "Would you like to preach?" That was his cue! (I can read the man's mind: *I thought you'd never ask!*) Without hesitation, he delivered the goods. He started in Genesis and preached all the way through to the ministry of Christ completely from memory! He had no notes. He did it extemporaneously.

The response was overwhelming. Luke informs us that the next Sabbath the whole town showed up to hear the message he would deliver. The same was true then as it is today: people are hungry for the Word of God. When you have hungry hearts and great food served well, there's no problem getting people to come for the spiritual feast. Finding people who long to be fed the nourishing meat of God's truth is no great challenge.

Therefore, my advice is simple: When you have the unexpected opportunity to share the good news, share it. But be careful not to dump the whole truckload. If you're sitting on a plane and the opportunity presents itself, don't preach through the whole Old Testament before getting to the heart of the Gospel. Tell that hungry soul how to find a piece of bread. As you lift up Christ, tell him of your own spiritual journey. If done courteously and interestingly, he will hang on every word, just as they did with Paul. And the response was overwhelmingly positive.

As Jesus promised, "When I am lifted up from the earth, I will draw all men to myself" (John 12:32 NIV).

# GRACE TO THE SAVED

### *Read Acts 13:14–52*

*P*aul's message emphasized the gospel to the lost and grace to the saved. That is a wonderful paradigm for any minister or ministry to adopt. As I've studied the life of Paul, particularly in his later years, I find two prominent themes woven like threads through the tapestry of his ministry.

First, *to the lost he presented the Gospel:* "Let it be known to you, brethren, that through Him forgiveness of sins is proclaimed to you, and through Him everyone who believes is freed from all things, from which you could not be freed through the Law of Moses" (Acts 13:38–39).

Imagine the impact our churches would have on our communities if each Christian committed to sharing the Gospel once a week with someone who expresses a need.

Second, *his message included large doses of grace for the saved.* Just as the lost don't understand the Gospel, the saved rarely understand grace. There are few activities more exhausting and less rewarding than Christians attempting to please the people around them by maintaining impossible legalistic demands. What a tragic trap, and thousands are caught in it. When will we ever learn? Grace has set us free! That message streamed often through the sermons and personal testimonies of the apostle Paul.

The lost need to hear how they can go from the island of debris, filled with misery and guilt, to the land of peace and forgiveness, flowing with mercy and grace. We build those bridges when we lovingly and patiently communicate the Gospel. You don't have to have a seminary degree. You don't have to know a lot of the religious vocabulary. In your own authentic, honest, and unguarded manner, share with people what Christ has done for you. Who knows? It may not be long before you will know the joy of leading a lost sinner from the darkness of death's dungeon across the bridge to the liberating hope of new life in Christ. Once they've arrived, release them. Release them into the magnificent freedom that grace provides. Don't smother them with a bunch of rules and regulations that put them on probation and keep them in that holding tank until they "get their lives straightened out." Making us holy is the Spirit's work. You be faithful to dispense the Gospel to the lost and grace to the saved. Then leave the results in the Lord's hands.

## TANGLED IN THE TANGIBLES

*Read Acts 13:45—48*

*W*hen Paul was rejected, he didn't quit. As my good friend and wise mentor, Howie Hendricks, often says, "Where there's light, there are bugs!" The brighter Paul's light, the more the bugs. And in that situation, those bugs had stingers filled with poison.

What grit! Paul didn't back down an inch in his response to open rejection. The result? Not surprisingly, the Gentiles in the crowd rejoiced in the good news he had for them. How exciting! What started as a smoldering ember of religious curiosity burst into flames of faith.

Why were Paul and Barnabas able to persevere? Neither man set his affections on temporal things. What discipline. If you want to get caught in the net of disillusionment, allow yourself to get tangled in the tangibles. You'll not only run shy of courage, you'll sink like a rock in a country pond. Why? Because others' opinions will start to mean everything. When you allow their responses to be the ballast, then their applause becomes essential to keep you afloat, and their assaults drag you straight to the bottom. That formula for failure can be found in all people-pleasing ministries. You're doomed to disillusionment if you don't focus on the eternal.

Lee Iacocca, not long after leaving the automobile business, said, "Here I am in the twilight years of my life still wondering what it's all about. I can tell you this: fame and fortune is for the birds."

You may be one who lives your life pursuing fame and fortune, depending on the applause of others. Bad plan. To begin with, fortune has shallow roots. The winds of adversity can quickly blow it all away. "Riches make themselves wings" writes Solomon, "they fly away as an eagle toward heaven" (Proverbs 23:5 KJV). And fame is as fickle as the last response from the crowd. Learn a dual lesson from this fine man who had wisdom far beyond most of us. When you're praised and applauded, don't pay any attention. And when you're rejected and abused, don't quit. It wasn't human opinion that called you into the work you're doing. So don't let human responses or criticisms get you sidetracked. Keep going.

Don't get tangled in the tangibles!

# ELUSIVE POPULARITY

### Read Acts 14:1–20

*R*emarkably, though laying lifeless in a pool of his own blood, Paul got right back up and walked back into the city from which he had been dragged and left for dead. I mean, is this missionary determined or what? True grit.

Let me ask you a couple of questions: Can you imagine being so hated that people literally pick up rocks and strike you repeatedly until you're unconscious and left for dead? Here's another one: If they stone you in Abilene, are you going stay in Abilene overnight? Okay, make that Phoenix or Bakersfield. Not a chance! You're going to take as quick a flight to a place as far away from there as possible. Get serious—if you're operating strictly from a horizontal viewpoint, you don't want to be within a thousand miles of that place when the sun rises the next dawn.

That is, of course, unless you're called and fully committed to the vertical perspective. Then you stick it out. You don't quit. Neither do you retaliate or throw a pity party. You go to sleep night after night, trusting in the same God who called you to serve there—convinced that He is sovereign and in absolute control.

That's exactly what Paul did. As a matter of fact, he entered that same city and spent the night there (14:20). He picked himself up off the dusty ground, pushed aside the larger stones, wiped the blood from his face and hands, gathered his composure, and climbed right back into the pulpit. They could not drive him away. Welcome to an authentic ministry!

You'd think he'd demonstrate a little caution and common sense. After all, Lystra is a dangerous, unpredictable city. Paul was stoned and left for dead! They wanted him gone, but God called him to minister there.

Listen to me: A ministry that lasts is a ministry that relentlessly perseveres through periods of enormous persecution. It is not fickle. It does not need the applause of people. It rejects being enshrined as a god. Authentic ministry delivers the truth of God, no matter how jagged the edges or perilous the threats. The ministry of Paul and Barnabas dripped with that kind of determination. Does yours?

# AUTHENTIC MINISTRY

### ✦ *Read Acts 14:1—20* ✦

*P*aul's ministry was saturated with the Word of God. Fifteen times in chapters thirteen and fourteen the phrases "God's Word," the "Word of truth," the "teaching of the Lord," the "Law and the Prophets," and the "Good News" are mentioned (13:5, 13:7, 13:12, 13:15a, 13:15b, 13:32, 13:44, 13:46, 13:48, 13:49, 14:3, 14:7, 14:15, 14:21, 14:25).

On that first journey Paul took with him just enough to live on, sufficient clothing to cover his nakedness, a heart full of hope in God's truth, and a confidence in God that would keep him faithful. That's what held him together. That's what steeled him against the tightening jaws of mistreatment in the ministry.

Could it be that you've grown a little soft in the past few months in your commitment to time spent in the Scriptures? It may be happening to you just as it happens to me from time to time. Please heed this gentle warning: If you're getting ready to go off to school, or preparing to take on new ministry responsibilities, or getting ready to launch a new phase of your career, don't do it without first establishing a regular time to meet alone with the Lord, preparing yourself for the new challenge by spending time in His Word. Your spiritual future depends on it. Without that commitment to saturate your life with God's Word, you step into the unknown future at your own risk. I urge you to spend sufficient time with the Lord so you might be strengthened within. It can begin with as little as fifteen minutes each day.

Some of you are thinking, I don't have fifteen minutes a day! Try cutting your lunch break short so you've got time on the other end to spend reading through a Psalm or two or digesting one of the New Testament letters.

If Paul could saturate his life in the Word of God, you and I can too. You are touching some people in your sphere of influence that likely no one else will touch. Be known for your biblical commitment, your biblical counseling. Be known for your biblical advice. Be appreciated for your biblical stand on moral values. It all starts with your investment of time in the Bible. Go there. Become saturated with the Word of God. That in itself will carry you miles down the road toward establishing an authentic ministry.

# DISAPPOINTING RESULTS

*Read Acts 14:1–20*

*A* sentence in the diary of James Gilmore, pioneer missionary to Mongolia, has stayed with me since the day I first read it. After years of laboring long and hard for the cause of Christ in that desperate land, he wrote, "In the shape of converts I have seen no result. I have not, as far as I am aware, seen anyone who even wanted to be a Christian."

Let me add some further reality to that statement by taking you back to an entry in Gilmore's journal made in the early days of his ministry. It expressed his dreams and burdens for the people of Mongolia. Handwritten in his journal are these dreams: "Several huts in sight. When shall I be able to speak to the people? O Lord, suggest by the Spirit how I should come among them, and in preparing myself to teach the life and love of Christ Jesus."

That was his hope. He longed to reach the lost of Mongolia with the Gospel of Jesus Christ. How different from his entry many years later, "I have not, as far as I am aware, seen anyone who even wanted to be a Christian."

What happened in between? He encountered the jagged edge of an authentic ministry. When I write about succeeding in the work of the Lord, I'm not promising success as we define it in human terms. I'm not saying because you are faithful to proclaim the Word of God your church will be packed. Some of God's most faithful servants are preaching their hearts out in places where the church is not growing. A great temptation for those in that difficult setting is to turn to some of the other *stuff* that holds out the promise of more visible results. Don't go there. Stay at it. God is at work.

Thinking of preparing for a life of ministry? Does the thought of standing before crowds of people and delivering the Word of God with passion and conviction appeal to your sense of adventure? I need to ask you one more time: Is there anything else in this world that would bring you greater enjoyment? If so, go there. Don't even hesitate.

But if you know the Lord has called you into His work, and you would not be fulfilled doing anything else, then go there and never look back, even if the results often seem disappointing.

# GOOD ATTITUDE

### *Read Acts 14:1–20*

*I*n his book, *Man's Search for Meaning,* Viktor Frankl wrote these amazing words:

"We who lived in the concentration camps can remember the men who walked through the huts comforting others, giving away their last pieces of bread. They may have been few in number, but they offer sufficient proof that everything can be taken from a man but one thing: The last of his freedoms is to choose his own attitude in any given set of circumstances—to choose one's own way."[14]

I could not be in greater agreement. We make a choice every waking moment of our lives. When we awaken in the morning, we choose the attitude that will ultimately guide our thoughts and actions through the day. I'm convinced our best attitudes emerge out of a clear understanding of our own identity, a clear sense of our divine mission, and a deep sense of God's purpose for our lives. That sort of God-honoring attitude encourages us to press on, to focus on the goal, to respond in remarkable ways to life's most extreme circumstances.

It was that kind of remarkable attitude Paul and Barnabas consistently maintained throughout their missionary journey. The two Antioch-sent servants faced and overcame countless and extreme obstacles with a relentless determination to stay focused on the goal.

We all need a reliable game plan for facing extreme circumstances. The situation that now looms in front of you may be fixable, or it may seem impossible to overcome in your own strength. It might be the result of your own actions, or you may be an innocent victim, caught in the backlash of someone else's consequences. Whatever the case, we can easily become intimidated, even fearful, and eventually immobile when facing such obstacles. The only way to move beyond that sort of paralyzing stalemate is to learn to accept and trust God's plan. You release the controls and wait for Him to move. And while you wait, maintain a good attitude.

# MISSION ACCOMPLISHED

### *Read Acts 14:21–28*

*W*hen Paul returned to places he had been before, there were no regrets. The end of Acts 14 chronicles the return trip Paul and Barnabas made back to home base, Antioch. En route, they visited many of the cities where they had earlier preached the Gospel. They returned to Lystra, where Paul had been stoned, then on to Iconium. They backtracked through Pisidia and Pamphylia, then down again to Perga and Attalia. Exhausted yet exuberant, they sailed across the deep-blue waters of the northeastern Mediterranean, destination Antioch—their first missionary enterprise now in the log books.

Retracing their steps, they stopped to encourage and strengthen the disciples they had made. They planted churches and appointed elders. There's no mention of lengthy attempts to reconcile the wrongs they had suffered. There were no angry outbursts, no regrets. Their focus remained the same: pursuing an authentic ministry for the glory of God.

In all that Paul did, the glory went to God. Whatever else you may remember, don't forget this. Luke writes, "And when they had arrived and gathered the church together, they began to report all things that *God had done* with them and how *He had opened a door of faith to the Gentiles*" (14:27, italics added). Is that great, or what? No big-time press conferences extolling a successful campaign. No self-serving interviews for some Christian radio station drawing attention to their hardships and successes. None of that. They reported everything that God had done *through them.* I love it.

Paul never forgot it was all about what God had done, not what he had accomplished. The work may be ours to do, but the glory belongs to God. The responsibility is ours to embrace, but the credit is the Lord's alone. There's to be no embezzling of glory. It all belongs to Him. That attitude never fails to put everything in proper perspective.

My challenge to you is to live a carefully examined life in an unexamining age. That will result in your maintaining a carefully examined ministry in a day when virtually anything goes. Whatever happens, keep your eyes on the goal. However difficult, don't quit. Though the obstacles are extreme, the stakes are eternal.

# POSITIVE SEPARATIONS

### ✄ *Read Acts 15:30—41* ✄

*L*et's be painfully candid here. I've had my own share of arguments, and you've had yours. I've had some that were never reconciled. Thankfully, most ended in a renewed friendship. I've learned through the years a few strategies that have proven effective in facing difficult disagreements.

1. *When in a disagreement, work hard to see the other point of view.* That begins with listening. Include in the formula three qualities that don't come easily: honesty, objectivity, and humility. That's the full package for handling conflict God's way. None of that comes naturally. They come to full bloom as products of the Spirit-filled life.

2. *When both sides have validity, seek a wise compromise.* For those who were reared as I was, even the thought of compromise makes you bristle. If you've got backbone, you don't give in. You stand firm, regardless. I appreciate an individual with backbone—true grit. But one who *never* bends, one who refuses to negotiate toward resolution? Hardly. I admire more someone who willingly and graciously seeks a suitable solution to disagreement, without in any way compromising biblical principles.

3. *When the conflict persists, care enough to work it through rather than walk out.* Slamming a phone down in the middle of a conversation or breaking through the screen on the front door as you stomp into the street solves nothing. Nor does a lengthy, manipulative silent treatment benefit either party. Or bolting from a marriage. Or quitting your job in a huff. That's not how to handle disagreements. Work it through. Stay at it. It's some of the hardest work you'll do, but it's also the most rewarding.

4. *When it cannot be resolved, graciously agree to disagree without becoming disagreeable.* I think Paul and Barnabas did that. Paul never takes a shot at Barnabas when he later wrote to the churches they had planted. In all of his letters, you'll not find one slam against his former companion. And there's no evidence of Barnabas licking his wounds either.

Honestly, not all separations lead to bad endings. Some of the greatest seminaries were birthed from a crucible of conflict. Some significant churches started as a result of an ugly split. It's never too early to start moving on.

Phillip Melanchthon, that persuasive tempering force in Martin Luther's life, put it best in these few words: "In essentials *unity*. In non-essentials *liberty*. In all things *charity*."

# "Forgive Them"

*Read Acts 15:35—41*

ather, forgive them for they don't know what they're doing." Jesus managed to
utter those penetrating words through bleeding, cracked lips, swollen from the
noonday sun. Impaled on that cruel, Roman cross, He interceded on behalf of
His enemies. What a magnificent model of forgiveness!

He paid the penalty in full for the sins of the world, the just for the unjust. As a result of
His sacrificial death, reconciliation was made between man and God. He's our model for correctly resolving disputes. Ultimately, it's a matter of forgiveness.

"Father, forgive them . . ."

What a way to live!

Before going on, you may have some honest reflecting to do. I invite you to revisit your
own unhealed wounded past. It may date back many years, it may bring to mind the face of
a parent, child, friend, former mate, fellow employee, boss, coach, pastor, or sibling. They've
wounded you. The pain has lingered all these years. You can't even hear their name or see a
photograph without all the anger and mistrust flooding your soul like a river overtaking its
banks.

My friend, it's time to move on. Seek a solution. Get help from someone else, if you
must. But get on with it. Whatever it takes to be free, do that.

Right now, I invite you to stand all alone at the foot of the cross, look up to Him, and
deliberately release it all. See Him hanging there, bleeding and dying, and embrace His forgiveness, for you and for your enemy. By forgiving, you're not condoning their sin. You're
simply leaving that to God. That's *His* turf, not yours. That's grace. And you can offer it to
others because you don't deserve it either.

Got a little homework to do? Get started on it before it gets too late and you lose your
way home.

# THE ULTIMATE AUTHORITY

### ✤ *Read Acts 16:1—10, 17:1—11* ✤

*A*man from Macedonia had said, "Come over and help us." God had in mind a seller of purple, an exploited slave girl, and a rugged, brutal Roman jailer. When you travel as God would have you travel, like Paul, you're sensitive to doors that open and at peace with doors that close.

Later, Paul appealed to Rome. Upon discovering he had tortured Roman citizens, the ruling magistrate shook with fear. Realizing he had illegally acted against these two men, the official begged Paul and Silas to leave Philippi to avoid further civil unrest.

The consummate church founder forged ahead, flanked by the faithful companionship of his co-workers. Next stop: Thessalonica. Paul, in keeping with his MO returned to his preferred place to start, in the synagogue. Many believed, including a large number of Greek men and influential women. That was sufficient to stir jealousy among the Jewish leaders to the point that Paul and his team were forced to escape under the cloak of darkness (17:10).

From there, they entered Berea and again preached in the local synagogue. A more sophisticated crowd than the folks in Thessalonica, the Bereans' eagerness led them to examine "the Scriptures daily, to see whether these things were so" (17:11).

I can't pass up this opportunity to say what a fine example they were to emulate. No matter how gifted or charismatic or well-trained and experienced your Bible teacher or pastor may be, form the healthy habit of checking what is being said against the Scriptures.

Architects and construction people use precise measurement to ensure a precise result. They don't go by how they feel. Both carefully mark their work by inches and by feet. Not even seasoned builders rely on guesses and hunches. They stay with the standard. The Scriptures are your measuring tool for making sure the teaching you receive is straight and true. Keep comparing.

As you grow in your spiritual life, the triangles need to be congruent between what's being said and what has been written in the Bible. If you can't support it with the Scriptures, there's something missing in the teaching. Don't believe the teacher. If he or she contradicts the divine standard, you're building on sand. Stay with the Scriptures. They remain your ultimate authority for faith and life.

# Traveling Well

### ✸ *Read Acts 16:11–15* ✸

hether you are traveling as a missionary or in the midst of your personal profession, God would have you travel as Paul traveled. I observe four enduring principles that will help you maximize your effectiveness for Christ, wherever you may go.

1. *When you travel, don't go alone.* Stay close to at least one other person, ideally your mate. If not your mate, a family member. If not a family member, a close companion. But stay close. Think back. Call to mind those with whom Paul traveled. If at all possible, avoid traveling alone. If you're lonely, a companion is there to lift your spirits. If you get into trouble, a companion is there to help get you through. Two are better than one. Three are better than two.

2. *When you travel, don't lose touch with home.* Stay accountable. Paul's heart stayed close to home. While away, he stayed in touch. When he returned he gave his reports. When he was with his men, he willingly gave an account of his ministry. When he wrote the letters, he was often vulnerable.

3. *When you travel, don't believe everything you hear.* Someone has said, "An authority is anyone who's one hundred miles away from home." Because I'm fairly well known, when I travel, people show up thinking they're going to be impressed. If they were around me more, they'd know better. When you travel, occasionally you'll meet folks who will almost worship you. (It happened to Paul.) Don't let them. On the opposite extreme, others will reject and mistreat you. Don't be derailed by naysayers. A few may even conspire against you. Keep your eyes on the goal. Focus on the Lord, and none of that will get you down.

4. *When you travel, don't become aloof.* It's easy in the busyness of travel to become a wax figure. Untouchable. Picking up the "circuit lingo," the clichés of the road, and losing touch with reality. Resist that sort of superficiality. Stay available. Stay real. People need a real, authentic *you*. Not perfect, *authentic*.

By observing these four principles, you will maximize your impact for Christ and travel well.

# Despite Your Circumstances

### ❧ *Read Acts 16:16—40; Philippians 1:12* ❧

few people in the first century had a deeper understanding of God's grace than the apostle Paul. Redeemed from a life of vicious brutality as a rigid legalistic Pharisee, the man turned the corner, repented, and through Christ's empowering became a gentle soul, gracious and affirming. Understanding. Forgiving. Approachable. He reached the place where he was willing not only to offer hope to the Gentiles, but to live among them, though he himself would bleed pure Jewish blood.

No one that I know endured the level of hardship Paul did as a good solider of Christ. What makes him all-the-more amazing is this: Never once does he leave a hint of complaint over being chained to a burly Roman soldier or about the inconvenience of being confined to such cramped quarters. The man simply would not grumble. By God's grace, he lived above it all. I repeat, he had learned the secret of contentment.

The great temptation is to allow that to embitter you—to turn you into someone who lives under a dark cloud, where doom and gloom characterize your outlook. Life's hard. You live in a situation that resembles a house arrest. You feel chained to your past, unable to escape the restrictive circumstances. Maybe you've lived this way so long that negative thinking has become a habit. You can't imagine thinking any other way.

I've got wonderful news: There is hope beyond your circumstances. You can live above them. If a man named Paul could live above his unbelievably trying circumstances, so can you. But Christ must become your central focus. He, alone, can empower you and teach you to live above the duress of adversity. Your external circumstances may not change, but deep within, *you* will. As Christ is allowed first place in your thoughts, changes will occur. Those changes will be evident to your mate, your children, your friends, and your coworkers. Instead of seeing yourself as a victim, you will begin to realize a strength that is not your own. The result? You will make a difference because of the way you respond to the circumstances that once defeated you. To the people closest to you, your contentment *despite your circumstances* will be nothing short of heroic.

Cling to hope! Focus on Christ, despite your circumstances.

# SECRET TO CONTENTMENT

### *Read Acts 16:16—40; Philippians 1:12—18*

*P*aul. is under house arrest in rented quarters; he refuses to focus on that. He is far from home, and his future is uncertain; he doesn't let that concern him. He is bound to a Roman guard every day; no problem. Because he has made Christ the object of his life, contentment has replaced frustration. He's taught himself to live above his circumstances. The benefits?

First, *the progress of the gospel is accelerated; it's never delayed.* In his letter to the Christians in Philippi, Paul passionately confesses, "I want you to know, brethren, that my circumstances have turned out for the greater progress of the gospel" (Philippians 1:12). Because of Paul's attitude regarding his predicament, his testimony spread like a firestorm through the ranks of the Roman guard. Systematically, God's Spirit leveled the towering pride of the Roman military.

Second, *when you live above your circumstances, the edge of the message is sharpened; it's never dulled.* Paul exclaimed that his chains had become the reason the entire palace guard had come under the hearing of the gospel. That was no insignificant statistic. By Paul's account, the message of Christ's love permeated the ranks of the imperial guard, which some scholars suggest were as many as nine thousand. Amazingly, the revival started with one Roman soldier chained to one man—but not just *any* man. That forced union became a springtide of grace to the whole Praetorian Guard.

There's a third benefit to living above your circumstances: *the courage of others is strengthened, never weakened.* Paul's unlikely converts were not sheepish about their new-found faith in Christ. I take it that they didn't hold back. Rather, they grew increasingly more courageous in their witness. I find that so exciting!

The secret to Paul's contentment did not emerge from a manual on how to live the Christian life or from a workshop on positive thinking. He didn't have access to a stack of self-help scrolls promising to shore up his sagging self-confidence. Paul's secret was not found in a program, but in a Person. Christ made the difference. He taught His servant to endure all situations, every circumstance, each difficult challenge, no matter how adverse, through His power. Paul released all rights to His Master and, in turn, He released all the strength Paul needed.

# LEARNED CONTENTMENT

*Read Acts 16:16–40; Philippians 2:1–18*

*P*aul recommends an attitude of unselfish humility. Quite remarkably, you never read where Paul said to his Roman guard, "I need you to do me a favor. Next time you happen to be near one of the Emperor's assistants, urge him to get me out of this dump. I shouldn't be here in the first place. I've been here for one year, seven months, four days, five hours, and nine minutes, and that's long enough." Paul's attitude of unselfish humility prevented him from keeping meticulous records of the wrongs done to him in Rome, or anywhere else for that matter. He was there by divine appointment. He willingly submitted to his situation.

Christ modeled the great emptying-out principle that permeated Paul's remarkable life. If we want to learn contentment, developing an attitude of unselfish humility is the perfect place to begin. Start with family or neighbors. Model it before your employees or clients. You won't believe the impact that sort of selfless mental attitude will have on the people. You won't have to wave flags or pass out tracts. Just demonstrate an attitude of unselfish humility. The results will amaze you.

Paul exhorts believers to have an attitude of joyful acceptance. Paul minced no words about how believers should relate to one another. "Do all things without grumbling or disputing; that you may prove yourselves to be blameless and innocent, children of God above reproach in the midst of a crooked and perverse generation, among whom you appear as lights in the world" (Philippians 2:14–15).

Paul knew the stakes were high as the secular world scrutinized the fledgling first-century followers of Christ. For Christians to grumble and dispute over circumstances put the credibility of the gospel at risk. Therefore, he sought an attitude of joyful acceptance, free of petty disputes and bickering. He pled for authentic joy. Nothing is more contagious. Paul said, "Don't complain; be joyful!" That's the ticket. Joy attracts. Grumbling repels. A choice sense of humor is wonderfully appealing.

My mentor, Ray Stedman, used to say, "We live in a world of crooks and perverts. What an opportunity to be winsomely different!" I love that kind of attitude. Joyful acceptance lights up this dismal planet!

# AN ATTITUDE OF STRONG DETERMINATION

*Read Acts 16:16—40; Philippians 2:1—18*

aul commands believers to possess the attitude of strong determination. He confesses, "Brethren, I do not regard myself as having laid hold of it yet; but one thing I do: forgetting what lies behind and reaching forward to what lies ahead, I press on toward the goal for the prize of the upward call of God in Christ Jesus" (Philippians 3:13–14).

At a time when many people in his place would be looking back in regret, wondering what life would have been like in a different profession, Paul repudiates the past and looks with confidence to the future. His strong determination kept him focused on the ultimate goal—pleasing Christ all the way to the goal, even in his chains. It's the picture of a runner running for the tape at the end of the race, straining forward in strong determination. Paul said, "I'm not looking back. I'm stretching for the prize." True grit on display.

No rusty Roman chains could deter Paul from reaching for the goal of pursuing the prize of Christ. He pressed on, determined to remain focused on his mission.

I was reading to Cynthia from *Sports Illustrated* about a ninety-year-old basketball scout that still does work for the Detroit Pistons. That's right—the man is ninety years old! He still gets on a plane, checks those prospects out, and brings back a reliable report. I love it! He said he flew past sixty-two without even a thought of retirement. Strong determination.

I read somewhere, "We wonder at the anatomical perfection of a da Vinci painting. But we forget that Leonardo da Vinci on one occasion drew a thousand hands." Leonardo possessed that same strong determination Paul modeled in Rome. Thomas Edison came up with the modern light bulb after a thousand failed attempts. By the man's own admission, it was mainly strong determination that gave the incandescent light to the world, not an inventor's creative genius.

But we're not talking about college athletes or persistent, brilliant inventors. We're talking about being a determined servant of Christ. There's no easy route to spiritual maturity. It doesn't happen overnight. Remember, it's a grueling journey at times. So, don't bother to publish a pamphlet on all the obstacles you face. Don't become famous for complaining. The apostle says, "Forget the past; reach for the tape. Keep running." Develop and maintain an attitude of strong determination.

# AN ATTITUDE OF GENUINE THANKSGIVING

### *Read Acts 16:16—40; Philippians 2:1—18*

*P*aul had an attitude of genuine thanksgiving: "Devote yourselves to prayer, keeping alert in it with an attitude of thanksgiving; praying that at the same time for us as well, that God may open up to us a door for the word, so that we may speak forth the mystery of Christ, for which I have also been imprisoned; in order that I might make it clear in the way I ought to speak" (Colossians 4:2–4).

Here's a man in his sixties who has been preaching for years asking for prayers for a clearer delivery. There was no pretense with Paul. No degree of success or number of years in the ministry gave him a false sense of ultimate accomplishment. He knew he had not yet arrived. He was convinced his preaching could be improved. And so with a genuinely thankful heart, he entreated his fellow believers for their prayers. Can you see the power of that kind of attitude? Very refreshing.

No wonder the man had such lasting impact for Christ. His secret bled through every one of his letters. He had learned to be content in all things. But we can't leave the ink of these truths to simply sit and dry on the page. We must embrace the same secret for ourselves if we are to have the same lasting impact. Some personal reflection is in order.

Let's turn the spotlight away from the man housed in Rome back then and focus it on you and your life, wherever you find yourself right now. Are you making a difference in the lives of those closest to you by the way you respond to your circumstances? Are others inspired by your faith, or are they discouraged by your fears? Are the attitudes of unselfish humility, joyful acceptance, strong determination, and genuine thanksgiving evident in the way you respond to circumstances? Maybe it's time to make some changes. Let's see if I can help.

Start by refusing to let your situation determine your attitude. When your attitude overshadows your situation, transformation really begins. As we saw in Paul, the power to transform stubborn attitudes of fear and bitterness, anger and defeat, comes from Christ. The Lord our God stands ready to pour his strength in you. He alone has the power to deliver you from those relentless foes and send you soaring.

Keep an attitude of genuine thanksgiving.

# HIS ONLY PRIORITY

*❧ Read Acts 17:1–9; 1 Thessalonians 2:1–6 ❧*

*P*aul's style of leadership was neither aloof nor secretive. He lived among them. They knew his address. He talked to them. He didn't preach a sermon and then conveniently slip out the back door during the benediction. He remained approachable, accessible, and real. His life was an open book. Most would agree, that kind of leader is refreshing. They've got nothing to prove, no secrets to hide, no pretense or air of self-importance, never feeling compelled to remind you of their qualifications for the job. That was Paul. He was believable. John Stott writes,

> Paul's ministry in Thessalonica had been public. It was exercised in the open before God and human beings for he had nothing whatever to hide. Happy are those Christian leaders today, who hate hypocrisy and love integrity, who have nothing to conceal or be ashamed of, who are well known for who and what they are, and who are able to appeal without fear to God and the public as their witnesses! We need more transparency and openness of this kind today.

A leader who lives his life in the open has nothing to guard or fear. But if he is always on the move, forever hiding behind locked doors and drawn blinds, the public has reason to suspect he's not genuine. Be careful about following a leader who is inaccessible and invulnerable.

Please remember, however, his ministry was no bed of roses. He literally limped into Thessalonica, his body bruised and tender from being beaten and imprisoned in Philippi. Thankfully, I've never had to endure such brutal persecution. Paul did. But here's the good news: it didn't impede his resolve. He writes, "After we had already suffered and been mistreated in Philippi, as you know, we had the boldness in our God to speak to you the gospel of God amid much opposition (1 Thess. 2:2).

One of the secrets of the man's success can be stated in three words: *he plodded on*. He led the same way whether the winds were at his back or blowing hard against him. Opposition and hardship didn't matter. The only priority that mattered to Paul was that Christ was proclaimed. Every trail he blazed led others to the cross.

How do your personal priorities align with Paul's?

# SENSITIVE LEADERS

*Read Acts 17:1—9; 1 Thessalonians 2:1—6*

Good leaders are sensitive to the needs of others. Paul compared his ministry to a mother who tenderly cares for the needs of her children. I love that word picture. I watched my wife nursing our children when they were tiny, without giving one thought to her own needs. It has been my joy as well to witness my grown daughters caring for our grandchildren too. It's a precious sight to behold.

Watching my wife and daughters gently cradle their little ones close to their breasts, and lovingly providing for their needs, helps me understand what Paul meant by "gentleness." His ministry was marked by a gentle nurturing of the flock. Paul says, "I was like a mother nursing a child, in my manner among you."

If God has placed you in a leadership responsibility, I urge you to cultivate a spirit of gentleness. It is after all a fruit of the Spirit (Galatians 5:23). Your tenderness will work wonders in the lives under your care.

In the aftermath of the September 11 tragedy, the world watched in wonder as powerful leaders spent time tenderly listening to the gut-wrenching stories of rescue workers and grieving New Yorkers. Mayor Rudolph Giuliani impressed the world day after day standing before the people of that great city chronicling the grim progress reports from ground zero. He spoke softly and compassionately, sometimes with tears, as the gruesome figures stuck in his throat. Somehow he made it through each meeting. Holding back his tears seemed as futile as trying to recover victims from the ten-story mound of twisted Trade Center rubble. Americans needed to see gentle leaders weep.

So do Christians. Spiritual leaders need to be just as real, as gentle, as understanding, and as empathetic. You and I appreciate spiritual leaders who consistently reveal their human sides. Contrary to popular opinion, Paul, the strong-hearted, passionate, gritty leader was also known for his gentleness and grace.

Are you known for yours?

# AFFECTIONATE LEADERS

*Read Acts 17:1–9; 1 Thessalonians 2:1–6*

ood leaders have affection for people. Paul writes, "Having thus a fond affection for you, we were well-pleased to impart to you not only the gospel of God . . ." (1 Thess. 2:8). Is that great, or what? Paul didn't shrink from sharing his emotions with his flock. That strong man, an apostle of Christ, looking back on the Thessalonians said, "Oh, what an affection I had for you. How dear you were to me." Those are affectionate words of intimacy.

To keep this simple and easy to remember, I want to suggest that affection for people can be demonstrated in two ways: *small yet frequent acts of kindness* and *stated and written words of appreciation*. Those you lead should have a few notes of appreciation and encouragement from you by now. They should be growing accustomed to your expressions of affection that include small yet frequent acts of kindness. No one is so important that he or she is above kindness. That aspect of leadership takes courage and a spirit confident in God's grace.

I came across a couplet that summarizes this point nicely:

*Life is mostly froth and bubble. Two things stand in stone.*

*Kindness in another's trouble. Courage in your own.*

I'm grieved by strong leaders who consistently walk over people. We wonder how people like that make it into significant places of influence. Here's some free advice: If you don't enjoy people, please, do us all a favor, don't go into leadership. Choose another career stream. Everyone will be better off. Say no when you're offered an opportunity to lead.

Neither the world nor the ministry needs more bosses. Both need more leaders— servant-hearted souls to lead as Paul led, with sensitivity and affection toward others. Love and affection, when appropriately given, fills the gap when words alone fail to comfort. If people know you love and value them, they'll go to the wire for you. Paul told the Christians at Thessalonica that he loved them. They never got over it.

# AFFIRMING LEADERS

*❦ Read Acts 17:1–9; 1 Thessalonians 2:1–11 ❧*

ood leaders are enthusiastically affirming. Again, Paul writes, "You are witnesses, and so is God, how devoutly and uprightly and blamelessly we behaved toward you believers; just as you know how we were exhorting and encouraging and imploring each one of you as a father would his own children" (1 Thess. 2:10–11). He started with a mother tenderly caring for her children. Now we see a father encouraging and exhorting his kids.

Ever sat on hard bleachers, in front of the father of the high school quarterback? He's his own cheer section. Why? He's a dad! The kid on the field's going, "Dad, come on, knock it off." But his old man's standing up there, yelling at top volume, loving very minute of it.

Perhaps you've longed for more affirmation from your father. Let's face it, encouragement goes a long way in preparing a child for life. No one should be getting more encouragement from us than our own children.

Pretty convicting stuff, isn't it?

What's true of our physical children is also true of God's children. Good leadership balances the tender nurturing of a mother with the loving affirmation of a father. Encouragement is like an oasis in the desert. It brings needed refreshment to weary individuals whose souls are parched from time spent in the desert of self-doubt. There's also the desert of failure when we've tried so hard to succeed and the desert of no progress when we so want something to happen but it doesn't. And there's the desert of family rejection, abuse, and a thousand other arid, barren landscapes of life.

In those desert experiences you long for an oasis where you're able to get a cool drink of water. Though it didn't come from your father, at last it comes from the affirming words of a leader, who, in speaking, dips his ladle deep in ice water, and as he pours it out, it cools your spirit and refreshes your soul.

Affirming leaders create loyal followers.

# BRINGING IT HOME

### 🪶 *Read Acts 17:1–9; 1 Thessalonians 2:1–6* 🪶

hat is it going to take to convince us that the last will be first and the first will be last? For some it will take a lifetime, for others only a few semesters in seminary.

Each May, at the end of the spring term at Dallas Seminary, we have the joy of listening to the school's top preachers. They're nominated and selected by pastoral-ministry professors. One year a talented young man preached on that pivotal passage in John 13 where Jesus washes His disciples' feet. After a compelling exposition of that simple text, the young senior class preacher leaned low into the microphone, looked across the faces in Chafer Chapel, and asked his fellow students, "Do you want to have a great ministry . . . or do you just want to be great?"

The packed chapel went silent. Nobody blinked. I'll never forget his question. None of us will. I hope he never does either.

In a single question he captured the crucial issue: greatness. Not as the world defines it. But greatness according to the standard of Almighty God. Great leaders are servants first. Like Paul . . . like his Master Jesus Christ.

This is for you, and this is for me. If you've never submitted fully to the Master, this is your moment. If you're still arrogant, you probably won't be struck down with blindness or find yourself shackled in a Roman prison. That was Paul's experience. But now that I have your attention, I suggest you take a good look within.

You do know how strong-willed and proud you are. So do the people you lead. You know how slow you are to encourage and how reluctant you are to affirm. They do too. You know if you're greedy. You know if you're self-serving. Frankly, it's time to give all that up. We're back to the crucial question: Do you want to have a great ministry, or do you just want to be great?

How you answer will determine how you lead.

# POWERFUL PREACHING

### ✥ *Read Acts 17:10–34* ✥

*I*f you are responsible for communicating biblical truth, consider yourself a preacher (at least for the now)—you are a communicator of God's Word. If that describes you, these next four principles are especially for you. Pay close attention, read thoughtfully and carefully, as I apply this to whatever may be your ministry.

First, *always stay on the subject—Christ.* For Paul it was always about Christ. Though explaining the altar of the unknown God of Athens, everything for Paul pointed to Christ. Preaching that doesn't exalt Christ is empty preaching. Paul wrote to the Corinthian believers, "For I determined to know nothing among you except Jesus Christ, and Him crucified" (1 Corinthians 2:2). For Paul, to live was Christ and to die was gain.

Second, *always speak the truth without fear.* Do not be overly impressed with those who have come to the class or who sit in the church where you serve. And it makes no difference how much they're worth or how little they contribute.

Third, *always start where your audience is.* Paul hooked those men in his first sentence. You can, too, if you spend some time thinking about it. Know your audience well enough to build a bridge quickly. Find a way to get into their world and then build a bridge to Christ. Remember: begin with the familiar in order to acquaint them with the unfamiliar.

Fourth, *always surrender the results to God.* Once they have heard the message, your part ends. Your task is to communicate truth. It's God's job to draw people to Himself. You prepare the patient; He does the surgery. They don't need manipulation. There's enough of that going on. You don't need to follow them out to their car or push them into a corner. God will reach them, just as He did in Athens. Leave the results to God.

When your heart is right, it's amazing what you're able to see. And when you see it clearly, it's remarkable how God can give you the words to say. You may be amazed how God uses you, just as He did Paul in that ancient metropolis so many years ago. When his moment arrived, he was ready.

When your moment comes, stand and deliver. God will give you courage as you tell others of his Son. There is no greater honor on earth.

# THINGS UNSEEN

*Read Acts 18:1—17; 2 Corinthians 4:7—15*

P aul viewed whatever happened to him through the eyes of faith. That remarkable trait allows him to be numbered among giants of the faith like Moses, who, according to Hebrews 11, "left Egypt, not fearing the wrath of the king; for he endured, as seeing Him who is unseen" (11:27). Like Moses, Paul endured the hard times by focusing on the eternal. He used his trials as reminders to focus on things not seen. When your heart is right, you can do that.

Awhile back Cynthia and I traveled to Houston for an Insight for Living event. While there we enjoyed a brief visit to the home of some good friends. Being down in the city in which I was reared reminded me of a home she and I had been in many years before. The place had a huge stone fireplace, big enough to crawl into. I relish those rare occasions when I can sit by a roaring fire and read or listen to classical music. I'm a fireplace guy!

Anyway, etched into the massive piece of timber that formed the mantle of that magnificent fireplace were these words:

"If your heart is cold, my fire cannot warm it."

Cynthia and I will never forget those words above that great stone hearth. There's no fire in the world that can warm a cold heart. A cold heart stays riveted on the hardship and refuses to see beyond the present. Paul's heart blazed with the fire of faith, allowing him to see the unseen. That's what kept him together under pressure. His heart stayed warm.

Nothing of what touched Paul externally would cool him deep within. Rather, it fueled his inner flame. The longer the persecution continued, the hotter his fire for God. He focused on the One who works His eternal purposes in the unseen realm when all around him gave way. Adversity strengthens our faith, consuming the dross of fear and unbelief as it melts away doubts.

"Faith is being sure of what we hope for and certain of what we do not see" (Hebrews 11:1 NIV). Hold on to faith!

# THE POWER OF WEAKNESS

*Read Acts 18:1—17; 2 Corinthians 11:22—28*

*P*aul pressed ahead through a mind-boggling series of intense hardships. Are they Hebrews? So am I. Are they Israelites? So am I. Are they descendants of Abraham? So am I. Are they ministers of Christ? I have more claim to this title than they. I have worked harder than any of them. I have served more prison sentences! I have been beaten times without number. I have faced death again and again. I have been beaten the regulation thirty-nine stripes by the Jews five times. I have been beaten with rods three times. I have been stoned once. I have been shipwrecked three times. I have been twenty-four hours in the open sea.

In my travels I have been in constant danger from rivers and floods, from bandits, from my own countrymen, and from pagans. I have faced danger in city streets, danger in the desert, danger on the high seas. danger among false Christians. I have known exhaustion, pain, long vigils, hunger and thirst, doing without meals, cold, and lack of clothing.

Apart from all external trials I have the daily burden of responsibility for all the churches.

On top of all that, the Lord gave him a thorn in the flesh. The Lord answered his desperate prayers to remove the thorn—whatever it may have been—in a most unexpected manner. The Lord simply answered, "My grace is sufficient for you, because power is perfected in weakness."

Surprised? "You mean, I don't have to be super strong and endure each trial relying on my own resources?" It's not like that at all. In fact, the only way you qualify to receive His strength is when you admit your weakness, when you admit you're not capable and strong, when, like Paul, you're willing to boast in nothing but your weakness and God's power.

# GENUINE HUMILITY

*Read Acts 18:1–17; 2 Corinthians 11:22–28*

e'd rather admire Paul for his strength in trials. We want to applaud his fierce determination against vicious persecution. If the man were alive today, he would not tolerate our congratulations. "No, no, no. You don't understand. I'm not strong. The One who pours his power into me is strong. My strength comes from my weakness." That's no false modesty. Paul would tell us, "Strength comes from embracing weakness and boasting in that." It is that kind of response that brings divine strength and allows it to spring into action.

J. Oswald Sanders, in his book, *Paul, the Leader,* writes, "We form part of a generation that worships power—military, intellectual, economical, scientific. The concept of power is worked into the warp and woof of our daily living. Our entire world is divided into power blocs. Men everywhere are striving for power in various realms, often with questionable motivation."

The celebrated Scottish preacher, James Stewart, made a statement that is also challenging: "It is always upon human weakness and humiliation, not human strength and confidence, that God chooses to build His Kingdom; and that He can use us not merely in spite of our ordinariness and helplessness and disqualifying infirmities, but precisely because of them."

That's a thrilling discovery to make. It transforms our mental attitude toward our circumstances.

Let's pause long enough here to consider this principle in all seriousness. Your humiliations, your struggles, your battles, your weaknesses, your feelings of inadequacy, your helplessness, even your so-called "disqualifying" infirmities are precisely what make you effective. I would go further and say they represent the stuff of greatness. Once you are convinced of your own weakness and no longer trying to hide it, you embrace the power of Christ. Paul modeled that trait wonderfully, once he grasped the principle. His pride departed and in its place emerged a genuine humility that no amount of hardship could erase.

# STOP AND SURRENDER

*Read Acts 18:1–17; 1 Corinthians 11:22–28*

S o much for Paul. How about you? Fast forward to the twenty-first century. Are you afflicted and burdened excessively? Do you feel as if you're under such intense pressure these days that you, too, are close to despair? I have some surprising news: you're exactly where God wants you to be. It took all these years to get you this low, this needy. Now, look up!

Are you feeling crushed and confused, misunderstood and beaten down? Resist the temptation to roll up your sleeves and muster a self-imposed recovery plan. This is your opportunity! Rather than fighting back, surrender. Embrace your weakness. Tell your heavenly Father that you are trusting in the strength of His power. If Paul could do it, so can you. So can I.

At this moment I am facing a few impossible situations. No doubt, so are you. To be honest, I'm too weak to handle any of them. So are you. I'm often near tears. I'm frequently discouraged. There's hardly a week that passes that I don't slump into a mild feeling of discouragement. Sound familiar? Admit it! Some nights I don't sleep well. There are times that I absolutely weep out of disappointment in some individual's failure . . . or my own. You too? You and I need to face the fact that we will never be able to handle any of these pressures alone. When we acknowledge this, and not until, His strength will be released in us.

Are you ready to face the next battle with a new strategy? Okay, *start by surrendering.* Instead of returning to your same-old method—doing a month of mental push-ups, talking yourself into looking strong and acting brave, putting on the gloves and stepping into the ring with swagger, relying on your own strength to win and succeed and impress. *Stop and surrender.* Drop to your knees and cry out to God. Admit your inadequacies, and declare your inability to keep going on your own.

If you're finally ready to step aside and let Him have His way, say so; then do it. He will honor your admission of weakness by showing Himself strong through you. But if you don't, He won't.

It's your call.

# ALL IN THE FAMILY

### *Read Acts 23:11–22*

ot one assassin but forty of them! Forty determined terrorists, operating under cover of secrecy. All of them vowing, "We will not eat or drink until we've killed him." The plan was treacherous and set in motion by those who wanted him dead. What they hadn't counted on was an unlikely ally for Paul. His nephew had overheard everything and made tracks to warn his uncle.

Remarkably, Paul's nephew plays a major role in his survival. He is not mentioned by name, and we never hear of him again. Then how did he know about the ambush? Only God knows.

Meanwhile, the Roman commander was feeling relieved, proud of his wise handling of the situation. His musings were interrupted by a reluctant knock at the door. The news couldn't be good. One of his centurions reports that the young man with him has some important information about a conspiracy to kill Paul. The Roman commander wasn't about to let some scrappy band of fanatics spoil his plan to bring Paul safely to Rome. So he pulled out all the stops.

Uniformed, armed, and trained soldiers. Four-hundred seventy-two to forty rag-tag conspirators. Nice odds. Talk about overkill. The guy would not be outdone. He made sure no one could get to Paul. Remember God's promise? "You must witness at Rome." This is just part of that divine plan. It was as if God said, "I know what I am doing. I will escort you down to Caesarea by the Sea with full protection. You are in My hand." A massive official escort—that would work just fine.

What a comforting story. Despite the odds stacked against him, Paul was never removed from God's protective hand. And neither are you.

Are you feeling alone, mistreated, misunderstood, forsaken? Remember this true account. God is at work. He's there, working behind the scenes. He'll work it out. He has a plan. Just when you're convinced the bottom is about to drop out from under you, He steps in and lifts you to safety. For Paul, he used an unlikely and virtually anonymous ally, a nameless nephew who comes out of the shadows at precisely the right time. God's timing is always perfectly synchronized with His will. Remember that. And be comforted.

# STRAIGHT THINKING

*Read Acts 23:11–22*

*H*ave you ever felt the ground move under your feet? Do you know what it's like to pitch from side to side in a small boat on strong seas? Have you ever had to run for cover, dodge bullets, or duck out of the way of advancing troops? Remarkably, some people around the world could answer, *Yes!* to all three questions. Most of us only imagine such scenes.

Still, everyone sooner or later faces the reality of feeling as if life is spinning out of control. That may describe you today. Left unchecked, fear will run its course and paralyze you to the point of helplessness. If you're not careful, you'll spend your days wringing your hands and obsessing over your encroaching circumstances. That will cause you to focus on what might happen instead of what God has promised.

Not Paul. He understood something about the sovereignty of God. That clear understanding allowed him to think straight and remain calm in crisis. That kind of straight-thinking calmness is rooted in the promises of God's Word. Take, for example, the promise in Psalm 46: "God is our refuge and strength, a very present help in trouble. Therefore we will not fear, though the earth should change, and though the mountains slip into the heart of the sea; though its waters roar and foam, though the mountains quake at its swelling pride" (Psalm 46:1–3).

Like Paul, we need to learn to think straight, even if the foundations of the earth shift beneath our feet. That takes a heart willing to trust His Word, submit to His plan, then deliberately and consciously relax.

If He was able to stir up four hundred seventy-two earthly bodyguards to get Paul from Jerusalem to Caesarea, safely and securely, He will have no trouble getting you from here to wherever He wants you to be, safely and securely. After all, how many angels are there?

And by the way, when you think straight about all this, you'll realize you only need one.

# GRACE LEADS YOU HOME

### ✦ *Read Acts 24:1–9* ✦

Long before my mother died, she and a neighbor friend compiled a book of God's promises taken from the Scriptures. Each made her own. My mother used that little book as a primer for her prayers. After she died, my brother and sister and I viewed that tender compilation as part of her legacy to us. The book swelled with handwritten promises from the Bible.

She must have written out hundreds of promises drawn directly from the Bible. Promise after promise after promise. My name was connected to some of them. "For Charles, I claim this promise," she wrote on one of the pages. For Orville and Luci she claimed scores of others and recorded them in her book.

My friend, go back to the Book. Search for the promises God offers you in His Word. I suggest you start with the Psalms. Look for the promises there. They are myriad. Become familiar with them. Live in them. Walk with them. In some special cases, memorize them. Let them be your guide and comfort. Like Paul, you'll be able to withstand the fiercest storms of criticism when you stand firmly on the promises of God.

I don't know where you are or what you face today. It's quite possible you're living under the pressure of negative criticism. I know that's true if you're in the ministry. Somebody may be determined to "prove" things about you that you know are absolutely false. My advice is to learn from Paul: remain calm. Rest your case with your Lord. Take your battles to Him in prayer. With a clear conscience and committed to the truth, lay your case out before Him. Start there. And the Judge of all truth will guide you to your next step. Don't quit. Don't stop. Don't tell yourself that you really are the kind of person others say you are. If what is being said against you is not true, don't believe it. Count on the Lord to give you the strength and courage to stand on the truth. His grace has brought you safe this far, and it will be His grace that leads you home.

Trust me on that; even better, *trust Him.*

# MODERN-DAY HEROES

### ❧ *Read Acts 26:1–32* ❧

*M*omentarily forgetting the difference in rank and status, Paul now spoke face to face with Agrippa. He engaged him on his knowledge of the Scriptures. He then listened for Herod's reply. It was a reply heard around the world: "Do you think that in such a short time you can persuade me to be a Christian?" (26:28 NIV). What a question! The apostle's enthusiasm could no longer be contained. In unguarded abandon, he exclaimed, "I would to God, that whether in a short or long time, not only you, but also all who hear me this day, might become such as I, except for these chains."

That may have been the crowning moment of Paul's entire life. Chains on his wrist rattled as the prisoner raised his arms to deliver that closing line. What an epochal moment! His words brought proud Agrippa so close to the throne of grace he nearly bowed before the King of kings!

*When you stand tall for Christ, you're so focused that you feel invincible.* Now don't allow that thought to slip past too quickly. You may have never experienced that sort of bold abandon because you've not allowed yourself to be in a challenging situation. Most play it safe. It's more convenient to let someone else do the talking. It's easier to let another climb to the heights and risk falling.

However, when the day arrives and you decide to stand tall for what's right, your focus on that all-important issue will give you a feeling of invincibility. The odds will mean nothing. You will be unimpressed with other folks sitting or standing in front of you. Neither credentials nor titles will intimidate you. Your convictions will carry you forward in a strength not your own. Like Paul, you will have become God's voice for that hour.

*When you stand tall for Christ, you are so passionate that you don't realize your ultimate impact.* Standing for the principle at stake is all that matters. Paul's audience simply got up and left. On the exterior it looked like the hearing had been a waste of time. Yet who can say? Who knows what Agrippa dreamed of that very night and in the nights that followed Paul's speech? I wouldn't be surprised if compromising Festus continued to squirm at Paul's compelling witness.

Only God knows the true impact of Paul's heroic stand that day by the sea. Ultimately, only God knows the impact of yours as well.

# STANDING TALL IN HIGH PLACES

*Read Acts 26:1–32*

ecently, I read a stirring speech delivered by the late Mother Theresa at the 44th National Prayer Breakfast—a prestigious event that occurred while Bill Clinton served as President. In the course of her speech, delivered without pretense, the gracious nun from Calcutta spoke plainly and courageously about the evils of abortion and the devastation that dreadful lapse in morality continues to have on our already splintered culture. While she read from a carefully prepared manuscript, no one in the room moved a muscle. In fact, many of the well-dressed dignitaries smiled nervously, appearing cool and collected on their refined exteriors, but churning wildly within.

Like Paul, the frail figure of a woman spoke her words and exited the room as silently as she entered. As the ancient political officials had sat glaring at Paul, so the nobility of Washington sat silent, their consciences throbbing in their chests.

I'm convinced that many people, given the situations faced by some of the heroes we've mentioned, would rise to such heroic deeds. I believe you have the potential in you to stand against enemies of righteousness who defy the power of Almighty God, or to speak out boldly against blatant injustice and outright discrimination. I believe many who pick up this book would be willing to have been numbered among the brave rescue workers at the World Trade Center and the Pentagon or even among those who died thwarting another air disaster on the flight that crashed in Pennsylvania.

The challenge comes in those private, unguarded moments when you face opposition to truth—in the halls of the university, in a company board room, at the school PTA meeting, in the athletic director's office, or while seated on a plane. In those times, will you stand tall and speak the truth when a principle is at stake? Will you announce what you believe, graciously yet firmly?

You may never be summoned to stand before kings and queens or be invited to address the political elite or high-ranking military officers; but you will have your own opportunities to stand and deliver. As you determine in your heart to stand tall, God will lay those opportunities before you when you least expect it. You can count on it.

When He does, will you be ready?

# ANCHOR OF STABILITY

*Read Acts 27:1—26*

*T*he anchor of stability holds firm when your navigation system fails. It's easy to lose your bearings in the storm. You can't find your way through the circumstances you face. Life rolls along fairly smoothly until suddenly the seas grow rough. Unseen problems occur. They were not in the forecast. In Luke's words, "All hope for being saved" is abandoned.

Those are treacherous moments when we reach the point of abandoning hope. At that difficult, gut-wrenching moment, God says, "Don't be afraid, I have a plan."

People facing intense adversity find it difficult to focus on anything other than the towering waves and stinging winds. Paul firmly announces, "Be of good cheer . . . we've heard from the Lord that none will be lost."

We find stability in storms through what God has said. Your tendency will be to turn to another source for strength rather than the Word of God. Don't go there! The only anchor of stability that will hold you firm, no matter how intense the gale-force winds, is God's written Word.

All this reminds me of a statement made by one of the ancient Jewish prophets, which supports the reliability of God and His Word. The following words flow from the seasoned hand of Isaiah: "But now, thus says the LORD, your Creator, O Jacob, and He who formed you, O Israel, 'Do not fear, for I have redeemed you; I have called you by name; you are Mine! When you pass through the waters, I will be with you; and through the rivers, they will not overflow you'" (Isaiah 43:1–2).

What encouraging words! "Do not fear, I have called you by name." What a great thought!

Isaiah was not writing of literal waters or actual rivers. His figure of speech emphasized encroaching circumstances that threatened the stability of one's faith. When the waters rise to dangerous depths, when difficulties reach maximum proportion, when your ship seems to be disintegrating board by board and starting to sink by life's inevitable storms, God is faithful. He promises, "I will be with you." He is your anchor.

# ANCHOR OF UNITY

*Read Acts 27:27–32*

The scene breathed life-threatening fears. Imaginations ran wild. Paul knew that staying together was the secret to their survival. The temptation was strong to abandon ship and let each person fend for himself. That's no way to survive a storm. As the water grew shallower, fear of shipwreck intensified. But Paul warned that allowing the men to escape meant certain death.

The spiritual application is obvious. Our tendency in dire straits is to cut and run. It's easier at the moment to walk out of a troubled marriage than to face it and work toward restoration. Human nature wants to retreat to a place where each one of us can be all alone, lock the door, and pull the blinds. Alienated, we sink further into depression. Tragically, some turn to alcohol, drugs, or worse, to a revolver.

If that in any way describes you, you need the support of family, friends, and especially God's people. It's easier to lower the dinghy and jump in all alone. I want to warn you against escaping. Instead, I urge you to stay with others aboard ship. Don't leap and try to make it on your own. Lock arms. Stay in touch with those who love you the most, who will be with you no matter what. You need the presence of God's people surrounding you when the bottom has dropped out of your life. Despite what you think, it's doubtful you can make it on your own. In our case, we had a few close friends of the ministry praying and a unified board encouraging us. Relocating was a challenging experience, but not a lonely one. You and I are designed by God to make it together. The anchor of unity holds us close.

You will need the anchor of unity many times in your life, just as Paul did. So hold on to unity!

# ANCHOR OF RENEWAL

### *Read Acts 27:33–38*

C an you imagine fighting a storm for two weeks and getting virtually no nourishment? That's what the men on Paul's ship experienced. Even more amazing, that's how most people respond to life's storms. We run our tanks dry fighting the battles on our own, and we end up physically weak, emotionally drained, and unable to sleep. The anchor of renewal guards against that sort of anatomical depletion. Instead, Paul encouraged the men to eat and be renewed. But first he prayed. They all prayed!

Can you imagine that scene? The storm raged about them, while almost three hundred men bowed in prayer as Paul gave thanks for the meager fare, then everybody on board joined together in the meal.

Your personal nourishment is crucial during times of storm. In panic moments, you'll cut a corner on your meals. You'll also fail to get sufficient sleep. It won't be long before you will set aside prayer altogether, and you'll find yourself drained, spiritually. Increased emotional pain mixed with decreased spiritual renewal can be lethal to your faith.

Spiritual renewal comes primarily through prayer. Few disciplines are of greater importance when all seems bleak. Simply talk it out. Wrestle with the reason for the storm. Seek His direction. Don't let up until you're satisfied you've got the Lord's mind. That's what Paul modeled on the deck of that rugged ship.

For some of the men on board, I'm confident it was the first time in their lives they had prayed. Certainly, it was the first time they had prayed to Almighty God! It may have been the only time in their lives they'd ever heard a prayer offered for a meal. In the middle of a howling wind-and-rain storm, they paused and witnessed a reverent, humble man offering a prayer of gratitude to the Lord God, Maker of heaven and earth, Captain of the winds and waves. That encouraged them. It was simple, but its impact was profound. Paul had shown them the anchor of renewal—a glimpse of hope.

# ANCHOR OF REALITY

### ✦ *Read Acts 27:39–44* ✦

*A*ll those going through a storm need to be engaged in the process. No one is promised a magical escape clause. Passivity is faith's enemy. It isn't an acceptable option to fold our arms and wait for the storm to pass.

It may mean some hard work. It may require humbling yourself before God and others. It might mean a season of counseling where a trained, compassionate individual helps you reorder your life. You may be required to admit several wrong actions and seek reconciliation as you make restitution. Whatever the case, you'll need to be involved. Reality mandates that type of mature response. It's part of throwing the anchor of reality and trusting God to bring you to shore.

The best plan for surviving a storm is preparation. No seasoned fishermen or responsible ship captain sets across the open sea without a thorough knowledge of the vessel's equipment and without making sure all is in proper working order. They rarely leave without having first spent sufficient time going over the navigation charts—studying the weather patterns and acquainting themselves with dangerous passages.

And they never leave port without anchors. That's for certain. No one wants to be shipwrecked. But the reality is, it happens, not only on the open sea, but also in life.

The secret of survival is what you do ahead of time in calmer waters. If your life is storm-free as you read this book, I urge you to take advantage of this peaceful lull. Spend time in God's Word. Study the inspired charts He has given you for the journey of life. Deepen your walk with Him through prayer and personal worship.

Then, when the inevitable winds of adversity begin to blow—and they most certainly will blow—you'll be ready to respond in faith, rather than fear. Don't wait. Check those anchors while it's smooth sailing. You'll be glad you did.

# An Urgent Charge

### ✠ *Read 2 Timothy 4:1–16* ✠

*P*aul wrote with urgency, "I solemnly charge you in the presence of God and of Christ Jesus, who is to judge the living and the dead, and by His appearing and His kingdom: preach the word; be ready in season and out of season; reprove, rebuke, exhort, with great patience and instruction" (4:1–2). In other words, stick with the preaching plan God has promised to bless and use. Deliver the biblical goods! Be a man or woman of the Word!

Don't attempt to be so creative and cute that folks miss the truth. No need for meaningless and silly substitutes that entertain but rarely convict the lost and edify the saved. Teach the truth. Will you notice something here? This exhortation is not addressed to the hearer, it's for the speaker. The one who is to do this is the one proclaiming the message. Be ready to do it in season and out of season. Being ready implies being prepared both mentally and spiritually.

In essence, Paul says, "Don't be lazy. Do your homework. Don't stand up and start with an apology that you didn't quite have adequate time to prepare. That doesn't wash." And do so faithfully—when it's convenient and when it's not.

Sadly, in an alarming number of churches today, God's people are being told what they *want* to hear rather than what they *need* to hear. They are being fed warm milk, not solid meat. A watered-down gospel may attract large crowds (for a while), but it has no eternal impact. I've not been able to find any place in the Scriptures where God expresses the least bit of concern for drawing numbers. Satisfying the curious itching ears of our post-modern audiences is an exercise in futility.

The task of ministry is to deliver Truth. Frankly, I intend to continue doing just that, by God's grace, until the day He calls me home. And I think there is an ever-increasing number of believers who long for nourishing messages based on the Word of God, not human opinion.

The world urgently needs more Christians with the fervor and faith of Paul. Will you be one of them? Will you answer the charge? If so, there's no better time than now to begin.

Jesus said, "Go and make disciples of all nations . . . and I will be with you" (Matthew 28:19–20 NIV). there is no greater challenge and no more comforting promise. Believe it. Trust it. And by the grace of God, go do it!

*Abraham: A Man of Trust & Faith*

*Samuel: The Boy Who Heard God's Voice*

*Saul: The King Who Disappointed God*

# HOLDING TOO TIGHTLY

### ✤ *Read Genesis 22:1–2* ✤

ach of our children grew to become a self-sustaining, responsible servant of Jesus Christ, in his or her own way. As God intended from the beginning, we released them to follow their destinies.

Some of you reading these words did not release your children in this way. Perhaps you have lost your child through death, a terrible crime, divorce, or some other horrible tragedy. Let me be clear about this. While God is the sovereign ruler of all and nothing is beyond His power or knowledge, a horrible tragedy is *never* a cruel, merciless act on God's part. God did not find delight in making you endure such grief. Yes, as with Job, He *permitted* it, but He is not the author of evil. The evil intent of a world that has been twisted by sin took your child from you.

God hates not only sin, He also hates death. He hates it so much that He sent His Son to destroy death by dying and rising again. Death is called in the Scriptures our "last enemy" (1 Corinthians 15:26). Ultimately, the Lord will have the last word in this fight against evil, and He spoke that word to us through Jesus Christ. Put simply: *Death is the will of a world gone wrong. Resurrection is God's final triumph over evil.*

Whether we lose our children by tragedy or design, this much is true: Anything we hold dear, we must learn to hold loosely. Let's face it, if we hold anything too tightly, it probably has *us* rather than our having *it.* And God will not allow that for your sake or the sake of your loved one.

Ultimately, the decision to hold anything loosely—especially as it applies to relationships—is an act of faith. Human instinct would have us clutch the things we adore most. Releasing them, presenting them to God, requires that we trust Him to do what is right. When we do this for our children, the lasting impact we leave is a practical model of faith. And I can think of no better way to teach our children about the God we worship than by modeling our trust in Him *daily.*

# THE TEST

### ✦ *Read Genesis 22:1–2* ✦

*W*hy? Why would a good and loving God ask an obedient and faithful man to do this? The answer can be found in the original language of Moses, the inspired, human author of Genesis. The Hebrew word *nasah,* translated "tested" in Genesis 22:1, has the idea of proving the quality of something, usually by putting it through a trial of some kind. God wanted to prove the validity—the authenticity—of Abraham's faith.

Remember, though, that God is omniscient. He knows all things, including the future. He knew the heart of Abraham better than Abraham did. The purpose of the test was not to satisfy God's curiosity. This was not an experiment. The appointed patch of ground at the top of a lonely mountain in the land of Moriah was to be Abraham's proving ground. This would be the time and place where any question about his faltering faith—so evident in his lying (twice) to save his skin and his pathetic attempt to fulfill the covenant through his wife's handmaid—would be put to rest. His family would see his faith, his friends would see it, we would see it by virtue of this record, and probably most important of all, Isaac would see it. If ever faith would be put on display, this would be the day.

The issue in question: did Abraham love the gift of God or God Himself?

Allow me to put Abraham's test on hold and rush into the twenty-first century. This has to be one of the toughest questions any parent has to consider: *Do I adore the gifts God gives me more than I adore the Giver? Have I begun to worship the relationships that God has granted me rather than the One who gave me these delights?*

Don't be too quick to answer.

The word *worship* comes from an Anglo-Saxon term meaning "worthship." When we worship something, we are affirming its value to us. We do that with our actions as well as with our hearts. A parent must ask, *Do I assign more worth to my child than I do my God?* To answer that question, follow the trail of your sacrifices. Tally the results. Be painfully honest now. For whom do you sacrifice more—or more often?

# GENUINE FAITH

*Read Genesis 22:3–8; Hebrews 11:8–19*

had to read this passage several times before I saw Abraham's clearly implied statement of faith. His words and his demeanor are so understated, so matter-of-fact, that it's easy to miss the drama of this scene. If I were about to sacrifice my only son, who embodied all the promises that God had ever made to me, I would have been overcome with emotion. "I don't understand why God is making me do this, but I will do as He says. So I'm going up that mountain to sacrifice my son on that altar, then I'm going home to mourn this terrible loss for the rest of my life!"

According to the book of Hebrews, Abraham knew three important facts. First, Isaac was to be the vehicle of God's promises; therefore, Isaac must live. Second, God always keeps His promises. Third, God's power is absolute, even over the power of death. The only logical conclusion that remained was that somehow, against all natural reason, after killing Isaac and allowing the fire to completely consume him, God would miraculously restore the life of Isaac—the boy he dearly loved.

Obviously, Abraham didn't tell Isaac everything he knew about what was to happen on the mountain. We can't be sure why he withheld that information. Maybe to spare his son unnecessary fear or dread. We don't know. But I do know that when God does a transforming work in you that involves a trial, He's not testing other people; He's testing you. Because this experience is designed for you, it isn't necessarily required or even appropriate for you to share the whole story with everyone else. Or, for that matter, with anyone else. Occasionally, strength is mustered in keeping it to ourselves . . . completely.

Isaac finally asked the obvious question. They have a knife, wood, and fire for the sacrifice. "Where is the sacrifice?" I love Abraham's answer. "God will provide." The Hebrew uses an idiom that sounds just like something a dad would say today. "The Lord will see to that for Himself, son." Can you hear his calm, reassuring tone? "God will provide for Himself. That's up to Him. We're doing His will. It's up to Him to work out the details He didn't give to us. Our responsibility is to trust Him. This is a risk we will share together."

# FAITH INVOLVES RISK

*Read Genesis 22:9*

Some people live so carefully they absolutely refuse to take risks. Everything has to be carefully regulated and kept under control . . . their control. Borders defined, guidelines spelled out, every dime accounted for, no surprises. And after having expended so much time and effort trying to live safely, they end life never having accomplished anything of lasting value. They built nothing, tried nothing new, invested in no one.

Not Abraham! His faith had matured to the point that his absolute confidence in God's character gave him the freedom to throw caution to the wind and risk everything to obey. What a perfect lesson in theology for his son.

Now, Abraham didn't raise a fool for a son. Isaac could piece all the clues together. He does that as the story continues. We read that they came to the place of which God had told him. Abraham built the altar there, arranged the wood, and then began to search everywhere for his son, for he had run away and hidden from his father.

I've heard this passage preached countless times, and I've never heard anyone talk about the quiet faith of this remarkable young man. He's the sacrifice, yet he allowed himself to be bound up and placed onto that altar! Obviously, this son learned his theology well from his father—a father who released his son because he completely trusted his God. By the way, Isaac didn't learn such faith on his way up the mountain that morning. He'd been cultivating it over the years, thanks to his father who modeled it often.

Some of you parents may find yourselves in a similar situation as you read these pages. Your relationship with your child may have reached a point where you have no other choice but to commit him or her completely to God's care. You would love to work out the details, but you cannot. You know the Lord is good, and you have prayed for a resolution, but nothing has changed. Only God can intervene. And because that is true, you can take your cues from Abraham.

Place your relationship with that son or daughter on the altar today. Surrender him or her to the Lord as an offering. Take this risk. Mentally place your boy or girl on top of the wood, and step back from the altar. Trust God. In His time, He will provide.

# RELEASE YOUR GRIP

*Read Genesis 22:10—14*

 his isn't a movie. As far as Abraham was concerned, the drama didn't have a surprise ending. The knife goes up in order to bring it down into his son's chest or across his throat, and what will happen next is the death of his boy. This is real! This is faith in the wild where the stakes are incredibly high—life and death! Suddenly, at the last possible moment, God intervened:

But the angel of the LORD called to him from heaven and said, "Abraham, Abraham!" And he said, "Here I am." He said, "Do not stretch out your hand against the lad, and do nothing to him; for now I know that you fear God, since you have not withheld your son, your only son, from Me." (Genesis 22:11–12)

As the Lord stopped Abraham's hand midplunge, And he said, in effect, "You've passed the test, My faithful friend. You've proven to Me who is first, My aging son. You have also proven that your faith has reached full maturity. Your willingness to give up your only son has demonstrated that while you love the gift, you love the Giver more."

Then Abraham raised his eyes and looked, and behold, behind him a ram caught in the thicket by his horns; and Abraham went and took the ram, and offered him up for a burnt offering in the place of his son. And Abraham called the name of that place The LORD Will Provide, as it is said to this day, "In the mount of the LORD it will be provided." (Genesis 22:13–14)

After this, hundreds of years and ancient sands have covered the site. However, this very mountaintop would one day accommodate a city and a temple. It would become the capital of God's covenant kingdom and His house of worship until, finally, it would be the place where Christ, the King and consummate sacrifice, would die. Moriah, Jerusalem, the place where another Father held His Son loosely, laid Him on an altar, and sacrificed Him for us. On this mountain in the region of Moriah—a place renamed "The Lord will provide"—a ram became Isaac's substitute, and Christ became ours.

# FAITH REVEALS GOD

### *Read Genesis 22:1–14*

*I*n this fascinating story of faith and sacrifice and trust and surrender, I see the characteristics of a God who asked nothing of Abraham that He didn't demand of Himself. Because it is so significant, I cannot resist sharing with you three powerful truths about our God that I see illustrated here.

*God the Father showed us how to live when He released His dear Son to us.* Nine months before that wondrous night in Bethlehem, the Father sent His Son. Christ willingly left His seat of absolute power in heaven, set aside the voluntary use of His divine authority, and became a helpless infant. As a human, subject to all the pains and sorrows and limitations that affect us all, He would mature, learn, minister, suffer . . . and die. If the Father was willing to release His own Son to us, what could be so much more precious to us that we would withhold it from Him?

*God the Son showed us how to die when He released Himself to the Father.* Isaac's quiet obedience to his father illustrates this beautifully. He gave himself over to the will of his father and allowed himself to be placed on an altar without a fight. That's exactly what the Son of God did at Calvary. When our faith is mature, we'll not fear death.

*God the Spirit will show us how to live and die as we learn how to release whatever has us in its grip.* (That last phrase wasn't a mistake.) As long as we're owned by whatever we're clutching, we'll never be given over completely to the Holy Spirit. This would be an excellent moment for you to do some self-analysis. To what, to whom are you clinging? Let it go. Let them go.

The Lord may be in the process of taking it from you. He'll gently tug on it at first, giving you the opportunity to release your grip. If you resist, He'll eventually have to pry your fingers away, and I can assure you that it will hurt. My advice? Voluntarily release it. Trust the Lord to provide. He has another ram in the thicket. You can't see it right now, but He has it waiting. Only after you have placed your sacrifice on the altar will you be ready to receive God's provision.

# ISRAEL'S DARK SETTING

### ❧ *Read Judges 21:25; 1 Samuel 1:1–28* ❧

*T*he setting is Israel before the glory days of King David. There has been a long period—a couple hundred years—of intermittent warfare, cycles of events during which Israel would suffer invasion followed by famine; then a judge would emerge and win a temporary peace. During the peace, the people would sin, and the down-spiraling cycle would kick in again. Another invasion followed by defeat, resulting in yet another famine, growing more severe each time. This story takes place during a lull in the violence, a restful season of relative peace. Days were unusually quiet and uneventful.

The people of Israel have settled back into a lax lifestyle that could be described as downright complacent. Their attitude toward God and His vision for them as a nation has become indifferent, a little ho-hum and boring. Their leader, the high priest, is Eli, an old man whose eyesight has begun to grow dim. Unless something changes, he will turn the reins of leadership over to his two rebellious sons, Hophni and Phinehas, who helped him minister in the tabernacle, which was the place of worship during this period of Israel's history.

There's more to the setting, so bear with me. A few years earlier, a woman named Hannah was a regular visitor to the temple. She spent most of her time in prayer, begging God for the gift of a son. She vowed to the Lord that if He would grant her request, she would give the boy back to Him. The Lord finally gave her a son, whom she named Samuel. Appropriately, the name means "asked of God." Soon after he was weaned, she fulfilled her promise and placed Samuel in the care of Eli, the aging, almost blind, high priest of Israel. Eli was responsible for Samuel's welfare and education. He was tutoring him in spiritual things, preparing him for a lifetime of service to God.

The whole land of Israel, stuck in a political and spiritual "slick," was half-asleep, yawning its way from one day to the next. God is silent. Everyone's passive. No one has visions, except maybe a few charlatans. Sounds a little like today, doesn't it?

# THE VOICE OF GOD

### ❧ *Read 1 Samuel 2:1–3:18* ❧

*E*li and Samuel were probably taking their turn sleeping in the tabernacle to keep the lamp lit. They slept in little rooms or closets near that special area of God's presence. It was when Samuel heard a voice call his name that he sat up in his little pallet and called back, "Yes?" No one answered.

You can't always tell from Scripture whether God's voice is audible or "heard" by some other means. When Saul (later Paul) was on the road to Damascus, he heard the voice of the resurrected Jesus talking to him in a vision, and the sound could be heard by his entourage. It was audible. In Genesis 6, God spoke to Noah and gave him specific instructions. We might assume that the voice was audible—that is, he heard spoken words with his ears— but the Lord may have "spoken" to him mind to mind. We don't know for sure. God's voice to Daniel sounded like thunder, but centuries earlier to Elijah, He spoke with "a noiseless sound." In Samuel's case, God spoke in such a way that Samuel literally heard His voice. He spoke with the voice of a normal Hebrew man so that the boy thought it was Eli calling to him from the other room.

Eli probably thought Samuel had been dreaming, so he sent him back to bed.

The LORD called yet again, "Samuel!" So Samuel arose and went to Eli, and said, "Here I am, for you called me." But he answered, "I did not call, my son, lie down again." Now Samuel did not yet know the LORD, nor had the word of the LORD yet been revealed to him. (1 Samuel 3:6–7; emphasis added)

The last sentence represents the storyteller's clarifying comment to the reader, who already knew of Samuel as a powerful prophet of God. It's the author's way of saying that this occurred before the Lord had initiated a personal relationship with the boy. Keep this in mind, as it will become an important part of the story as it unfolds. By the way, in the Old Testament, having a personal relationship with the Lord in the way we have come to know it by the new covenant and the indwelling Holy Spirit was a rare and truly awesome privilege. I think we take this privilege far too lightly!

# Watching the Kids

*✦ Read 1 Samuel 3:1–18 ✦*

*E*li was a great preacher, a fine priest. As the high priest, he was responsible, once each year, to enter the Most Holy Place and offer an atoning sacrifice on behalf of the nation. No one else had that privilege. He judged, he instructed the people in matters of worship, he gave counsel, he devoted his entire life to serving in the tabernacle of God and ministering to the needs of His people. But he was a passive, inactive father who indulged his sons. Those boys of his were a piece of work!

According to the Law of Moses, they were to burn the fat as an offering and take whatever didn't burn from the altar. In this way, they were to receive only what the Lord provided. Eli's worthless sons defied God's instructions and reserved the choicest cuts of meat for their dinner table.

Along with their audacious disrespect for the sacrifices of God, they were perverse men who took sexual advantage of the women who came to worship. And they did so without shame, right there in the house of God. And Eli knew it! You would think that a genuine man of God like Eli would be outraged. Remember, he also served as Israel's judge, meaning that his responsibility was to carry out justice on behalf of God. These sons of shameless lust should have been carried to the edge of town and stoned to death. Instead, they receive a mild scolding. How pathetic is *that?*

God has preserved fascinating stories for us to leave us with enduring lessons. Fathers in particular need to take heed. It has been my observation that Eli's paralysis of leadership is not uncommon . . . even among those in ministry. As a father whose vocation is service to the Lord, I have made it my intentional mission to avoid the failure of Eli. I urge you to do the same.

To avoid his fate, each one of us today must recognize that our family could very easily end up like Eli's. Yes, any family can come unraveled—an elder's family, a pastor's family, a missionary family whose father walks with God and pours his heart into a church—rich, poor, healthy, strained. And that includes *your* family.

# DISINTEGRATING FAMILIES

*Read 1 Samuel 3:1–18*

T he temptation of any child of vocational Christian ministers is to see the work of the ministry as just another thing, just another religious occupation. Breaking through the wall of "public religion" must be the intense responsibility of the parent-minister if his or her children are to understand that this isn't a business, a slick profession, or an entertainment arena where Mommy or Daddy puts on a performance.

The key word is *authenticity*. Not perfection, for no one gets it right all the time. But *being real*. Admit your faults, own them completely, ask for forgiveness, be quick to give it, allow children plenty of room to fail, and let them see you live your life behind the scenes with love, grace, and humor. All of that takes time and effort, both of which will cost you productivity on the job. Consider it a priceless sacrifice . . . a permanent investment.

Disintegrating families have parents who refuse to face the severity of their children's actions. Eli knew how horrible his sons had become, yet did nothing! I've seen parents in such denial that they cannot bring themselves to admit that their child has a serious problem with drugs or pornography or sexual promiscuity or stealing—behavior that any other normal person would consider a red flag. Yet they act as though the crisis will resolve itself if given a little patience. Wrong.

If you have children who are young, you have children who are impressionable. That's the time to make your most important investment in them. To wait until they're as tall as you, you will have already allowed them to sow seeds of self-destruction.

If your children are nearly adults, take responsibility for your part in their poor choices, then do whatever is necessary to save them. Because you've waited so long, there are few options that don't have grave consequences in the short term. So consider the long term, and do what you must. It is never too late to start doing what is right.

# GET INVOLVED

### ❧ *Read 1 Samuel 3:19–21* ❧

*D*isintegrating families fail to respond quickly and thoroughly to the warnings of others. Listen to their teachers. They may seem biased against your child, but they rarely are. Take the early warnings seriously, and get involved soon. Listen to your pastor or your youth leader. Listen to the uniformed officer with a badge who rings your doorbell.

Don't be so quick to jump to your child's defense. Take time to hear the report in full. Ask direct, hard questions to be sure you have the whole picture. Then take time to reflect on what you have heard. If it resonates, causing you to think that it might be accurate, then dig deeper and go to whatever measure is necessary to make certain you have it resolved.

Disintegrating families rationalize wrong behavior, and thereby become part of the problem. Eli participated in his sons' behavior. We know this because Eli got fat on the food his boys had stolen from the altar.

As for Samuel, the boy who heard God's voice, the closing words of this episode tell us that the sleepy, spiritual indifference that had lulled Israel into complacency was about to come to a screeching halt. A man of action was on the scene, and Israel's spiritual drift was about to end. Even as a little boy, he not only heard the Lord, but he obeyed His voice.

As you ponder all of this, especially as you evaluate the condition of your family, remember that hearing the truth isn't enough. Action is the ticket. Only on the rarest occasions does the Lord bless someone for merely listening to Him. Faith is an action. That means His blessings almost always lie on the other side of obedience. According to Scripture, knowledge alone merely puffs up, but with action comes humility (1 Corinthians 8:1). Besides, problems like those of Eli do not solve themselves. They multiply and intensify with the slow and silent passing of time.

If you have reached the conclusion that your family is in danger, choose to do something rather than nothing. Refuse to be like Eli. In the end, after achieving public success in ministry, God considered Eli a failure at home . . . and judged him for it.

Don't go there.

# "WE WANT TO BE LIKE EVERYONE ELSE"

### ✦ *Read 1 Samuel 8:1–9:27* ✦

*F*rom the time that Joshua died until Saul took the throne of Israel, the Hebrew government was not a monarchy like most surrounding nations. Theologians refer to it as a *theocracy*—"God-rule." The Lord ruled over Israel, issuing His decrees and governing through prophets and priests. Each major region looked to a judge for what most other cultures would expect from a king. He (occasionally, she) led the people in battle, decided civil cases, and enforced God's laws.

Samuel judged all Israel with God reigning as king over the Hebrew people. In this way, the Israelites were like no other nation on earth in that they could claim God as their leader, the invisible Creator, the God of Abraham, Isaac, and Jacob, the Almighty One who crushed Egypt, parted the Red Sea, and conquered Canaan. But, much in the same way that the wandering generation tired of manna, the people grew tired of the theocracy. Three factors drove their desire for a king.

First, Samuel was old and no longer able to keep pace with the demands of the nation. Second, his sons had disqualified themselves by losing the respect of the people. And third, "we want to be like all the nations."

Before we move on, let's not bypass an important point of interest. On previous pages we observed the failure of Eli to guide his sons. Now we see little evidence to suggest that Samuel did any better. Scripture doesn't offer as detailed information about his parenting, but the remarkable similarity between Samuel's sons and those of Eli leaves us with little else to conclude. Eli was a great priest and a faithful judge, but a lousy father. Samuel, sadly, followed in his footsteps. His sons became unfit as leaders like those of Eli.

This was a pivotal moment in the life of Israel. Take special note of the Lord's assessment of their decision. "They have not rejected you, but they have rejected Me from being king over them."

In effect, the Lord said, "You are determined to go down this path—one that will certainly cause you sorrow—and I will not stop you. You have rejected My way for your own. Therefore, you will lie in the bed you have made."

# SAD DAY

### ❧ *Read 1 Samuel 10:1—11:15* ❧

*W*hen the people located their new king, they celebrated. And why not? This was a glorious day. Saul was tall, strong, modest, and had the full support of his nation. From a *human* point of view, this was a beautiful start to a new era.

But from God's point of view, this was a sad day. His people had rejected Him as king, replacing Him with someone as impressive as a handsome film star. Unlike all those cheering people, God knew that this was not the beginning of Israel's glory days. A disaster would soon begin to happen.

Almost overnight Saul's popularity index was off the chart. He had demonstrated himself to be a brave and capable warrior, an able general, and a strong leader. When the Ammonites attacked, he acted decisively and firmly, and he did so with honor. This won the confidence of the people and earned him a great endorsement speech by Samuel. But don't forget that this story is a tragedy. This is a roofline life, and Saul has reached his peak.

Following his burst of glory, Saul's life began to unravel. He became a victim of himself: full of pride, impatience, rebellion, jealousy, and attempted murder. Over a long and painful stretch of years, he shriveled into a twisted, maniacal, pathetic figure. Eventually, he would commit suicide. Evil had begun to pour into his life like sewage flowing into a harbor, deep beneath the surface, under cover of night. No one could see it. In fact, for a long time, no one could even smell it, but slowly and ever so surely it polluted the waters of his mind and soiled his soul.

One of the chief qualities I look for in a prospective staff member or employee is modesty. I want a confident man or woman, but one who finds the job a little daunting. That tells me that he or she has a healthy view of the role we're looking to fill. It is daunting! A modest person will be more likely to rely upon the Lord to succeed, and will be much less likely to fail. I am always leery of people who seek the limelight.

# SAUL'S DISOBEDIENCE

### *Read 1 Samuel 13:1—15*

Saul's disobedient actions involved at least three major errors.

First, *kings weren't supposed to offer sacrifices on behalf of the community.* Kings could offer sacrifices for themselves, but never for the nation. That was done only by priests.

Second, *it was Samuel who was to convey the Lord's battle plans.* Saul was to wait for him. However, since Saul kept his eye on the sundial and his dwindling army, he gave in to panic and rushed ahead on his own. This reduced the sacrifice to a pointless ritual that looked more pagan than Hebrew. Gentile generals decided where, when, and whom to attack, mobilized their troops, *then* sacrificed to their gods to gain favor. The Hebrew sacrifice was different; it was to be an act of submission, not bribery.

Third, and most important to our study, *Saul made the decision to trust himself at the crisis point.* His decision to sacrifice and attack was based on good common sense (from an earthly perspective). Just like Israel's desire to have a human king and their ready acceptance of Saul based on his outward appearance, the new king was ready to advance on the enemy with a human strategy. Probably a good one, but human, nonetheless.

Saul's faith failed. He saw his army evaporating like water and the town of Michmash teeming with his enemy. He saw that the appointed seven days had passed and that Samuel was late. So he tossed aside any pretense of decorum and protocol. He, in effect, put on the priestly garb along with his crown and signet and tried to make the altar his own special instrument of power—something he had no right to do.

Confrontation is rarely pleasant but frequently necessary. We all need a Samuel, someone who cares more about our character than our image or comfort. Often, that kind of loving honesty calls for sharp words. "You have played the fool" is never easy to hear, but when it comes from the mouth of a trusted, godly friend, we *must* hear it and take heed.

# RATIONALIZATIONS

### ✤ *Read 1 Samuel 15:1–35* ✤

*E*ven though I have known people like this, still, I cannot fathom Saul's perspective. How can anyone be so clueless? He disobeyed the Lord's direct command by keeping not just a few things under the ban, but keeping everything having any value. On top of having no sense, Saul had no shame. Instead of being humiliated by his own guilt, he erected a monument to himself to commemorate the day. At least Achan had the good sense to be ashamed of his sin. Not Saul! Somehow he managed to twist events and rearrange facts to portray himself as God's champion.

Samuel's response is priceless: "What then is this bleating of the sheep in my ears, and the lowing of the oxen which I hear?" (1 Samuel 15:14).

Amazing how simple facts can so easily prick a deceiving heart.

I see two timeless principles at work in the story of Saul that deserve our attention.

First, *how you finish is far more important than how you start.*

No one graduates from college thinking, *Okay, now how can I fail?* No bride or groom tells the wedding guests, "Enjoy the party; this thing won't last more than a couple of years." Only when a woman or man finishes well can we call that life a success. A good beginning does nothing to guarantee a good ending. Happy endings are the result of good choices and consistent discipline put in sequence over a lifetime and faithfully maintained.

Second, *rationalization is disobedience because it refuses to accept the truth.* I've heard it said that the most destructive lie is the one you tell yourself. Rationalizing is an insidious form of self-delusion. It starts small—usually with something innocent—and quietly twists the mind to spin the truth in convenient ways. In the end, the self-deluded mind rationalizes everything so conveniently, so automatically, that the person has no concept of how preposterous his or her thinking and behavior have become. And—never forget this—no one is immune.

# ENDNOTES

1. Boris Pasternak, source unknown.
2. A. W. Tozer, *The Root of the Righteous* (Camp Hill, Penn.: Christian Publications, 1986), 137.
3. Arthur Gordon, "A Foolproof Formula for Success," *Reader's Digest* (December, 1966), 88.
4. Amy Carmichael, from *Rose from Brier* (Fort Washington, Penn.: Christian Literature Crusade, 1973), 12. Used by permission.
5. A.W. Tozer, *The Root of the Righteous* (Camp Hill, Penn.: Christian Publications, 1986), 137.
6. Vance Havner, *It Is Toward Evening* (Westwood, N.J.: Fleming Revell, a division of Baker Books, 1968), 39–40.
7. Douglas Southall Freeman, *R.E. Lee* (New York: Charles Scribner's Sons, 1947), 3:216.
8. George Keith, "How Firm a Foundation," third stanza, 1787.
9. V. Raymond Edman, *In Quietness and Confidence* (Wheaton, Ill.: Scripture Press, 1956), 63.
10. Lawrence J. Crabb, Jr., *The Pressure's Off* (Colorado Springs: WaterBrook, 2002), 183. All rights reserved.
11. C.S. Lewis, *A Grief Observed* (New York: Harper & Row, 1961), 17–18. C.S. Lewis Pte. Ltd. 1961. Extract reprinted by permission.
12. "Amazing Grace," John Newton. Public Domain.
13. "O Worship the King," Robert Grant, 1833. Public Domain.
14. Viktor E. Frankl, *Man's Search for Meaning* (New York: Pocket Books, Simon and Schuster, 1976). Used by Permission.

# The Great Lives Series

In his Great Lives from God's Word Series, Charles Swindoll
shows us how the great heroes of the faith offer a model of
courage, hope, and triumph in the face of adversity.

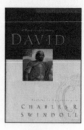

**DAVID**
A Man of
Passion and
Destiny

**ESTHER**
A Woman of
Strength and
Dignity

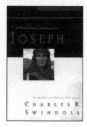

**JOSEPH**
A Man of
Integrity and
Forgiveness

**MOSES**
A Man of
Selfless
Dedication

**ELIJAH**
A Man Who
Stood With
God

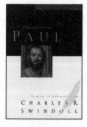

**PAUL**
A Man of
Grace and Grit

**JOB**
A Man of
Heroic
Endurance

W PUBLISHING GROUP™
www.wpublishinggroup.com